To Rich,

Grateful to have a friend and mentor like you. Happy to share with you my work with passion!

Edward.
Oct 2012

CHILDREN'S ISSUES, LAWS AND PROGRAMS

CHILD PROTECTION IN CHINESE SOCIETIES

CHALLENGES AND POLICIES

Children's Issues, Laws and Programs

Additional books in this series can be found on Nova's website under the Series tab.

Additional e-books in this series can be found on Nova's website under the e-book tab.

China in the 21st Century

Additional books in this series can be found on Nova's website under the Series tab.

Additional e-books in this series can be found on Nova's website under the e-book tab.

CHILDREN'S ISSUES, LAWS AND PROGRAMS

CHILD PROTECTION IN CHINESE SOCIETIES

CHALLENGES AND POLICIES

KO LING CHAN

EDITOR

Nova Science Publishers, Inc.

New York

The Optimus Study was initiated and funded by the UBS Optimus Foundation

Additional color graphics may be available in the e-book version of this book.

LIBRARY OF CONGRESS CATALOGING-IN-PUBLICATION DATA

Child protection in Chinese societies : challenges and policies / editors, Edward Ko Ling Chan.
p. cm.
Includes index.
ISBN 978-1-61942-879-9 (hardcover)
1. Child abuse--China. 2. Children--Legal status, laws, etc.--China. 3. Children's rights--China. 4. Child welfare--China. I. Chan, Edward Ko Ling.
HV6626.54.C6C45 2011
362.70951--dc23
2012000557

Published by Nova Science Publishers, Inc. † New York

CONTENTS

PREFACE

This book introduces the current situations of child victimization in the Chinese populations to readers, discusses the relevant political and legal systems as well as health and social services, and puts forward some recommendations for effective child protection with an emphasis on the unique cultural values and situations in the Chinese populations. Grounded in the recent and contemporary research and scholarly inquiry, this is a vital book for understanding trends and current situations in China, as well as an essential read for those who work, research, teach or study in the area. This book is the only one available to date to present a comprehensive and critical review of child maltreatment and victimization in China whilst promoting a multi-disciplinary collaboration to child protection.

Chapter 1 – This chapter reviewed 56 empirical studies on the prevalence and risk factors of various types of violence against children in Chinese societies. The reviewed studies were published between 1988 and 2009 and examined various forms of child abuse among the Chinese population. The vastly ranging estimates of the prevalence of child abuse in Chinese societies in these studies revealed that child maltreatment is highly pervasive among the Chinese population. Physical child abuse and corporal punishment had the highest prevalence rates, followed by psychological abuse, neglect, and sexual abuse. However, the studies also showed that there is a tendency to underreport child abuse due to a lack of awareness of the definitions of child maltreatment, a reluctance to expose a family's shame, and a cultural conceptualization of child abuse that is different from official definitions in Western countries. These studies also discussed various psychological, behavioral, and interpersonal consequences of each type of abuse.

Chapter 2 – Child victimization accompanied by injury has imposed a heavy demand on health services in China. However, efforts to recognize it as a public health problem have been hampered by the absence of reliable estimates of the prevalence of the different types of victimization. The objective of the population surveys is to investigate the prevalence and risk factors of child victimization, with specific emphasis on child sexual abuse. A multistage stratified sampling procedure was adopted to identify eligible participants from Hong Kong and180 communes in 5 cities in mainland China. Face-to-face interviews were conducted with 8,945 Chinese parents of children younger than 18 years of age. A total of 3 321 children and 18 341 students, aged 15-17 years, were successfully interviewed. The lifetime prevalence rates of child sexual victimization and child victimization, as reported by household parents, were 1.3% and 35.2% respectively. The lifetime prevalence rates of child sexual victimization and child victimization, as reported by household children and school students were 3.1% to 8% and 50.1% to 71.7%, respectively, which were significantly higher than those reported by parents. The findings provide reliable estimates of child victimization which will facilitate the allocation of resources. The associations between child victimization and family violence highlight the value of screening for multiple types of violence when one type has been detected.

Chapter 3 – The major findings related to child victimization and child sexual abuse in China were presented in the last chapter. In this chapter, the interpretation of the findings and possible explanations of some controversial issues will be discussed. The major issues include the underreporting of child victimization by parents, prevalence of childhood sexual abuse in Chinese populations, difficulties encountered in the study process, and recommendations.

Chapter 4 – The authors present an in-depth case analysis to provide a comprehensive understanding of the issues related to child sexual abuse in China. The case was an adult survivor from child sexual abuse recruited in Hong Kong. Through the framework of control and power, they argue that perpetrators systematically avoid being held responsible for their actions. They will go to great lengths to hide the truth. It is difficult for victims and their family members to seek help. The impact of sexual abuse on the victims is not only determined by the event itself, but also by the methods and attitudes adopted to handle the event. While people around the victim can assist him/her in healing, they can also impede the process and do more harm than good.

Chapter 5 – The construction and development of the continental legal system in Mainland China has been influenced by the international and national environment. Since 1949, the child protection legal system in Mainland China has gone through three stages: inception, establishment, and preliminary development. Throughout this period of development, significant advancements have been made in areas such as the goals of legislation; the principles, conceptualization, and content of child protection; child protection in criminal, civil, and administrative justice; and the supervision and execution of law on child protection. The basic spirit of the principles on the best interests of the child, non-discrimination, respecting the child's views, and protecting of child's rights to survival and development established in the United Nations Convention on the Rights of the Child (CRC) are also reflected in the relevant legislation in mainland China. The child's right to survival, development, to be protected and participation have been clearly stipulated by the Protection of Minors Act in China. To date, has formed a legal framework for the child protection system, with the Constitutional Law as the core, and coordinated by the Protection of Minors Act and other laws, as well as a large number of related regulations and policy measures. Nevertheless, the current situation regarding the legal protection of children in mainland China faces the following challenges: (a) the influence of traditional values in legislation and the enforcement of laws; (b) inadequate integration of systems and standards in legislation; (c) the lack of standard content; and (d) deficient enforcement.

Chapter 6 – Ensuring a child's rights of access to justice and dignity is one of the fundamental principles of the United Nations Convention on the Rights of the Child (CRC). Since the 1980s, China has explored the issue of establishing a juvenile justice system. However, the current Penal Code and Criminal Procedure Law still contain no judicial diversion mechanism for children, and thus the issue of juvenile justice remains a law in the making. In addition, the absence of a unified child protection system with appropriate mandates increases the risk of vulnerable groups of children, especially migrant children in cities and left-behind children, coming into conflict with the law. The double insufficiency in the judicial sector and the administrative sector reveals the need to accelerate the reform of juvenile justice and to establish a comprehensive child protection system in China. The chapter will first examine the interdependency of the child protection system and the juvenile justice system from the perspective of child rights and then review the situation in China by focusing on the ongoing juvenile justice reform and local innovative pilot practices. This will be followed by an analysis of the success of these measures and the challenges that remain. Finally, practical recommendations on ways forward will be presented.

Chapter 7 – Cyberbullying is a global and alarming problem, and this has led to calls for regulation at the national, regional and international level. Yet, the resort to direct and sole legal means to tackle cyberbullying has remained controversial. The alternative model of co-regulation combining legal intervention, education, and regulation from the telecommunications industry has been adopted, in various degrees, in Europe and North America. Drawing from their lessons, this chapter first maps out the problem of cyberbullying in Hong Kong, Taiwan and Mainland China, then explains why the current legal regimes in the three jurisdictions have failed to address adequately the problem of cyberbullying. This is followed by discussion on current attempts on anti-bullying policies made by the education authorities in Hong Kong and Taiwan. Finally, it argues why a co-regulatory and integrated approach involving all stakeholders should be implemented to tackle the problem.

Chapter 8 – The policies and social services related to child welfare and child protection in Mainland China and Hong Kong are examined. The traditional Chinese cultural characteristics of filial piety and familism have a great influence on the perspectives and behaviors of the Chinese. The legal and social service delivery systems in Mainland China and Hong Kong are quite different. Hong Kong is relatively more mature in terms of the development of a child protection system, although there is still much room for improvement. The development of child protection services in Mainland China can use the experiences of Hong Kong as reference points, while the new initiative in Mainland China can, in turn, create a positive force to push Hong Kong to further improve its system.

Chapter 9 – China faces many complex new challenges in light of the current trends of rapid economic growth, urbanization, massive domestic migration, dislocation and separation of family members, changing family structures, increasing cost of basic social services, rising disparities, and increasing frequency of natural disasters. In this current context, children and their families are increasingly exposed to new social welfare and child protection risks, with poverty acting as a contributing factor to the risk of child protection violations. As it has become more difficult for the Chinese government to manage these risks and vulnerabilities through vertical social protection programs, China is beginning to shift from an issues-based approach to social welfare and child protection toward a more comprehensive, multisectoral child welfare and child protection system as the most effective way to address new challenges. This new system comprises a social welfare system that provides (a) universal benefits to support social protection and services for all children and their families, and within this, (b) a child protection system that targets the most vulnerable children. UNICEF is supporting the Chinese government to strengthen its social welfare system for children at three basic levels: (a) at the upstream and national level, supporting the development of child-sensitive national social protection, social assistance and child protection policies, laws, and frameworks; (b) at the intermediate or provincial level, developing strategies, mechanisms, and plans that facilitate the implementation of national child welfare and child protection laws and policies; and (c) at the community level, piloting and demonstrating effective, affordable, and sustainable intersectoral child welfare and child protection packages and models within diverse local settings for possible government replication (this component also feeds into policy development). Within this social welfare framework, UNICEF is supporting China to move toward the establishment of a child protection system; this involves policy and legal reforms aimed at a strengthening a systems approach to child protection which is integrally linked with the social welfare and justice systems. Support is also being provided to demonstrate and develop community-based child protection service models that prevent and respond to violence, abuse, exploitation, and neglect.

Chapter 10 – News about child abuse is reported almost daily. It has been recognized as a social problem and not just a family matter of child discipline. Different professionals need to work together for the prevention of child abuse. This chapter reviews the milestones in child protection and examines what has been done and achieved in the past three decades. The World Health Organization (2002) recommends a public health approach to the early identification of child abuse. To improve the system in Hong Kong, it will be necessary to conduct research and strategic evaluations, strengthen professional development, and build bridges between sectors. On the issue of the ways ahead, the following strategies are suggested in this chapter: 1) develop a data link system and conduct a prevalence study so as to inform policies and practices; 2) ensure a home visitation to each family, including cross-border families with newborn children; 3) put effective preventive services into the mainstream; 4) establish a review mechanism for cases of serious and fatal child abuse; 5) show concern for the child victims of psychological abuse and for children who are emotionally disturbed; 6) impose a total ban on corporal punishment as it is a form of violence and an infringement of children's rights; 7) set up a mandatory sex offenders registry; 8) conduct a review of sentencing options and require every convict to receive therapy and treatment; 9) put in place laws and ways to protect unattended children; and 10) establish an independent child commission to look into all child-related issues. Every child is precious. It is everyone's responsibility to ensure that each child is protected and develops in a safe environment. What our society will be like depends on how determined we are to provide a nonviolent environment at home and in society for our children today.

Chapter 11 – With rising public awareness of HIV/AIDS, the living condition of children orphaned by HIV/AIDS has gradually become a focal issue in society. Since the onset of this disease, children orphaned by HIV/AIDS have emerged as a new social group. Struggling with family difficulties, social stigma, and other difficulties, these children have become a typical vulnerable group in society. It is therefore necessary to explore the living condition and unmet basic needs of children orphaned by HIV/AIDS so as to establish a certain social psychological care model and social support system to meet their needs and enable their healthy development. This chapter aims to examine the living condition and social environment of HIV/AIDS orphaned children, to analyze their needs, and to suggest ways to build an effective social support system for them through field investigations.

Chapter 12 – As the world's economy has grown, the child mortality rate due to infectious and contagious diseases has dropped significantly. However, while the latest developments in medical research and technologies are improving the health of children, the situation with regard to child injuries and deaths has worsened considerably. Accidental child injury can be fatal, and it has a significant impact on both families and society. It has been recognized as an essential child health issue by international academic communities. This chapter explains the importance and the necessity of child safety education by reviewing the literature and presenting typical cases. It then introduces the strategies used to organize educational programs. It discusses in detail how to cultivate a harmless environment for children and provides accompanying guidance on educating parents and suggestions to the government and society on the protection of children.

Chapter 13 – Hong Kong professes to have zero tolerance toward violence against children, and the government claims that child protection is already built into various policies and systems. Yet, every day, many children still experience different forms of violence, whether at home, in school, in the community, or in the virtual world. Child protection is often viewed in terms of programs targeting different forms of maltreatment, but to tackle the root causes of child abuse, a comprehensive approach that respects and protects the basic rights of the child as laid down in the United Nations Convention on the Rights of the Child (hereinafter, the "Convention") is required. In its concluding observations on the report on the Convention submitted by Hong Kong in 2005, the United Nations Committee on the Rights of the Child urged Hong Kong to establish a human rights institution to monitor children's rights and to implement the Convention. A motion to set up a Commission on Children was passed in the Legislative Council in 2007, but as this was a nonbinding motion, no action has yet been taken. Using examples of recent concerns in Hong Kong, this chapter discusses why no time should be lost in establishing a children's commission if Hong Kong is to turn zero tolerance toward violence against children from a slogan into a reality.

Chapter 14 – Child maltreatment has been recognized as a major public health problem in Chinese communities and worldwide. Around 50 to 90 children under 18 die of external causes in Hong Kong annually; 5% of these cases are due to "assaults." The Child Fatality Review conducted in Chinese communities elsewhere identified a significant number of child deaths due to unnatural causes that were related to neglect and a lack of proper care. In a review of 494 suspected child abuse cases reported in Hong Kong hospitals from June 1997 to August 1999, 58% were substantiated as child abuse and 1% (5 children) had died from serious head injuries. Child abuse is a prevalent problem worldwide, and in western countries, official statistics from child protection registries or statistics on offenses against children are considered to be important social indicators. However, most Chinese communities lack an effective surveillance system to monitor and report key epidemiological data on child abuse and thus to describe the real situation and address the need for child protection. In 2010, the Hong Kong Child Abuse Collaborative Research Team produced the first database of abuse-related hospital admissions in Chinese. From 2001 to 2008, there were 5,430 admission cases that were later discharged with a diagnosis of child maltreatment syndrome. In contrast to the significant decline in the annual incidence of child maltreatment syndrome in England, there has been an upsurge in maltreatment admissions in Hong Kong. The annual incidence rate has followed a simple linear curve and has increased from 32.5 to 73 per 100,000 (R^2 0.96, $p<0.0001$). The alarming rise in child maltreatment and the unequal distribution of cases in Hong Kong demonstrate the need to recognize child abuse as an important social indicator which warrants further investigation to delineate its underlying causes and to recommend appropriate prevention strategies. There is an obvious need to build up a more effective child abuse surveillance system in order to improve child protection in Chinese communities. The authors' team is working on an innovative project commissioned by the government to integrate the social service sector's Child Protection Registry (CPR) and the health sector's

Child Abuse Database in order to provide a clearer picture and epidemiology of child maltreatment and to explore the feasibility of integrating existing key databases, which could then serve as a child abuse surveillance model in Chinese communities.

SECTION 1.
CHILD VICTIMIZATION IN CHINESE SOCIETIES: CURRENT SITUATIONS

This section provides an overview on the current situations of child victimization, including child maltreatment and other types of violence victimization, in Chinese societies. It starts with a review on relevant past studies and extends the discussion with the findings of two new empirical studies in China in later chapters.

Chapter 1 presents the results of a literature review on previous research on child maltreatment in the Chinese populations in the last two decades (1988-2009). The prevalence rates, risk factors and consequences of the problem are explored. The review also focuses on possible factors leading to the reporting or underreporting of child maltreatment, with a special emphasis on the great influence of the Chinese cultural values on the Chinese societies.

In addition to the past research on child maltreatment, Chapter 2 and Chapter 3 provide details of a new empirical study using a national, representative sample in China. While the former introduces the study methodology and offers a variety of reliable estimates on the problem, the latter puts forward some explanations of the findings as well as some recommendations for the making of relevant policies.

Case studies, which facilitate deeper understanding of a problem, are as important as their large-scale empirical counterparts. In Chapter 4, a case of child sexual abuse is analyzed. What happened to the case during childhood? How have these experiences affected her life later on? This chapter presents the details of a real-life example of the adult survivors from childhood sexual abuse in China.

In: Child Protection in Chinese Societies
Editor: Ko Ling Chan
ISBN: 978-1-61942-879-9

Chapter 1

CHILD MALTREATMENT IN CHINESE SOCIETIES: A COMPREHENSIVE REVIEW

Ko Ling Chan
Department of Social Work and Social Administration
University of Hong Kong, Pokfulam, Hong Kong

ABSTRACT

This chapter reviewed 56 empirical studies on the prevalence and risk factors of various types of violence against children in Chinese societies. The reviewed studies were published between 1988 and 2009 and examined various forms of child abuse among the Chinese population. The vastly ranging estimates of the prevalence of child abuse in Chinese societies in these studies revealed that child maltreatment is highly pervasive among the Chinese population. Physical child abuse and corporal punishment had the highest prevalence rates, followed by psychological abuse, neglect, and sexual abuse. However, the studies also showed that there is a tendency to underreport child abuse due to a lack of awareness of the definitions of child maltreatment, a reluctance to expose a family's shame, and a cultural conceptualization of child abuse that is different from official definitions in Western countries. These studies also discussed various psychological, behavioral, and interpersonal consequences of each type of abuse.

Keywords: Child maltreatment, Child abuse and neglect, Chinese, Prevalence, Risk factors

INTRODUCTION

Child abuse is a serious public health problem that is receiving increasing public attention in China. During the past decades, researchers have begun to identify a different pattern of child abuse among the Chinese population (Samuda, 1998). There are cultural and traditional features among the Chinese that potentially allow for more physical violence and psychological abuse against children. Traditional Chinese culture advocates family harmony, parental loyalty, respect for parents, and familial piety. In other words, the child is obligated to show respect and obedience to his/her parents regardless of what the parents may do (Shen, 2009). The authoritarian parenting style practiced by the Chinese is harsh, restrictive, domineering, physically coercive, and controlling (Nelson, Hart, Yang, Olsen, and Jin, 2006). Chinese parents believe that the infliction of physical pain as a form of discipline is necessary not only to maintain obedience but also to train children to have the strength to endure physical hardship in the future (J. T. F. Lau, Liu, Yu, and Wong, 1999; Tang, 1996). Therefore, within Chinese culture, there is a high tolerance of physical punishment, regardless of the socioeconomic background of the parents (Fong, 1997). Psychological abuse and neglect are also unrecognized in Chinese culture, as scolding, beating, and shaming children is often done deliberately in front of others and in public in order for discipline to be effective (J. T. F. Lau, Liu, and Cheung, 1999; J. T. F. Lau, Liu, Yu, et al., 1999). Due to this unique familial culture in Chinese families, culture-specific epidemiological studies are needed to understand the prevalence, patterns, and risk factors of child abuse in order for the government to be able to provide effective prevention and intervention services for victims and families (Ma, Yau, Ng, and Tong, 2004). Moreover, the negative impact of child abuse on the mental health, behavior, and physical wellbeing of victims is highly relevant to our society's future and has important implications in terms of the costs to society.

The scope of this review focuses on journal articles and book chapters located in databases including the Criminal Justice Abstract, Criminology, MEDLINE, PsycINFO, Psychology, Social Services Abstracts, Sociology, and Sociological Abstracts. Keyword terms including Chinese, China, Hong Kong, Taiwan, child, children, adolescent, abuse, maltreatment, violence, aggression, and victimization yielded 660 articles, 515 of which were excluded from this review. The 515 irrelevant articles were mostly about substance abuse, spousal abuse, alcohol abuse, patients with psychological symptoms, crime and violence, juvenile delinquency, HIV, and suicidal ideation. We also excluded child abuse studies of people of other ethnicities because the focus of our review was limited to the Chinese. A second round of screening narrowed the 145 articles down to 56; 89 articles with a focus on interventions and perceptions of child abuse were excluded as no information could be obtained from them. The final 56 articles included reports on the situation in Chinese populations in Mainland China, Hong Kong SAR, and Taiwan and among the large Chinese communities in Singapore and America. Various forms of child maltreatment, such as physical abuse, sexual abuse, psychological abuse, neglect, bullying, child abduction, slavery, and trafficking, were included in the scope of the review as were hospital and clinical records of child maltreatment among the Chinese population. Accounts of community knowledge of child abuse are also presented in the review to show how cultural beliefs may be risk factors of child victimization among Chinese communities. The current laws and regulations concerning child abuse within various Chinese communities are also included in this review of the most current child abuse research in Chinese societies.

CHINESE COMMUNITIES

This chapter provides a comprehensive review of child abuse in Chinese societies in Mainland China, Hong Kong, Macau, Taiwan, and Singapore and among immigrants in Canada and the United States. However, most Chinese people reside in Mainland China, Hong Kong, Macau, and Taiwan, and these societies differ in terms of their socio-political-economic structure. This can best be illustrated by the United Nation Human Development Index (HDI), which is a recent statistical measure that takes account of a country's average achievement in relation to three basic aspects of human development: health, knowledge, and a decent standard of living (UNDP, 2010). According to the HDI rankings, while Hong Kong and Singapore are classified as countries with "very high human development" comparable to the United States and United Kingdom, China is only classified as a country with "medium human development." In general, Mainland China is still undergoing fairly rapid economic development while, at the same time, striving to achieve a better balance between economic and social development. It can therefore be said that Chinese societies are distinctive in terms of their economic and social development status.

In China, there are four municipalities (Beijing, Tianjin, Shanghai, and Chongqing) directly under the central government, 23 provinces (Anhui, Fujian, Gansu, Guangdong, Guizhou, Hainan, Hebei, Heilongjiang, Henan, Hubei, Hunan, Jiangsu, Jiangxi, Jilin, Liaoning, Qinghai, Shaanxi, Shandong, Shanxi, Sichuan, Taiwan, Yunnan, and Zhejiang), five autonomous regions (Guangxi Zhuang, Inner Mongolia, Ningxia Hui, Tibet, and Xinjiang Uygur), and two special administrative regions (Hong Kong and Macau). This chapter reviews studies of child abuse in Chinese populations in general rather than exclusively in Mainland China, Hong Kong, and Macau.

Hong Kong and Macau, both of which were colonies for many years, are very much alike. Chinese people in Hong Kong and Macau are exposed to both Chinese and Western cultures, in particular those of the United States, the United Kingdom, and Portugal. The official language in Hong Kong is still English, even though sovereignty over the region was returned to China in 1997. The legal system in Hong Kong is basically adapted from the common law system of the United Kingdom, although it is now being integrated into the Mainland legal system. In Macau, Portuguese was the official language until the handover of sovereignty in 1999. Significant cultural differences are also found within Mainland China, which has more than 19 ethnic groups, the Han being the dominant group in terms of numbers (Chiu, 2001). Nearly 90% of the population of Mainland China, Hong Kong, and Macau are Han Chinese. There are also huge differences between the people in rural areas and those in the cities and between Northern China and Southern China. In Southern China, regions such as the Pearl River Delta and Shanghai have a longer history of economic development and exposure to Western cultures.

Singapore is a multiethnic society; however, Chinese do make up the majority (77%) of the population (Leow, 2001). Similarly, Canada, which is known for its multiculturalism, had a population of around 1,029,000 Chinese in 2002. The Chinese form the largest visible minority group in Canada (Statistics Canada, 2001). The United States has also experienced one of the most significant demographic changes recently with a rapid increase in the number of Chinese immigrants. More than 80% of Chinese residents in the United States are either foreign born or have at least one foreign-born parent. The largest proportion of the Asian population in the United States is made up of 2,314,537 non-Taiwanese Chinese (United States Census Bureau, 2003). Although North America might have a different concept of child abuse, Chinese parents living there maintain their traditional parenting style and their high tolerance of physical discipline (Kwok and Tam, 2005; Meston, Heiman, Trapnell, and Carlin, 1999). However, there is a lack of research on child abuse among Chinese populations in Western countries, and this impedes Western social practitioners from gaining a culturally-relevant understanding of the patterns and dynamics of child abuse specifically among the Chinese. In order to grasp the concept, types, and patterns of child abuse commonly found in Chinese communities, Chinese immigrants in foreign countries were included in the review. Chinese populations are indeed heterogeneous; therefore, caution should be exercised in interpreting findings from studies because no one study can represent all of the Chinese people in these societies.

DEFINITION OF CHILD ABUSE

The terms child abuse and child maltreatment have overlapping meanings and are often used interchangeably in reports and documents, including this review. The World Health Organization (WHO) has provided a general definition of child abuse:

> Child abuse or maltreatment constitutes all forms of physical and/or emotional ill-treatment, sexual abuse, neglect or negligent treatment or commercial or other exploitation, resulting in actual or potential harm to the child's health, survival, development or dignity in the context of a relationship of responsibility, trust or power (Krug, Dahlberg, Mercy, Zwi, and Lozano, 2002).

A coherent definition of child abuse in research is important because different conceptualizations of child abuse may result in underreporting (J. T. F. Lau, Liu, Yu, et al., 1999). This review covers familial child abuse and also nonfamilial abuse and violence against children.

TYPES AND MAGNITUDE OF CHILD ABUSE IN CHINESE SOCIETIES

Physical Abuse

In general, estimates of the prevalence of child physical abuse (CPA) vary widely, from 1.1% (J. T. F. Lau, Liu, Yu, et al., 1999) to 95% (Samuda, 1998). The prevalence rates of minor physical victimization and severe physical abuse range from 2.0% (J. T. F. Lau, Liu, and Cheung, 1999) to 62.4% (Tang, 1996) and from 1.1% to 46.1% (Tang, 1998a), respectively. The prevalence rate of corporal or physical punishment ranges from 4.1% (J. T. F. Lau et al., 2005) to 95% (Samuda, 1998). These huge discrepancies in rates may be accounted for by differences in sample size and gender composition in these studies. Males are often found to have a higher chance of experiencing physical punishment than females; one study found that 3.1% of males were injured a result of beatings in the 6-month period prior to the study, while only 2.4% of females had this experience (J. T. F. Lau et al., 2005). Studies have also reported that males are more likely to be beaten without provocation (J. T. F. Lau et al., 2005; Tang and Davis, 1996), and one study reported that girls are more likely to be beaten for no apparent reason (J. T. F. Lau, Liu, and Cheung, 1999). Overall, CPA seems to be more prevalent among Chinese communities.

Researchers have argued that corporal punishment should be distinguished from physical abuse as corporal punishment is meant to inflict pain, not injury, for the purpose of discipline while physical abuse refers to physical aggression and violence that inflicts pain and injury on children (Tang, 2006). Many Chinese hold the belief that "the rod makes an obedient son," and Chinese parents believe that they are entitled to discipline their own children within their private property using any amount of force they choose (Qiao and Chan, 2005), although most disapprove of causing injury to children (Meston et al., 1999). It should also be noted that corporal punishment has been found to be significantly associated with age: the younger the respondents, the more likely it is that they have received corporal punishment from their parents (J. T. F. Lau, Liu, and Cheung, 1999). In J. T. F. Lau, Liu, and Cheung's (1999) study of 95,788 adolescents, more than 7.1% of the respondents who were aged 12 or below had experienced corporal punishment while only 1.2% of the respondents aged 19 or above had had such an experience. This echoes most of the research, which has reported that victims of CPA tend to be younger children, ranging in age from 4 to14 years (Leung, Wong, Chen, and Tang, 2008; Samuda, 1998; Tang, 2006; W. C. W. Wong, Chen, Goggins, Tang, and Leung, 2009). From this, it may be concluded that corporal punishment can be viewed as a subtype or milder form of physical abuse which often happens during early childhood.

The perpetrators of CPA are usually the victims' biological parents (A. C. W. Lee, Li, and So, 2006), younger than 40 years old, and with a low level of marital satisfaction and education (Tang, 2006). Minor physical assaults are more likely to be perpetrated by parents with a college education than by parents who only completed high school (A. S. Lau, Takeuchi, and Alegria, 2006). Severe physical assaults perpetrated by mothers are more prevalent among girls than boys (Chan, 2005). Lastly, perpetrators of CPA are also likely to be perpetrators of spousal violence (Chan, 2005).

Victim-related risk factors for CPA are as follows: male (Tang, 1996); being the only child of the family, which indicates that the parents have no prior child-rearing experience (Tang, 1998b); engaging in fights with peers (J. T. F. Lau, Liu, and Cheung, 1999); excessive academic pressure (J. T. F. Lau et al., 2005; Le and Wallen, 2009); and low educational attainment (Tang, 2006). Other demographic and social factors that put a family more at risk of CPA include low socioeconomic status (W. C. W. Wong et al., 2009); single-parent families; temporary housing (J. T. F. Lau et al., 2005); unemployment; mothers in white collar or professional jobs (Tang, 1996); parental alcohol or substance abuse (J. T. F. Lau et al., 2005; J. T. F. Lau, Liu, and Cheung, 1999; Yen, Yang, Chen, et al., 2008); poor family function and frequent conflicts (Yen, Yang, Yang, et al., 2008); relationship distress; low social support; low self-esteem; low social desirability; depressive symptoms; and the presence of spousal violence (Chan, 2005).

The magnitude of the impact of CPA on the victims is highly dependent on the individual victim's perceived normativeness of physical discipline; greater perceived normativeness is less strongly associated with adverse child outcomes (Lansford et al., 2005). Psychological outcomes include depression, aggression, anxiety, psychiatric morbidity, self-perceived bad health, somatic illnesses, high sensation seeking, and managing anger violently (Chan, 2005;

Duong, Schwartz, Chang, Kelly, and Tom, 2009; Lansford et al., 2005; J. T. F. Lau, Chan, Lam, Choi, and Lai, 2003; J. T. F. Lau, Liu, and Cheung, 1999; Nelson et al., 2006; Xu, Farver, and Zhang, 2009; Yen, Yang, Chen, et al., 2008). CPA also leads to various externalizing behavioral problems, including substance use, cigarette smoking, and sexual and self-harm behaviors (J. T. F. Lau et al., 2003; J. T. F. Lau et al., 2005). On the interpersonal level, CPA victims have poorer familial relations and more fights with their peers (J. T. F. Lau, Liu, and Cheung, 1999).

Sexual Abuse

In general, the prevalence rate of child sexual abuse (CSA) ranges from around 2.5% (Yen, Yang, Yang, et al., 2008) to 22.1% (Sun et al., 2008), 17.9% of which is intrafamilial abuse (Ho and Mak, 1992). Incidences of 22.1% among females and 14.7% among males were reported in a retrospective study conducted among 1,307 college students (Sun et al., 2008); these findings are comparable with those of a study conducted in the United States in which 14.2% of men and 32.3% of women reported having experienced CSA (Briere and Elliott, 2003).

Some studies have concluded that victims of CSA are more likely to be prepubertal females (Cheung et al., 2004; Tang, 2002) and not the only child in the family (Chien, 2009). A study conducted among college students (Sun et al., 2008) found that (a) CSA incidence increased with age among the female victims, (b) 54.7% of the male students first experienced CSA between the ages of 12 to 16, and, (c) female victims who experienced CSA before the age of 14 accounted for 11.4% of the overall female incidence rate (22.1%). In general, studies have found that the average age of first CSA experience is between 11.5 (Chen, Dunne, and Han, 2006) and 12.2 years (Ho and Mak, 1992) and ranges from 4 to 15 years. Furthermore, victims of intrafamilial CSA tend to be younger, under the age of 10 (Ho and Mak, 1992), and extrafamilial cases are highly skewed toward the preadolescent or adolescent period. In particular, the mean age of the onset of sexual abuse in Chinese societies is older than that reported in the West (Wyatt, 1985); this could be explained by the later onset of puberty among the Chinese (Ho and Mak, 1992).

Tang (2002) surveyed 2,147 Hong Kong college students and found significant gender differences regarding their childhood CSA experiences. While 72% of the perpetrators were people known to the victims, the males were three times more likely than the females to be sexually abused by their friends and the females were twice as likely than males to be sexually abused by strangers. The average age difference between the victims and the perpetrators at the time of the abuse was 14 years, but the difference was greater for the female victims than for the male victims. The males were also more likely than the females to experience repeated sexual abuse (Tang, 2002). Tang (2002) also reported on the duration of CSA among the college respondents: 45% of the CSA happened only once, 36% occurred more than once but lasted less than a year, 5% continued for 1 to 2 years, 12% continued for 2 to 5 years, and 3% lasted for over 5 years (Tang, 2002).

Studies have shown that the following groups are at risk of experiencing CSA: females (Chen, Dunne, and Han, 2004; Tang, 2002); indigenous boys (Yen, Yang, Yang, et al., 2008); children who are not the only child (Chien, 2009); lower socioeconomic class children; children in single-parent families (Ho and Mak, 1992); and children in families where there are frequent family conflicts (Yen, Yang, Yang, et al., 2008). The perpetrators of CSA are typically adults, mostly aged between 31 and 50 (Ho and Mak, 1992), and at least 5 years older than their victims (Ma et al., 2004), and 88% (Tang, 2002) to 96.3% (Ho and Mak, 1992) of them are males. In Ho and Mak's (1992) study, 62.4% of the perpetrators were friends of the victims or members of their households, 37.3% were strangers, 11.9% were fathers, 3% were elder brothers, and 3% were stepfathers or male cohabitors. Multiple incidences of CSA tend to be perpetrated by family members, especially parents, who reside with the victims (Ma et al., 2004).

In Tang's (2002) study, 62% of the CSA victims remained silent and did not report their experience of abuse. Even when the victims did make a report, 56% of their cases were not followed up, 8% were advised by others to keep silent, 8% were scolded or ridiculed, and only 3% were actually referred to social workers (Tang, 2002). Repeated or multiple-abuse CSA victims are more likely to tolerate the abuse longer before they disclose it to anyone. Younger CSA victims under 12 years of age tend to disclose the abuse to their own family members, while older victims over the age of 12 tend to tell their friends and professionals (Ma et al., 2004).

The reported psychological and social impacts of CSA on Chinese victims include depression, suicidal ideation, alcohol abuse, sexual behavior, eating disorders, violence, cigarette use, low self-esteem (Chen et al., 2004), a sense of disempowerment, fear for personal safety, anxiety, psychiatric disorders, impairment of mental health (Sun et al., 2008), social isolation, interpersonal difficulties, and clinginess (T. Y. E. Luo, 1998). Another consequence of CSA is traumatic sexualization. Features of traumatic sexualization include hyper-sexuality, the increased salience of sexual issues, preoccupation with thoughts about sex, confusion about sexual identity and norms, and aversion to sex or intimacy. Victims engage in compulsive sexual behaviors, a variety of sexual practices, and high levels of masturbation; they become sexually dysfunctional, have a high turnover of partners, and avoid or have phobic reactions to heterosexual intimacy (T. Y. E. Luo, 1998; Y. Luo, Parish, and Laumann, 2008). In incestuous CSA cases, female victims express more anger toward their mothers than the father-abusers (T. Y. E. Luo, 1998). CSA victims also have a heightened vulnerability to revictimization (Y. Luo et al., 2008).

Psychological Abuse and Neglect

In general, the prevalence rate of psychological abuse against children ranges from 0.8% (Hong Kong Medical Coordinators on Child Abuse, 2003) to 78.3% (Leung et al., 2008). Studies have shown that the victimization rate of neglect ranges from 1.7% (Hong Kong Medical Coordinators on Child Abuse, 2003) to 36% (Chan, 2005) and that 18% of adults admit to neglect in the preceding year (Chan, 2005). Most studies have not adequately addressed gender differences because they did not compare the rates of female and male victimization.

Risk factors for victims of emotional victimization, especially outside the home, include being involved in violent offending, being a gang member, and experiencing dating abuse. All of these risk factors increase the risk of emotional victimization four or five fold. Although emotional victimization tends to happen among females, sex was not consider as a significant risk factor in the study conducted by Le and Wallen (2009). Studies have found that within the home, fathers commit more emotional abuse than mothers, while mothers neglect their children slightly more than fathers (Rhee, Chang, Weaver, and Wong, 2008). Nonviolent discipline is commonly carried out by Chinese mothers (Chan, 2005), although with their daughters, mothers use more physical coercion while fathers use more psychological control (Nelson et al., 2006).

As in the case of physical abuse, the public and the profession have only just become aware of the phenomenon of psychological abuse and neglect. Therefore, relevant research is still in its infancy. This lack of awareness and conceptualization can be illustrated by the results of a study that found that only around 13% of females and males were able to mention psychological abuse without being prompted by the interviewer and only 20% of both females and males were able to talk about neglect. In this study, it was only after prompting from the interviewer that more than three quarters of the respondents stated that they felt that child neglect is common in Hong Kong and over 40% felt that psychological abuse is common (J. T. F. Lau, Liu, Yu, et al., 1999). In other words, there may be a lack of cultural recognition of psychological abuse and neglect, especially within Chinese societies.

Compared to Western societies, Chinese societies show a lower awareness of psychological abuse and neglect as forms of child maltreatment. Chinese parents typically have no concept of or concern about the potential damage these forms of child maltreatment can have on a child's self-respect and self-esteem because they regard shaming and scolding as effective discipline methods (J. T. F. Lau, Liu, and Cheung, 1999; J. T. F. Lau, Liu, Yu, et al., 1999). The Chinese parenting style, which is often referred to as *guan* (discipline), tends to be harsh, restrictive, domineering, and controlling (Nelson et al., 2006), and children are expected to *chiao shun* (filial piety) their parents by showing them the utmost respect and giving them their unquestioning obedience. These values, which often demand rigid gender and family roles, actually result in a higher chance of psychological abuse and neglect among Chinese populations (Rhee et al., 2008). However, not many parents are aware of the impact of such authoritative parenting. Psychological control by parents is associated with physical and relational aggression in children (Nelson et al., 2006), and emotional abuse can lead to serious violence in the child (Ngo and Le, 2007). Harsh parenting by parents can affect the regulation of children's emotions; this, in turn, may lead to aggression at school, and it is also associated with peer acceptance difficulties. Interestingly, compared to the father, harsh parenting by the mother has been shown to have a stronger effect on the regulation of a child's emotions but a lesser effect on the child's aggression; harsh parenting from fathers has a greater impact on sons than daughters (Chang, Schwartz, Dodge, and McBride-Chang, 2003).

Neglect is not limited to parents: it also exists in welfare institutions. Lee (1997) documented the reality of orphanages in China and found that the 1989 nationwide ratio of deaths to new admissions among institutionalized children was around 57.9%. Such a high mortality rate was a consequence of intentional starvation and malign neglect. However, in response to allegations and complaints, the Chinese government simply covered up the problems and controversy in order to suppress criticisms of the conditions inside the orphanages (W. C. Lee, 1997).

School Bullying

As in many countries, school bullying is a major source of victimization among youths. Research indicates that school bullying has a variety of negative consequences for both bullies and victims. The increasing problem of school bullying within the Chinese cultural context is of particular interest and should be included in the discussion of child abuse.

In 2001, Wong and colleagues (2008) surveyed 7,025 Hong Kong primary school children aged 10 to14. They found that the prevalence rate of victimization from physical bullying in the 6-month period prior to their study was 68%; 14% of these cases involved children who had been bullied over 10 times. Another study reported that (a) in the 30-day period prior to the interview, the rate of the victimization from bullying was 20%; and (b) in the 6-month period prior to the interview, 62% of the reported victimization was verbal, 32% was physical, 28% involved social exclusion, and 13% involved extortion (Hazemba, Siziya, Muula, and Rudatsikira, 2008). In Wong and colleagues' (2008) study, 87% and 68% of the students reported witnessing verbal bullying and physical bullying respectively during the previous 6 months, while 66% and 40% of the students respectively reported having witnessed exclusion and extortion in schools within the previous 6 months (D. S. W. Wong, Lok, Lo, and Ma, 2008). With regard to gender differences and subtypes of bullying, they found that (a) nearly 32% of boys engaged in physical bullying, while only 16% of the girls were involved in this type of bullying; and (b) about 40% of the boys had experienced physical victimization within a classroom setting, while only 22% of girls had had the same experience (D. S. W. Wong et al., 2008). Therefore, comparatively speaking, boys are involved in more physical bullying and are also being more physically bullied by their schoolmates, while girls are involved in more emotional victimization (Le and Wallen, 2009). This gender difference is similar to that identified in studies from the West; these studies found that boys are more likely to be involved in physical and verbal forms of bullying, while girls are more involved in relational forms of abuse (Wang, Iannotti, and Nansel, 2009).

Wong and colleagues found that (a) the prevalence rates of the perpetration of bullying in the 6-month period prior to their study were 52% (verbal bullying) and 24% (physical bullying), (b) 61% of the student participants admitted using at least one bullying tactic, and (c) 13% of the students used three or four types of tactics (D. S. W. Wong et al., 2008). They also found that the bullies commonly reported that they did not know how to control their temper or that they wanted to take revenge after being victimized themselves; more than one third of the bullies aimed to take revenge after being victimized by others, and nearly a quarter of the victims also indicated that they would take revenge sometime in the future. Similar findings were reported in a study that analyzed a nationally representative sample of adolescents in the United States. In that study, the prevalence of frequent involvement in school bullying in the 2-month period prior to the survey was 29.9%: 13.0% as bullies, 10.6% as victims, and 6.3% as both (Nansel, Overpeck, and Pilla, 2001). From the above patterns, it can be concluded that bullying and victimization may actually create a vicious cycle (D. S. W. Wong et al., 2008). Without proper intervention, it can be predicted that school bullying will become widespread across campuses as more and more students will become involved in, and affected by, it.

There are some risk factors that increase the likelihood of children being bullied in school, including feelings of loneliness, worry, sadness, and hopelessness; cigarette smoking, alcohol use, and being a truant (Hazemba et al., 2008). Unsatisfactory relationships with peers, parents, or siblings; low self-esteem; low family engagement; stressful life events; and poor academic achievement are also risk factors associated with the likelihood of being victimized by bullies. Also, the less students feel that their school provides a harmonious environment, the higher the chances of them being involved in bullying (D. S. W. Wong et al., 2008). Violent values (e.g., exposure to gangs, violent comics, and action films) and delinquency (e.g., delinquent peer affiliations, previous arrest history, and being a gang member) also increase the likelihood of children being bullied and bullying others (Le and Wallen, 2009; D. S. W. Wong et al., 2008).

Although bullying is viewed as normative in schools, it is socially unacceptable to almost all children. Wong and colleagues (2008) identified the impact of bullying on schoolchildren. Bullied children are frightened by physically aggressive acts that could lead to bodily harm. Social exclusion and verbal insults have adverse psychological effects. Most importantly, school bullying may also be the precursor of general juvenile delinquency or youth violence. Growing up in an aggressive environment may increase the likelihood of school children becoming involved in violence in the future (D. S. W. Wong et al., 2008).

Child Trafficking and Slavery

Trafficking in children has become a serious problem in China in the last two decades. UNICEF experts have even predicted that if the trend is not stopped, China will become the center of human trafficking in Asia (Pochagina, 2007). Due to the one-child policy in China, the prohibition of ultrasound examinations for the purpose of determining the sex of the fetus, and the preference for male offspring, a market has been created for abandoned or abducted children. Children, especially girls, are abducted for sale and exploitation in the sex business and in industry. Moreover, they are bought and sold not only as workers or servants, but also as daughters or future brides for sons. Pochagina's (2007) article is the only one to date to have thoroughly described the current child trafficking situation in China. There are unknown numbers of underground criminal organizations in China that specialize in the abduction and sale of children for illegal adoption, child slavery, and exploitation in the sex business. Thus, it is difficult to make a precise assessment of the number and gender of the children sold due to the secretive nature of the business and the high risks and difficulties involved in obtaining information.

Pochagina (2007) summarized the important risk factors behind the increase in the supply of trafficked children, including poverty; an inappropriate family planning policy; unplanned pregnancies; the large number of abandoned infant girls, children with congenital defects, and runaway children; the ignorance of underage girls looking for jobs in big cities; and dysfunction and violence in the family. The increasing demand for underage children is due to the development of sex tourism; gender imbalance; the desire of foreigners to adopt Chinese children; the demand for cheap or free labor in factories, households, and farms; weak control by local authorities; and corruption among law enforcement bodies and officials (Pochagina, 2007).

One form of child slavery in China is the "*Mui Tsai*" system, which involves rich families purchasing young girls, either directly from poverty-stricken parents or indirectly through kidnapping, as servants; these girls receive no salary, but they are provided with food and lodging. The Hong Kong government did not impose any restrictions on the *Mui Tsai* system until 1922, when the Anti-*Mui Tsai* Society was formed by members of churches and labor unions who argued against this form of slavery. However, in 2005, the case of an 11-year-old girl with multiple injuries who was admitted to hospital for evaluation as a suspected case of child abuse was reported; the details of the case bore a remarkable resemblance to the practice of *Mui Tsai*. When she was 10 years old, this girl's parents received HKD$1,000, and she was sent from Mainland China to be a servant to her paternal aunt in Hong Kong. The young girl was subordinate to everyone in her aunt's household. Not only did she work long hours, she was also subjected to physical and verbal abuse (A. C. Lee and So, 2006). All in all, the concept of child protection is still developing in Chinese societies, even in well-developed societies such as Hong Kong. Therefore, trafficking and slavery still remain among the most urgent problems that hinder the minimization of child victimization.

Risk Factors of Child Maltreatment

Child abuse is a complex phenomenon with multiple causes. Thus, it is crucial to identify and understand the risk factors of child abuse in order to prevent and address the problem. Besides the specific risk factors of different subtypes of child abuse mentioned above, there are also cultural values and attitudes that foster the occurrence of child abuse.

Tang (1998) has suggested that the definition and the perception of child maltreatment are typically shaped by cultural norms. Thus, it is not surprising to find that there is a lack of cultural recognition of such a problem within Chinese culture. Historically and culturally, the Chinese have different attitudes to child-rearing practices, especially the use of physical force for discipline, compared to Western countries. Filial piety is highly valued in Chinese populations, and a high percentage of Hong Kong adults believe that corporal punishment and shaming and scolding children are parental rights and effective discipline methods (J. T. F. Lau, Liu, and Cheung, 1999); it is ingrained to the point where the children themselves accept the abusive behaviors of their parents as a necessary part of discipline. Despite the fact that there is increasing public concern about the issue of child abuse, most Chinese parents do not understand the various mental health and behavioral consequences of child abuse (Dunne, Chen, and Choo, 2008). It is still very difficult to distinguish between physical maltreatment and physical discipline as child maltreatment is understood by the Chinese as the parents having malicious intent; therefore, it is impossible for China to treat all domestic violence cases as crimes of child abuse (Qiao and Chan, 2005). This may be a major risk factor that contributes to the widespread phenomenon of child abuse within the Chinese community.

Second, the ever-growing economy in China is also a risk factor. Families living in rural areas and in poverty still have difficulties supporting themselves. Together with the pressure created by the one-child policy, these difficulties have further cultivated the traditional preference for boys over girls as boys have a greater physical capacity to do hard work than girls. This gender preference has given rise to a large number of infant girls being abandoned; children who suffer from congenital defects and disabilities are also abandoned in large numbers. This gender bias therefore causes neglect and abandonment. Moreover, it is not surprising to find that parents have little time to communicate and care for their children when they have to work for long hours and away from home. All of these factors create a conducive environment for child victimization. When children are unsupervised by their parents, they may be at an increased risk of becoming involved in and exposed to violence and abuse outside the home. This further increases the chance of aversive and harsh parenting due to the misconduct and behavioral problems of the children. In other words, parents who are living in poverty are being caught in a catch-22 situation which fosters child victimization inside and outside home.

Third, the cultural belief that family problems should be kept strictly within the family may also give rise to child abuse. The studies reviewed in this article have shown that child abuse is highly pervasive among the Chinese and that it is very likely that underreporting occurs. Lau (1999) concluded that there are three general causes of underreporting among Chinese victims. First, in Lau's (1999) study, the majority of people said they would not report child abuse cases to the police or social workers; people also showed a low level of awareness of various forms of child abuse, and their conceptualization of child abuse was very different from Western official definitions of abuse (J. T. F. Lau, Liu, Yu, et al., 1999). In particular, it is unknown whether the lower prevalence of sexual abuse in males is due to lower vulnerability among Chinese boys or their greater reluctance to report sexual abuse compared to Chinese girls (Ho and Mak, 1992). Since the majority of CSA perpetrators are males, male victims may feel reluctant to disclose the abuse for fear of being identified or viewed as having a homosexual orientation. Also, younger victims tend to disclose the abuse to family members, and according to Chinese traditional beliefs, shameful family matters should not be disclosed to others; therefore, victims are most often scolded or ignored (Tang, 2002). Thus, embarrassment, shame, and the tendency to avoid family disgrace inhibit both victims and abusers from seeking help, which may further increase the likelihood of repeated victimization.

To conclude, cultural beliefs and childrearing practices, from the principle of filial piety to unquestioning obedience; poverty; and attitudes toward seeking help may facilitate the occurrence of child abuse within Chinese communities. Nonetheless, the study of child abuse among Chinese societies is still in its infancy. Future research should investigate these culture-specific factors in a more systematic and rigorous manner.

CHILD PROTECTIVE FACTORS IN CHINESE CULTURE

In general, the Chinese are a diversified population spread across many different societies. In particular, some of the culture-specific risk factors mentioned above may also be considered as protective factors. Thus, caution should be taken when interpreting the culture-specific risk factors.

The essence of familism and harmony within Chinese culture may actually give Chinese people a certain degree of resilience against child maltreatment. Chinese culture emphasizes maintaining family harmony and integrity as a way of preserving the family as an ideal and intact unit (Feng, Chen, Wilk, Yang, and Fetzer, 2009). Therefore, this may reduce the chances of conflicts occurring. When conflict does arise, Chinese people use different methods to cope with the problem so as to preserve peace and unity within the family, and this reduces the likelihood of them maltreating their children. At the same time, the Chinese have a great tendency to avoid losing face. As child abuse, once disclosed or discovered, would cause the entire family much disgrace and shame, the fear of disgrace and shame makes Chinese people less likely to allow child abuse to take place in the home.

Although it is often argued that family harmony strongly influences the victims, especially their help-seeking behavior after being abused, the essence of preserving harmony and family cohesion still stands as a buffer against revictimization. Once intentional or unintentional child maltreatment has occurred, family members may make their best efforts to cure the damage done to the family's harmony and prevent future disturbance (Zhai and Gao, 2009). This holistic family effort can thus protect Chinese children from becoming victims of maltreatment.

Policy and Regulation Regarding Child Protection

No child wants to grow up in an unsafe environment. While it is true that everyone has the responsibility and power to stop child abuse from happening, local governments are expected to assume responsibility for caring for vulnerable people. Despite the fact that child maltreatment is underreported among Chinese communities, there have been remarkable achievements in protecting children's rights in Mainland China, Hong Kong, and Taiwan.

Based on the current status of China's socioeconomic development, even though child welfare provision is still underdeveloped, the current laws of China have made provision for the prohibition of child maltreatment. In general, all policies and laws can be categorized into three levels: international, national, and provincial. Two of the major international documents relating to children's rights that the Chinese government has signed and ratified are the Convention on the Rights of the Child and the United Nations Declaration of the Rights of the Children. At the national level, the 2001-2010 National Program of Action for the Development of Children serves as the guidelines that outline the national action to be taken to further promote healthy and sustainable child development in China. In addition, the primary law governing child protection is the PRC Law on the Protection of Minors, which was originally passed in 1991 and then revised in 2006. The newly revised Law on the Protection of Minors was enacted on June 1, 2007. This law defines the responsibilities of families, schools, and the government with regard to the protection of children's rights and the judicial protection of these rights. The Protection of the Rights of Women and Children within the PRC Law, the Law on the Protection of Children, Article 49 of the Constitutional Law of the PRC, and Article 3 of the Marriage Law are also important laws that state that child maltreatment is prohibited in China (Qiao and Chan, 2005). Furthermore, there are different regulations and policies that have been established at the provincial level that further promote the work and importance of child protection within the country. In general, Mainland China declares that it protects a wide range of children's rights through domestic legislation and by ratifying and joining relevant international conventions and treaties. However, the reality is still debatable; the enforcement of laws and policies especially remains a huge problem.

Hong Kong, on the other hand, has a highly integrated legislative system and a mature child welfare system. First, the Procedural Guide for Handling Child Abuse Cases was revised in 2008 to further strengthen the efforts and collaboration of different professionals in handling the problem of child abuse in Hong Kong. In addition, units exist within the government body that work together to serve the best interests of children, such as the Family and Child Protective Services Unit (FCPSU) within the Social Welfare Department (SWD); the child abuse investigation units (CAIUs) within the Hong Kong Police Force; and the Child Protection Special Investigation Team (CPSIT), which is jointly run by the police and the SWD. The Child Protection Registry (CPR) has also been set up in recent years to facilitate the better handling of child abuses cases. Apart from keeping a record of reported cases and providing a case-checking function, the CPR also produces an annual statistical report that includes information on the general profile of newly reported child abuse cases; this information informs the future planning and development of government units and nongovernmental organizations concerned with child abuse prevention and intervention. Most importantly, a list of ordinances and offences can be referred to as and when necessary and appropriate. The primary law that governs child protection is the Protection of Children and Juveniles Ordinance (CAP 213), which should be discharged by a police officer or social worker, as authorized by the Director of Social Work, whenever a situation warrants protecting a child or juvenile from assault, ill treatment, neglect, sexual abuse, and harm. As far as sexual abuse is concerned, the Crimes Ordinance (CAP 200) and the Prevention of Child Pornography Ordinance (CAP 579) are used in cases of offenses such as incest, rape, abduction, trafficking, and child pornography. Nonetheless, it should be noted that a legal definition of child abuse is absent within Hong Kong's legislative system; thus, specific abusive acts are dealt with under a number of different ordinances.

In Taiwan, a significant degree of progress has been achieved over the past 50 years in relation to the development of children's rights. Various laws regarding child protection and welfare have been promulgated according to the Taiwanese Constitution, the most significant being the Child Welfare Law (Amendment), the Juvenile Welfare Law, the Law to Suppress Sexual Transactions Involving Children and Juveniles, and the Law to Prevent Family Violence.

To conclude, Chinese societies have increasingly recognized the significance of child protection and welfare. Nonetheless, we believe that continuous efforts are needed to monitor whether laws and regulations are fully utilized and executed by relevant government departments to help and protect victims.

CONCLUSION

This chapter has provided a comprehensive review of the studies on child abuse in Chinese societies and has provided researchers with the information required to conduct further research. The reviewed studies varied in their methodology, measures, and samples, and they thus yielded a wide range of prevalence figures. Although the Chinese government has become more open to conducting domestic violence research, the situation in China has still not developed to the level where child maltreatment can be understood and treated as a social problem (Qiao and Chan, 2005). More research on child abuse is needed in order to provide a clearer understanding of the situation that will lead to proper responses by the Chinese government.

REFERENCES

Briere, J., and Elliott, D. M. (2003). Prevalence and psychological sequelae of self-reported childhood physical and sexual abuse in a general population sample of men and women. *Child Abuse and Neglect, 27*(10), 1205-1222.

Chan, K. L. (2005). *Study on child abuse and spouse battering: Report on findings of household survey.* [A Consultancy Study Commissioned by the SWD of HKSAR]. Hong Kong: Department of Social Work and Social Administration, The University of Hong Kong.

Chang, L., Schwartz, D., Dodge, K. A., and McBride-Chang, C. (2003). Harsh parenting in relation to child emotion regulation and aggression. *Journal of Family Psychology, 17*(4), 598-606.

Chen, J. Q., Dunne, M. P., and Han, P. (2004). Child sexual abuse in China: A study of adolescents in four provinces. *Child Abuse and Neglect, 28*(11), 1171-1186.

Chen, J. Q., Dunne, M. P., and Han, P. (2006). Child sexual abuse in Henan province, China: Associations with sadness, suicidality, and risk behaviors among adolescent girls. *Journal of Adolescent Health, 38*(5), 544-549.

Cheung, P. C. H., Ko, C. H., Lee, H. Y. M., Ho, L. M. C., To, W. W. K., and Ip, P. L. S. (2004). Correlation of colposcopic anogenital findings and overall assessment of child sexual abuse: Prospective study. *Hong Kong Medical Journal, 10*(6), 378-383.

Chien, M.-h. (2009). The current relationships of Taiwanese women with a history of childhood sexual abuse to their non-offending mothers. *Journal of Social Service Research, 34*(4), 29-39.

Chiu, M. C. (2001). Politicizing Han-Chinese masculinities: A plea for court mandated counselling for wife abusers in Hong Kong. *Feminist Legal Studies, 9*(1), 3-27.

Dunne, M. P., Chen, J. Q., and Choo, W. Y. (2008). The evolving evidence base for child protection in Chinese societies. *Asia-Pacific Journal of Public Health, 20*(4), 267-276.

Duong, M. T., Schwartz, D., Chang, L., Kelly, B. M., and Tom, S. R. (2009). Associations between maternal physical discipline and peer victimization among Hong Kong Chinese children: The moderating role of child aggression. *Journal of Abnormal Child Psychology, 37*(7), 957-966.

Feng, J. Y., Chen, S. J., Wilk, N. C., Yang, W. P., and Fetzer, S. (2009). Kindergarten teachers' experience of reporting child abuse in Taiwan: Dancing on the edge. *Children and Youth Services Review, 31*(3), 405-409.

Fong, R. (1997). Child welfare practice with Chinese families: Assessment issues for immigrants from the People's Republic of China. *Journal of Family Social Work, 2*(1), 33-47.

Hazemba, A., Siziya, S., Muula, A. S., and Rudatsikira, E. (2008). Prevalence and correlates of being bullied among in-school adolescents in Beijing: Results from the 2003 Beijing Global School-Based Health Survey. *Annals of General Psychiatry, 7*(6), 1-6.

Ho, T. P., and Mak, F. L. (1992). Sexual abuse in Chinese children in Hong Kong: A review of 134 cases. *Australian and New Zealand Journal of Psychiatry, 26,* 639-643.

Hong Kong Medical Coordinators on Child Abuse. (2003). Management of child abuse in Hong Kong: Results of a territory-wide interhospital prospective surveillance study. *Hong Kong Medical Journal, 9*(1), 6-9.

Kwok, S. M., and Tam, D. M. Y. (2005). Child abuse in Chinese families in Canada - Implications for child protection practice. *International Social Work, 48*(3), 341-348.

Krug, E.G., Dahlberg, L.L., Mercy, J.A., Zwi, A.b. and Lozano, R. (2002). World report on violence and health. Geneva, Switzerland: World Health Organization.

Lansford, J. E., Chang, L., Dodge, K. A., Malone, P. S., Oburu, P., Palmerus, K., et al. (2005). Physical discipline and children's adjustment: Cultural normativeness as a moderator. *Child Development, 76*(6), 1234-1246.

Lau, A. S., Takeuchi, D. T., and Alegria, M. (2006). Parent-to-child aggression among Asian American parents: Culture, context, and vulnerability. *Journal of Marriage and the Family, 68*(5), 1261-1275.

Lau, J. T. F., Chan, K. K., Lam, P. K. W., Choi, P. Y. W., and Lai, K. Y. C. (2003). Psychological correlates of physical abuse in Hong Kong Chinese adolescents. *Child Abuse and Neglect, 27*(1), 63-75.

Lau, J. T. F., Kim, J. H., Tsui, H. Y., Cheung, A., Lau, M., and Yu, A. (2005). The relationship between physical maltreatment and substance use among adolescents: A survey of 95,788 adolescents in Hong Kong. *Journal of Adolescent Health, 37*(2), 110-119.

Lau, J. T. F., Liu, J. L. Y., and Cheung, J. C. K. (1999). Prevalence and correlates of physical abuse in Hong Kong Chinese adolescents: A population-based approach. *Child Abuse and Neglect, 23*(6), 549-557.

Lau, J. T. F., Liu, J. L. Y., Yu, A., and Wong, C. K. (1999). Conceptualization, reporting and underreporting of child abuse in Hong Kong. *Child Abuse and Neglect, 23*(11), 1159-1174.

Le, T. N., and Wallen, J. (2009). Risks of non-familial violent physical and emotional victimization in four Asian ethnic groups. *Journal of Immigrant Minority Health, 11,* 174-187.

Lee, A. C., and So, K. T. (2006). Child slavery in Hong Kong: Case report and historical review. *Hong Kong Medical Journal, 12*(6), 463-466.

Lee, A. C. W., Li, C. H., and So, K. T. (2006). The impact of a management protocol on the outcomes of child abuse in hospitalized children in Hong Kong. *Child Abuse and Neglect, 30*(8), 909-917.

Lee, W. C. (1997). Death by default: A policy of fatal neglect in China's state orphanages - Human RightsWatch/Asia. *Journal of Asian Studies, 56*(2), 476-477.

Leow, B. G. (2001). *Census of population, 2000.* Singapore: Department of Statistics.

Leung, P. W. S., Wong, W. C. W., Chen, W. Q., and Tang, C. S. K. (2008). Prevalence and determinants of child maltreatment among high school students in Southern China: A large scale school based survey. *Child and Adolescent Psychiatry and Mental Health, 2*(1), 27-34.

Luo, T. Y. E. (1998). Sexual abuse trauma among Chinese survivors. *Child Abuse and Neglect, 22*(10), 1013-1026.

Luo, Y., Parish, W. L., and Laumann, E. O. (2008). A population-based study of childhood sexual contact in China: Prevalence and long-term consequences. *Child Abuse and Neglect, 32*(7), 721-731.

Ma, E. Y. M., Yau, D. C. W., Ng, W. W., and Tong, S. L. (2004). Characteristics of child sexual abuse cases referred for psychological services in Hong Kong: A comparison between multiple incident versus single incident cases. *Journal of Child Sexual Abuse, 13*(2), 21-39.

Meston, C. M., Heiman, J. R., Trapnell, P. D., and Carlin, A. S. (1999). Ethnicity, desirable responding, and self-reports of abuse: A comparison of European- and Asian-ancestry undergraduates. *Journal of Consulting and Clinical Psychology, 67*(1), 139-144.

Nansel, T. R., Overpeck, M. P., Ramani S., Ruan, W. J., Simons-Morton, B., and Scheidt, P. (2001). Bullying behaviors among US youth: Prevalence and association with psychosocial adjustment. *Journal of the American Medical Association, 285*(16), 2094-2100.

Nelson, D. A., Hart, C. H., Yang, C. M., Olsen, J. A., and Jin, S. H. (2006). Aversive parenting in China: Associations with child physical and relational aggression. *Child Development, 77*(3), 554-572.

Ngo, H. M., and Le, T. N. (2007). Stressful life events, culture, and violence. *Journal of Immigrant Health, 9,* 75-84.

Pochagina, O. (2007). Trafficking in women and children in present-day China. *Far Eastern Affairs, 35*(1), 82-101.

Qiao, D. P., and Chan, Y. C. (2005). Child abuse in China: A yet-to-be-acknowledged 'social problem' in the Chinese Mainland. *Child and Family Social Work, 10,* 21-27.

Rhee, S., Chang, J., Weaver, D., and Wong, D. (2008). Child maltreatment among immigrant Chinese families: Characteristics and patterns of placement. *Child Maltreatment, 13*(3), 269-279.

Samuda, G. M. (1998). Child discipline and abuse in Hong Kong. *Child Abuse and Neglect, 12,* 283-287.

Shen, A. C. T. (2009). Long-term effects of interparental violence and child physical maltreatment experiences on PTSD and behavior problems: A national survey of Taiwanese college students. *Child Abuse and Neglect, 33*(3), 148-160.

Statistics Canada. (2001). *Visible minority population, by province and territory (2001 Census).* Retrieved from http://www.statcan.ca/english/Pgdb/demo52b.htm.

Sun, Y. P., Zhang, B., Dong, Z. J., Yi, M. J., Sun, D. F., and Shi, S. S. (2008). Psychiatric state of college students with a history of childhood sexual abuse. *World Journal of Pediatrics, 4*(4), 285-290.

Tang, C. S. K. (1996). Adolescent abuse in Hong Kong Chinese families. *Child Abuse and Neglect, 20*(9), 873-878.

Tang, C. S. K. (1998a). Frequency of parental violence against children in Chinese families: Impact of age and gender. *Journal of Family Violence, 13*(2), 113-130.

Tang, C. S. K. (1998b). The rate of physical child abuse in Chinese families: A community survey in Hong Kong. *Child Abuse and Neglect, 22*(5), 381-391.

Tang, C. S. K. (2002). Childhood experience of sexual abuse among Hong Kong Chinese college students. *Child Abuse and Neglect, 26*(1), 23-37.

Tang, C. S. K. (2006). Corporal punishment and physical maltreatment against children: A community study on Chinese parents in Hong Kong. *Child Abuse and Neglect, 30*(8), 893-907.

Tang, C. S. K., and Davis, C. (1996). Child abuse in Hong Kong revisited after 15 years: Characteristics of victims and abusers. *Child Abuse and Neglect, 20*(12), 1213-1218.

United Nations Development Programme (UNDP) (2010). *Human development report 2010 20th anniversary edition.* New York: United Nations Development Programme.

United States Census Bureau. (2003). *Facts for features Asian American heritage month: May 2003*. Retrieved from http://www.census.gov/Press-Release/www/2003/cb2003-ff2005.html.

Wang, J., Iannotti, R. J., and Nansel, T. R. (2009). School bullying among adolescents in the United States: Physical, verbal, relational, and cyber. *Journal of Adolescent Health, 45*(4), 368-375.

Wong, D. S. W., Lok, D. R. P., Lo, T. W., and Ma, S. K. (2008). School bullying among Hong Kong Chinese primary schoolchildren. *Youth and Society, 40*(1), 35-54.

Wong, W. C. W., Chen, W. Q., Goggins, W. B., Tang, C. S., and Leung, P. W. (2009). Individual, familial and community determinants of child physical abuse among high-school students in China. *Social Science and Medicine, 68*(10), 1819-1825.

Wyatt, G.E. (1985). The sexual abuse of Afro-American and White-American women in childhood. *Child Abuse and Neglect, 9*(4), 507-519.

Xu, Y. Y., Farver, J. A. M., and Zhang, Z. X. (2009). Temperament, harsh and indulgent parenting, and Chinese children's proactive and reactive aggression. *Child Development, 80*(1), 244-258.

Yen, C. F., Yang, M. S., Chen, C. C., Yang, M. J., Su, Y. C., Wang, M. H., et al. (2008). Effects of childhood physical abuse on depression, problem drinking and perceived poor health status in adolescents living in rural Taiwan. *Psychiatry and Clinical Neurosciences, 62*(5), 575-583.

Yen, C. F., Yang, M. S., Yang, M. J., Su, Y. C., Wang, M. H., and Lane, C. M. (2008). Childhood physical and sexual abuse: Prevalence and correlates among adolescents living in rural Taiwan. *Child Abuse and Neglect, 32*(3), 429-438.

Zhai, F., and Gao, Q. (2009). Child maltreatment among Asian Americans: Characteristics and explanatory framework. *Child Maltreatment, 14*(2), 207-224.

In: Child Protection in Chinese Societies
Editor: Ko Ling Chan

ISBN: 978-1-61942-879-9

Chapter 2

CHILD VICTIMIZATION IN CHINA: PREVALENCE AND RISK FACTORS

Ko Ling Chan
Department of Social Work and Social Administration
University of Hong Kong, Pokfulam, Hong Kong

ABSTRACT

Child victimization accompanied by injury has imposed a heavy demand on health services in China. However, efforts to recognize it as a public health problem have been hampered by the absence of reliable estimates of the prevalence of the different types of victimization.

The objective of the population surveys is to investigate the prevalence and risk factors of child victimization, with specific emphasis on child sexual abuse. A multistage stratified sampling procedure was adopted to identify eligible participants from Hong Kong and180 communes in 5 cities in mainland China. Face-to-face interviews were conducted with 8,945 Chinese parents of children younger than 18 years of age. A total of 3 321 children and 18 341 students, aged 15-17 years, were successfully interviewed.

The lifetime prevalence rates of child sexual victimization and child victimization, as reported by household parents, were 1.3% and 35.2% respectively. The lifetime prevalence rates of child sexual victimization and child victimization, as reported by household children and school students were 3.1% to 8% and 50.1% to 71.7%, respectively, which were significantly higher than those reported by parents.

The findings provide reliable estimates of child victimization which will facilitate the allocation of resources. The associations between child victimization and family violence highlight the value of screening for multiple types of violence when one type has been detected.

Keywords: Child victimization; Child sexual victimization; Intimate partner violence; Elder abuse; In-law conflict

INTRODUCTION

Child victimization involving injury has imposed a heavy demand on health services in China. However, efforts to recognize this as a public health problem have been hampered by the absence of reliable estimates of the prevalence of different types of victimization. Research on child victimization in Mainland China has not developed to the level where child victimization can be understood and treated as a social problem.

To fill the gap in our understanding of child victimization in order to inform policy making designed to prevent it, the Optimus Study, funded by the Optimus Foundation in Switzerland, was launched in China in 2007. The Optimus Study is a multinational research project on victim experiences among children and young people with a special focus on sexual assaults. The purpose of this project is to support high quality epidemiological study on child victimization that provides reliable data from representative studies. The ultimate goal is to develop evidence-based prevention and intervention. The Optimus Study in China is the one of two projects; its study period lasted from 2007 to 2010.

The Optimus Study in China consisted of population (household and school) surveys. The objective of the study was to investigate the prevalence and risk factors of child victimization in China, with a specific emphasis on child sexual abuse (CSA).

RESEARCH DESIGN AND METHODOLOGY

Sample Selection and Procedure

We used the combination of a household-based survey and a school-based survey to gather information about child victimization in China. The household-based survey involved (a) parents with children aged 17 or under and (b) children aged 15 to 17, and the school-based survey involved students aged 15 to 17. The former survey was used because it was the most feasible way to assess child victimization among young children (aged 0-14); the latter survey was employed because it was believed that it would be less subject to underreporting.

We adopted a multistage sampling procedure to identify eligible participants in Hong Kong and five cities in Mainland China (Shanghai, Shenzhen, Tianjin, Wuhan, and Xi'an). The five mainland cities share similar characteristics in terms of social, economic, political, and cultural development which can be differentiated from the characteristics of Hong Kong, a former British colony that was returned to Chinese sovereignty in 1997.

Household-Based Survey (Parents)

In the first stage of the household-based survey, two urban administrative districts and one rural/suburban administrative district were randomly sampled from each of the five mainland cities. In the next stage, three neighborhoods, towns, or villages were randomly selected from each administrative district. Communes or smaller districts were then further sampled from each selected neighborhood, town, or village. A total of 36 communes were sampled in each mainland city. We used the official registers of households and temporary migrants as the sample frame for eligible families. In the final stage, one of the parents or caregivers of any child aged 17 years or under was randomly sampled by selecting the parent/caregiver with the most recent birthday.

A slightly different sampling method was used to identify eligible families in Hong Kong. We randomly sampled 14,422 living quarters from the Register of Quarters, which is maintained by the Census and Statistics Department of the Government of Hong Kong. In the first stage, eligible households were randomly selected with stratification based on housing type and geographic region. Next, as in the final sampling stage used in the mainland cities, one of the parents or caregivers of any child aged 17 years or under was randomly selected.

The parents of 8,945 children under 18 years of age were successfully interviewed, giving an overall response rate of 76.8%.

Household-Based Survey (Children)

When an eligible household sampled by the above multistage stratified procedure had a child aged 15 to 17 years, this child was selected to participate in the survey. If the family had more than one eligible child, the child whose birthday was the most recent was selected.

With the consent of their parents, a total of 3,321 children aged 15 to 17 were successfully interviewed. Their parents were also interviewed to respond to the parent questionnaire.

School-Based Survey (Students)

We used a two-stage stratified procedure to identify eligible student participants. First, about 150 schools from the mainland cities and Hong Kong were randomly sampled. Next, eligible students, who were aged 15 to 17, were randomly sampled.

A total of 18,341 students aged 15 to 17 were successfully interviewed, giving an overall response rate of 76.5% at school level and 95.8% at individual level.

The sampled parents, children, and students were invited to participate in the study. All of the participants provided written informed consent prior to the interviews, which were conducted face-to-face by trained interviewers. The participants were asked to provide information about their family as well as about themselves. With regard to the parent participants, if they had more than one child under the age of 17 at the time of the study period, the child with most recent birthday was selected as the assessment target.

Ethical Issues

Participation in the present study was on a voluntary basis. Items on sensitive issues were grouped into a separate self-administered questionnaire which was completed and sealed in an envelope by the participants themselves. All of the participants were told that they could omit answering any question they wished. Each completed survey was assigned a record identifier. To ensure anonymity, apart from the record identifier, no information about the participant's name, address, or school was recorded on the questionnaire or in the data files. Whenever possible, all interviews were conducted in a quiet place in the absence of other family members or students. Training on the ethical issues related to working with participants who report violence was provided to all of the interviewers. The interviewers also gave the participants an information card containing details of social services related to violence prevention.

The study was conducted in compliance with the principles enunciated in the 1996 or later version of the Declaration of Helsinki and the Hospital Authority of Hong Kong Investigator's Code of Practice in Undertaking Clinical Research. The Institutional Review Board of the University of Hong Kong and the Hospital Authority Hong Kong West Cluster provided ethical approval for the whole study. The local institutional review board in each mainland city provided approval for the study at that study site.

Measures

We used a battery of instruments that has already been extensively pilot tested in Shanghai and Hong Kong for feasibility and acceptability.

Child Victimization

Child victimization was assessed using the Juvenile Victimization Questionnaire (JVQ; Finkelhor, Hamby, Ormrod, and Turner, 2005), a 34-item scale covering five aspects (modules) of violence victimization among children and adolescents: (a) conventional crime; (b) child maltreatment; (c) peer and sibling victimization; (d) sexual victimization; and (e) witnessing and experiencing indirect victimization. In the present study, the "child version" of the questionnaire was used with the child and student participants, while the "caregiver version" was used with the parents who were interviewed as proxies for the target children. In accordance with the original study (Finkelhor et al., 2005), there was no gender preference or exclusion in the selection of the proxies. The Chinese JVQ has demonstrated good internal consistency in previous validation studies, with a Cronbach's alpha value exceeding .70 for all subscales and .89 for the scale as a whole (Chan, Fong, Yan, Chow, and Ip, 2011). In the present study, the Cronbach's alpha value ranged from .60 to .87 for all subscales and was .76 for the total scale.

Intimate Partner Violence (IPV)

The validated Chinese version of the Revised Conflict Tactics Scale (CTS2) was used to assess the prevalence of parental IPV (Chan, 2004). The original CTS2 has demonstrated satisfactory internal consistencies, cross-cultural reliability, and criterion validity (Straus, 2004; Straus, Hamby, Boney-McCoy, and Sugarman, 1996). The subscales of physical assault, psychological aggression, sexual violence, and injury were used in this study. The parent participants were asked to report whether they had been victimized by any of these types of IPV in the year preceding the interview or during their lifetime. The child and student participants were asked if they had witnessed any IPV between their parents. The Chinese CTS2 showed satisfactory reliability in the present study, with alpha values ranging from .74 to .86.

Elder Abuse

A Chinese version of the elder abuse measure has been developed based on the constructs of the CTS. The scale, which includes the subscales of physical violence, injury, psychological aggression, and neglect, was used to measure the elder abuse experienced by the grandparents of the sampled families since the age of 60; the participants were asked to act as proxies for the target grandparents in reporting experiences of elder abuse. These subscales have been used in past studies of elder abuse in Hong Kong and have demonstrated good reliability (Yan and Tang, 2003, 2004). In the present study, the Cronbach's alpha values for the physical and psychological aggression subscales were .87 and .86, respectively.

In-Law Conflict

In-law conflict was measured by the modified version of the psychological aggression subscale of CTS2 and two items assessing the presence of physical violence and injury. The parent participants were asked about their experiences of conflict with their parents-in-law, while the child and student participants were asked about their experiences of witnessing such conflict. The original psychological aggression subscale of CTS2 measures psychological abusive behaviors between the couples. These items were adapted by changing the subjects involved in in-law conflict. The participants reported any violence victimization by their parents-in-law. The internal consistency of the psychological aggression subscale ranged from .92 to .93 in the present study.

Depression

The Beck Depression Inventory version II (BDI-II) was used to assess the symptoms corresponding to the criteria for diagnosing depressive disorders (Beck, Sterr, and Brown, 1996). The BDI-II consists of 21 groups of statements and requires participants to choose one statement in each group that best describes how they have felt during the previous 2 weeks. The Chinese version of the BDI-II has been shown to have satisfactory validity and reliability (α ranging from .86 to .87; Leung, 2001). The internal consistency of the BDI-II in this study was .90.

Health Status

The 12-item Short Form Health Survey (SF-12v2) was used to assess the health status of the participants (Ware, Kosisnki, and Keller, 1996). The items in the SF-12v2 allow for the calculation of a physical (PCS) and a mental (MCS) component summary which reflect a participant's physical and mental health. In previous studies, the Chinese version SF-12v2 has demonstrated satisfactory validity (Lam, Tse, and Gandek, 2005) and reliability, with an alpha value of .62 for the PCS and .75 for the MCS (Fong et al., 2010). In the present study, the internal consistency of the PCS and MCS of the Chinese SF-12v2 was .83 and .75 respectively.

Demographic Variables

A series of questions was used to collect information on the demographic, socioeconomic, and family characteristics of the participants and the members of their families. The parent participants provided age, gender, education level, employment status, and disability status information about themselves, their partners, and the target children. Questions were also asked about the marital status of parents and the annual income of the family during the study period. The student participants were asked to provide their own demographic background, such as age, gender, and education level.

Statistical Analysis

We treated the questionnaires collected from all of the sites in Mainland China and Hong Kong as one integrated dataset for analysis. Regional differences are not the main concern of the analyses included in this chapter. We believe that based on the sampling strategies, the present study's sample can be generalized to the Chinese population.

The missing items in this study were not serious. With regard to the sensitive part of the questionnaire (JVQ), the percentages of missing items for JVQ (nonsexual victimization) items were 2.8-4% (parents), 0.4-1.6% (household children), and 0.7-3% (students). For the most sensitive part of the questionnaire (JVQ sexual victimization), the percentages of missing items were 10.7% (parents), 11.4-11.5% (household children), and 0.9-2.0% (students). The missing parts of the questionnaires were left as missing values.

We summarized the demographic characteristics and calculated the lifetime and preceding-year prevalence rates of various kinds of child victimization, IPV, elder abuse, and in-law conflict. Gender comparisons of the prevalence rates were performed using Fisher's exact test.

Separate logistic regression analyses were conducted to examine the association of demographic factors and family violence with child sexual victimization (CSV) in the preceding year. Another series of logistic regression analyses was also conducted to investigate the impact of CSV on health outcomes, namely depression, general physical health, and mental health, as measured by SF-12. The goodness of fit of all of the logistic regression models was assessed by the Hosmer and Lemeshow (H-L) test. A p-value of <0.05 was considered statistically significant, and all of statistical analyses were performed in SPSS version 17.

PROFILE OF THE RESPONDENTS

Household Data (Parents)

Demographic information, including the characteristics of the children such as gender, age (measured in years), living place, and education level, was obtained in the parent interviews. Information was also collected on the parents' characteristics, including marital status, household income, employment status, and highest education level. Data on 8,945 parents and their families were obtained in the present sample.

Parents' Characteristics

In the present sample, 57.7% (n = 5,165) of the participants were mothers and 42.3% (*n* = 3,780) were fathers. Fathers were, on average, older than the mothers. The mean age of the fathers was 41.4 (*SD* = 7.6), which was slightly greater than the mean age of the mothers (38.5, *SD* = 6.6). Most of the parents (93.9%) were either cohabiting or married; only 2.5% were separated or divorced, and 1.9% were widowed. About 1.7% did not report their marital status, which led to missing information. In this study, the fathers had generally attained a higher education level than the mothers. Significantly more fathers than mothers had received a tertiary education (16.2% vs. 13.3%, respectively). A similar trend was found in the proportion of participants who had attended secondary 4 to 7 (Fathers: 31.3% vs. Mothers: 30.4%). About 52.6% of the mothers and 47.2% of the fathers reported having an education level of secondary 3 or below.

Financial status of the families. In this study, 51.1% of the sample had an annual household income above the median income of the present sample, while 40.7% had one that was below the median. About 8.2% of the participants did not disclose this information.

We calculated the "unemployment rate" by dividing the number of unemployed workers by the overall labor force. Unemployed workers were those who were not working during the study period but were willing, able, and available to work for pay and were actively searching for work. The unemployment rate of the fathers was higher than that of the mothers (8.2% vs. 5.6%). Gender role expectation could be one possible explanation for the gender difference in the unemployment rates. Mothers are expected to stay at home to take care of the children and do the housework, whereas fathers are expected to work and earn money for the family. Therefore, the homemakers, who were mostly the mothers, were not considered as "unemployed workers" as they were not actively searching for another job to replace their current role. By excluding the homemakers from the calculation (making the numerator smaller), it was to be expected that the unemployment rate of the mothers would be lower.

Children's Characteristics

Table 1 shows that among the 8,945 child participants, 33% of their families were from Hong Kong, 16.8% were from Xi'an, 14.5% were from Shenzhen, 13.2% were from Tianjin, 11.9% were from Shanghai, and 10.7% were from Wuhan. The distribution of the sample of children by gender is also shown in the Table.

Children's age. The mean age of the children of the parent participants was 11.3 (*SD* = 5.0). With reference to Figure 1, 3,513 children (39.3%) were 15 to 17 years old, 22.8% were 11 to 14 years old, 16.7% were 7 to 10 years old, and 13.5% were 3 to 6 years old. Only 7.8% were infants or toddlers under 3 years old.

The girls were significantly older than the boys. The mean age of the girls was 11.5 (*SD* = 5.0), which was higher than that of the boys (11.2, *SD* = 5.1). No significant gender difference was found between the age group distributions.

Table 1. Distribution of the Sample of Children by Site (N = 8,945)

Site	Total (*N* = 8,945)	Boys (*n* = 4,710)	Girls (*n* = 4,235)
Hong Kong	2,949 (33.0%)	1,539 (32.7%)	1,410 (33.3%)
Shanghai	1,062 (11.9%)	511 (10.8%)	551 (13.0%)
Shenzhen	1,297 (14.5%)	730 (15.5%)	567 (13.4%)
Tianjin	1,178 (13.2%)	611 (13.0%)	567 (13.4%)
Wuhan	953 (10.7%)	537 (11.4%)	416 (9.8%)
Xi'an	1,506 (16.8%)	782 (16.6%)	724 (17.1%)

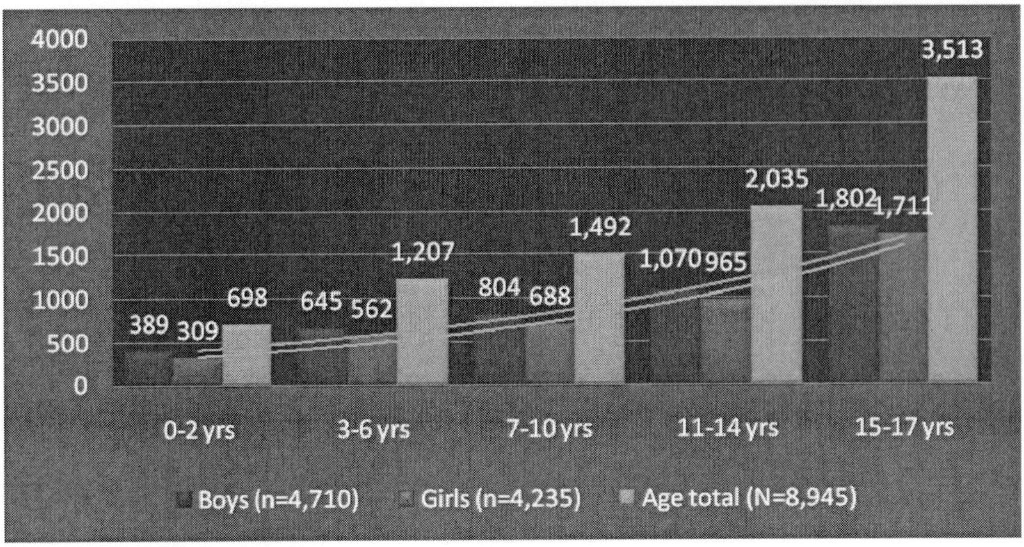

Figure 1. Age of the Children in the Sample (N = 8,945).

Children's education level. In line with the ages of the children, 27.2% of the children were in secondary 1 to 3, 27.0% in primary school, 21.9% in secondary 4 to 7, and 20.1% in preprimary school; only 0.6% were receiving education at tertiary level or above.

Figure 2 shows that the distribution patterns of education level were different across gender. In percentage terms, more boys were attending primary school (28.6%) than secondary 1 to 3 (26.1%). However, the reverse pattern was found in girls: in percentage terms, more girls were in secondary 1 to 3 (28.5%) than in primary school (25.3%).

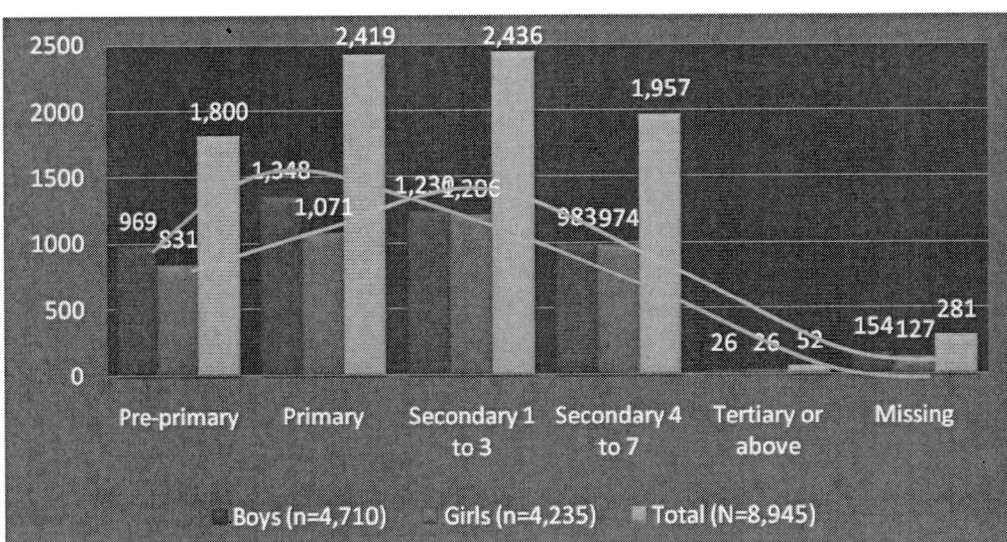

Figure 2. Education Level of the Children in the Sample (N = 8,945).

Household Data (Children Aged 15-17 Years)

Demographic information, including the child's characteristics and parents' characteristics, was obtained in the interviews with the children. A total of 3,321 children aged 15 to17 were recruited in the present sample.

Parents' Characteristics

In the present sample, 52.7% of the parents were mothers and 47.3% were fathers. Fathers were, on average, older than the mothers. The mean ages of the fathers and the mothers were 45.4 (*SD* = 6.1) and 42.4 (*SD* = 4.7) respectively. The mean age difference between the parents was 3.4 years (*SD* = 3.9). Most of the parents in the current sample (Fathers: 95.2%; Mothers: 91.3%) were either cohabiting or married. Mothers were more likely to be separated or divorced (4.2%) or widowed (3.3%) than athers (2.4% and 1.1%, respectively). About 1.4% of the fathers and 1.3% of the mothers did not report their marital status. Overall, fathers were more likely to have received a higher education than mothers. Significantly more fathers than mothers had received a tertiary education (13.1% vs. 10.4%, respectively). The pattern was similar for secondary 4 to 7 level education (29.0% vs. 29.6%, respectively). About 55.9% of the mothers and 51.9% of the fathers reported having a secondary 3 or below education level.

Financial status of the families. Fathers had a significantly higher earning ability compared to mothers. About 44.2% of the fathers had a level of income status below the median, compared to 31.0% of the mothers. Nearly one third of the fathers had a mid to high income level, compared to only 16.3% of the mothers. On the other hand, about 14.5% of the mothers had a low level of income, compared to 11.2% of the fathers. In addition, a higher percentage of mothers than fathers reported having no income (25.2% vs. 6.4%, respectively). Also, more mothers than fathers failed to report this information (13.0% vs. 7.6%, respectively). The rate of unemployment was higher among fathers than mothers (8.8% vs. 6.0%).

Disability. About 0.9% of the parents of the child participants had some kind of disability. The most obvious disabilities among the parents were physical disabilities (0.8%), followed by mental illness (0.1%). There was only one parent with an intellectual disability or autism in the current sample.

Assistance for disability. Most of the parents with a disability (Fathers: 93.7%; Mothers: 95.8%) did not receive any assistance. Among those parents, significantly more fathers than mothers reported the need for assistance (0.9% vs. 0.5%, respectively).

Children's Characteristics

Slightly more boys (50.7%) than girls (49.3%) were recruited in the current sample. Nearly all of the children were Chinese; only 1.2% of the children (1.4% for boys and 1.0% for girls) reported being of another race or ethnicity.

Table 2 shows that among the families of the 3,321 child participants, 35.3% were from Hong Kong, 17.8% were from Xi'an, 16.5% were from Tianjin, 15.0% were from Shanghai, 12.1% were from Wuhan, and 3.3% were from Shenzhen. The distribution of the sample of children by gender is also shown in this table.

Table 2. Distribution of the Sample of Children by Site (N = 3,321)

Site	Total (*N* = 3,321)	Boys (*n* = 1,683)	Girls (*n* = 1,638)
Hong Kong	1,171 (35.3%)	582 (34.6%)	589 (36.0%)
Shanghai	499 (15.0%)	228 (13.5%)	271 (16.5%)
Shenzhen	109 (3.3%)	60 (3.6%)	49 (3.0%)
Tianjin	549 (16.5%)	290 (17.2%)	259 (15.8%)
Wuhan	403 (12.1%)	226 (13.4%)	177 (10.8%)
Xi'an	590 (17.8%)	297 (17.6%)	293 (17.9%)

Children's age. The mean age of the child participants was 16.1 (*SD* = 0.8). No significant gender difference was found among the age group distributions.

Children's education level. The education levels of the child participants are presented in Figure 3. Over half of the children were attending secondary school; 53.3% were studying in secondary 4 to 7 and 39.0% in secondary 1 to 3. About 1.4% of the children were studying in primary school or at tertiary level or above. Only 0.5% of the children were in preprimary education. The distribution pattern of the educational attainment achieved by the boys was similar to that of the girls.

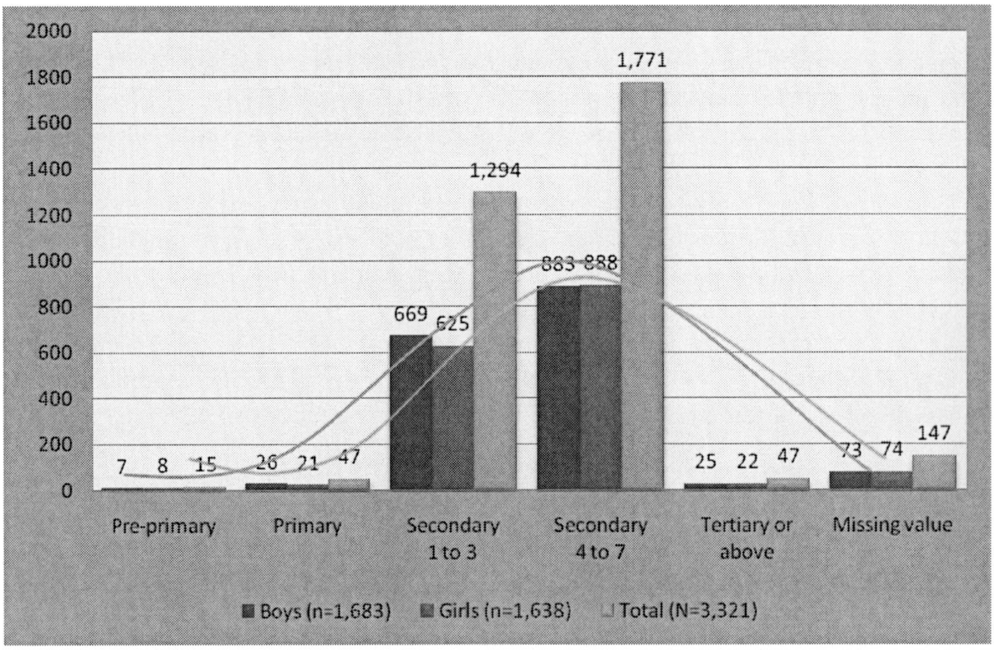

Figure 3. Education Level of the Child Participants (*N* = 3,321).

Siblings. About 61.5% of the children reported having siblings (Mean number = 1.5, *SD* = 0.6). A gender difference was found in terms of the average number of siblings within a family. The girls were more likely to have more siblings (*n* = 1.5, *SD* = 0.6) than the boys (*n* = 1.4, *SD* = 0.6).

Children's disability. About 0.2% of the child participants had a disability of some kind. The most commonly reported disabilities among the children were physical disabilities (0.1%). Only three children reported a certain degree of intellectual disability, and none suffered from a mental illness or autism.

Assistance for disability. Most of the children with a disability (91.7%) did not receive any assistance. The boys were more likely than the girls to have disability assistance (0.5% vs. 0.4%, respectively), although the difference was not significant.

School Data (Children Aged 15-17 Years)

Demographic information, including the parents' and children's characteristics and family structure, was obtained in the school interviews. A total of 18,341 children aged 15 to 17 were recruited from among 150 schools in the five mainland cities and Hong Kong.

Parents' Characteristics

Most of the parents in the current sample were either married or cohabiting (90.2%); 6.0% were separated or divorced, and 1.6% were widowed. About 2.3% of the parents did not report their marital status.

Overall, fathers were more likely to have received a higher education than mothers. Significantly more fathers than mothers had received a tertiary education (18.8% vs. 15.9%, respectively). The pattern was similar for the secondary 4 to 7 education level (26.7% vs. 24.7%, respectively). About 47.1% of the mothers and 41.9% of the fathers reported having a secondary 3 or below education level. With regard to the gender differences among the education levels attained by the parents (as reported by the students), the results showed that families with a girl had a lower level of educational attainment than families with a boy. Significantly more boys reported having a father (20.2%) or a mother (17.1%) who had received a tertiary level or above education compared to the girls (17.3% for fathers and 14.5% for mothers).

Unlike the unemployment rate reported by household, the rate of unemployment was similar among the fathers and mothers (5.8% vs. 5.9%). However, more of the girls reported having an unemployed father (5.3% for boys vs. 6.4% for girls), whereas the boys were more likely to report having an unemployed mother (6.0% for boys vs. 5.8% for girls).

Financial status of the families. In the present sample, 45.8% had a mid to high annual household income, 22.0% had a low to mid income level, and 15.0% had a low income level. About 8.9% of the families had no income, and about 8.3% of the participants did not disclose this information. Significantly more boys than girls reported that their family had a mid to high income level (48.8% vs. 42.4%, respectively).

In line with the income status of the families, only 7.4% of the families in the current study were receiving social security. Regarding the gender differences, more girls (7.5%) than boys (7.2%) reported receiving family social security.

Children's Characteristics

Table 3 shows that among the 18,341 student participants, 21.4% were from Hong Kong, 20.8% were from Shenzhen, 18.4% were from Tianjin, 17.3% were from Xi'an, 11% were from Shanghai, and 11% were from Wuhan. The distribution of the student participants by gender is also shown in this table.

Children's gender. Slightly more boys (53.3%) than girls (46.7%) were recruited in the current sample.

Children's age. The mean age of the student participants was 15.9 (*SD* = 1.0). No significant gender difference was found among the age group distributions.

Children's education level. The education levels of the student participants are presented in Figure 4. Over half of the students were in secondary 3 or above; about 14.1% were in secondary 2 and only 0.9% were in secondary 1. Gender differences were present in the pattern of educational attainment achieved by the students: More girls (86.0%) than boys (84.1%) were in secondary 3 or above, whereas more boys (14.9%) than girls (13.3%) were in secondary 2.

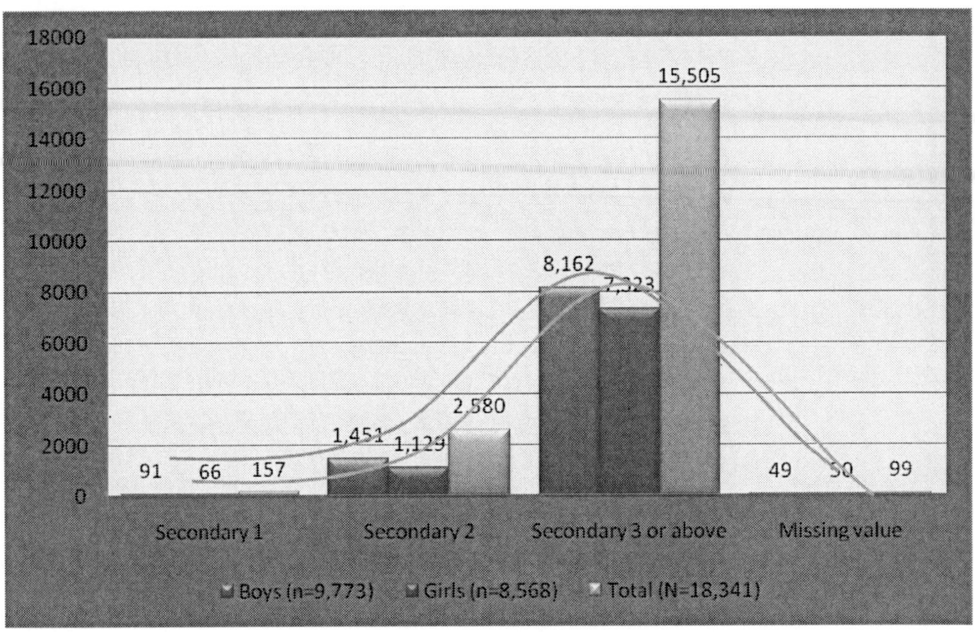

Figure 4. Education Level of the Student Participants (*N* = 18,341).

Siblings. About 59.3% of the children reported having siblings (Mean number = 0.9, *SD* = 1.0). The girls were more likely to have siblings than the boys (55.0% for boys vs. 64.1% for girls).

A gender difference was also found in the average number of siblings within the family. Compared to the boys (*n* = 0.9, *SD* = 1.1), the girls were more likely to have more siblings (*n* = 1.0, *SD* = 1.0).

Table 3. Distribution of the Student Sample by Site (N = 18,341)

Site	Total (N = 18,341)	Boys (n = 9,773)	Girls (n = 8,568)
Hong Kong	3,926 (21.4%)	1,882 (19.3%)	2,044 (23.9%)
Shanghai	2,032 (11.1%)	1,227 (12.6%)	805 (9.4%)
Shenzhen	3,806 (20.8%)	2,184 (22.3%)	1,622 (18.9%)
Tianjin	3,372 (18.4%)	1,807 (18.5%)	1,565 (18.3%)
Wuhan	2,030 (11.1%)	1,187 (12.1%)	843 (9.8%)
Xi'an	3,175 (17.3%)	1,486 (15.2%)	1,689 (19.7%)

CHILD VICTIMIZATION

Reported by Household Parents

Lifetime Prevalence

The overall lifetime prevalence of child victimization was 35.2%. Of the reported victimization cases, 21.3% were conventional crime, 14.0% were peer and sibling victimization, 13.1% were witnessing and experiencing indirect victimization, and 11.7% were child maltreatment. Only 1.3% of the parents reported sexual victimization among their children.

Preceding-Year Prevalence

The overall prevalence of child victimization in the preceding year was 29.4%. The distribution of types of child victimization in the preceding-year prevalence figures was similar to that found in lifetime prevalence. Conventional crime was the most commonly reported type of child victimization (15.8%), followed by peer and sibling victimization (11.6%), witnessing and experiencing indirect victimization (11.2%), and child maltreatment (9.0%). Only 1.1% of the parents reported sexual victimization among their children in the preceding year.

Gender Differences in Child Victimization

Table 4 shows that gender differences were found in both lifetime and preceding-year prevalence rates of child victimization. The boys were more likely than the girls to have experienced conventional crime, child maltreatment, peer and sibling victimization, and overall child victimization in their lifetime and during the preceding year. The p-values of the gender differences were found to be significant among the rates of lifetime conventional crime (23.3% for boys vs. 19.1% for girls), lifetime peer and sibling victimization (16.2% for boys vs. 11.5% for girls), and overall lifetime child victimization (36.9% for boys vs. 33.2% for girls). With regard to the preceding-year prevalence rates, the gender differences were significant in conventional crime (17.1% for boys vs. 14.3% for girls), peer and sibling victimization (13.5% for boys vs. 9.4% for girls), and overall child victimization (31.1% for boys vs. 27.6% for girls).

More boys than girls had experienced child victimization, especially conventional crime and peer and sibling victimization, in their lifetime and during the preceding year. Two possible reasons for this difference are the different behavioral expectations parents have for boys and girls and the importance of the male gender-role socialization of boys in the eyes of parents. In Chinese families, parents often have higher expectations for boys than for girls. Physical punishment often occurs within Chinese culture, which accepts beating as a way of helping to produce a competent male to inherit the leadership of the family clan. Influenced by violent parenting styles, boys tend to accept and follow the use of violence in solving problems, and this makes them more hostile and aggressive. In addition, boys who are under greater pressure in terms of parental expectations are not only more achievement oriented (which may easily provoke peer and sibling rivalry) but also more likely to engage in criminal activities under stressful conditions. Therefore, it is to be expected that boys will experience more victimization incidents than girls, especially during childhood.

Table 4. Prevalence of child victimization as reported by household parents

Child victimization	Lifetime prevalence %				Preceding-year prevalence %			
	All (*N* = 8,945)	By gender			All (*N* = 8945)	By gender		
		Boys (*n* = 4,710)	Girls (*n* = 4,235)	p*		Boys (*n* = 4,710)	Girls (*n* = 4,235)	p*
Conventional crime	21.3	23.3	19.1	<0.001	15.8	17.1	14.3	.001
Child maltreatment	11.7	12.5	10.8	.012	9.0	9.5	8.4	.097
Peer and sibling victimization	14.0	16.2	11.5	<0.001	11.6	13.5	9.4	<0.001
Witnessing and experiencing indirect victimization	13.1	13.5	12.8	.316	11.2	11.2	11.3	.971
Sexual victimization	1.3	1.4	1.2	.483	1.1	1.2	1.0	.450
Overall	35.2	36.9	33.2	<0.001	29.4	31.1	27.6	.001

CI = confidence interval. *By Fisher's exact test.

Reported by Household Children (Aged 15-17 Years)

Lifetime Prevalence

Among the child victims, 34.3% of the abuses were conventional crime, 25.4% were witnessing and experiencing indirect victimization, 19.7% were peer and sibling victimization, and 18.6% were child maltreatment. Only 3.1% reported sexual victimization in their lifetime.

Preceding-Year Prevalence

Among the child victims, 20.9% of the abuses were conventional crime, 18.0% were witnessing and experiencing indirect victimization, 12.7% were peer and sibling victimization, and 11.8% were child maltreatment. Only 2.8% of the children reported sexual victimization in the preceding year.

Gender Differences

Table 5 shows that no significant gender difference was found in relation to the lifetime and preceding-year prevalence of each type of child victimization except in the case of peer and sibling victimization, which had a higher prevalence rate among the boys than the girls. This difference may have been due to the boys being more likely to have been involved in or exposed to physical activities with peers that ended in victimization.

Table 5. Prevalence of child victimization as reported by household children (aged 15-17)

Child victimization	Lifetime prevalence %				Preceding-year prevalence %			
	All (N = 3,321)	By gender: Boys (n = 1,683)	Girls (n = 1,638)	p*	All (N = 3,321)	By gender: Boys (n = 1,683)	Girls (n = 1,638)	p*
Conventional crime	34.3	34.2	34.5	0.826	20.9	19.8	22.0	0.114
Child maltreatment	18.6	19.5	17.6	0.180	11.8	12.6	11.1	0.197
Peer and sibling victimization	19.7	21.4	17.9	0.011	12.7	13.8	11.6	0.054
Witnessing and experiencing indirect victimization	25.4	24.9	25.9	0.547	18.0	17.4	18.6	0.388
Sexual victimization	3.1	3.5	2.7	0.208	2.8	3.2	2.4	0.182
Overall	50.1	50.1	50.1	0.420	36.9	36.5	37.2	0.380

CI = confidence interval. *By Fisher's exact test.

Reported by School Students (Aged 15-17)

Lifetime Prevalence

Among all of the reported incidents of child victimization, 57.1% were conventional crime, 40.3% were witnessing and experiencing indirect victimization, 32.6% were peer and sibling victimization, and 28.1% were child maltreatment. Only 8.0% of the children reported sexual victimization in their lifetime.

Table 6 shows that in the current sample, gender differences among the lifetime prevalence rates of child victimization were significant in relation to conventional crime, peer and sibling victimization, witnessing and experiencing indirect victimization, and sexual victimization. The boys were more likely than the girls to have experienced conventional crime (59.0% for boys vs. 55.0% for girls), peer and sibling victimization (36.9% for boys vs. 27.7% for girls), and sexual victimization (9.2% for boys vs. 6.5% for girls), whereas the girls were more likely to have witnessed and experienced indirect victimization (38.6% for boys vs. 42.3% for girls).

Preceding-Year Prevalence

Among all of the reported incidents of child victimization, 43.1% were conventional crime, 32.7% were witnessing and experiencing indirect victimization, 25.3% were peer and sibling victimization, and 21.7% were child maltreatment. Only 6.3% of children reported sexual victimization in the preceding year.

Table 6 shows that in the current sample, gender differences among the preceding-year prevalence rates for child victimization were significant in relation to conventional crime, peer and sibling victimization, witnessing and experiencing indirect victimization, and sexual victimization. The boys were more likely than the girls to have experienced conventional crime (44.7% for boys vs. 41.3% for girls), peer and sibling victimization (29.3% for boys vs. 20.8% for girls), and sexual victimization (7.8% for boys vs. 4.7% for girls), whereas the girls were more likely to have witnessed and experienced indirect victimization (31.7% for boys vs. 33.8% for girls).

Table 6. Prevalence of child victimization as reported by school students (aged 15-17)

	Lifetime prevalence %				Preceding-year prevalence %			
Child victimization	All (*N* = 18,341)	By gender Boys (*n* = 9,773)	Girls (*n* = 8,568)	p*	All (*N* = 18,341)	By gender Boys (*n* = 9,773)	Girls (*n* = 8,568)	p*
Conventional crime	57.1	59.0	55.0	0.000	43.1	44.7	41.3	0.000
Child maltreatment	28.1	28.8	27.3	0.027	21.7	22.2	21.0	0.061
Peer and sibling victimization	32.6	36.9	27.7	0.000	25.3	29.3	20.8	0.000
Witnessing and experiencing indirect victimization	40.3	38.6	42.3	0.000	32.7	31.7	33.8	0.002
Sexual victimization	8.0	9.2	6.5	0.000	6.3	7.8	4.7	0.000
Overall	71.7	72.0	71.3	0.000	60.0	60.4	59.5	0.000

CI = confidence interval. *By Fisher's exact test.

OTHER TYPES OF FAMILY VIOLENCE

The study also investigated the prevalence of several kinds of family violence, including IPV, elder abuse, and in-law conflict. The main purpose of presenting these figures is to examine their association with CSA; this association is discussed in the next section. The prevalence rates of the three types of violence, as reported by household parents, are presented below.

Intimate Partner Violence (IPV)

As shown in Table 7, the most pervasive IPV was psychological abuse, the prevalence rate of which was 32.8% over lifetime and 26.2% in the preceding year. There were fewer reports of physical abuse (Lifetime: 6.7%; Preceding Year: 4.6%). The lifetime and preceding-year prevalence rates of sexual abuse were 4.7% and 4.2% respectively, whereas the prevalence rates of injury were 2.1% (lifetime) and 1.5% (preceding year). Gender differences were found in relation to several forms of IPV. The women were significantly more likely than the men to have been physically and psychologically abused by their partners over their lifetime.

Table 7. Prevalence of parents' intimate partner violence (IPV) victimization (N = 8,763)

IPV	Lifetime prevalence % (95% CI)				Preceding-year prevalence % (95% CI)			
	Total	By gender			Total	By gender		
	(*N* = 8,763)	Male (*n* = 3,822)	Female (*n* = 4,941)	p*	(*N* = 8,763)	Male (*n* = 3,822)	Female (*n* = 4,941)	p*
Physical	6.7 (6.2-7.2)	5.9 (5.2-6.6)	7.4 (6.8-8.1)	.005	4.6 (4.2-5.0)	4.3 (3.7-4.9)	4.7 (4.1-5.3)	.430
Injury	2.1 (1.8-2.4)	2.2 (1.7-2.7)	2.0 (1.6-2.4)	.601	1.5 (1.2-1.8)	1.8 (1.4-2.2)	1.3 (1.0-1.6)	.055
Psychological	32.8 (31.8-33.8)	30.4 (28.9-31.9)	34.7 (33.4-36.0)	<.0001	26.2 (25.3-27.1)	25.4 (24.0-26.8)	26.8 (25.6-29.0)	.154
Sexual	4.7 (4.3-5.1)	4.3 (3.7-4.9)	5.1 (4.5-5.7)	.116	4.2 (3.8-4.6)	3.9 (3.3-4.5)	4.5 (3.9-5.1)	.219

CI = confidence interval. *By Fisher's exact test.

Elder Abuse

Table 8 presents the lifetime and preceding-year prevalence rates of different forms of elder abuse. Similar to IPV, the most pervasive form of elder abuse was psychological abuse

(Lifetime: 22.5%; Preceding Year: 11.5%). The lifetime and preceding-year prevalence rates of neglect were 11.2% and 5.2% respectively, whereas the lifetime and preceding-year prevalence rates of physical abuse were 6.9% and 2.8% respectively. The least common form of elder abuse was injury: lifetime prevalence was 1.0% and preceding-year prevalence was 0.5%. The men were more likely to have experienced various forms of elder abuse over their lifetime and in the preceding year.

Table 8. Prevalence of elder abuse against grandparents in the sample families (N = 8,807)

Elder abuse	Lifetime prevalence % (95% CI)			Preceding-year prevalence % (95% CI)		
	Grandfather* or Grand-mother †	Grandfather	Grand-mother	Grandfather or Grand-mother	Grand-father	Grand-mother
Physical	6.9 (6.4-7.4)	6.0 (5.5-6.5)	4.7 (4.3-5.1)	2.8 (2.5-3.1)	2.4 (2.1-2.7)	2.1 (1.8-2.4)
Injury	1.0 (0.8-1.2)	0.8 (0.6-1.0)	0.7 (0.5-0.9)	0.5 (0.4-0.6)	0.3 (0.2-0.4)	0.3 (0.2-0.4)
Psychological	22.5 (21.6-23.4)	20.4 (19.6-21.2)	18.7 (17.9-19.5)	11.5 (10.8-12.2)	10.5 (9.9-11.1)	9.4 (8.8-10.0)
Neglect	11.2 (10.5-11.9)	9.7 (9.1-10.3)	9.1 (8.5-9.7)	5.2 (4.7-5.7)	4.6 (4.2-5.0)	4.2 (3.8-4.6)

CI = confidence interval. *Grandfather = father of a participant. †Grandmother = mother of a participant.

In-law Conflict

The figures in Table 9 indicate that the parent participants were more likely to report psychological in-law conflict, the lifetime prevalence and preceding-year prevalence rates of which were respectively 11.1% and 9.5%.

Table 9. Prevalence of in-law conflict against parents (N = 8,763)

In-law conflict	Lifetime prevalence % (95% CI)			Preceding-year prevalence % (95% CI)		
	Total (*N* = 8,763)	Male (*n* = 3,822)	Female (*n* = 4,941)	Total (*N* = 8,763)	Male (*n* = 3,822)	Female (*n* = 4,941)
Physical	1.4 (1.2-1.6)	1.3 (0.9-1.7)	1.6 (1.3-1.9)	1.2 (1.0-1.4)	0.9 (0.6-1.2)	1.3 (1.0-1.6)
Injury	1.3 (1.1-1.5)	1.2 (0.9-1.5)	1.5 (1.2-1.8)	1.1 (0.9-1.3)	0.9 (0.6-1.2)	1.2 (0.9-1.5)
Psychological	11.1 (10.4-11.8)	10.7 (9.7-11.7)	11.5 (10.6-12.4)	9.5 (8.9-10.1)	9.3 (8.4-10.2)	9.6 (8.8-10.4)

CI = confidence interval.

The lifetime and the preceding-year prevalence were respectively 1.4% and 1.2% for physical conflict and 1.3% and 1.1% for injury. In the current sample, the mothers tended to experience more in-law conflict in terms of psychological abuse, physical abuse, and injury than the fathers.

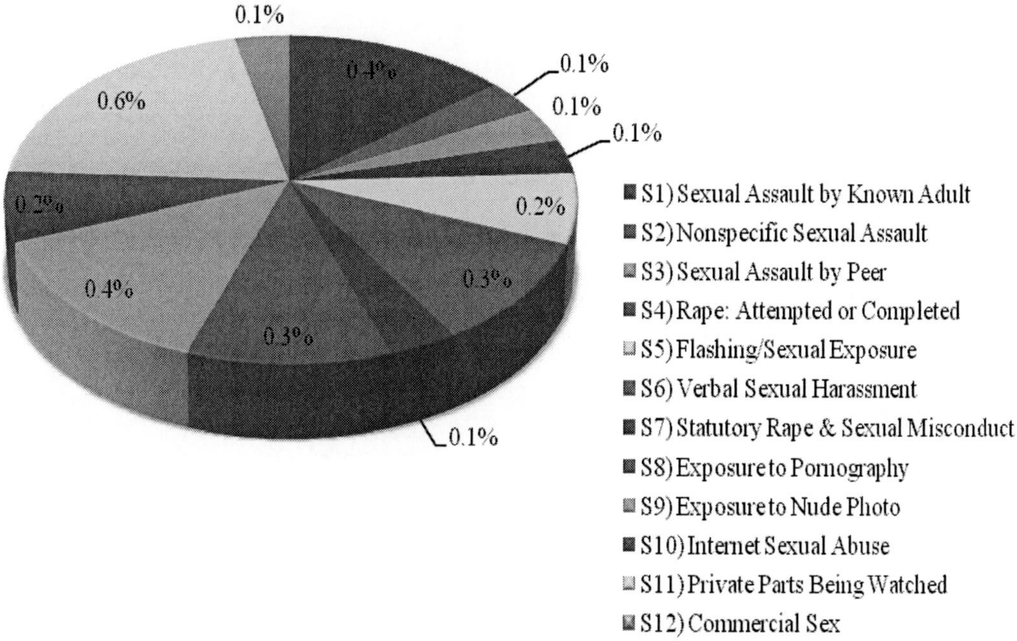

Figure 5. Lifetime Prevalence of Child Sexual Victimization by Type (N = 8,945).

CHILD SEXUAL VICTIMIZATION (CSV)

Reported by Household Parents

Lifetime Prevalence

In the current study, CSV was measured by 12 items. Sexual violence accounted for only 1.3% of all of the assaults against child victims. As shown in Figure 5, the most prevalent types of CSV were being watched private parts (i.e. others exposed their private parts to the children) (0.6%), sexual assault by a known adult (0.4%), and exposure to nude photos (0.4%). The least pervasive types of CSV were nonspecific sexual assault (0.1%), sexual assault by peer (0.1%), attempted or completed rape (0.1%), and statutory rape and sexual misconduct (0.1%).

Gender Differences

Figure 6 presents the lifetime prevalence rate of each type of CSV by gender. No significant gender difference was found among these 12 items.

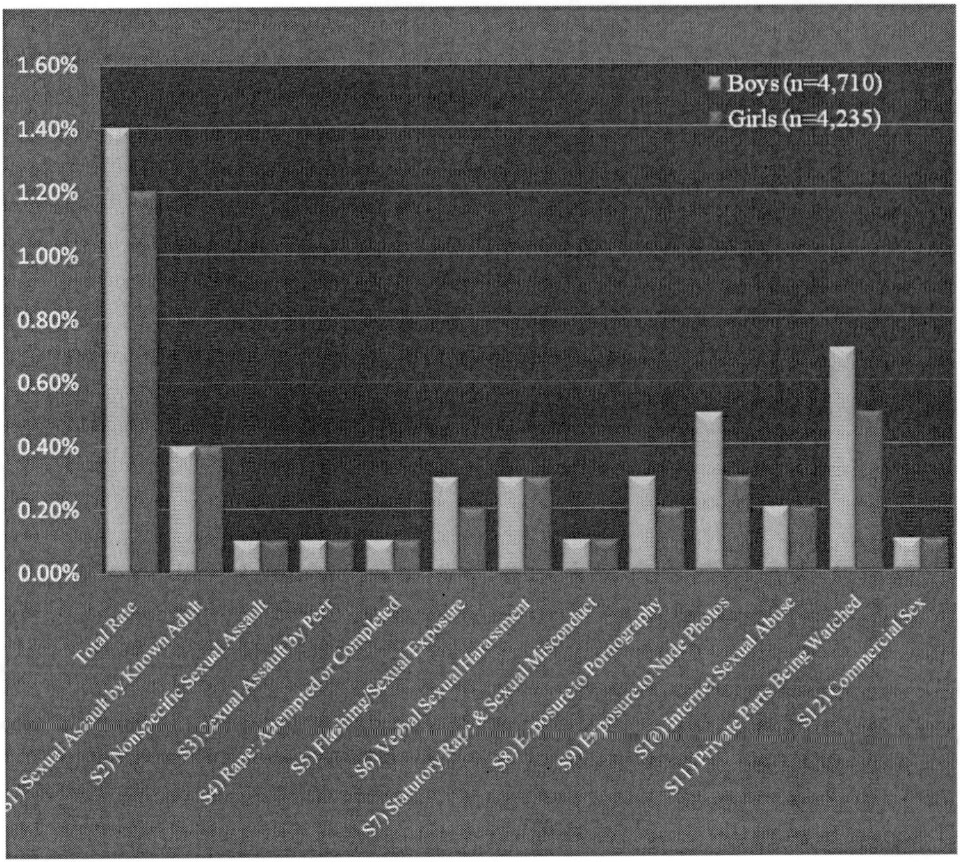

Figure 6. Lifetime Prevalence of Child Sexual Victimization by Type and Gender (N = 8,945).

Age Differences

Table 10 shows that significant age differences were found in the lifetime prevalence of CSV. Children aged 0 to 2 and 12 to 14 had a higher rate of overall CSV (2.0%). Both age groups were more likely to have been exposed to commercial sex (2.0%) compared to the other age groups. Children aged 0 to 2 were more likely to have experienced flashing/sexual exposure (0.4%), and children aged 3 to 5 had a higher rate of nonspecific sexual assault (1.0%). Among all of the age groups, children aged 12 to 14 had a higher rate of exposure to pornography (0.6%), exposure to nude photos (1.0%), and watched private parts (1.3%).

Similar trends were observed for verbal sexual harassment and exposure to pornography: the rates increased between the ages of 3 and 5, then declined between the ages of 6 and 11, and increased again between the ages of 12 and 14 before dropping again between the ages of 15 and 17. The trends for exposure to nude photos and being watched private parts were also similar: the rates were stable in early childhood, but there was a sudden increase between the ages of 12 and 14, followed by a sharp drop between the ages of 15 and 17.

It is worth noting that these were responses from the household parent participants' point of view on the lifetime sexual victimization experienced by their children. These results may represent the actual pattern of such incidences in real life. Another possibility is that the parents did not actually know what happened to their children.

Table 10. Lifetime prevalence of child sexual victimization by type and age group (N = 3,513)

	Children Age (years); %					χ^2
	0-2	3-5	6-11	12-14	15-17	
Sexual Victimization	2.0	1.5	1.2	2.0	0.7	.005
S1) Sexual Assault by Known Adult	0.8	1.0	0.4	0.4	0.2	.015
S2) Nonspecific Sexual Assault	0.0	0.1	0.0	0.2	0.0	.088
S3) Sexual Assault by Peer	0.0	0.1	0.0	0.2	0.1	.542
S4) Rape: Attempted or Completed	0.0	0.1	0.0	0.2	0.0	.271
S5) Flashing/Sexual Exposure	0.4	0.1	0.2	0.2	0.2	.915
S6) Verbal Sexual Harassment	0.2	0.5	0.2	0.5	0.1	.236
S7) Statutory Rape and Sexual Misconduct	0.0	0.1	0.0	0.2	0.0	.088
S8) Exposure to Pornography	0.2	0.3	0.1	0.6	0.2	.107
S9) Exposure to Nude Photos	0.4	0.4	0.3	1.0	0.1	.001
S10) Internet Sexual Abuse	0.0	0.4	0.1	0.4	0.1	.134
S11) Private Parts Being Watched	0.6	0.6	0.5	1.3	0.2	.002
S12) Commercial Sex	2.0	1.5	1.2	2.0	0.7	.005

Gender Differences among Children in the 15-17 Age Range

Table 11 shows the lifetime prevalence of CSV for children in the 15 to 17 age range. No significant gender difference was found in these 12 items.

Table 11. Lifetime prevalence of child sexual victimization between the ages of 15 and 17 by type and gender (N = 3,513)

	15-17	Children (15-17) Gender, %		T-test
		Boys	Girls	
Sexual Victimization	0.7	0.9	0.5	.455
S1) Sexual Assault by Known Adult	0.2	0.3	0.1	.625
S2) Nonspecific Sexual Assault	0.0	0.0	0.0	-
S3) Sexual Assault by Peer	0.1	0.2	0.1	1.000
S4) Rape: Attempted or Completed	0.0	0.1	0.0	1.000
S5) Flashing/Sexual Exposure	0.2	0.3	0.3	1.000
S6) Verbal Sexual Harassment	0.1	0.2	0.1	1.000
S7) Statutory Rape and Sexual Misconduct	0.0	0.0	0.0	-
S8) Exposure to Pornography	0.2	0.3	0.1	.625
S9) Exposure to Nude Photos	0.1	0.2	0.0	.500
S10) Internet Sexual Abuse	0.1	0.1	0.1	1.000
S11) Being Watched Private Parts	0.2	0.3	0.1	.375
S12) Commercial Sex	0.0	0.0	-	0.0

Reported by Household Children (Aged 15-17 Years)

Lifetime Prevalence

Figure 7 shows that 3.1% of all of the child victimization incidents reported were sexual victimization. The most prevalent type of sexual victimization was verbal sexual harassment (1.7%), followed by exposure to pornography (0.7%) and flashing/sexual exposure (0.6%). The least pervasive type of sexual victimization was commercial sex (0.1%).

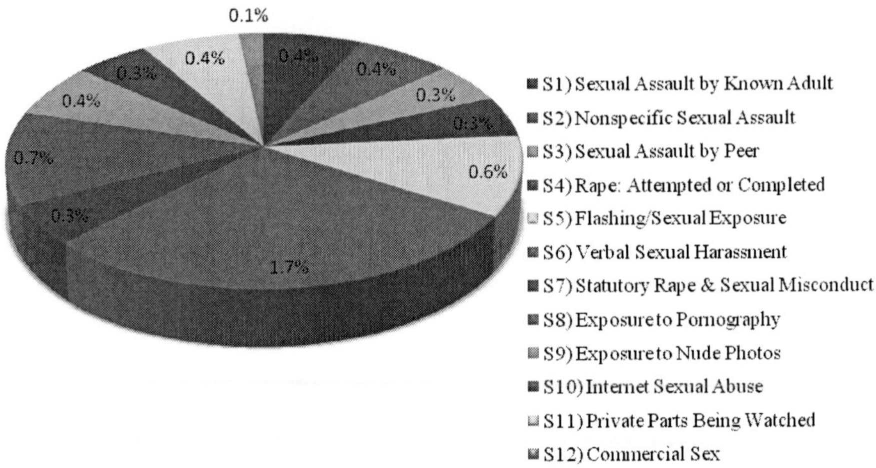

Figure 7. Lifetime Prevalence of Child Sexual Victimization by Type (N = 3,321).

Gender Differences

Figure 8 shows the lifetime prevalence of CSV by type and by gender. No significant difference was found across gender.

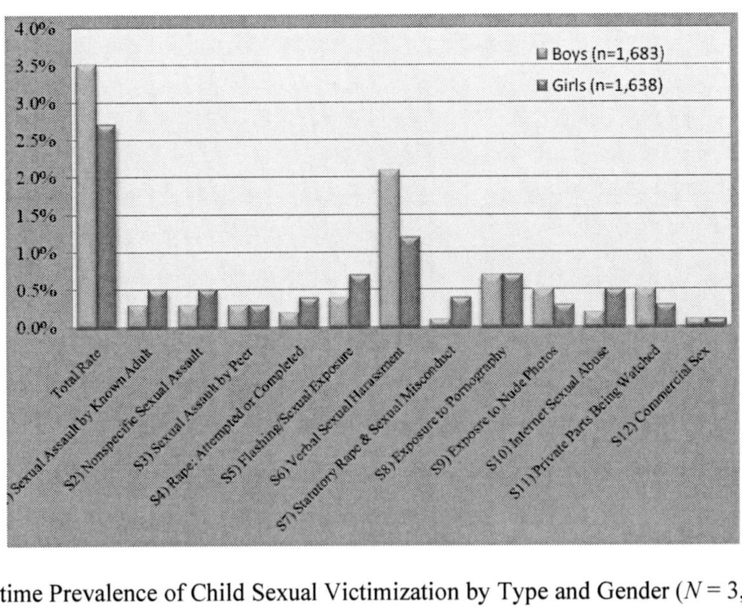

Figure 8. Lifetime Prevalence of Child Sexual Victimization by Type and Gender (N = 3,321).

Reported by School Students (Aged 15-17 Years)

Lifetime Prevalence

Among all of the child victimization incidents reported, 8.0% were sexual victimization. Figure 9 shows that the most prevalent types of sexual victimization were sexual assault by known adult (3.8%), nonspecific sexual assault (3.4%), and exposure to pornography (3.4%). The least pervasive type of sexual victimization was commercial sex (1.6%).

Gender Differences

Figure 10 shows the lifetime prevalence of CSV by type and by gender. The findings show that the boys were more likely than the girls to have experienced CSV in general (9.3% for boys vs. 6.6% for girls). The p-values of gender differences were found to be significant among the rates of all forms of CSV: sexual assault by known adult (4.5% for boys vs. 3.0% for girls), nonspecific sexual assault (4.3% for boys vs. 2.4% for girls), sexual assault by peer (3.2% for boys vs. 1.9% for girls), attempted or completed rape (2.5% for boys vs. 1.9% for girls), flashing or sexual exposure (2.9% for boys vs. 2.1% for girls), verbal sexual harassment (3.5% for boys vs. 2.2% for girls), statutory rape and sexual misconduct (3.4% for boys vs. 2.1% for girls), exposure to pornography (4.4% for boys vs. 2.4% for girls), exposure to nude photos (2.5% for boys vs. 1.4% for girls), internet sexual abuse (2.4% for boys vs. 1.6% for girls), being watched private parts (4.1% for boys vs. 2.0% for girls), and commercial sex (2.0% for boys vs. 1.1% for girls).

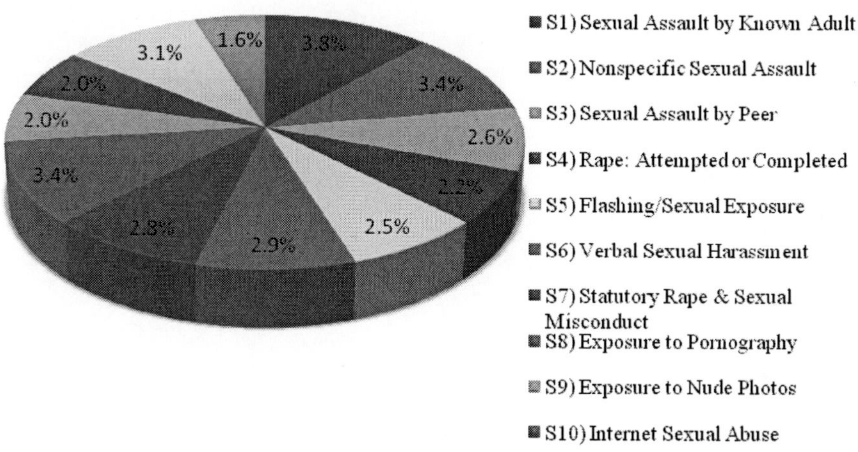

Figure 9. Lifetime Prevalence of Child Sexual Victimization by Type (N = 18,341).

Risk Factors of Child Sexual Victimization

We conducted logistic regression analyses to test for the association between demographic characteristics and family violence using the dataset of household parents. Table 12 shows the final regression model. The characteristics of the children (e.g., age) were associated with greater odds of lifetime and preceding-year CSV (OR = 0.95; 95% CI = 0.91,

0.99 and OR = 0.95; 95% CI = 0.90, 0.99, respectively). Other factors, such as parents' approval of violence, also increased the odds of lifetime CSV (OR = 1.04; 95% CI = 1.00, 1.08). Having siblings was also a significant predictor of lifetime CSV (OR = 1.71; 95% CI = 1.04, 2.80) and preceding-year CSV (OR = 1.75; 95% CI = 1.02, 3.00).

The characteristic of violence within the family was also found to increase the odds of CSV. Lifetime IPV was associated with greater odds of lifetime CSV (OR = 3.08; 95% CI = 1.49, 6.34) and preceding-year CSV (OR = 3.83; 95% CI = 1.81, 8.12). Preceding-year IPV was also a significant predictor of CSV in the preceding year (OR = 3.34; 95% CI = 1.46, 7.63). Lifetime elder abuse was also found to increase the odds of both lifetime and preceding-year CSV (OR = 3.21; 95% CI = 1.43, 7.22 and OR = 3.1; 95% CI = 1.31, 7.35, respectively).

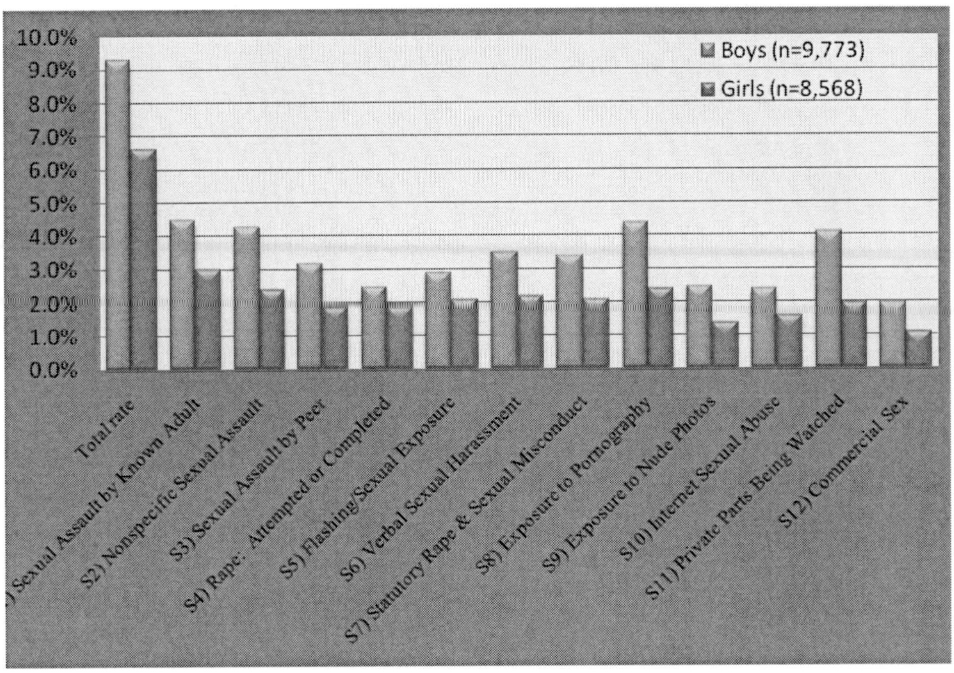

Figure 10. Lifetime Prevalence of Child Sexual Victimization by Type and Gender (N = 18,341).

Table 12. Demographic Characteristics of Parents and their Association with Child Sexual Victimization

Demographic characteristics	Crude OR Lifetime prevalence of Child Sexual Victimization		Crude OR Preceding-year prevalence of Child Sexual Victimization	
	(95% CI)	p-value	(95% CI)	p-value
Site				
Mainland	0.77 (0.468, 1.273)	0.310	0.69 (0.403, 1.173)	0.170

Demographic characteristics	Crude OR Lifetime prevalence of Child Sexual Victimization		Crude OR Preceding-year prevalence of Child Sexual Victimization	
HK	1.000		1.000	
Parents' characteristics				
Parents' education				
Secondary 3 or below	0.89 (0.445, 1.764)	0.730	1.14 (0.523, 2.506)	0.735
Secondary 4-7	1.43 (0.715, 2.875)	0.310	1.58 (0.706, 3.524)	0.267
Tertiary or above	1.000		1.000	
Unemployed	1.13 (0.490, 2.63)	0.768	1.36 (0.582, 3.165)	0.480
Marital status				
Widowed	0.78 (0.107, 5.637)	0.802	–	–
Divorced/separated	1.99 (0.617, 6.407)	0.249	2.34 (0.722, 7.557)	0.157
Married/cohabiting	1.000		1.000	
Family Income Level				
None to low	1.15 (0.568, 2.312)	0.703	1.23 (0.582, 2.58)	0.592
Low to mid	0.89 (0.527, 1.493)	0.652	0.82 (0.461, 1.472)	0.513
Mid to high	1.000		1.000	
Children's characteristics				
Gender (child)				
Boy	1.2 (0.754, 1.903)	0.445	1.22 (0.736, 2.009)	0.444
Girl	1.000		1.000	
Age (mean) (Child)	0.95* (0.911, 0.991)	0.017	0.95* (0.904, 0.991)	0.019
Siblings				
Yes	1.71* (1.043, 2.798)	0.034	1.75* (1.018, 3.001)	0.043
No	1.000		1.000	
Psychological and behavioral characteristics				
Violence approval	1.04* (1.002, 1.076)	0.040	1.03 (0.993, 1.075)	0.107
Support	1.02 (0.949, 1.091)	0.623	1.05 (0.978, 1.138)	0.168
Violence characteristics				

Table 12. (Continued)

Demographic characteristics	Crude OR Lifetime prevalence of Child Sexual Victimization		Crude OR Preceding-year prevalence of Child Sexual Victimization	
IPV lifetime physical/injury/sexual (total)	3.08** (1.494, 6.335)	0.002	3.83*** (1.806, 8.123)	0.000
IPV preceding-year physical/injury/sexual (total)			3.34** (1.460, 7.631)	0.004
Elder abuse lifetime physical/injury (total)	3.21** (1.430, 7.215)	0.005	3.1* (1.307, 7.352)	0.010
Elder abuse preceding-year physical/injury (total)			1.2 (0.158, 9.098)	0.861
In-law conflict lifetime physical/injury/ psychological	1.65 (0.671, 4.064)	0.275	1.94 (0.777, 4.843)	0.156
In-law conflict preceding-year physical/injury/ psychological			1.4 (0.475, 4.113)	0.543

Impact of Child Sexual Victimization

Using the dataset of household parents, we investigated the impact of CSV on children using logistic regression analyses. As shown in Table 13, depression was associated with greater odds of both lifetime CSV (OR = 1.05; 95% CI = 1.02, 1.08) and preceding-year CSV (OR = 1.05; 95% CI = 1.02, 1.09). However, the associations between CSV and physical health and mental health were not significant in the present study.

Table 13. Impact of Child Sexual Victimization

Demographic characteristics	Crude OR Lifetime prevalence of Child Sexual Victimization		Crude OR Preceding-year prevalence of Child Sexual Victimization	
	(95% CI)	p-value	(95% CI)	p-value
Psychological and behavioral characteristics				
Depression	1.05** (1.02, 1.083)	0.001	1.05** (1.02, 1.087)	0.001
Physical health	0.99 (0.962, 1.017)	0.451	0.99 (0.957, 1.016)	0.367
Mental health	0.98 (0.957, 1.011)	0.245	0.98 (0.951, 1.011)	0.203

Comparison of the Prevalence of Child Victimization and Child Sexual Abuse from Different Reports

Table 14 presents the rate of each type of child victimization as reported by four different groups of participants: household parents with children aged 0 to 17, household parents with children aged 15 to 17, household children aged 15 to 17, and school students aged 15 to 17.

With regard to CSV, these reports found that 0.7% to 8.0% of children had been victims of sexual violence. The most prevalent types of CSA were sexual assault by known adults (0.2%-3.8%), exposure to pornography (0.2%-3.4%), sexual assault by nonspecific people (0-3.4%), and being watched private parts (0.2%-3.1%). No significant gender difference was found among the prevalence rates of different types of CSA.

Table 14. Comparisons between the Lifetime Prevalence Rates of Child Victimization Reported by Different Samples

Child Victimization	Household parents (children 0-17) % (n = 8,945)	Household parents (children 15-17) % (n = 3,513)	Household children (15-17) % (n = 3,321)	School students (15-17) % (n = 18,341)
Overall child victimization	35.2	32.4	50.1	71.7
Conventional crime	21.3	19.3	34.3	57.1
Child maltreatment	11.7	10.5	18.6	28.1
Peer and sibling victimization	14.0	11.2	19.7	32.6
Witnessing and experiencing indirect victimization	13.1	14.0	25.4	40.3
Sexual victimization	1.3	0.7	3.1	8.0
S1) Sexual Assault by Known Adult	0.4	0.2	0.4	3.8
S2) Nonspecific Sexual Assault	0.1	0.0	0.4	3.4
S3) Sexual Assault by Peer	0.1	0.1	0.3	2.6
S4) Rape: Attempted or Completed	0.1	0.0	0.3	2.2
S5) Flashing/Sexual Exposure	0.2	0.2	0.6	2.5
S6) Verbal Sexual Harassment	0.3	0.1	1.7	2.9
S7) Statutory Rape and Sexual Misconduct	0.1	0.0	0.3	2.8
S8) Exposure to Pornography	0.3	0.2	0.7	3.4
S9) Exposure to Nude Photos	0.4	0.1	0.4	2.0
S10) Internet Sexual Abuse	0.2	0.1	0.3	2.0
S11) Being Watched Private Parts	0.6	0.2	0.4	3.1
S12) Commercial Sex	0.1	0.0	0.1	1.6

Comparing the prevalence rates reported by the different samples, household parents were more likely to underestimate the prevalence of CSV. The rate of CSV was generally higher among the reports by children. This is possibly because the parents did not want to disclose actual incidents as this would be considered as a family shame or simply because they were not aware of what had happened to their children. Among the four sources of information, school students reported the highest rate of overall CSV and of each type of sexual abuse. Children in the household setting may not have felt as free as those in the school setting during the survey, hence their underreporting in comparison to the school children. The evidence revealed discrepancies between the rate of CSV reported by the household children and the school children, and these should be further analyzed in future studies. The evidence also showed that underreporting was obvious in the sample of household parents. It is therefore recommended that the findings from the school survey should be used as the key findings to estimate the prevalence of CSA in China.

Conclusion

The findings of the Optimus Study provide reliable estimates of child victimization which will facilitate the allocation of resources. The associations between child victimization and family violence highlight the value of screening for multiple types of violence when one type has been detected. The present research fills in the existing research and information gaps with regard to the incidence and prevalence of child victimization in China. This study has significant policy implications. The interpretation of the findings has to be made carefully in order to facilitate evidence-based planning and implementation of these programmes, and provide a rationale for resource allocation.

References

Beck, A. T., Sterr, R. A., and Brown, G. K. (1996). Manual for the Beck Depression Inventory. Antonio, TX: Psychological Corporation.

Chan, K. L. (2004). Correlates of wife assault in Hong Kong Chinese families. *Violence and Victims, 19,* 189-201.

Chan, K. L., Fong, D. Y. T., Yan, E., Chow, C. B., and Ip, P. (2011). Validation of the Chinese Juvenile Victimization Questionnaire. *Hong Kong Journal of Paediatrics, 16*(1): 17-24.

Finkelhor, D., Hamby, S. L., Ormrod, R. K., and Turner, H. A. (2005). The Juvenile Victimization Questionnaire: Reliability, validity, and national norms. *Child Abuse and Neglect, 29,* 383-412.

Finkelhor, D., Ormrod, R. K., and Turner, H. A. (2007). Poly-victimization: A neglected component in child victimization. *Child Abuse and Neglect, 31,* 7-26.

Fong, D. Y. T., Lam, C. L. K., Mak, K. K., Lo, W. S., Lai, Y. K., Ho, S. Y., and Lam, T. H. (2010). The Short Form-12 Health Survey was a valid instrument in Chinese adolescents. *Journal of Clinical Epidemiology, 63,* 1020-1029.

Lam, C. L., Tse, E. Y., and Gandek, B. (2005). Is the standard SF-12 Health Survey valid and equivalent for a Chinese population? *Quality of Life Research, 14,* 539-547.

Leung, R. K. W. (2001). *A validation of the traditional Chinese (Hong Kong) versions of the Beck Anxiety Inventory and the Beck Depression Inventory-II (BDI-II).* Hong Kong, China: University of Hong Kong.

Straus, M. A. (2004). Cross-cultural reliability and validity of the Revised Conflict Tactics Scales: A study of university students dating couples in 17 nations. *Cross-Cultural Research, 38,* 407-432.

Straus, M. A., Hamby, S. L., Boney-McCoy, S., and Sugarman, D. B. (1996). The Revised Conflict Tactics Scales (CTS2): Development and preliminary psychometric data. *Journal of Family Issues, 17,* 283-316.

Ware, J. E., Kosisnki, M., and Keller, S. D. (1996). A 12-item Short-form Health Survey: Construction of scales and preliminary tests of reliability and validity. *Medical Care, 34,* 220-233.

Yan, E. C. W., and Tang, C. S. K. (2003). Proclivity to elder abuse: A community study on Hong Kong Chinese. *Journal of Interpersonal Violence, 18,* 999-1017.

Yan, E. C. W., and Tang, C. S. K. (2004). Elder abuse by caregivers: A study of prevalence and risk factors in Hong Kong Chinese families. *Journal of Family Violence, 19,* 269-277.

In: Child Protection in Chinese Societies
Editor: Ko Ling Chan

ISBN: 978-1-61942-879-9

Chapter 3

Child Victimization in China: Interpretation of Findings and Recommendations

Ko Ling Chan
Department of Social Work and Social Administration
University of Hong Kong, Pokfulam, Hong Kong

Abstract

The major findings related to child victimization and child sexual abuse in China were presented in the last chapter. In this chapter, the interpretation of the findings and possible explanations of some controversial issues will be discussed. The major issues include the underreporting of child victimization by parents, prevalence of childhood sexual abuse in Chinese populations, difficulties encountered in the study process, and recommendations.

Keywords: Child victimization, Underreporting, Gender Differences

Introduction

The major findings related to child victimization and child sexual abuse in China were presented in the last chapter. In this chapter, the interpretation of the findings and possible explanations of some controversial issues will be discussed.

Low Prevalence Rates of Child Victimization Reported by Parents

Based on a large national representative sample of parents recruited from China, this study provides both the most reliable prevalence estimates and a more comprehensive profile of child victimization in China: 35% of the children in the study had been victimized in their lifetime. A comprehensive definition of child victimization, covering conventional crime, child maltreatment, peer and sibling victimization, sexual victimization, and witnessing and experiencing indirect victimization, was used. The lifetime prevalence rate of child victimization, as reported by parents, was 21% for conventional crime, 12% for child maltreatment, 14% for peer and sibling aggression, 13% for indirect exposure to violence, and 1% for sexual victimization. When compared to figures from previous studies, this study revealed a lower prevalence of child victimization in China than in the United States, where the annual prevalence rate lies between 30% and 53% for conventional crime, 10% and 14% for child maltreatment, 53% and 59% for peer and sibling victimization, 29% and 36% for witnessing violence, and 2% and 10% for sexual victimization (Finkelhor, Hamby, Ormrod, and Turner, 2005; Finkelhor, Ormrod, and Turner, 2009; Finkelhor, Ormrod, Turner, and Hamby, 2005; Finkelhor, Turner, Ormrod, and Hamby, 2010). However, these U.S. rates are comparable to the prevalence rates reported in this study by the children and students aged 15 to 17.

Based on the rates reported by parents, this study may reflect the true difference between China and the United States in terms of the prevalence of child victimization. Given the one-child policy in operation in Mainland China, parental supervision of children in China is generally strict. The chance of victimization by people other than parents may therefore be reduced (Sun, Li, Ji, Lin, and Semaana, 2008). Another possible explanation for the discrepancy in the prevalence rates could be the difference between the information sources used in previous research and the present study. Most of the studies by Finkelhor and colleagues (Finkelhor et al., 2009; Finkelhor, Hamby, et al., 2005; Finkelhor, Ormrod, et al., 2005) used a combination of reports by proxies and children, while we only used parent reports. Findings on the comparison of reports by proxies and children are mixed. On one hand, children's self-reports have been found to show higher rates of victimization when compared to the reports of proxies (Kolko, Kazdin, and Day, 1996); on the other hand, Finkelhor et al.'s (2005) study showed no significant difference in the rates reported by the two groups. Unless a clearer conclusion is reached by future studies, we cannot deny the possibility that the lower rates of child victimization found in the present study may have been due to the differences between the reports of the proxies and the children.

Another possible explanation of the lower prevalence rate reported by parents is underreporting. Parent reports of child maltreatment may involve a response bias and thus result in significant underestimates (Kaufman, Hilliker, Lathrop, and Daleiden, 1993; Kolko, Kazdin, and Day, 1996). Factors affecting the reliability of parent reports may include shame, denial, and fear of future legal consequences (Appel and Holden, 1998; Cicchetti and Olsen, 1990); memory deficits due to the passage of time (McGee, Wolfe, Yuen, Wilson, and Carnochan, 1995); and limited ability to recall information due to posttraumatic stress disorder (PTSD) symptoms when the parent informant also experiences domestic violence (Biriere, 1992).

Cultural values may also exert an influence on the perception, tolerance, and reporting of child maltreatment. Past studies have often reported a higher tolerance toward parental physical aggression as a disciplinary practice among Chinese populations (Hong and Hong, 1991; Wong et al., 2009). The Chinese concept of face (*mien-tzu*) may play an important role in the reporting of violence (Chan, 2009). Since perpetrating child maltreatment is socially undesirable and may lead to one "losing face" and bringing shame on the family (Ho, 1990), the abusive parent may refrain from disclosing violent acts. Therefore, a greater need to save face may increase the tendency for parents to underreport and may also explain the discrepancy between parent and child reports.

PREVALENCE OF CHILDHOOD SEXUAL ABUSE (CSA) IN CHINESE POPULATIONS

Differences among the Household and School Surveys

The overall prevalence rates of CSA, as reported by the different sample groups, varied in the present study. Only 1.3% of the CSA cases were reported by parents; a higher rate was found among the household child reports (3.1%), and the highest rate was found among the student reports (8.0%). Such a discrepancy in the prevalence rate across different sources of information is in line with previous findings where child self-reports have revealed a higher rate of violence victimization than parent or proxy reports (Kolko, Kazdin, and Day, 1996). Parents are likely to provide underestimates of child victimization as they may have little knowledge about victimization incidents experienced by their children outside the family context. Other possible factors affecting the reliability of parent reports may include shame, denial, and fear of future legal consequences (Appel and Holden, 1998; Cicchetti and Olsen, 1990); memory deficits due to the passage of time (McGee, Wolfe, Yuen, Wilson, and Carnochan, 1995); and limited ability to recall information due to PTSD symptoms when the parent informant also experiences domestic violence (Biriere, 1992).

Although the reporting discrepancy between parents and children is not yet conclusive (e.g., Finkelhor and colleagues (2005) found no difference between parent and child reports), the present study does provide evidence to support the view that child self-reports may be a more reliable source of information, which is consistent with previous international (McGee, Wolfe, and Wilson, 1997; Richters and Martinez, 1993; Winegar and Lipschitz, 1999) and local (Chan, forthcoming) studies. A large and representative study in Hong Kong using a parent-child matched sample has shown that Chinese parents, regardless of their gender, tend to underreport severe forms of child abuse (Chan, Forthcoming).

The use of child reports is not free from limitations. Maltreated children may underreport the amount of abuse they have experienced (Jouriles, Mehta, McDonald, and Francis, 1997; McGee et al., 1995) as they often feel a sense of loyalty toward the abusive family or parent (Jaffe, Sudermann, and Reitzel, 1992) or suffer from PTSD symptoms that hinder their accurate recall of information (DeVoe and Graham-Bermann, 1997). Methodological differences may also contribute to the variance in rates across respondents. In this study, the children may have been more willing to disclose their experiences of victimization in the questionnaires because their anonymity and confidentiality were assured. This may have been especially true for the school children as they were surveyed without the presence of their parents. The school settings without parental supervision may have been perceived by the children as a safer and freer environment in which to disclose sensitive matters. Moreover, the data collection process in the present study was conducted in class rather than on an individual basis. The questionnaires were collected in groups. The children would therefore have felt more reassured that their identities would not be disclosed. Indeed, studies using student samples often reveal higher rates of CSA victimization compared to other studies conducted in the same country or region (Chen et al., 2004; Chen, Dunne, and Wang, 2003).

Comparing the prevalence of CSA as reported by the different sample groups, the household parents in this study were more likely to underestimate the rates of CSA. The prevalence of CSA was generally higher among the children's reports. Among all of the sample groups in the present study, the school students reported the highest rate of overall CSA and of each type of sexual abuse. It is therefore recommended that the findings from the school survey be used as the key findings to estimate the prevalence of CSA in China.

Comparison with Previous Studies

Nonetheless, even omitting the parent reports in which underreporting may have occurred, the present findings on CSA prevalence still appear to be at the lower end of the self-reported rates shown in previous studies, which range between 2% and 59% (Alikasifoglu et al., 2006; Campbell, Greeson, Bybee, and Raja, 2008; Catania et al., 2008; Figueiredo et al., 2004; Finkelhor, Moore, Hamby, and Straus, 1997; May-Chahal and Cawson, 2005). The relatively low CSA rates reflect differences between Chinese and Western populations in terms of CSA victimization. In fact, past research has often found CSA rates ranging from 2% to 14% among Chinese populations (Chen et al., 2004; Hong Kong Medical Coordinators on Child Abuse, 2003; Y. Luo, Parish, and Laumann, 2008a; Tang, 2002; Yen, Yang, Yang, Su, Wang, and Lan, 2008) and from 4% to 7% among other Asian populations (Ashcroft, Daniels, and Hart, 2003; Jirapramukpitak, Prince, and Harpham, 2005; Kim and Kim, 2005). According to a study conducted by Ashcroft, Daniels, and Hart (2003), the prevalence of CSA among an Asian American sample was less than 7%, which was lower than the rate among a Native American sample (16%) and the average prevalence among all samples (8%). A similar trend has also been shown in another study, in which the CSA prevalence rate among Asian or Pacific Islanders was lower than the rate among their American counterparts (8% and 28%, respectively) (Rohde et al., 2008). The lower CSA victimization rate in China might be attributed to differences in the risk factors or protective factors across cultures. Given the one-child policy operating in China and the fact that Chinese families tend to live in extended families (Zeng, 2002), supervision of children by parents or grandparents is generally strict and close. The tendency for Chinese youths to live with their parents is higher than among their Western counterparts (Chan and Straus, 2008). This study's findings showed a high percentage of parents who were either cohabiting or married (93.9%) and a lower rate of family violence. These are factors associated with better parenting capacity and are thus crucial to child protection (Donald and Jureidini, 2004; Mikton and Butchart, 2009). The chance of CSA victimization by people other than parents may therefore be reduced (Sun et al., 2008).

Another possible explanation for the lower CSA victimization rates among Chinese children compared to Western children could be the difference in cultural beliefs which might lead to reporting bias. "Face," which can be defined as "prestige; dignity; honor; respect; status" (Carr, 1993), is one of the major principles governing the social lives of Chinese people (Eberhard, 1967). Face can be lost when a person is criticized, fails, or acts in ways that are not accepted as being the social norm. Disclosure of CSA victimization, either by oneself or by one's immediate family member, may lead to feelings of shame and losing face.

To avoid losing face, which can be extremely unpleasant, Chinese people may be less willing to report CSA victimization than Westerners; this could explain the relatively lower prevalence rate found in the present study.

Gender Differences in the Prevalence of CSA Victimization

In this study, a gender difference was found in the CSA victimization rates as reported by school children. Specifically, more boys than girls reported an experience of CSA victimization, thus providing a piece of contrary evidence to the more common finding that girls are more likely to experience CSA victimization (Cawson, Wattam, Brooker, and Kelly, 2000; Fergusson, Horwood, and Lynskey, 1996; Finkelhor, Ormrod, Turner, and Hamby, 2005; Finkelhor, Turner, Ormrod, and Hamby, 2009; Jirapramukpitak et al., 2005; May-Chahal and Cawson, 2005; Priebe and Svedin, 2008). However, the finding that boys are more likely to experience CSA victimization is not limited to the present study. A similar gender difference has been revealed in past studies, in particular those conducted in "high anonymity settings" such as schools (Madu and Peltzer, 2000; Yen et al., 2008) and computer-assisted settings (Y. Luo et al., 2008). According to the sexual script theory, boys (or males) are (a) more likely to be predicted to be the perpetrators and (b) less expected to be the victims of sexual abuse than girls (or females) (Banyard et al., 2007; Hartwick, Desmarais, and Hennig, 2007; O'Sullivan, Byers, and Finkelman, 1998). Holding this traditional sexual script concept, boys might be less likely to disclose CSA victimization as this may violate the expectations others have of males. However, the anonymous nature of school or computer-assisted settings, which involve neither individual face-to-face interviews nor the presence of known others, might facilitate the reporting of CSA by boys and thus lead to a higher prevalence of victimization compared to studies conducted in other settings (e.g., household).

The differences between the expectations of Chinese parents for sons and daughters may also contribute to the lower CSA victimization rates among girls. After toddlerhood, Chinese girls are often discouraged from engaging in boyish behaviors such as hanging around or playing outside. Instead, they are more likely to be expected to stay at home under their parents' supervision (Zhao, 2003).

Also, the high value placed on female virginity in Chinese societies may encourage parents to be more protective toward their daughters to prevent them being sexually abuse (Zhou, 1989).

Such strict parental supervision might therefore reduce the likelihood of Chinese girls experiencing sexual victimization (especially by nonfamily members), thus resulting in a relatively lower CSA prevalence rate compared to boys.

In addition, the traditional insistence on female virginity may act as a barrier to girls disclosing their experiences of CSA victimization to others. The loss of virginity at a young age may dishonor the family, thus leading to a loss of face which is unpleasant for both the girl and her family. Therefore, to avoid any fear and shame, Chinese girls may tend to refrain from disclosing their CSA experiences to others.

Gender Differences in the Prevalence Rates of Child Victimization

Gender differences were found in both the lifetime and the preceding-year prevalence rates of child victimization. The boys were more likely than the girls to have experienced conventional crime, child maltreatment, peer and sibling victimization, and overall child victimization in their lifetime and during the preceding year. As well as the importance of the male gender-role socialization of boys in the eyes of parents, another reason for this difference may be the different behavioral expectations parents have for boys and girls. Parents often have higher expectations for boys than girls in Chinese families. Physical punishment often occurs within Chinese culture, which accepts beating as a way of helping to develop a competent male to inherit the leadership of the family clan. Influenced by violent parenting styles, boys tend to accept and follow the use of violence in solving problems, and this makes them more hostile and aggressive. In addition, boys under greater pressure of parental expectations are not only more achievement oriented (which may easily provoke peer and sibling rivalry) but also more likely to engage in criminal activities in stressful conditions. Therefore, it is to be expected that boys will experience more victimization incidents than girls, especially during childhood.

Children who experience one kind of victimization are at greater risk of experiencing other forms of victimization. In other words, victimization of any one type makes an individual very vulnerable to subsequent different forms of revictimization (Finkelhor et al., 2007). In this study, the boys were more likely to have experienced child victimization than the girls; this may explain why more boys than girls reported an experience of CSA victimization.

Reflection on the Study Process

Due to the extensive scale and dimension of this study, we conducted surveys in five major Chinese cities beside Hong Kong, namely, Shanghai, Shenzhen, Tianjin, Wuhan, and Xi'an. Despite the valuable survey results we obtained from these surveys, we also encountered some difficulties as a result of cultural differences and the environment. Below, we discuss the major difficulties we encountered in both the household and school surveys and what we did to overcome these challenges.

Overall Difficulties Encountered in the Study

(1) *Sensitivity of Topic:* Besides the cultural differences between Mainland China and Hong Kong, the Mainland Chinese community is relatively more traditional and conservative than the Hong Kong community; this can be seen in the views of the two communities on child maltreatment and CSA. This increased the difficulty of persuading participants, especially the schools, to take part in the survey. Also, for those participants who were illiterate or had a low education level, the researchers had to conduct the questionnaire verbally, and sometimes the participants felt too embarrassed to answer the questions. With the assistance of computer-administered questionnaires, such difficulties could be relieved.

(2) *Design of Questionnaire:* The design of the questionnaire needed to take into consideration the cultural differences between, and the terminology used in, Hong Kong and China. Even though we modified the questionnaires many times, the researchers still had to spend more time providing further explanation to the participants, especially those who had a lower education level.

(3) *Cultural Differences:* In general, the Chinese have a different definition of child maltreatment, including the use of physical abuse and psychological aggression, due to their culture being more traditional compared to western culture; in fact, most forms of child maltreatment are acceptable to Chinese families (please refer to Chapter 2 on the background of traditional Chinese culture). Given this attitude toward child maltreatment and child abuse, some of the participants did not understand the purpose or the significance of this study. The researchers in Xi'an even came across some teachers who strongly refused to allow their students to participate or criticized the study as being harmful to children's growth and development. Their misunderstanding of the study and their unsupportive attitudes increased the difficulty of conducting this survey. The research team had to spend more time explaining the study to school principals and teachers in order to engage them in the study process.

Resolutions

(1) *Hiring of Researchers:* Hiring experienced researchers and teachers as team leaders and selecting researchers who spoke the local dialects facilitated the smooth running of the surveys.

(2) *Training for Researchers:* Providing additional training to and conducting test surveys with all researchers in order to ensure that they understood thoroughly the survey content, the questionnaire details, and, most importantly, the significance of the survey allowed all of the researchers to (a) gain the confidence to persuade the participants to take part in the survey and (b) explain details to participants patiently if they lost interest in the middle of the survey.

(3) *Support for Researchers:* We supported the researchers in a humane way by purchasing insurance for them, especially those who had to travel extensively to rural areas with adverse conditions.

(4) *Connection with Local Community:* To establish good local relations, we established relationships with the local communities, residential committees, and government officials though frequent communications, taking the initiative in seeking their approval for the study, and coordinating with the households and schools.

Limitations of the Study

As in any study based on self-reporting, recall bias, especially reporting bias, may have affected the results of this study. The time frame used to measure violence may have been one of the factors that contributed to recall bias. We used one year as the reference boundary and asked respondents to recall any violent incidents before and after that point. Previous research has highlighted that a year may be both a long time period over which to recall victimization that may occur more frequently and a relatively short period in which to recall rarer incidents (Finkelhor, Ormrod, and Turner, 2007). However, while underreporting may occur when respondents have forgotten an incident, overreporting can also occur when they "telescope" other types of victimization from earlier periods into the 1-year time frame (Finkelhor et al., 2007).

Another limitation was the use of parent reports as a source of information. As mentioned previously, the evidence on whether underreporting is present in parent reports is still inconclusive (Finkelhor, Hamby, et al., 2005; Kolko et al., 1996). Unless more conclusive evidence is presented, there is a possibility that parent reports provide an underestimate as parents might not know about victimization incidents involving their children or be unwilling to disclose them. Gender differences between parent reports may also be a barrier to presenting an accurate interpretation of the study's findings. Similar to past research (Finkelhor et al., 2009; Finkelhor, Hamby, et al., 2005), our study recruited caregivers randomly without preference or exclusion of any gender. However, differences may have existed between the fathers' and mothers' knowledge or reporting of the victimization of their children. Future studies should consider comparing reports between parents to minimize any effect of gender difference on the results.

Recommendations

Child victimization is expensive to societies. Estimates of the medical and mental health costs of child victimization are required to address this newly prioritized problem as such estimates would greatly facilitate the development of effective measures to help the victims (Chan and Cho, 2010). This study provides a reliable estimate of the rates of various forms of child victimization, and this will aid the determination of an accurate estimation of the medical, mental health, and social costs. Reliable estimates of such prevalence rates may facilitate better resource allocation in healthcare and mental health settings. In addition, our data revealed strong associations between previous experience of the three main types of family violence and the likelihood of child victimization. Child protection services and services for intimate partner violence (IPV) or family violence should therefore screen for all of these other forms of maltreatment. Multidisciplinary collaboration between health professionals and nongovernmental organizations should be undertaken so as to provide better integrated prevention programs with the capacity to address the coexistence of multiple forms of violence within the same nuclear family.

Our findings show that child victimization is prevalent in China. However, there is still limited recognition and identification of this problem. The lack of a formal definition and the underuse of coding systems for child abuse, such as the International Classification of Diseases (ICD-10; World Health Organization, 2004), in health settings have been major barriers to successful interventions for victims. Routine screening is uncommon in most hospitals in Mainland China, including those dedicated to children.

Hong Kong has developed very different practices for the screening and identification of child maltreatment cases. A multidisciplinary case conference is held once a case of suspected child maltreatment is identified by a social worker or medical professional. Following the Procedural Guide for Handling Child Abuse Cases (Revised 2007; Hong Kong Social Welfare Department, 2010), the participants in the case conference, drawn as needed from the medical, social work, police, teaching, and other professions, decide if child abuse has been established; if it has, a welfare plan is devised for the protection of the abused child. Hong Kong has modeled this system on the practices of the World Health Organization and western societies. This model would probably be a highly useful exemplar for the development of Mainland China's health system.

Training practitioners and formalizing the procedures for identifying child victimization and establishing an official database of cases for the use of frontline professionals may be effective first steps toward addressing the problem in Mainland China. Given the strong association between child victimization and other family violence, screening for the latter when there are child victims may be a useful means of detecting multiple types of violence and hence reducing revictimization.

The Optimus Study in China will surely provide valuable information for the surveillance of these issues in China. We have already started the first important step in conducting high quality studies. We will continue to work hand in hand to further develop quality research that will inform policy changes.

REFERENCES

Alikasifoglu, M., Erginoz, E., Ercan, O., Albayrak-Kaymak, D., Uysal, O., and Ilter, O. (2006). Sexual abuse among female high school students in Istanbul, Turkey. *Child Abuse and Neglect, 30,* 247-255.

Appel, A. E., and Holden, G. W. (1998). The co-occurrence of spouse and physical child abuse: A review and appraisal. *Journal of Family Psychology, 12*(4), 578-599.

Ashcroft, J., Daniels, D. J., and Hart, S. V. (2003). Youth victimization: Prevalence and implications. Retrieved from http://www.ojp.usdoj.gov/nij

Banyard, V. L., Ward, S., Cohn, E. S., Plante, E. G., Moorhead, C., and Walsh, W. (2007). Unwanted sexual contact on campus: A comparison of women's and men's experiences. *Violence and Victims, 22,* 52-70.

Biriere, J. (1992). Methodological issues in the study of sexual abuse effects. *Journal of Consulting and Clinical Psychology, 60,* 196-203.

Campbell, R., Greeson, M. R., Bybee, D., and Raja, S. (2008). The co-occurrence of childhood sexual abuse, adult sexual assault, intimate partner violence, and sexual harassment: A mediational model of posttraumatic stress disorder and physical health outcomes. *Journal of Consulting and Clinical Psychology, 76*(2), 194-207.

Carr, M. (1993). Chinese "face" in Japanese and English (Part 2). *The Review of Liberal Arts, 85,* 69-101.

Catania, J. A., Paul, J., Osmond, D., Folkman, S., Pollack, L., Canchola, J., et al. (2008). Mediators of childhood sexual abuse and high-risk sex among men-who-have-sex-with-men. *Child Abuse and Neglect, 32,* 925-940.

Cawson, P., Wattam, C., Brooker, S., and Kelly, G. (2000). Child maltreatment in the United Kingdom: A study of the prevalence of abuse and neglect. *NSPCC,* 1-20.

Chan, K. L. (2009) Protection of face and avoidance of responsibility: Chinese men's account of violence against women. *Journal of Social Work Practice, 23*(1), 93-108.

Chan, K. L. Comparison of parent and child reports on child maltreatment in a representative household sample in Hong Kong. *Journal of Family Violence,* Forthcoming.

Chan, K. L., and Cho, E. Y. N. (2010). A review of cost measures for the economic impact of domestic violence. *Trauma, Violence, and Abuse, 11*(3), 129-143. doi: 10.1177/1524838010374371

Chan, K. L., and Straus, M. A. (2008). Prevalence and correlates of physical assault on dating partners. *The Open Social Science Journal, 1,* 5-14.

Chen, J., Dunne, M. P., and Han, P. (2004). Child sexual abuse in China: A study of adolescents in four provinces. *Child Abuse and Neglect, 28,* 1171-1186.

Chen, J., Dunne, M. P., and Wang, X. (2003). Childhood sexual abuse: An investigation among 239 male high school students. *Chinese Mental Health Journal, 17*(5), 345-347.

Cicchetti, D., and Manly, J. T. (2001). Operationalizing child maltreatment: Developmental processes and outcomes. *Development and Psychopathology, 13,* 755-757.

Cicchetti, D., and Olsen, K. (1990). The developmental psychopathology of child maltreatment. In M. Lewis and S. M. Miller (Eds.), *Handbook of developmental psychopathology* (pp. 261-279). New York: Plenum.

DeVoe, E., and Graham-Bermann, S. A. (1997). *Predictors of posttraumatic stress symptoms in battered women and their children.* Paper presented at the The Second International Conference on Children Exposed to Family Violence.

Donald, T., and Jureidini, J. (2004). Parenting capacity. *Child Abuse Review, 13,* 5-17.

Eberhard, W. (1967). *Guilt and sin in traditional China.* Berkeley, CA: University of California Press.

Fergusson, D. M., Horwood, J., and Lynskey, M. T. (1996). Childhood sexual abuse and psychiatric disorder in young adulthood: II. Psychiatric outcomes of childhood sexual abuse. *Journal of the American Academy of Child and Adolescent Psychiatry, 34*(10), 1365-1374.

Figueiredo, B., Bifulco, A., Paiva, C., Maia, Â., Fernandes, E., and Matos, R. (2004). History of childhood abuse in Portuguese parents. *Child Abuse and Neglect, 28,* 669-682.

Finkelhor, D., Hamby, S. L., Ormrod, R., and Turner, H. (2005). The Juvenile Victimization Questionnaire: Reliability, validity, and national norms. *Child Abuse and Neglect, 29,* 383-412.

Finkelhor, D., Moore, D., Hamby, S. L., and Straus, M. A. (1997). Sexually abused children in a national survey of parents - Methodological issues. *Child Abuse and Neglect, 21*(1), 1-9.

Finkelhor, D., Ormrod, R. K., and Turner, H. A. (2007). Poly-victimization: A neglected component in child victimization. *Child Abuse and Neglect, 31*(1), 7-26. doi: 10.1016/j.chiabu.2006.06.008

Finkelhor, D., Ormrod, R. K., and Turner, H. A. (2007). Re-victimization patterns in a national longitudinal sample of children and youth. *Child Abuse and Neglect, 31,* 479-502.

Finkelhor, D., Ormrod, R. K., and Turner, H. A. (2009). Lifetime assessment of poly-victimization in a national sample of children and youth. *Child Abuse and Neglect, 33*(3), 403-411. doi: 10.1016/j.chiabu.2008.09.012

Finkelhor, D., Ormrod, R., Turner, H., and Hamby, S. L. (2005). The victimization of children and youth: A comprehensive national survey. *Child Maltreatment, 10*(5), 5-25.

Finkelhor, D., Turner, H., Ormrod, R., and Hamby, S. L. (2009). Violence, abuse, and crime exposure in a national sample of children and youth. *Pediatrics, 124*(5), 1-13.

Finkelhor, D., Turner, H. A., Ormrod, R. K., and Hamby, S. L. (2010). Trends in childhood violence and abuse exposure: Evidence from two national surveys. *Archives of Pediatrics and Adolescent Medicine, 164*(3), 238-242.

Hartwick, C., Desmarais, S., and Hennig, K. (2007). Characteristics of male and female victims of sexual coercion. *Canadian Journal of Human Sexuality, 16,* 31-44.

Ho, C. K. (1990). An analysis of domestic violence in Asian American communities: A multicultural approach to counseling. *Women and Therapy. Special issue: Diversity and complexity in feminist therapy: I, 9*(1-2), 129-150.

Hong, G. K., and Hong, L. K. (1991). Comparative perspectives on child abuse and neglect: Chinese versus Hispanics and Whites. *Child Welfare, 74,* 189-204.

Hong Kong Medical Coordinators on Child Abuse. (2003). Management of child abuse in Hong Kong: Results of a territory-wide interhospital prospective surveillance study. *Hong Kong Medical Journal, 9*(1), 6-9.

Hong Kong Social Welfare Department. (2010). *Procedural guide for handling child abuse cases: Revised 2007.* Hong Kong, China: Hong Kong Social Welfare Department.

Jaffe, P. G., Sudermann, M., and Reitzel, D. (1992). Child witnesses of marital violence. In R. T. Ammerman and M. Hersen (Eds.), *Assessment of family violence: A clinical and legal sourcebook* (pp. 313-331). New York: John Wiley.

Jirapramukpitak, T., Prince, M., and Harpham, T. (2005). The experience of abuse and mental health in the young Thai population: A preliminary survey. *Social Psychiatry and Psychiatric Epidemiology, 40,* 955-963.

Jouriles, E. N., Mehta, P., McDonald, R., and Francis, D. V. (1997). Psychometric properties of family members' reports of parental physical aggression toward clinic-referred children. *Journal of Consulting and Clinical Psychology, 65,* 309-318.

Kaufman, K. L., Hilliker, D. R., Lathrop, P., and Daleiden, E. L. (1993). Assessing child sexual offenders' modus operandi: Accuracy in self-reported use of threats and coercion. *Sex Abuse, 6,* 213-229.

Kim, H. S., and Kim, H. S. (2005). Incestuous experience among Korean adolescents: Prevalence, family problems, perceived family dynamics, and psychological characteristics. *Public Health Nursing, 22*(6), 472-482.

Kolko, D. J., Kazdin, A. E., and Day, B. T. (1996). Children's perspective in the assessment of family violence: Psychometric characteristics and comparison to parent reports. *Child Maltreatment, 1,* 156-167.

Luo, Y., Parish, W. L., and Laumann, E. O. (2008). A population-based study of childhood sexual contact in China: Prevalence and long-term consequences. *Child Abuse and Neglect, 32,* 721-731.

Madu, S. N., and Peltzer, K. (2000). Risk factors and child sexual abuse among secondary school students in the Northern Province (South Africa). *Child Abuse and Neglect, 24*(2), 259-268.

May-Chahal, C., and Cawson, P. (2005). Measuring child maltreatment in the United Kingdom: A study of the prevalence of child abuse and neglect. *Child Abuse and Neglect, 29,* 969-984.

McGee, R. A., Wolfe, D. A., and Wilson, S. K. (1997). Multiple maltreatment experiences and adolescent behavior problems: Adolescents' perspectives. *Development and Psychopathology, 9,* 131-150.

McGee, R. A., Wolfe, D. A., Yuen, S., Wilson, S. K., and Carnochan, J. (1995). The measurement of child maltreatment: A comparison of approaches. *Child Abuse and Neglect, 19,* 233-249.

Mikton, C., and Butchart, A. (2009). Child maltreatment prevention: A systematic review of reviews. *Bulletin of World Health Organization, 87,* 353-361.

O'Sullivan, L. F., Byers, E. S., and Finkelman, L. (1998). A comparison of male and female college students' experiences of sexual coercion. *Psychology of Women Quarterly, 22,* 177-195.

Priebe, G., and Svedin, C. C. (2008). Child sexual abuse is largely hidden from the adult society: An epidemiological study of adolescents' disclosures. *Child Abuse and Neglect, 32,* 1095-1108.

Richters, J. E., and Martinez, P. (1993). The NIHM Community Violence Project I: Children as victims and witnesses to violence. *Psychiatry: Interpersonal and Biological Processes, 56,* 7-21.

Rohde, P., Ichikawa, L., Simon, G. E., Ludman, E. J., Linde, J. A., Jeffery, R. W., et al. (2008). Associations of child sexual and physical abuse with obesity and depression in middle-aged women. *Child Abuse and Neglect, 32,* 878-887.

Sun, S., Li, L., Ji, G., Lin, C., and Semaana, A. (2008). Child behaviour and parenting in HIV/AIDS-affected families in China. *Vulnerable Children and Youth Studies, 3,* 192-202.

Tang, C. S. K. (2002). Childhood experience of sexual abuse among Hong Kong Chinese college students. *Child Abuse and Neglect, 26,* 23-37.

Winegar, R. K., and Lipschitz, D. S. (1999). Agreement between hospitalized adolescents' self-reports of maltreatment and witnessed home violence and clinician reports and medical reports. *Comprehensive Psychiatry, 40*(5), 347-352.

Wong, W. C. W., Leung, P. W. S., Tang, C. S. K., Chen, W. Q., Lee, A., and Ling, D. C. (2009). To unfold a hidden epidemic: Prevalence of child maltreatment and its health implications among high school students in Guangzhou, China. *Child Abuse and Neglect, 33*(7), 441-450.

World Health Organization. (2004). *International classification of diseases (ICD).* Geneva, Switerland: World Health Organization.

Yen, C. F., Yang, M. S., Yang, M. J., Su, Y. C., Wang, M. H., and Lan, C. M. (2008). Childhood physical and sexual abuse: Prevalence and correlates among adolescents living in rural Taiwan. *Child Abuse and Neglect, 32,* 429-438.

Zeng, Y. (2002). A demographic analysis of family households in China, 1982-1995. *Journal of Comparative Family Studies, 33*(1), 15-34.

Zhao, X. (2003). Chinese Americans. In C. R. Ember and M. Ember (Eds.), *Encyclopedia of sex and gender: Men and women in the world's cultures.* New York: Springer.

Zhou, X. (1989). Virginity and premarital sex in contemporary China. *Feminist Studies, 15,* 279-288.

In: Child Protection in Chinese Societies
Editor: Ko Ling Chan

ISBN: 978-1-61942-879-9

Chapter 4

CASE STUDY OF AN ADULT SURVIVOR OF CHILD SEXUAL ABUSE

Anna Wai Man Choi and Ko Ling Chan
Department of Social Work and Social Administration
University of Hong Kong, Pokfulam, Hong Kong

ABSTRACT

We present an in-depth case analysis to provide a comprehensive understanding of the issues related to child sexual abuse in China. The case was an adult survivor from child sexual abuse recruited in Hong Kong. Through the framework of control and power, we argue that perpetrators systematically avoid being held responsible for their actions. They will go to great lengths to hide the truth. It is difficult for victims and their family members to seek help. The impact of sexual abuse on the victims is not only determined by the event itself, but also by the methods and attitudes adopted to handle the event. While people around the victim can assist him/her in healing, they can also impede the process and do more harm than good.

Keywords: Adult survivor; Child sexual abuse; Power and control; Patriarchy; Chinese

INTRODUCTION

In this chapter, we present an in-depth case analysis to provide a comprehensive understanding of the issues related to child sexual abuse in China. No case study can ever be generalized to the whole of society, but it can provide a deep understanding of the phenomenon. Below, we provide an in-depth analysis of an adult survivor of child sexual abuse. Section I presents the details of the case and the sexual abuse incident; Section II presents the analysis of the case.

CASE STUDY—"DO I DESERVE ALL THIS?" (NARRATED BY CINDY* [AN ALIAS])

My Family

Regarding my family, I don't want to call my parents "Daddy and Mommy," so I will refer to them as Mr. and Mrs. Cheung for now.

Pitiful Mom - Mrs. Cheung

Mrs. Cheung is in her fifties. She had a difficult life during her early childhood. Her biological father passed away when she was still a toddler. At the age of three, she followed her mother (Cindy's grandma) and came to Hong Kong. Her life did not get any easier after her arrival in Hong Kong. At a young age, she had to complete her studies while also taking care of the household chores. Her mother was bad tempered and often mistreated her verbally and physically. Mrs. Cheung left home at the age of 11 and has lived an independent life ever since. Later on, my Grandma cohabited with another man; I have called this man Grandpa ever since I was a child. Both Grandma and Grandpa treated me well; they visited me and bought toys for me to have fun with. However, Mrs. Cheung did not like Grandpa much.

Hard-Working Dad - Mr. Cheung

Mr. Cheung, who is 60 years old, also had a miserable life; he had been denounced during the Cultural Revolution in China. He was the second of six children in his family. He tried smuggling himself into Hong Kong several times before the age of 18, but he failed and was put in jail. During his incarceration, he was hung up and beaten. Finally, he made it to Hong Kong. As he was illiterate and uneducated, he could only secure jobs that required heavy labor. Nonetheless, he worked with painstaking effort and saved as much money as he could, and this allowed him to start up his own company when I was at elementary school. His diligence is all that I admire about him.

Our Family Becomes Well-off

Mr. and Mrs. Cheung dated for 8 years after their friends introduced them to each other. Shortly after they got married, my brother and I were born. We lived in a small place; the four of us shared a wooden hut that was less than 100 square feet. We were later allocated public housing when I started my elementary school. By then, Mr. Cheung had already established his own business, which gradually improved our living standard.

When I reached high school, Mr. and Mrs. Cheung and I moved into a spacious private housing apartment, while my brother and Grandma stayed behind in the public housing. Mr. and Mrs. Cheung believed that this arrangement would keep me away from bad influences. They also wanted to offer me my own room; I was really grateful for that. Both flats were in the same district. Although they were not too far apart, we still had to travel to and fro by

* Cindy is a 31-year-old married woman. She is of average height with shoulder-length straight hair. She has common features, wears glasses, and looks younger than she actually is. She was very cooperative throughout the interview. She was willing to share her experiences and feelings. She said that she hoped her story would empower other victims, just as a magazine interview with a victim of sexual abuse had once inspired her.

public transport. My brother and I often spent time in the playgrounds around the area, and Grandma used to take care of our daily living needs. All in all, we often spent time together.

My Childhood

Life as a Spoiled Child

Since the day I was born, I was pampered and taken care of just like a princess.

When we were still living in the wooden hut, Mr. Cheung worked from dawn to dusk while Mrs. Cheung took care of my brother and me. Every Sunday, Grandma and Grandpa would come and visit us. They love us so much, sending us toys and dolls all the time.

After we moved into public housing, Mr. Cheung's business began to grow quickly and so Mrs. Cheung decided to help him at work. Therefore, Grandma took on responsibility for raising us. By that time, Grandpa had already passed away, and so Grandma had moved in with us. Those days were the golden days of our family. Every Sunday, we would all go for dim sum in the morning and Mr. and Mrs. Cheung would go shopping with us. We often dined out and lived a luxurious life. I still remember how I used to travel a lot during my elementary school years. I can honestly say that I had everything I needed in terms of material comforts, and Mr. and Mrs. Cheung were also willing to spend time communicating with me. I felt close to them.

Trapped in Hell

However, I sometimes felt as though I was in Hell because I was subjected to cursing, blaming, and beatings.

Grandma was very strict about our behaviors and attitudes. Whenever we disobeyed her or skewed slightly away from her requirements, she would use corporal punishment on us with whatever came to hand. On one occasion when my brother was making a noise while he was eating, she picked up a spoon and hit him on the mouth with it. She would report our misconduct to Mr. and Mrs. Cheung, which would lead to another round of punishment. Mrs. Cheung used a bamboo stick to physically punish us without cause. She would not intervene when she saw Grandma or Mr. Cheung abusing or punishing us; her inaction may have been due to the fact that she had been raised the same way.

As for Mr. Cheung, he would often wear only his undergarments when he was at home. He also preferred to us to be naked whenever he was physically punishing us. On one occasion, he took my brother's clothes off and tied his hands and legs to a bamboo rod and beat him up badly. He took a photo of it and has kept it ever since as a memento.

In addition, Mr. and Mrs. Cheung did not accept the idea of giving us pocket money, even when both of us were in high school. They believed that as long as we voiced our needs, they would have the final decision on whether or not to get items for us. They also prohibited us from having unnecessary contacts and connections with people outside the family, such as friends and classmates. We were asked not to release our contact numbers to others and not to spend time with neighbors. We were not allowed to have any playtime with classmates and had to return home straight after class. We would only be excused for coming home late if we had a note either from school or a teacher; otherwise, we would be punished verbally and physically if we were late.

Mr. and Mrs. Cheung always claimed that they did all of these things for our own good. At that time, I seemed to understand their good intentions; hence, I tried my very best to measure up to their standards. When, at times, I did not measure up to their expectations, I too felt that I should be punished. However, I also felt like I was the only child in such a pitiful state, as they never tried to get to the bottom of things. Likewise, we were totally shut off from the outside world—the first time I knew what potato chips tasted like was when I attended my classmate's birthday party!

The Rebellion

More often than not, I felt like I was trapped between two extremes: heaven, where I was surrounded by love and attention, and hell, where I was severely mistreated and maltreated.

I remember that back then I tried stealing money from home, snacks from the supermarket, and much more when I was still in Primary 5 and 6, and Mr. and Mrs. Cheung punished and humiliated me. Although I understand that all of these incidents were my fault, I still wonder why they never tried to understand me and the reasons for my behavior better. There was no trust, communication, listening, or understanding, only punishment and maltreatment.

When I was in Form 1, the other children began to reject and abandon me. I attribute this to the fact that I might not have known how to act around others. The other children found me too arrogant and cocky to be friends with. I then started to pick fights at school. My school refusal behavior intensified in Form 2: I would only turn up at school to register my attendance; then, I fled from all classes and only returned when the school day was over. I never gained Mr. and Mrs. Cheung's trust during this time of my life. They would often stalk me to on my way to school. I was annoyed by their actions; they never learned how to respect and trust me.

This was also the time when I met my first boyfriend (hereinafter, "Boyfriend #1"). Boyfriend #1 was about the same age as I was; he had dropped out of school right after Form 2 and spent his days wandering the streets with friends. After we had been dating for about a year, we had sex. During the second semester of Form 2, I gradually showed up less for school and spent most of my days feeling abused, aggrieved, and discontented.

The Transformation of my World - Summer of Form 3

One day during summer of my Form 3 year, Mr. and Mrs. Cheung went to work as usual. I was on my own that day, and so I invited my boyfriend to come up. However, Mrs. Cheung suddenly showed up and discovered that my boyfriend and I were spending time alone together in the house. She suspected that I had already lost my virginity to him, and she scolded me. In the heat of the moment, my boyfriend left. That night, when Mr. Cheung returned home from work, Mrs. Cheung told him everything. They locked me inside a room, and Mr. Cheung took off all of my clothes and maltreated me continuously. He even attempted to throw me out of the window. Fortunately, he let me go when Mrs. Cheung, who was in tears, begged him not to harm me.

Once I retrieved my clothes, I used them to cover up my body and returned to my own room. Not long after that, Mr. Cheung entered my room and locked the door. I did not realize that there was anything wrong about this. I thought that, as was his usual practice, he had come in to explain the reasons behind my punishment. Unfortunately, this was not the case. He forced me onto the bed and used his hands to cover up my mouth so that I could not make a sound. I knew that both my brother and Mrs. Cheung were right outside the door with the keys as they were worried that Mr. Cheung would beat me. However, I was unable to utter a word when he sexually assaulted me. While he was doing this, he kept on questioning me, saying "Did he do the same thing as I did?" Once he had had enough, he put on his shorts, walked out of the room, and left the house. My mind went blank at that split second. All of a sudden, I felt so messed up…until I heard the sound of the gate and knew that he had left the house. I immediately ran into the toilet and locked myself in. I wanted to commit suicide but was too afraid to do so. I spent hours sitting and gazing into space. A few hours later, Mrs. Cheung and my brother knocked on the door to check whether I was alright.

Once I stepped out of the toilet, I calmly called my boyfriend and suggested to him that he should leave his house. I explained to him that I was worried that Mr. Cheung was on his way to find him. As my immediate goal was to protect him from harm, I did not have enough time to explain to him in detail what had happened. Then, I told Mrs. Cheung that "Daddy messed me up (i.e., sexually assaulted me), I want to leave." This was not the first time I had told Mrs. Cheung about such experiences. Recalling my early high school days, I had a blurry memory of Mr. Cheung pressing hard on me while I was asleep. It startled me when he touched my private parts. I woke up and asked him what he was doing. He claimed that he was just taking me to my bed like he always did. After that event, I informed Mrs. Cheung immediately. She did not believe me, and I put the whole event to the back of my head. But this time, Mrs. Cheung gave me my identification card and a few hundred dollars. I thought that she believed me and supported my decision to leave.

Runaway from Home

I still remember that, on that night, when I was running toward the bus station, I was only wearing my pajamas and slippers and I was covered in bruises. When I got on the bus, the bus driver asked me whether my case should be reported to the police. I felt a sense of warmth inside me; it was not until that moment that I realized I actually had a way out, namely, to report the incident to the police.

When I arrived at the home of Kaka, my best friend, I immediately told her everything. She listened to me attentively and then went with me to find my boyfriend. Once he knew the story, he was furious and wanted to find Mr. Cheung. I stopped him from doing so; I said, "I know he will be in trouble if I ever bring this to the attention of the police." By that time, I was certain that he had committed the offense of having unlawful sexual intercourse with a girl under the age of 16. However, taking the rest of my family's interests into consideration, I did not want to send him to jail.

After running away from home, I stayed at Kaka's home for a while. I started to miss going to school when I saw Kaka and the rest of my fellow schoolmates busy with their schoolwork while I stayed at home. All I did was sleep. As I had dropped out of school before the beginning of the summer, there was no reason for me to return to it anymore. At the same time, the school did not care that I had dropped out.

A month later, I moved into my boyfriend's home where he lived with his parents and brothers. The place was not spacious; therefore, I had to share a bed with my boyfriend. His parents often asked why my parents disliked me, why I was not going to school or working but rather idly spending my time at home, and why my parents were not looking for me anymore. I did not know how to answer their questions and so I remained silent and cried myself to sleep every night.

The Attitudes of Mrs. Cheung and Grandma

Coincidentally, my boyfriend lived in the same block as my grandmother. I could therefore visit her to get meals so as to reduce my expenses. Mrs. Cheung and I would meet up every week. However, she was terrified by the idea that Mr. Cheung would find out sooner or later and beat me up. She would secretly bring along clothes and belongings for me every time we met up.

As a matter of fact, a few months after I ran away from home, a group of gangsters came to my boyfriend's home searching for me, and I believe that this was arranged by Mr. Cheung. Fortunately, at the time they arrived, both my boyfriend and I were having a chat on the staircase, and they did not find us. We would not have escaped if they found us, as they were equipped with metal rods and weapons.

Every week when I met with Mrs. Cheung, she would try to persuade me to find a job, which annoyed me extremely. Whenever I brought up the incident of sexual abuse, Mrs. Cheung would feel sick to her stomach. She would also try to convince me to forget about the incident and not to mention it to anyone ever again. I could never understand Mrs. Cheung's extreme fear of Mr. Cheung. I had no idea whether she feared that he would hurt me again or whether she just could not cope with the truth. I doubted that it was true that I would heal over time once I forgot about the incident. Ever since the incident, Mrs. Cheung had suffered from insomnia. Feeling burnt out from work, she also suffered from different kinds of pains. As for me, I had an emotional breakdown and cried a lot. All of these experiences taught me not to speak about the incident anymore.

As for Grandma, she adopted a similar attitude whenever I mentioned the incident. She strongly suggested that I should never bring the matter up again. Although she was very worried that I would be maltreated again if I ever returned home, she still advised me to beg for forgiveness so that I could return home. I did not understand why it was my fault and why I had to ask for forgiveness.

On one occasion, Mrs. Cheung and Grandma yelled at me and complained that I always dressed inappropriately. I often wondered whether this was true. I thought that I could dress casually at home, just like Kaka and her sister did in their home. I did not understand why I could not do the same. I was confused and felt misunderstood as Mrs. Cheung and Grandma never took my side.

Meeting Daddy Again

Two years after I ran away from home, Mr. and Mrs. Cheung wanted to travel to Australia. However, my brother refused to go with them. Mr. Cheung then demanded my immediate return so that I could serve as their translator during their trip. As I had not travelled for a long time and wanted to take care of Mr. and Mrs. Cheung and Grandma, I agreed to travel with them. Both Mrs. Cheung and Grandma were excited about our first reunion. In order to please Mr. Cheung, Mrs. Cheung claimed that I was the one who was paying for the expenses.

A sense of fear arose in me immediately when I first saw Mr. Cheung at the airport. I felt uneasy, uncomfortable, and frightened whenever he was around me, talking or initiating any physical contacts, such as touching and patting my shoulders and arms. Not wanting to spoil the pleasant atmosphere, I tried to suppress my reactions and act normally. One day, Mr. Cheung and I joined a snorkeling course. Hence, we were both in our swimsuits. While we were snorkeling, he lightly patted my leg, which made me feel extremely resentful and uncomfortable. After the snorkeling, I was very tired and I slept on his shoulder during the return trip. This gave me a sense of warmth and closeness to him, just like I used to have when I was young.

After the trip, Mr. Cheung occasionally asked Mrs. Cheung to invite me over for dinner. Sadly, on these occasions, he would humiliate me harshly using foul language and accuse me of being a prostitute. Another time, Mr. Cheung bought me a down jacket. Mrs. Cheung was so excited about this; she said that I should choose one that I liked. I honestly felt disgusted about this. I never wore the jacket; I just kept it in my closet.

All in all, I could not understand how Mr. Cheung could act as though nothing had happened. I also could not comprehend the happiness and bliss that Mrs. Cheung and Grandma displayed when they saw Mr. Cheung treating me better.

Searching among the Chaos

Boyfriend #1

Not long after I moved into Boyfriend #1's home, I tried to find a job. At the age of 15, I found my first job as a sales representative in a cake shop, but it only lasted for a few days. In fact, during the next 10 years, I had many different jobs. None of these jobs lasted that long—a few days to a year. I never really knew why I quit jobs: sometimes I was upset after being bullied or worried about being criticized; other times, I worried a lot for no apparent reason. I would just walk away, without any explanation or following up on any salary payments I was owed. I did not make any statement about my resignation as I did not have a clue about why had resigned.

More often than not, I suffered from sleeping problems. My body always went numb when I was asleep. A sense of sadness and insecurity often overwhelmed me, and this was reflected in my need to indulge in substance abuse every week and to stuff my bed full of dolls. Every now and then, I would throw tantrums, and I even cut my wrists. Even now, the scars remain.

After moving in with my boyfriend, his family members gradually came to accept me. They started to treat me as one of the family, maybe even as a daughter-in-law. His grandmother would leave me items as keepsakes. Even after our breakup, they all continued to treat me well; they did not want us to break up. They are now my godparents.

Sometimes, I think that my boyfriend did not do enough to keep me, especially in terms of handling the fact that I had been sexually abused. I guess he thought that I had done something inappropriate, but I could not figure it out. On the other hand, I certainly understand that he was too young to have the knowledge and skills required to handle my experience wisely. Mrs. Cheung never liked him; she believed that it was completely his fault that Mr. Cheung sexually assaulted me. She even declined my wish to give birth to his baby and arranged for me to have an abortion.

After 6 years, I broke up with him. I gradually realized that he did not understand me. He never had a stable job. He even got involved with gangsters and started fights. Also, I felt annoyed when he always asked me to mimic pornography when we were having sex, and this led to arguments.

Boyfriend #2

I met my second boyfriend (hereinafter, "Boyfriend #2") when I was working in a fashion boutique. He was a drug addict and would amble around my shop with his friends. We had a sexual relationship after our second date. I felt as though I had the freedom to choose someone else besides Boyfriend #1. I slowly walked away from Boyfriend #1 by rejecting his good intentions and occasionally spending my nights with Boyfriend #2. When Boyfriend #1 found out about this, he found himself another girlfriend, and this made things even more complicated. Thus, I made the decision to move in with Boyfriend #2, who spent most of his time alone in his apartment; his parents did not care about him. Comparatively speaking, his apartment was bigger than the home of Boyfriend #1, and I felt carefree and relaxed there. I could do whatever I wanted to and enjoy life. Sometimes, he took drugs with his friends while I was drinking next to them. I gradually got used to consuming more alcohol. Even when he went away for drug addiction rehabilitation, I continued to live in his home.

However, regardless of what I said, he often suspected that I was keeping in contact with Boyfriend #1. Perhaps this was due to the fact that I did not handle the relationship well when it first started. Even when I told him that I was pregnant with his baby, he would not admit that it was his and asked me to have an abortion. Whenever I suggested a breakup, he would threaten to kill himself if I left. He also made it clear that he could not live without me. I cannot deny the fact that this made me feel important and significant.

Boyfriend #3 and Girlfriend #1

I was troubled about being involved in more than one relationship at a time. Therefore, I tried to find comfort in being a workaholic. During the day, I worked at the boutique. At night, I worked in a nightclub, where I got to know my third boyfriend. I did not like him much as a person, but I still treated him nicely. As he came from a well-off family, we lived a life of luxury. I realized that I had regained the sense of fruitfulness, in terms of material comforts, that I had once had when I was small. I quickly started a sexual relationship with him. I admit that I missed my first boyfriend and felt that what I was doing with Boyfriend #3 was wrong. Therefore, the relationship with Boyfriend #3 did not last long. During that period of time, I also met a girl who was a lesbian. Out of curiosity, I had a short yet intimate relationship with her.

Ever since the day I first ran away from my family, nothing was stable. I had also developed a tendency to shop for branded goods despite my financial instability. I was thus in great debt and lived that period of my life in chaos. I developed and maintained all of the above relationships at the same time, and I called everywhere my home.

I Want a Place Called Home

On one occasion, when I was seriously ill at Boyfriend #3's place, I called Mr. and Mrs. Cheung and asked them to send me to the hospital where Mrs. Cheung had had her bile duct surgery. After I was discharged from hospital, Mr. Cheung invited me to move back home. Unfortunately, he did not change his attitude toward me. He would still humiliate me without cause, and he disliked me for being sociable, especially when I was hanging out with my friends. He blamed me for tearing the whole family apart when I moved out. He claimed that he had a hard time explaining my absence and had to lie about it to my relatives. I could not be bothered with him anymore, and I therefore planned to run away to Kaka's house. Unfortunately, my brother discovered my plan. It ended really badly: Mr. and Mrs. Cheung spent time wandering around places looking for me.

My nomadic life began once again. I would spend some time at Kaka's place, some time at Boyfriend #2's apartment, and sometimes go back to my family. I did promise Mr. and Mrs. Cheung that I would cut my ties with friends who had a bad influence on me. Every day, I would go to work on time and come back home right after work, trying to be a good daughter. I did all of these things because I wanted a home so badly and did not want to wander around places anymore. I even tolerated it when both of them came to my workplace and spent hours spying on me.

As time went by, Mr. Cheung still felt reluctant about trusting me. He stalked me at my workplace; I also had to report to him whenever I went out. All of my painstaking efforts were not rewarded. Mr. And Mrs. Cheung only responded with indifference and dissatisfaction. To them, spending time with friends was a sin. To make things worse, Mr. Cheung never stop humiliating me. If I got dressed up, he accused me of being a prostitute. Although I spent more time with Mr. and Mrs. Cheung like I did when I was small, Mr. Cheung still denied what he did to me. Every time the incident was mentioned, he put all the blame on me; he said, "It was entirely your fault that the family was ruined when you walked away from us! I had to lie to our relatives, telling them that you were with a man or that you were a prostitute." Whenever I heard these comments, all I could do was cry.

Boyfriend #4

I found Boyfriend #4 when my relationship with Mr. and Mrs. Cheung deteriorated. He was a friend of Girlfriend #1, and he worked on construction sites. He was good looking and had a lot of female friends. At that time, many men pursued me. Thus, I felt like we were a perfect match when we started dating. I moved in with him not long after we started dating. Although his parents did not approve of me, I dismissed them and stayed in my boyfriend's room. We then managed to rent a place of our own. He started adopting different kinds of animals, including six cats, dogs, turtles, and fish, and keeping them at home. During the outbreak of avian flu in early 2000, I refused to allow him to adopt a chicken. Not only did he like animals, he also liked cross-dressing as a woman. He especially liked wearing women's lingerie, which aroused him sexually. During sexual intercourse, he wanted me to take the active male role and to accommodate his needs. We also shopped together for girls outfits. At the beginning, he confined his cross-dressing to home. None of his friends or family knew about it. However, I started to feel disgusted when he pleaded with me to allow him to cross-dress on our date nights. I was shocked when I found him waiting to pick me up from work in women's clothing.

My relationship with him only lasted about a year. Day by day, we argued more and more. I also had another abortion during that year with him. At the end, I wanted to help him kick his habit of cross-dressing and thus sought help from my friends. However, he was upset when he found out that I had disclosed his secret to others. He took his revenge by revealing my past to my friends. This was when I decided to end my unhappy relationship with him.

Meeting my Current Husband

Ming, my current husband, is a good friend of Boyfriend #4. Initially, I did not make much of an impression on him. He did not speak much when we met; he only looked at me. On the day before I broke up with Boyfriend #4, Ming admitted that he liked me after I prompted him. The next day, I broke up with Boyfriend #4 and he moved back to live with his parents. Ming started living with me from then on. Ming worked in the logistics industry. He took on a debt of over HKD100,000 to buy himself a truck in the hope of improving our lives. As a result, we barely had enough money to make ends meet, and so we started going out less and quitting drugs to reduce our spending.

At the same time, I started to work in the fashion boutique again. My boss trusted me and knew my capabilities, and therefore he appointed me as the supervisor for several shops. I built up a reputation as a successful manager in the industry. However, I was very demanding of the junior staff, and this led to a deterioration in my working relationships with them. The junior staff even complained to my boss. To appease the junior staff, my boss criticized me for being too demanding. On the other hand, he needed me to keep up the sales. I was very stressed, unhappy, and aggrieved.

Grandpa Passes Away

At that time, Grandpa, the most senior person in our family, was very sick, and I travelled frequently to the Mainland to visit him. Within a short time, he passed away, and the feeling that no one was there for me overwhelmed me once again. At that time, I went back to visit Grandpa with Mr. and Mrs. Cheung and my brother. Mr. Cheung told the rest of our family how bad I was, which led to even more criticism. That was when I first understood the meaning of "silence is golden." I was hoping to explain to Grandpa what had happened throughout the years. However, he passed away, and I never got the chance to make it up to him. Ever since he passed away, I have felt a sense of helplessness and hopelessness.

The Article

After arriving back in Hong Kong, I remained very emotional. I would break down and cry while I was at work. Even though my boss understood my need to apply for leave to visit my Grandpa, as a responsible supervisor, I knew that I should not take leave that frequently. This made it difficult for me to manage my team at work. I panicked and did not know how to face my junior staff; hence, I decided to run away from my job and quit.

I started to think about committing suicide. While I was cooking, I thought about cutting my hand. I did not want to work, and so I just stayed at home. Sometimes, Ming asked me to go work with him so that I had some company. One day, I read a magazine article of an interview with someone who had had a similar experience to mine. Based on the information in the article, I contacted the Against Child Abuse Association and got to know Mrs. Chan, a social worker.

Mrs. Chan referred me to a psychiatrist. I was diagnosed with depression. I had to both take medication and attend counseling sessions regularly. Ming joined me whenever I visited Mrs. Chan. We got married in 2006. After 2 years of counseling and treatment, I was getting better. I stopped taking my medication and reduced my counseling sessions 2 years later. Unfortunately, I relapsed into depression and lost interest in everything. I did not want to work and the thought of committing suicide recurred. I immediately contacted Mrs. Chan and started seeing a psychiatrist again. My situation has stabilized now. I am taking medication regularly, and I have started to look for part-time jobs. I am also planning to have children. I am now living in a harmony with my in-laws (father, mother, and sister).

My Wishes

I wish that I could have a job that I like, one that I can continue for a long time so that I no longer have to seek a new one.

I wish that I could control my emotions. I want to be emotionally stable. Sometimes, I am anxious and worried about what others think about me and whether they look down on me. Other times, I feel disappointed and sad when others do not give me the attention I think I deserve. All of these negative thoughts bombard me at the same time.

I also hope that Mr. and Mrs. Cheung will no longer be disturbed by or avoid the incident of sexual assault. Whenever I see them, I feel sorry for them and pity them. They have never known how to cope with the incident. I even thought of killing myself as a means of forcing Mr. Cheung to face the facts and also to offer forgiveness to him through my last words.

To be honest, I still feel confused about why Mr. Cheung sexually abused me. All these years, I have had a question for him that I have buried deep down inside me: “Why did you ever treat me like this?”

Case Analysis – The Emerging Power of Perpetrators

Power and control (DAIP, 2008; HKSWA, 2005) is a common and repetitive thinking pattern among most perpetrators except for the few that are mentally dysfunctional. This thinking pattern dominates their speech and behaviors. The perpetrators believe that the key to maintaining and consolidating their relationships with their spouses, children, and other family members is based on whether they are within their power and under their control.

The ideology of power and control often stems from unhealthy and improper concepts of intimate relationships. For example, perpetrators believe that they (a) are the most important person and are superior to their spouse and children and (b) have privileges over their spouse and children; they also require absolute obedience and service from their spouse and children. The shaping of such thinking patterns can be explicated in the following ways: (a) the perpetrators have been maltreated during their own childhood; (b) the perpetrators have witnessed domestic violence; (c) the patriarchal structure of the family; or (d) the gender inequality in the society.

Through the case of Cindy, this chapter attempts to explicate the development of the power and control of perpetrators so as to obtain a better and in-depth understanding of the circumstances, risk factors, and impacts of child maltreatment.

Risk Factors

Cindy's case not only reflects the interplay of power and control from her father; it also illustrates (a) the patriarchal authority and male domination that are strongly embedded within traditional Chinese culture and (b) the formation of domestic violence and its culture within the family. On the other hand, it also reveals how sexual violence can gradually be legitimized and even accepted within a family merely due to the power and control of the perpetrator.

The Ideology of the Perpetrators – Control and Power

The idea of being in control and power causes perpetrators to become self-centered. They do not know how to respect their spouses and children, believing that they have the responsibility to understand and take care of their own emotions. When conflicts arise that trigger the anger of the perpetrators, they will strongly insist that their spouses or children have failed to perform their duties. Thus, perpetrators justify their use of violence as a form of punishment and control by regarding it as a means of expressing their dissatisfaction with the misconduct of their victims (i.e., spouses and children).

In Cindy's case, both children (Cindy and her brother) were abused and maltreated, especially by their father, at an early age. Their father never explained or justified his abuse and beatings, and he imposed many restrictions on their daily lives: For example, he limited their contacts and connections with others outside school; absolute obedience was a must; and beatings would result if they could not measure up to his standards. All in all, by claiming that all of his actions were "for the good" of the children or that their behaviors were not good enough or against his rules, Cindy's father justified all of his abuse toward his children as valid and legitimate.

It is very common to find perpetrators using threats to maintain family cohesion. They will apologize in some way to their victims after the abuse and will compile different reasons to excuse themselves from the blame, just as Cindy's father did in this case. Cindy's father believed that being strict was the only parenting skill he needed to educate his own children. He did whatever it took—even scolding, humiliating and beating—to educate them. Perpetrators not only regard their methods as legitimate but may even put the blame for their use of violence on their victims. Under the long-term rule and parenting of Cindy's father, his power and control was gradually rationalized and accepted by his family members, which further consolidated his power within the family.

Patriarchy in Chinese Societies

Cindy's case serves as a demonstration of the development of the patriarchal system within a family. Grandma was asked to take good care of the children, which included taking charge of their behaviors and actions. If misconduct occurred, she punished them and reported them to their parents. Similarly, Mrs. Cheung also reported the misconduct of the children to the father. Both Grandma and Mrs. Cheung knew that Mr. Cheung would be harsh on the children, such as tying them up and beating them with their clothes off. Despite the fact that they feared and worried about Mr. Cheung's inappropriate parenting, they still obeyed and assisted him. This may have been due to the fact that they were worried that if they did otherwise, the children would be abused even more or that they actually identified with the parenting skills of the father.

This case illustrates clearly that the patriarchy system is evident within Chinese culture. While males dominate the leading positions, females are expected to follow a subordinate role (Chan, 2007). Under the supremacy of the patriarchy, all family members, including the spouse, children, and mother-in-law, are expected to obey the father. Moreover, the violence adopted by perpetrators not only applies to the children, but to every member of the family.

Multiple Types of Violence in the Family (WHO and ISPCAN, 2006)

Domestic violence encompasses a range of violent behaviors among family members, including spousal abuse, child abuse, and elderly abuse. According to the statistics, spousal abuse and child abuse shared a close link. When one type of domestic abuse arises within a family, this increases the chance of another type of domestic abuse occurring. In general, spousal abuse and child abuse will often co-occur within a family setting (Chan, 2005).

Multiple types of violence can be observed within Cindy's family, such as violence between the grandparents and the parents and by the parents on the children. Based on Cindy's narration, it is clear that her grandparents often had conflicts that resulted in fights. Although she was too young to remember all of the details of these fights, she did not forget about them. At the same time, Cindy also reported that she had observed a similar situation between her parents. Not only were her parents involved in serious arguments, it was also common for them to insult and humiliate each other, even in public. In Cindy's case, verbal abuse was adopted as an expression of power and authority. Not only would this have had an impact on the immediate victim of the verbal abuse; the children who witnessed the process would also have been profoundly affected. Furthermore, Cindy's father once knocked Mrs. Cheung down causing an injury on her waist. When Cindy moved out of the family home, her father prohibited Mrs. Cheung from meeting up with Cindy; he even threatened to beat up Mrs. Cheung if they ever met up. Mrs. Cheung had to be cautious about her moves in order to avoid being found out by Mr. Cheung. Mrs. Cheung was under enormous stress due to the threats and controlling behavior of Mr. Cheung, which can be considered as psychological abuse. Mr. Cheung threatened to cause harm to their children if Mrs. Cheung ever disobeyed his commands.

A major part of Cindy's life was dominated by child maltreatment. According to the World Health Organization (WHO) (1999), child maltreatment constitutes "all forms of physical and/or emotional ill-treatment, sexual abuse, neglect or negligent treatment or commercial or other exploitation, resulting in actual or potential harm to the child's health, survival, development or dignity in the context of a relationship of responsibility, trust or power".

In short, any behavior or neglect that put a child's physical and mental health at risk can be considered as a form of child maltreatment. In the case of Cindy, different types of abuse, such as physical, psychological and sexual abuse and neglect, can be observed. She was physically abused and attacked with different objects, such as bamboo, hangers, slippers, and folding stools. She was also forced to kneel overnight or tied to a bamboo rod. She also suffered a lot of psychological abuse: Mr. Cheung humiliated and insulted her and imposed social constraints on her.

Neglect is also evident in Cindy's case. She recalled the experience of her father abandoning her baby brother on the backstairs when he cried inside the cinema hall. Last, but not least, sexual abuse also occurred. Ever since Cindy and her brother were children, Mr. Cheung had only worn his underwear at home, and he insisted on them doing the same even after they had reached puberty. Furthermore, his act of punishing them naked and the sexual intercourse forced on Cindy resulted in psychological harm that may last for a lifetime.

Violence Culture

According to WHO (1996, 2002), violence is defined as the intentional use of physical force or power, threatened or actual, against oneself, another person, or against a group or community, that either results in or has a high likelihood of resulting in injury, death, psychological harm, mal-development, or deprivation.

Thus, violence refers to an intention to use violence and power on oneself, others, or a group, regardless of whether or not it results in an actual injury. In other words, the main consideration is the *intention* rather than the *consequence.* Therefore, cases where the perpetrators do not intend to cause injury or damage but use violence (e.g., corporal punishment) deliberately would also be considered to be a form of violence. In addition, violence takes different forms, such as physical, sexual, and psychological. Suicide and self-destructive behaviors are also considered as violence against oneself. Lastly, violence that results from the use of power, such as threats, intimidation, and neglect, is also considered to be a form of violence.

In Cindy's family, violence was a part of their lives. Even when they were having casual interactions, forceful hitting was involved; for example, Mr. Cheung used to bang Mrs. Cheung's head with toys during family playtime, which has resulted in Mrs. Cheung suffering from severe headaches ever since. The primary strategies of using corporal punishment within this family were insults, humiliation, spanking with a rod, assaults, and forcing the children to kneel down on the floor. Grandma had employed a similar approach to educating and parenting Mrs. Cheung when she was young. In general, hitting is considered to be a playful action, while corporal punishment is seen as a common and effective parenting strategy (WHO and ISPCAN, 2006).

Verbal abuse was also common within the spousal relationships in Cindy's family (i.e., between Mr. and Mrs. Cheung and between Cindy's grandparents). Mr. and Mrs. Cheung and Cindy's Grandpa and Grandma would often insult one another. Thus, it is not surprising to find that violence was tolerated and accepted within the family. Mr. Cheung claimed that he once tried to stop his son from crying by using a pillow to suffocate him or by neglecting him. He would even tie him up naked and take a picture as a memento. All of these incidents reflect the fact that violence was legitimized in Cindy's family, and this gradually established a culture of violence within the family.

Progressive Rationalization of Sexual Violence

The progressive rationalization of sexual violence can be readily observed in Cindy's case. First, Mr. Cheung would only wear his undergarments at home and would insist that Cindy and her brother do the same by using the weather as an excuse. He would also insist and expect his children to be naked when he was punishing them. Everyone in the family was used to this pattern of demand and discipline; for example, Cindy did not feel awkward being punished naked even when she was in high school. Cindy also recalled that it was her father who had helped her apply medication when she got a genital infection. None of the family members ever recognized that these behaviors and contacts were inappropriate.

As Cindy got older (i.e., high school age), her father would use the excuse of sending her to bed to touch her while she was asleep. Although Cindy told Mrs. Cheung about this, Mrs. Cheung did not trust Cindy enough to believe everything she said. On the other hand, Cindy also did not pay much attention to the clues that sexual violence was taking place. When Cindy was in Form 3, Mr. Cheung still punished her physically. Mrs. Cheung did not care about Cindy being naked; all she cared about was whether Mr. Cheung would abandon her. No one, not even Mrs. Cheung, Cindy's brother, or Cindy herself, ever noticed the slightest hint of sexual violence when Mr. Cheung locked himself in Cindy's room. Their focus was on whether Cindy would be physically injured. As a result, sexual abuse and violence were gradually accepted as the means of disciplining the children within this family. Their awareness of the danger of sexual abuse and violence was minimal and prevented them from realizing that such a danger was gradually emerging within their family.

Incident – The Perpetrator's Control over Victims and Family Members

In addition to controlling the everyday lives of their victims, the control and power which perpetrators have over their victims can manifest itself as abuse. Victims and family members are constrained behaviorally and psychologically by the perpetrator. They can do nothing to prevent or resist the perpetrator's power and control.

White Terror

When Mr. Cheung attempted to throw Cindy out of the window, Mrs. Cheung begged him to stop; when Mr. Cheung went into Cindy's room, Mrs. Cheung did nothing to prevent it. It is obvious that both Mrs. Cheung and her son were terrified by Mr. Cheung's use of violence. Although Mrs. Cheung was worried about Cindy's safety, all she could do was wait and observe passively at the door. Their unassertive approach may be attributed to their lack of awareness of sexual abuse and the long-term impact of the power and control imposed on them by Mr. Cheung. As the rest of the family conformed to Mr. Cheung's instructions without a struggle, they gradually got used to, tolerated, accepted, and permitted the use of violence. They believed that disobeying him would only result in more severe forms of violence; thus, it made sense to give in to him.

Regardless of whether he was physically, verbally, or sexually abusing Cindy, no one was there to stop Mr. Cheung's abusive behavior. It was certainly astonishing to find that Mr. Cheung could walk away from all of these incidents without a thought or care. He even placed the blame on Cindy. When he discovered that Cindy had moved out, he even claimed that he would maintain his attitude and behavior toward her. The case of Mr. Cheung demonstrates how a perpetrator's power and control impacts on his/her family members and victims.

Sexual Assault as a Means of Punishment

Ironic as it seems, Mr. and Mrs. Cheung once punished Cindy for dating because they were worried that she would lose her virginity. However, it was Mr. Cheung who sexually assaulted Cindy. He even questioned whether Cindy's boyfriend ever treated her in the same way. Mr. Cheung was furious about Cindy dating and losing her virginity. He saw such behavior as signs of disobedience. Thus, in order to regain his power and control over her, he forced Cindy to be stripped naked and abused her physically (by severely beating her) and verbally (by humiliating and threatening her). He even went into great lengths to express his dissatisfaction and anger sexually. It is also possible that Mr. Cheung resorted to using sexual violence as a way of expressing his extreme urge to regain control and possession of his own daughter. All that concerned Mr. Cheung was his need to have total power and control and be the center of the family. No one could ever escape from his rule and power.

The Condemnation of Victims

Mr. Cheung justified his punishment of Cindy by saying that it was due to her misconduct. He insulted Cindy, calling her a prostitute, and when he sexually abused her, he questioned whether Cindy's boyfriend treated her the same way as he did. He believed that by sexually abusing her and condemning her at the same time, this would allow him to deny responsibility for his abusive acts. By emphasizing to Cindy that she was no longer a virgin, Mr. Cheung was attempting to induce a sense of guilt in Cindy; he wanted her to take the blame and responsibility for being sexually abused. In general, perpetrators will often employ such condemnation tactics on their victims to relieve themselves of responsibility for the violence and abuse (Chan, 2006).

Postevent – The Understanding and Coping Strategies of Perpetrators, Victims, and Families

Sexual abuse is traumatic. During the posttrauma period, individuals, such as the victim, the perpetrator, and the people around them, are highly influential in the recovery and healing process. Below, we discuss this in relation to the case of Cindy.

Perpetrator: Father (Mr. Cheung)

Like typical perpetrators, Mr. Cheung not only denied the event and his responsibility, but also rationalized the incident, depicting himself as the righteous father. He adopted these strategies to avoid being blamed (Chan, 2006).

Denial: In regard to the sexual assault incident, Mr. Cheung never mentioned it. When Cindy confronted him, he did not admit that he had done such a thing to her.

Shunning Responsibility: Mr. Cheung kept on criticizing the misconduct of his daughter, such as going on dates, her complicated relationships with other boys, and running away from home. He regarded Cindy's running away from home as an elopement with her boyfriend rather than running away from home; thus, to him, it was valid to regard this as his daughter's fault. He therefore believed that it was right to humiliate and criticize Cindy in front of family members and relatives.

Violence Rationalization and Legitimization: Mr. Cheung considered punishing Cindy physically and verbally as a means of parenting and disciplining his daughter when she misbehaved. When Cindy ran away from home, he prohibited Mrs. Cheung from meeting up with her; he even threatened to kill Cindy if they did so. He rationalized and legitimized his use of violence as a means of punishing Cindy for running away from home.

Family Members: Mother (Mrs. Cheung), Grandma, Brother

On the one hand, both Mrs. Cheung and Grandma took care of Cindy and helped her while at the same time obeying Mr. Cheung and agreeing with him after the incident. They did not know how to react or respond or how to handle the event once it had happened.

Obedience to the Perpetrator: Mrs. Cheung and Grandma were afraid of Mr. Cheung, as was shown by their actions in concealing the truth, namely, that they kept in contact with Cindy and that they preferred to take good care of her. This indirectly reflected the power and control Mr. Cheung had over them. To a certain extent, they agreed with how Mr. Cheung justified blaming Cindy and his use of violence and maltreatment against his daughter. Not only did they never confront Mr. Cheung about the sexual assault, they even accepted his intentions and reasons: Cindy should be blamed for her misconduct; she had run away from home because she wanted to avoid facing and handling the incident. In the end, while Mr. Cheung returned to his normal routine, Cindy was accused of being an irresponsible daughter who ran away from home and lived a nomadic life.

Shame Stays Within the Home: Mrs. Cheung kept reminding her daughter not to mention the incident to anyone, especially her boyfriend. She believed that it would bring shame to the family. She was also worried that people would see her daughter in a bad light.

Emphasis on Family Orientation: Mrs. Cheung and Grandma seemed to forget about everything when Mr. Cheung asked Cindy to join them on the Australia trip. They valued family unity very much, more than the fact that Cindy had been harmed by Mr. Chan. They felt blissful and grateful that Mr. Cheung accepted Cindy again. They even asked Cindy to twist the facts by saying that she was paying for the trip. This reflects the fact that Mr. Cheung held a very high position within the family; everyone had to respect him.

Externalization of Responsibility: Mrs. Cheung always believed that it was Boyfriend #1's actions (taking Cindy's virginity) that ultimately led to the sexual assault of Cindy. Thus, Mrs. Cheung disliked him intensely because she thought that he was the reason why Cindy was punished by Mr. Cheung and subsequently ran away from home. At the same time, Mrs. Cheung and Grandma both stated that it was the inappropriate outfits that Cindy wore at home that caused the incident. They externalized responsibility for the incident not to the perpetrator but to the victim and her boyfriend.

Avoidance of the Incident: Whenever Cindy mentioned the sexual assault, Mrs. Cheung would show physical discomfort to stop her daughter from continuing her story. In addition, she would also try to convince Cindy that time would heal things as long as she stopped mentioning the incident. In order to persuade and convince Cindy, Grandma sided with Mrs. Cheung. As time passed, Cindy complied with their wishes and stopped mentioning the incident. The whole incident seemed to fade from the memories of everyone in the family. Even now, Cindy's brother does not know about the incident; he believes that Cindy left the house for her boyfriend.

Downplaying the Incident: All Mrs. Cheung cared about was whether Cindy would be physically injured by Mr. Cheung. Her primary concern was Cindy's physical safety. She even suggested that Cindy should go on a trip with Mr. Cheung alone to conciliate their father-daughter relationship, but Cindy eventually rejected this idea. In general, Mrs. Cheung focused her attention on safety over everything else, such as the fact that Mr. Cheung had sexually assaulted Cindy and that encouraging Cindy to be in close contact with her father might put her in further danger. She downplayed the incident and took part in concealing the truth. She was not alert to, or aware of, the potential that a similar incident could happen in the future.

Victim: Cindy

Based on relevant studies, it has been found that there are three major recovery factors for a sexually abused child: disclosing the abuse, making meaning of one's trauma, and developing supportive relationships (Anderson, Kim, and Hiersteiner, 2008). From Cindy's narration, we can obtain a better understanding of all of these recovery factors.

Emotion—Extreme Fear: Cindy described that her mind went blank when Mr. Cheung sexually assaulted her. She ran away from the scene and locked herself in the restroom for hours, thinking about killing herself by jumping off the building. She felt really confused and frightened. She has not been able to comprehend and digest the incident until now. Spacing out, confusion, and apprehension are all reactions that result from a traumatic event; they all signify extreme fear.

Coping—Consideration for Family Members and Boyfriend: After Cindy calmed down, she immediately informed her boyfriend to flee from his home in order to avoid Mr. Cheung finding him. When her boyfriend found out about the incident, he wanted to take revenge on Mr. Cheung. Cindy had to forbid him to do so; she stated that she did not want to take revenge on Mr. Cheung or report him to the police because she had to take her family into consideration. As she and her family were still dependent on Mr. Cheung, she decided not to seek any professional help outside the family.

Apprehension—Disclosure and Seeking Support: Whenever Cindy embarked on a new relationship, she would first disclose her experience to the other person. Some of her friends and supervisors also knew about her past. Cindy believed that it was Mr. Cheung's fault not hers and thus she did not mind mentioning the incident to others. She wanted to be understood by others. She was also not satisfied with how her first boyfriend handled the situation when he found out that she had been sexually assaulted by her father. Furthermore, Cindy even confronted Mr. Cheung about this. She then considered committing suicide hoping to make Mr. Cheung face and admit to his wrongdoings. When Grandpa passed away, Cindy felt extremely down and thought that she would never receive justice.

All Cindy wanted was to have someone—a family member, a significant other, or even the perpetrator—who would help her to achieve justice. She wanted others to understand and accept her. Internally, she understood that it was her father's responsibility not hers. However, she needed external support and understanding from the people around her. Unfortunately, none of them ever came to her. Her family did not accept her; rather, they had a negative opinion of her and cast accusations against her. All of this added to Cindy's suffering. Without positive affirmations, Cindy felt confused and perplexed most of the time.

Given that the nature of the relationship between the perpetrator and the victim in this case was a father and daughter, it was challenging for the victim to leave the family which included the perpetrator. Everyone's point of view mattered to Cindy, especially in terms of her self-recognition and affirmation. In this case, the victim was continuously being cast in a bad light. Her family labeled her as the irresponsible daughter who ran away from home and chose not to respond to her traumatic experience. The responses Cindy got on her path of meaning-making and support-seeking were all negative and disapproving, which was emotionally troubling for her.

Impact – The Aftermath of the Victim's Life

After such unfortunate events, Cindy decided to leave her family for good, and she embarked on her own independent, yet unstable, life. With regard to work, Cindy tried different jobs but none of these lasted very long (a few days to a year). Sometimes, Cindy became worried about being bullied or criticized and thus skipped work. Sometimes, when a sense of fear suddenly overwhelmed her, she would quit a job without giving any notice to her supervisor; she would not explain why she had quit or even pursue any pay she was owed. Due to her unstable work situation, she never had a steady income. Most of the time, she struggled to make ends meet; she borrowed from others, which once led her into great debt.

Cindy also had great difficulty interacting and maintaining her interpersonal relationships. During her high school years, she started fights with classmates and even bullied her brother's classmates. She would throw things at her boyfriend when they were fighting. Furthermore, even after leaving home and having a 6-year relationship with her boyfriend, she did not manage to develop relationships with any significant others. At one time, she maintained sexual relationships with two boyfriends that led to unwanted pregnancies. Looking back, Cindy felt extremely weary and tired. She regretted that her relationships had been such a mess. Fortunately, she has a healthy and steady relationship with her current husband which has lasted for more than 8 years.

In terms of her emotions, Cindy still constantly feels anxious, worried, fearful, and unhappy, and she lacks a sense of security. She does not sleep well, and she is preoccupied by self-destructive ideation and carries out self-destructive behaviors such as wrist cutting. A few years back, Cindy was referred to a psychiatrist and was diagnosed with depression. To make things worse, Cindy also had a drug problem before meeting her current husband. She used psychotropic drugs such as ecstasy several times a week to maintain a pleasant state of mind when she hung out with her friends. Only in recent years has she stopped taking drugs.

According to studies, sexual assault and abuse may have long-lasting effects on children, such as posttraumatic stress disorder and related symptoms, depression, sexual risk taking, substance abuse, and violent behavior (Feiring, Cimon, and Cleland, 2009). All of these effects were exhibited in Cindy's case.

Conclusion

The case of Cindy provides us with a better understanding of the background, development, and impacts of child sexual abuse, especially through the framework of control and power. Perpetrators are known to avoid being held responsible for their actions. They will go to great lengths to hide the truth. Thus, it is not surprising to find that it is difficult for victims and their family members to seek help. The impact of sexual abuse on the victims is not only determined by the event itself, but also by the methods and attitudes adopted to handle the event. While people around the victim can assist him/her in healing, they can also impede the process and do more harm than good.

REFERENCES

Anderson, K. M., and Hiersteiner, C. (2008). Recovering from childhood sexual abuse: Is a 'storybook ending' possible? *The American Journal of Family Therapy, 36*(5), 413-424.

Chan, K.L. (2006) The Chinese concept of face and violence against women. *International Social Work, 49*(1), 65-73.

Chan, K. L. (2005). *Study on child abuse and spouse battering: Report on findings of household survey.* [A Consultancy Study Commissioned by the SWD of the HKSAR]. Hong Kong: Department of Social Work and Social Administration, the University of Hong Kong.

Chan, K. L. (2007). Spousal violence in Chinese societies. In K. A. Kendall-Tackett and S. M. Giacomoni (Eds.), *Intimate partner violence* (10: pp. 1-19). Kingston, NJ: Civic Research Institute.

Feiring, C., Simon, V. A., and Cleland, C. M. (2009). Childhood sexual abuse, stigmatization, internalizing symptoms, and the development of sexual difficulties and dating aggression. *Journal of Consulting and Clinical Psychology, 77*(1), 127-137.

Hong Kong Social Work Association (HKSWA). (2005). *Professional guidelines for social workers in handling spousal abuse cases.* Hong Kong Social Work Association (in Chinese).

The Domestic Abuse Intervention Project (DAIP). (2008). Retrieved from http://www.duluth-model.org/

WHO Global Consultation on Violence and Health. (1996). *Violence: A public health priority.* Geneva: World Health Organization (document WHO/EHA/SPLPOA.2).

WHO and ISPCAN. (2006). *Preventing child maltreatment: A guide to taking action and generating evidence.* Geneva: World Health Organization.

World Health Organization. (1999). *Report of the consultation on child abuse prevention, 29-31 March 1999.* Geneva: World Health Organization. (document WHO/HSC/PVI/99.1).

World Health Organization. (2002). *World report on violence and health.* Beijing: People's Medical Publishing House (in Chinese).

Section 2. Legal Systems in Child Protection and Related Issues

After introducing the facts about current situations of child victimization in Chinese societies, this section goes on reviewing the legal systems related to child protection in the Mainland China and Hong Kong, a city which returned to Chinese sovereignty in 1997 after more than 100 years as a British colony.

Chapter 5 provides detailed information about the development of the legal system related to child protection in the Mainland China since 1949, when the People's Republic of China was formed. Also discussed are the influence of the United Nations Convention on the Rights of the Child (UNCRC) on child protection, and the obstacles to effective child protection in Mainland China nowadays.

Echoing with the previous chapter, Chapter 6 first addresses the insufficiency of the current child protection system in Mainland China, and then introduces the Juvenile Justice Reform which started from the 1980s. This chapter aims at reviewing the progress of the Reform in the last 30 years, examining the challenging remained, and making practical recommendations for the future development and reform of the Juvenile Justice System.

Chapter 7 shifts the focus to a more specific issue in child protection in Chinese societies. As noted in the chapter, cyberbullying has been an alarming problem. Understanding of cyberbullying itself as well as issues related is undoubtedly essential to tackle the problem. This chapter guides you through the problem, legal regimes, and anti-bullying policies in Mainland China, Hong Kong and Taiwan.

In: Child Protection in Chinese Societies
Editor: Ko Ling Chan
ISBN: 978-1-61942-879-9

Chapter 5

LEGAL DEVELOPMENTS AND CHALLENGES IN CHILD PROTECTION IN MAINLAND CHINA

Xuemei Wang
Chinese Academy of Social Sciences, P. R. China

ABSTRACT

The construction and development of the continental legal system in Mainland China has been influenced by the international and national environment. Since 1949, the child protection legal system in Mainland China has gone through three stages: inception, establishment, and preliminary development. Throughout this period of development, significant advancements have been made in areas such as the goals of legislation; the principles, conceptualization, and content of child protection; child protection in criminal, civil, and administrative justice; and the supervision and execution of law on child protection. The basic spirit of the principles on the best interests of the child, non-discrimination, respecting the child's views, and protecting of child's rights to survival and development established in the United Nations Convention on the Rights of the Child (CRC) are also reflected in the relevant legislation in mainland China. The child's right to survival, development, to be protected and participation have been clearly stipulated by the Protection of Minors Act in China. To date, has formed a legal framework for the child protection system, with the Constitutional Law as the core, and coordinated by the Protection of Minors Act and other laws, as well as a large number of related regulations and policy measures. Nevertheless, the current situation regarding the legal protection of children in mainland China faces the following challenges: (a) the influence of traditional values in legislation and the enforcement of laws; (b) inadequate integration of systems and standards in legislation; (c) the lack of standard content; and (d) deficient enforcement.

Keywords: Child protection, the Rights of minors, Legal protection system, Mainland China

INTRODUCTION

The legal system of child[1] protection (legislation, judiciary, and execution) is centered on the survival and development of the child. The establishment and development of the child protection legal system in Mainland China has been influenced by both international and national communities. The legal system of child protection in China originated in the 1970s after the downfall of the "Gang of Four."[2] Two factors further facilitated the construction of this system: first, the massive legislation by the government as well as the increasing more incidents of child victimization has gained much attention from the public; second, the increasing participation of China in international affairs, which brought out the important issue of human rights. Since the 1980s, China has (a) been actively involved in the implementation of the *United Nation's Convention on the Rights of the Child* (CRC), (b) participated in international human rights legislation, (c) increasingly emphasized the standard protection laid down in the international convention, and (d) become progressively aware of the need for the rights of children to be respected and protected by legislation and the judiciary's role in protecting children's rights. During the past 60 years, the development of a child protection legal system in China has gone through three stages: inception, establishment, and preliminary development. The following chapter will first discuss the development of China's child protection legal system. It will then go on to examine the challenges the system faces and its future prospects of legal child protection in China.

THE DEVELOPMENT STATUS OF LEGAL PROTECTION FOR CHILDREN IN CHINA

Child Protection Legislation

The inception period of the child protection legal system in China lasted from 1949 to the late 1970s. In terms of criminal policy, many provisions were introduced that adopted a more lenient approach to handling juvenile delinquency, but this was not a child protection legal system. In addition to the child protection provisions in the 1954 Constitution, a number of policies granted differential treatment for minors, for instance, the *Instruction on Dealing with Female Offenders, Juvenile Offenders, and Youth Offenders* (关于处理女犯、少年犯及青年犯的指示) issued by the Ministry of Public Security in 1951 and the Joint *Notice on the General Offenses Committed by Juveniles Not Subject to Be Arrest and Trial* (关于对少年儿童一般犯罪不予逮捕判刑的联合通知) issued by the Supreme People's Court, Supreme People's Procuratorate of PRC and the Ministry of Public Security in 1960. This period of child protection could be regarded as child protection through criminal policy.

[1] According to the *Convention on the Rights of the Child* and China's *Protection of Minors Act*, the terms "child", and "minor" (as used in the current chapter) have the same meaning. The terms "juvenile" and "youth" will also be used in this chapter: "juvenile" refers to a child aged 14 to 18, while "youth" covers a wider age range, including youths aged 18 to 28.

[2] After the death of Mao ZiDong on September 9, 1976, Wang HongWen, Zhang ChunQiao, Jiang Qing, and Yao WenYuan formed the "Gang of Four" to usurp the national leadership.

From the late 1970s to the late 1980s, the child protection legal system in China entered its period of establishment. In order to tackle the increasing juvenile crime rate after the Cultural Revolution, the Chinese state established an integrated mechanism based on the following: the 1979[3] *Report on the Emphasis on the Resolving of Juvenile Delinquency Problem by Disseminated by the Whole Party* (关于提请全党重视解决青少年违法犯罪问题的报告), the 1981 *Summary on Five-City Forum on Public Order* (五大城市治安座谈会纪要), and the 1985 notice *On Further Strengthen Youth Education, Juvenile Delinquency Prevention* (关于进一步加强青少年教育，预防青少年违法犯罪). The great attention paid to the crime rate among minors led to further relevant legislation by the state. At the same time, the increasing number of relevant studies on the criminal problem and the protection of minors, the founding of the China Youth Crime Research Society and other organizations, and the establishment of the first juvenile court demonstrated the practical and functional development of a comprehensive child protection system. Moreover, public awareness of juvenile delinquency increased during this period. However, a specific child protection law was missing; child protection provisions were scattered around the *Constitution of the People's Republic of China* (PRC), the *Marriage Law*, the *Criminal Law*, the *Criminal Procedure Law*, and others relevant laws. In 1988, the Ministry of Labour issued the *Notice of the Prohibition of Using Child Labour* (关于严禁使用童工的通知), after which the issue of establishing special legal protection for minors was raised.

From the late 1980s/early 1990s to the present day, child protection in China has been in its preliminary development stage: the legal framework of child protection has been formed. In 1987, the *Shanghai Youth Protection Ordinance* (上海市青少年保护条例) was passed. This was the first regulation in China especially enacted for juvenile protection. Since then, every province, autonomous area, and directly controlled municipality has enacted its own specialized regulations on the protection of minors. The Central Communist Youth League once again submitted the *Report on Proposal for the Enactment of the Law on Juvenile.* (关于建议制定青少年法律的报告) until the drafting of national law on child protection legislation commenced in 1989. In 1991, the promulgation and implementation of the *Protection of Minors Act* (未成年人保护法) further promoted the development of child protection and child protection legislation in local areas. In the same year, China ratified the CRC. This series of actions reflected the state's understanding of children's rights and the attention it was giving to the issue. In addition, the laws and regulations relevant to child protection have been consistently improved. During the Eighth Party Congress in 1994, legislation on juvenile crime prevention was planned. In 1999, the *Law on Preventing Juvenile Delinquency* (预防未成年人犯罪法), which underscores juvenile crime prevention, was adopted. This law further strengthened and improved the juvenile justice system and marked the completion of the social and, especially, the judicial protection system for juveniles. The core of the juvenile justice system is the provision of educational measures for preventing delinquency, the rehabilitation of minors, and the provision of correctional measures. Apart from national specialized legislation and several local laws on child protection, two particular laws related to minors were developed and revised: the *Law on*

---

[3] The provided statistics of crime cannot accurately reflect the exact situation of minors. For instance, the youth crime rate in 1983 was 60.2% and 70% in 1989. A large number of those who committed crimes were over 18.

Adoption (收养法) and the *Compulsory Education Act* (义务教育法). In addition, a series of regulations and policies relevant to child protection were introduced, including *The Regulations on Prohibiting of Using Child Labour* (禁止使用童工规定), *Provisions on the Special Protection of Minor Workers* (未成年工特殊保护规定), *Interim Measures for Administration of Family Foster Care* (家庭寄养管理暂行办法), *Interim Measures for the Education of Migrant Children* (流动儿童少年就学暂行办法), *Recommendation on the Compulsory Education of Children of Migrant Workers* (关于进一步做好进城务工就业农民子女义务教育工作的意见), and *Several Regulations on Hearing Criminal Cases Involving Minors* (关于审理未成年人刑事案件的若干规定). During this period, the *General Rules of Civil Law* (民法通则), the *Protection of the Disabled Act* (残疾人保障法), the *Women's Rights Act* (妇女权益保障法), the *Marriage Law* (婚姻法), the *Criminal Law* (刑法), the *Criminal Procedure Law* (刑事诉讼法), the *Education Act* (教育法), the *Mother and Infant Health Protection Act* (母婴保健法), the *Inheritance Law* (继承法), the *Law on Public Security Administration and Punishment* (治安管理处罚法), and other laws related to trafficking that are relevant to child protection were formulated and revised. In particular, the *Protection of Minors Act* was formulated to protect minors against all forms of violence, including child trafficking, child labor, bullying, and violence on campus. The new ideas injected into Chinese legislation marked the enhancement of child protection and reflected synchronization with international child protection issues. The primary Chinese-style child protection legal framework was formed by making the PRC Constitution the hub and encircling it with the *Protection of Minors Act* , the *Law on Preventing Juvenile Delinquency*, the *Compulsory Education Law*, the *Maternal and Infant Health Protection Act*, the *Law on Adoption*, and other laws and policy-based measures related to child survival and development.

The Characteristics of Child Protection Legislation

First, the purpose and principle of child protection legislation evolved from the original lenient treatment of minors to a focus on child survival and development. Initially, public awareness of children and their rights was very limited. The principle behind child protection legislation was mainly to curb and prevent juvenile crime. To reflect China's participation in international children's rights protection legislation and to sum up China's practical experience of domestic child protection, a child's right to survive and develop was included as a core concept. During the revision of the *Protection of Minors Act* in 2006, the principles of the CRC were incorporated into legislation pertaining to the *Protection of Minors Act* (Article 4), which stated that (a) the dignity of minors should be respected, (b) the characteristics and biological and mental growth of individual minors should be taken into account in regulations, and (c) minors have the right to protection and education.

Second, by incorporating international concepts of child protection, Chinese experiences of legislation, and the principle of showing respect to the community, the development of child protection in China is improving. For instance, children's rights were included in the revision to the *Protection of Minors Act* in 2006. This revision highlights the special priority given to child protection, judicial protection, self-protection, the responsibility of parents, and the importance of the family environment to a child's survival and healthy development. It also highlights the position of the government as the main law enforcement entity and strengthens the features of China's child welfare system.

Third, the child protection laws have also introduced strategies to ensure that children are fully protected. These strategies involve a concerted effort by various social sectors (e.g., official agencies) and social agencies and organizations (e.g., family, schools, society) and self-protection. For instance, according to the *Marriage Law* (Article 25), amended in 2001, the living expenses and educational fees of children born out of wedlock are the responsibility of both the father and the mother. Also, the *Interim Measures of Family Foster Care* (家庭寄养管理暂行办法) introduced in 2004 provide legal protection for orphans and abandoned children. These measures standardized and formalized the management of family foster care and legal responsibility in order to protect children in foster care.

Due to the significance of the family in child protection and the child's right to custody, the *General Rules of Civil Law* and the *Protection of Minors Act* stipulate that parents are the guardians of minors. The *Marriage Law*, the *Inheritance Law* , and the *Protection of Minors Act* stipulate a child's right to inherit. The inheritance rights of minors are protected by the courts when dealing with inheritance cases. Specifically, in a divorce case, if both parties cannot reach an agreement on the custody of a minor, the court should deliver its verdict based on particular principles to protect the minor's rights.

Lastly, the legislative system for child protection is provided by the corporation of the national government and local governments. The legislation on child protection originated at local level and from the experiences gained through communication with local governments. On the other hand, the national legislation on child protection functions as a guide to promote legal child protection at local level.

The Development of the Judicial System for Minors

The judicial system for minors consists of child protection through the criminal justice system, the civil justice system, and the administration of justice.

Child Protection in the Criminal Justice System

After the Cultural Revolution, between 1966 and 1976, regulations, judicial interpretations, and policies were restored and juvenile delinquent rehabilitation centers, specialized schools, and other specialized administrative agencies were reestablished. In 1984, a juvenile court was established in Shanghai. This is considered to be the first judicial system that was tailored-made for juveniles. The development of the juvenile judicial system subsequently went through three stages:

(1) 1984 to 1988: the establishment of the first juvenile courts and the promotion of the juvenile judicial system through the national courts.

(2) 1988 to 1995: the initial establishment and rapid development period. During this period, juvenile courts flourished throughout the country (reaching 3,694 near the end of 1998) and legal and social welfare systems were formulated and expanded

across provinces. This demonstrated the transition of the juvenile judicial system from local to national level.

(3) 1995 to the present: the predicament. Juvenile courts are often faced with a shortage of personnel, lack of cases, the instability of agencies, and other barriers. They have accordingly started to focus mainly on hearing criminal cases involving minors. From 2001 onward, the idea of focusing on juvenile criminal cases was further promoted and a pilot scheme was carried out. The juvenile judicial system has developed into a more resilient system that differs from the general judicial system in that it allows deferred prosecutions and has established the social survey system, the supervision order, community service, the round-table trial mode, and other initiatives. In addition, the exchange, collaboration and research with the international communities should be strengthened. The juvenile justice reform will become the next hot spot.

According to the relevant laws and regulations, state law stipulates the protection of the legitimate rights of minors in civil, administrative, and criminal proceedings. In judicial practice, cases involving minors must follow the principle of education and rehabilitation, with punishment being used as a supplemental measure. Also, when handling a juvenile criminal case, law enforcement agencies must be aware of the minor's biological and psychological characteristics and respect the dignity of the minor. Torture or any degrading acts are prohibited. Juveniles have the right (a) to apply for a restricted hearing, (b) to a defense, (c) to present new evidence, (d) to apply for reidentification or inquisition, (e) to ask questions, and (f) to appeal. During imprisonment, minors are entitled not to be insulted, their safety is ensured, and their legal property is inviolable. Juveniles are placed in custody and incarcerated separately from adults to prevent them being harmed and/or corrupted by adults. Mass media, such as television and newspapers, are forbidden to reveal the name, address, photo, or other personal identification of a juvenile who has been processed. During incarceration, juveniles have the right to receive education appropriate to the normal school curriculum and to continue their education and employment after incarceration.

Child Protection in the Civil Justice System

Child protection in the civil justice system involves issues such as child support, child custody, and adoption after divorce. The best interests of minors are prioritized in state laws. For instance, the *Marriage Law* stipulates that pregnant women or women who have just given birth to a baby in the previous six months are prohibited from applying for a divorce. After a divorce, parents are obligated to raise and educate their children. Also, when one party is responsible for bringing up the minor, the other party is required to bear responsibility for the minor's education and living expenses after a divorce. People's courts reserve the right to suspend visitations by parents (father or mother) that will harm the minor's biological and psychological development. *The Several Comments by the Supreme People's Court on Child Custody Problems in Hearing Divorce Cases* (最高人民法院关于人民法院审理离婚案件处理子女抚养问题的若干具体意见) issued in 1993 provided that in requesting change of rearing relationship to the child, the following cases shall be supported: (a) when the particular party who lives with the child is seriously ill or disabled; (b) when the particular party who lives with the child treats the child in an abusive way or in way that harms the child's biological and psychological health; (c) a minor aged 10 or above has the right to choose his/her guardian provided that chosen party is capable of providing the minor's living and education needs or that it is better for the children to live with one party while the other party has a serious or infectious disease that could have adverse consequences on the minor's biological and psychological health.

Child Protection in the Administration of Justice

At present, child protection in the administration of justice is based on three concepts: (1) special protection for minors in proceedings. The distinction between "education" and "infringe right" should be cleared up in order to protect their best interests; (2) special control on procedural discretion. The administrative organs should take into account protection of the child's rights and interests fully before it makes any decision; and (3) the necessity of administrative sanctions to protect minors. Since minors are especially vulnerable when faced with administrative power, the necessity of administrative punishment should be carefully considered being imposed.

Law Enforcement and Supervision in Child Protection

The one hand, specialized agencies for implementation of the laws on child protection need to be strengthened. In order to effectively protect children's rights, legislative, judicial, and relevant government departments and social organizations have established their own mechanisms. The Internal Affairs and Judiciary Committee of NPC is responsible for legislation and supervising its implementation. In line with the state, which functions as the main law enforcement entity, local relevant government departments have established institutions that are in charge of children's work. In addition to the State Council Committee on Women and Children, each province, autonomous region, and municipality has established a working committee for women and children or a committee for the protection of minors. Moreover, in order to fulfill its international obligations, the *Protection of Minors Act* was promulgated; this was followed by three state-level action plans: the *Programme Outline for the Development of China's Children in the 1990s* and *the National Program of Action for Child Development in China (2001-2010) and (2010-2020)*. The publication of *China's Action Plan on Anti-Trafficking in Woman and Child* (中国反对拐卖妇女儿童行动计划) (2001-2010) and the *National Human Rights Action Plan of China* (2009-2010) further reflected the enforcement of the *Protection of Minors Act*. Apart from these state-level plans, all of the provinces and most of the local areas in China have developed local child protection development plans. The Communist Youth League , the All-China Women's Federation, and relevant mass organizations combined 20 State ministries have developed integrated, multidisciplinary mechanisms to promote the implementation and enforcement of child protection related measures.

The other hand, the Supervision of Law Enforcement:

(1) Committees for the protection of minors, a provincial-level coordinating mechanism, have been established in 29 provinces, autonomous areas, and municipalities. Headed by the provincial government, these committees coordinate the criminal justice

system, relevant government departments, and NGOs to implement child protection policies. These committees have solved the problems of diffused responsibility, dispersed power, and unsolvable paradoxes. It has enforced the Protection of Minors Act in practice and has strategically linked up policy and practice work.

(2) Monitoring the enforcement. In 1992, 2003, and 2008, the Internal and Judicial Affairs Committee monitored and inspected the child protection system, which ultimately advocates the implementation of child protection based on the Protection of Minors Act.

(3) Inspection centers monitor and assess the procedures that police departments go through when handling juvenile delinquency cases. Any behaviors or procedures that are detrimental to the biological and mental health of minors are corrected and suggestions are provided to rectify the situation.

THE CHALLENGES IN DEVELOPING A CHILD PROTECTION LEGAL SYSTEM

Although the process of developing a child protection legal system has had its own unique style in Mainland China, the experience has demonstrated the incompleteness of the system. The establishment of authority, the legitimacy of the law, and the way to effectively enforce child protection in society need to be adjusted. At present, the development of legal child protection still faces challenges in various areas, such as the reform of the *Protection of Minors Act*, the welfare system, and the judicial justice system.

First, due to the influence of Chinese traditions, the protection of minors is still confined to the idea of "kids do not have their own rights". This idea is reflected in the child protection system. For instance, the child custody system and the child welfare system demonstrate the existing extreme concepts of the public with regard to responsibility for child protection. One extreme of the system overly emphasizes the responsibility of parents and family; thus, the state, specialized government organizations, and social welfare organizations do not need to fulfill their responsibilities. The other extreme of the system overgeneralizes the responsibility of the nation and society, which is a feature of the "whole-society" approach to the prevention of juvenile delinquency. This approach results in diffused responsibilities for various social organizations and social departments. In addition, juvenile jurisdiction is still mostly regarded as being more about juvenile criminal justice, overlooking the child protection ingredient.

Second, the standardization, formalization, and operation of legislation are still inadequate. Principles were overemphasized in the making of existing laws, and insufficient guidance was given regarding their application in practical situations. Thus, it may not be easy to operationalize these legal principles. The system lacks specificity, standards, and provisions, and so operating the system is difficult. For instance, implementing the provisions of the *Protection of Minors Act* is difficult due to insufficient rules and the lack of clearly listed regulations. The function of the law may therefore largely become advocacy rather than operations. This will lead to two major problems. First, the perpetrators of offenses against juveniles may not be sufficiently prosecuted. Second, the interpretation of the law will depend on the quality of the judge, thus leading to inconsistent and subjective judgments. If the laws are not ready to be operationalized, the responsibility of government departments will become ambiguous.

Third, substantive content is lacking. Although the pace of legislation is speeding up, the provisions regarding child protection still lacks standard content. The three prioritized development areas identified by the UN *Millennium Declaration* in relation to the child development issue in Mainland China were as follows: (a) regional disparity in economic development, (b) urgent child survival and development issues, such as the unmet needs of disadvantaged groups; and (c) inadequate resources allocated to child development, especially for vulnerable groups such as abused children, children without parental care, and children from deprived families. In addition, children are not treated as proactive agents in these pieces of legislation. The new laws are also not up to date in terms of social developments and unenacted practices such as the elimination of juvenile criminal records, the social survey system, the round-table court mode, and so on. To conclude, the making of laws to expand protection, law enforcement, and welfare support are strongly recommended.

Fourth, the level of enforcement is inadequate. The juvenile protection committee in each province is mainly a coordinating organization which does not have a law enforcement mechanism. The difficulty regarding law enforcement is mainly due to three factors. First, the existing child protection legislation is overly theoretical, which makes it hard to enforce. Second, there is no independent specialized institution which can directly process cases regarding child welfare protection, and therefore vulnerable children face difficulties when seeking assistance. Despite the fact that there are juvenile protection committees in local areas, these committees merely function as coordinating bodies. Third, the lack of a specialized juvenile justice system means that child protection jurisdiction is inadequate.

THE PROSPECTS FOR THE CHILD PROTECTION LEGAL SYSTEM

The challenges and problems above need to be corrected and improved through legislation, enforcement, maintenance, and system construction.

First, the active citizenship of children needs to be recognized by the public. The participation of children enables them to advocate their own rights. The traditional view, which does not treat children as independent individuals, needs to change. Children's voices and opinions need to be respected, and all decisions regarding the care and protection of children must be made in the child's best interests.

Second, the systemic and regulatory of laws need to be strengthened, formalized, and updated. In terms of legislation, all levels of state departments should bear the legal responsibility to intensify the legislation process. An independent child's rights protection institution should be established in order to effectively implement relevant laws.

Third, the National Programme of Action for Child Development should be earnestly implemented in China. During the implementation, the focus should be on rural areas, especially the impoverished groups in western China and ethnic minority areas. The quality of the health, education, and living environment of children needs to be improved in order to promote the healthy development of children and prevent child and juvenile crime.

Fourth, all child protection related systems (e.g., the child welfare system, the adoption and registration system for children born out of wedlock, the system of parents' rights, the guardianship system for minors, and the child support system) should be improved, and these systems should support the best interests of vulnerable minors. The responsibilities of the state, society, and family in relation to the protection of minors need to be emphasized, particularly the assistance provided by the state and society to families. For instance, the adoption law should be based on the best interests of children: every procedure, such as accessing applications, censoring, and investigations, should be carried out cautiously. With regard to recovery and rehabilitation, laws on regular checkups of children's physical and mental health, sexual harassment and abuse prevention, and substance victimization rehabilitation need to be introduced. All and all, the state should take multiple measures to expand the protection of minors so that homeless, poor, orphaned, and disabled children can receive more assistance and care.

Finally, the juvenile justice, juvenile criminal law, and juvenile rehabilitation systems should be improved. The establishment of a bail system for juveniles, the probation system, the elimination of criminal records system, the mechanism of judicial remedies, and the detention for reeducation system all need to be considered. The nature and proceedings of juvenile criminal law and juvenile court law also need to be formulated. The recovery and rehabilitation of juvenile offenders should be the prime concern in any legislation, and the protection of juvenile witnesses and victims should also be intensified.

References

Chen, F., and Le, Y. (2009). *The juvenile justice reform and development paper announced on the twenty-fifth anniversary conference of the national juvenile court* (全国法院少年法庭成立二十五周年纪念大会暨少年司法制度改革与发展论坛论文). Beijing: The PRC Government.

Lu, S., and Li, J. (2011). *The analysis of the accomplishments and problems of the implementation of the Protection of Minors Act.* Retrieved from. http://www.cctv.com/tvguide/tvcomment/tyzj/zjwz/8782.shtml.

Yao, J. (2003). *Becoming an adult: The construct of the juvenile justice system.* Beijing: The Chinese People's Public Security University Press.

In: Child Protection in Chinese Societies
Editor: Ko Ling Chan

ISBN: 978-1-61942-879-9

Chapter 6

JUVENILE JUSTICE REFORM AND CHILD PROTECTION SYSTEM: A CHINA CASE STUDY

Yinghui Song[1], Yuanqiong Hu[2], Ting He[1], Zhenhui Wang[1] and Min Jiang[2]

[1]College for Criminal Law Science, Beijing Normal University, Beijing, P. R. China
[2]Save the Children China Program, P. R. China

ABSTRACT

Ensuring a child's rights of access to justice and dignity is one of the fundamental principles of the United Nations Convention on the Rights of the Child (CRC). Since the 1980s, China has explored the issue of establishing a juvenile justice system. However, the current Penal Code and Criminal Procedure Law still contain no judicial diversion mechanism for children, and thus the issue of juvenile justice remains a law in the making. In addition, the absence of a unified child protection system with appropriate mandates increases the risk of vulnerable groups of children, especially migrant children in cities and left-behind children, coming into conflict with the law. The double insufficiency in the judicial sector and the administrative sector reveals the need to accelerate the reform of juvenile justice and to establish a comprehensive child protection system in China.

The chapter will first examine the interdependency of the child protection system and the juvenile justice system from the perspective of child rights and then review the situation in China by focusing on the ongoing juvenile justice reform and local innovative pilot practices. This will be followed by an analysis of the success of these measures and the challenges that remain. Finally, practical recommendations on ways forward will be presented.

Keywords: Child protection, Child rights, Juvenile justice, China

Introduction

Juvenile Justice and Child Protection System from the Perspective of Children's Rights

Every day, thousands of children in the world get caught up in justice systems that are designed for adults. The *Report of the Independent Expert for the United Nations Study on Violence against Children* (2006) estimated that at least 1 million children were deprived of their liberty in 1999,[1] despite the fact that international standards require that detention should be the last resort for children in conflict with the law. It is important to recognize that most of the children in conflict with the law are petty offenders or first-time offenders and that many of them are detained because of truancy, vagrancy, or homelessness.[2]

Looking at these children from another perspective has revealed that most of them are socioeconomic victims. Research conducted by Save the Children demonstrated that most of the children in conflict with the law face challenges in terms of their survival, education, care, and protection and in their relationships with their families and communities:[3]

> Many of them have had little or no access to education; many are working children. Some children have left their homes and taken to the streets to escape from violence and abuse at the hands of their families. Some are forced to make a living on the streets in order to survive. Others have been abandoned by their families and left to fend for themselves and sometimes for younger siblings. These children, who are abandoned and destitute, are also at high risk of sexual exploitation, trafficking and becoming involved in substance abuse and the drug trade through peer influence or the influence of adult criminals.[4]

In China, the average number of juvenile offenders between 1992 and 1996 was around 30,000-40,000 per year.[5] Ten years later, this number had increased dramatically; the number of juvenile offenders increased to 70,086 in 2004, 82,692 in 2005, and 83,697 in 2006.[6] In particular, the rapid socioeconomic transition that has taken place in China in recent decades has increased the complexity of the vulnerability of children and contributed to the rise in the number of juvenile offenders.

The wealth gap between rural and urban regions, the increasing divorce rate, and inequality in health care and social welfare provision have led to children migrating, living in poverty, being left behind in rural areas by migrant parents, and facing difficulties in gaining

---

[1] UN General Assembly (2006). *Report of the independent expert for the United Nations study on violence against children* (para. 61).

[2] *id.*

[3] Save the Children (2005). *The right not to lose hope: Children in conflict with the law - A policy analysis and examples of good practice* (p. 3).

[4] Save the Children (2004). *Juvenile justice: Modern concept of working with children in conflict with the law* (p. 11).

[5] W. Lin (2001). *Review of recent juvenile delinquency statistics in China: Analysis from judicial and legislative perspectives. Vol. 29(3).* Also available at the Chinese Society of Criminology: http://www.zgfzxxh.com/xhlw/201007/t20100729_392835.shtml, last visited on July 20, 2011.

[6] National Bureau of Statistics (2007). *The annual review of statistics 2007.* See also Research report of Chinese children's rights and interests, *Journal of China Youth Research (2008), Vol. 11.*

access to quality education, health care, family care and protection.[7] These children are at high risk of coming into conflict with the law.

Since the 1980s, China has been reforming its juvenile justice system; the intention of the reforms is to establish special institutions and procedures for children in conflict with the law. Over the last decade, local experiments have shown positive outcomes in terms of safeguarding children from violence and abuse in judicial proceedings.

However, the current Penal Code and Criminal Procedure Law still has no judicial diversion mechanism for children, and thus the issue of juvenile justice remains a law in the making.

In addition, the absence of a unified child protection system with appropriate mandates increases the risk of vulnerable groups of children, especially migrant children in cities and left-behind children, coming into conflict with the law.

United Nations Convention on the Rights of the Child and Child Protection System Building

Child Protection Under the United Nations Convention on the Rights of the Child

The United Nations Convention on the Rights of the Child (hereinafter, the "CRC") sheds light on the fundamental rights of children that should be respected, fulfilled, and protected. Article 3 of the CRC establishes the principle of protection for children; the best interests of the child have to be taken into account in all actions concerning children, including those regarding "courts of law, administrative and legislative bodies."[8]

A number of the provisions in the CRC explicate the child's right to protection and the corresponding state obligations toward children. The provisions cover a wide range of issues—economic exploitation, child labor, the effect of drug abuse on children, the sexual exploitation of children, children trafficking, child protection in armed conflicts, and harmful factors to enjoying welfare—and require states to make use of the highest level of resources available to take immediate or progressive action.

Articles 37 and 40 specifically regulate the rights of the child and the obligations of the state with regard to juvenile justice and children suffering torture, inhuman or degrading treatment, or deprivation of liberty.

The substantive rights under the CRC weave a net of the rights to protection that all children should enjoy. The interdependent and interrelated nature of these rights also calls for a systematic approach from states in order to facilitate and protect a child's enjoyment of each of these rights.

---

[7] W. Lin. (2001). Review of recent juvenile delinquency statistics in China: Analysis from judicial and legislative perspectives. *Journal of China Youth College of Political Science, 29*(3). Also available at the Chinese Society of Criminology: http://www.zgfzxxh.com/xhlw/201007/t20100729_392835.shtml, last visited on July 20, 2011.

[8] *Ref.* Article 3 of the United Nations Convention on the Rights of the Child.

Key Elements for Child Protection System Building

A systematic approach to addressing a child's right to protection requires building a child protection system. Essentially, the purposes of a child protection system are as follows:[9]

(1) To prevent and respond to abuse, exploitation, neglect, and violence.

(a) Setting legal, practice, and other standards; collecting data.

(b) Providing social services, including family tracing, reunification, psychosocial, and reintegration services.

(c) Mobilizing families and communities; raising public awareness; initiating legal actions.

(2) To develop and maintain linkage with other systems.

(a) Engaging with justice systems, national security systems, health systems, education systems, economic and social welfare systems.

(b) Ensuring that a central mechanism for joint work is effective for referrals and following up individual cases between systems.

(3) To prepare for and respond to shocks.

(a) Pre-emergency work to mitigate the negative effects on child protection and to meet the child protection needs generated by any emergency and its subsequent effects.

(b) Engaging in an optimal way with international humanitarian and protection agencies.

Achieving the above goals requires a child protection system to be dynamic in linking together all of the factors affecting children and addressing them in a coordinated and collaborative way. The chart below depicts the high-level features of child protection systems, including the dynamic that exists between the status of children (measured as outcomes), child protection goals, and the child protection system in relation to change, including social change.[10]

The dynamic between a child protection system and other specialized systems, such as justice and social welfare systems, is the key to making the system work. This dynamic requires collaboration and a support and referral mechanism to be in place. Such a mechanism, within the given context and with the boundaries of the interlinked systems defined, has implications for how one goes on to define functions, capacities, the process of care, governance, and accountability.[11]

---

[9] Save the Children (2008). *Child protection system in emergencies: A review of current thinking and experiences*.

[10] UNICEF, UNHCR, Save the Children, Chapin Hall. (2010). *Adapting a system approach to child protection: Key concepts and considerations* (p. 19).

[11] UNICEF, UNHCR, Save the Children, Chapin Hall (2010). *Adapting a system approach to child protection: Key concepts and considerations* (p. 20).

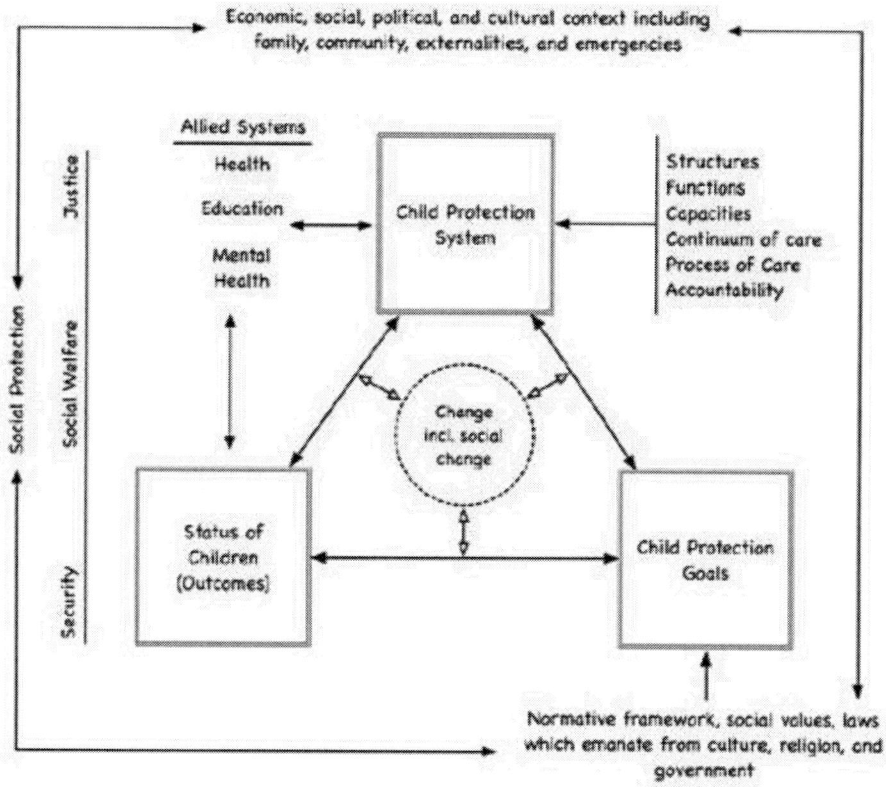

Figure 1. Child Protection Systems: Context and Dynamics.

Juvenile Justice and Child Protection

Juvenile justice under a child rights framework. Internationally, the emergence of juvenile justice as an international law issue started with the United Nations Standard Minimum Rules for the Administration of Juvenile Justice (hereinafter, the "Beijing Rules"), which was issued in 1985. Later on, a number of international standards, including the United Nations Rules for the Protection of Juveniles Deprived of their Liberty (hereinafter, the "Havana Rules") and the United Nations Guidelines for the Prevention of Juvenile Delinquency (hereinafter, the "Riyadh Guidelines"), specified the principles and practical guidelines to be followed by countries when handling cases involving children in conflict with the law.

Articles 37 and 40 of the CRC, as well as General Comment No. 10 issued by the United Nations Committee on the Rights of the Child (hereinafter, the "CRC Committee"), established the core elements of protection for children in conflict with the law together with the obligations of the state:

> Children differ from adults in their physical and psychological development, and their emotional and educational needs. Such differences constitute the basis for the lesser culpability of children in conflict with the law. These and other differences are the reasons for a separate juvenile justice system and require a different treatment for children. The protection of the best interests of the child means, for instance, that the traditional objectives of criminal justice, such as repression/retribution, must give way to rehabilitation and restorative justice

objectives in dealing with child offenders. This can be done in concert with attention to effective public safety.[12]

Therefore, the issue of juvenile justice requires a comprehensive policy response. As discussed in General Comment No. 10, the core elements of such a policy response include:[13]

(1) Prevention of juvenile delinquency.
(2) Intervention and diversion, including intervention without resorting to judicial proceedings and interventions within judicial proceedings.
(3) Age appropriate legislative and judicial settings.
(4) Guarantee of a fair trial, including the right to legal assistance.
(5) Measures such as pretrial alternatives and noncustodial punishments.
(6) Protection of rights during deprivation of liberty.

To achieve the prevention, rehabilitation, and restorative objectives of a comprehensive policy response to juvenile justice, the legal and judicial approach has to go hand in hand with the building of a child protection system in the broader social context.

Juvenile justice system and child protection. As argued by Save the Children's research, violence is a recurring theme in the lives of children in conflict with the law—and not only after they come into conflict with the law. Violence is a major root cause of children coming into conflict with the law in the first place. It is also a major consequence of inappropriate criminal justice responses to children's coping strategies and behaviors.[14] Similarly, it is also a direct consequence of failed care and protection responses by states and communities for children at risk because their traditional protective family environments have broken down.[15]

Therefore, addressing the issue of juvenile justice should not be isolated from examining the profound root reasons on which a child protection system plays an essential role in creating enabling environment for the entire childhood and preventing children from being in conflict with the law at the first place. To achieve the prevention and restorative objectives of justice, an enabling family and community environment is required; to implement noncustodial measures, an informed and functional community support system is essential. None of the objectives of a juvenile justice system can be completely achieved without examining the impact of contact with the judicial system on a child from the perspective of promoting the child's reintegration into society and encouraging the child to play a constructive role in society.[16]

---

[12] UN Committee on the Rights of the Child. (2007). *General comments no. 10: Children's rights in juvenile justice* (para. 10).
[13] UN Committee on the Rights of the Child. (2007). *General comments no. 10: Children's rights in juvenile justice.*
[14] Save the Children. (2005). *The right not to lose hope: Children in conflict with the law - A policy analysis and examples of good practice* (p. 4).
[15] *id. National human rights action plan* of *China* (2009-2010).
[16] UN Convention on the Rights of the Children. Article 40(1).

OVERVIEW OF JUVENILE JUSTICE REFORM AND THE CHILD PROTECTION SYSTEM IN CHINA

Legal System of Juvenile Justice in China

In China, legislation and regulations on juvenile justice can be categorized into three groups:

The Constitution of the People's Republic of China and Relevant Laws

The Constitution of the People's Republic of China (hereinafter, the "Constitution") formulates principles-based regulations on the problems of juvenile justice. These form the basis of all of the juvenile justice laws in the country, while other laws further clarify and detail the rules set out in the Constitution; for example, the 1997 Revised Criminal Law and each subsequent amendment [17] (the 1996 Revised Criminal Procedure Law,[18] the 2006 Revised Law on the Protection of Minors, and the 1999 Law on the Protection of Minors Prevention of Juvenile Delinquency, etc.) all contain a number of provisions setting out the rules on juvenile justice protection.

Relevant Judicial Interpretations and Departmental Rules and Regulations

With a view to enforcing the Constitution and the relevant regulations in the laws, the Supreme People's Court, the Supreme People's Procuratorate, the Ministry of Public Security, and other central ministries provide detailed and practical guidelines on juvenile justice in the form of judicial interpretations, departmental regulations, and jointly issued explanations or opinions containing guidance; for example, the 1991 Notice on Establishing Complement Working System for Handling Juvenile Criminal Cases jointly promulgated by the Supreme People's Court, the Supreme People's Procuratorate, the Ministry of Public Security, and the Ministry of Justice; the 1995 Rules on Handling Cases Involving Children in Conflict with the Law by Police Agencies issued by the Ministry of Public Security; the 2006 Explanations on Certain Issues about Applying Laws on the Hearing of Juvenile Criminal Cases issued by the Supreme People's Court; the 2006 Interpretations on Handling Juvenile Criminal Cases by the People's Procuratorate released by the Supreme People's Procuratorate; and the 2010 Several Opinions on Further Establishing and Perfectly Handling the Supplementary Working Systems of Juvenile Criminal Cases (hereinafter, the "Six Departmental Opinions") released by the Leading Group of Prevention on Juvenile Delinquency under the Central Committee of Integrated Administration, the Supreme People's Court, the Supreme People's Procuratorate, the Ministry of Public Security, the Ministry of Justice, and the Communist Youth League of China. In addition, provincial laws and regulations and other documents have been enacted in provinces, municipal cities, and

[17] The most recent revised version is the implementation of Amendment (VIII) to the Criminal Law which came into effect on May 1, 2011. Article 19 stipulates that a convicted person who was sentenced to less than five-years fixed-term imprisonment and was under 18 at the time of offending can be exempted from the corresponding obligation of reporting criminal records.

[18] In 2010, China formal launched the amending of the Criminal Procedure Law. The amendment will be completed in early 2012. See section II.3 for more details.

autonomous regions to enforce the Law on the Protection of Minors and the Law on the Prevention of Juvenile Delinquency.

Relevant International Standards

China has ratified and taken part in developing a set of United Nations conventions concerned with juvenile justice, and therefore it should abide by the principles, standards, and rules of these conventions; for example, China adopted *the Beijing Rules in 1985*, the CRC in 1989, and the Riyadh Guidelines and the Havana Rules in 1990.

In addition to this, international conventions and standards encourage all countries to establish judicial organs for children in conflict with the law that are separate from those for adults so as to achieve the objectives of protection, correction, prevention, and social reintegration. In China, article 55 of the Law on the Protection of Minors stipulates that organs of the public security procuratorate and courts should be in accord with the circumstances of a case; these bodies should set up a specialized organization or designate a special person to deal with cases of juvenile delinquency and cases involving the protection of child rights. Corresponding regulations are formulated in the judicial interpretations of the Supreme People's Court and the Supreme People's Procuratorate. There are the three main aspects of institutional reform related to criminal justice agencies:

Specialization of Juvenile Courts

In China, the development of juvenile courts can be divided into four stages: (1) 1984 to 1988: juvenile tribunals were piloted in some specific regional courts; (2) 1989 to 1993: juvenile courts and tribunals gradually expanded from certain pilot sites to the whole country; (3) 1994 to 2003: juvenile tribunals and courts provided a comparatively comprehensive system and working mechanism; (4) 1994 to the present: continued progress in juvenile court reform, the system improving with each working mechanism introduced. There are currently 2,219 juvenile courts in China, and these are basically in charge of all cases involving juvenile delinquency. The construction of juvenile courts has already been into regularity and institutionalization.[19]

Specialization of Prosecuratorate Organs

In 1986, the People's Procuratorate of Chang Ning District, Shanghai established the first Juvenile Prosecution Group in China, thus taking the lead in initiating a specialized juvenile prosecuratorate organ.[20] In 1992, the Supreme People's Procuratorate promulgated the Notice on Earnestly Launching Prosecution Work on Juvenile Delinquency, which called on all regions to establish a specialized organ to deal with cases of juvenile delinquency. As a result, a specialized exploration of prosecuratorate organs was launched throughout the country. Currently, over 40% of public prosecuratorate departments within the national prosecuratorate organs have set up a specialized team or assigned a particular person to deal with cases of juvenile delinquency, and some provincial cities have established an independent juvenile prosecution organ.

[19] The Central People's Government of the PRC (2009-2010). *Assessment report on the national human rights action plan of China*. Also available at http://www.gov.cn/jrzg/2011-07/14/content_1906151.htm, last visited on August 9, 2011.

[20] J. L.Yao. (2010). *Progress and expectation on the reform of the juvenile prosecuting system*. Retrieved from "Procuratorial Daily" (March 4, 2010), Issue 3.

Specialization of Police Investigation Units

A specialized juvenile policing organ has been established in some areas, but not yet established in the whole country, it may have a passive effect on the protection for children during the investigation process.

To further establish, consolidate, and perfectly develop a specialized organ for handling juvenile criminal cases, the Six Departmental Opinions issued in 2010 emphasized the stipulations on (a) strengthening the construction of specialized judicial organs and officers to deal with juvenile criminal cases; and (b) strengthening mutual coordination and cooperation in police stations, prosecuratorate organs and courts.

Policy Framework of Juvenile Justice in China

Juveniles do not share the same characteristics as adults. The formulation of policies, principles, and the designation of rules and regulations of juvenile criminal justice should be in the best interests of children and beneficial to their future development. In terms of differentiating treatment for juvenile, China insists on a general policy of "education, persuasion, and redemption", with emphases on the safeguarding of children's rights, assistance and educational correction for juvenile offenders. This policy forms the basis of the establishment of each fundamental principle of juvenile justice.

The first principle of juvenile justice is to prioritize educational correction, and consider punishment as a subsidiary measure. (see article 54 of the Law on the Protection of Minors and article 44 of the Law on the Prevention of Juvenile Delinquency). When dealing with juvenile delinquency cases, a judicial organ should ensure the proper handling of the case, finding the correct balance between punishment for crime committed and the principle of "education, persuasion and redemption." In addition, the general policy of handling criminal offenders in China is balancing "lenient, strict and complementary" under the jurisdiction, which is also applicable to the juvenile delinquency and should go hand in hand with the principle of juvenile case handling as above mentioned. Thus, for juveniles, though punishments remain valid for criminal behaviors, but division and the maximized margin of discretion in deciding non-punishment measures should be firstly pursued in the light of restorative goals, so that children have chances to repent and reintegrate into society.

The second principle is judicial diversion, for which article 46 of the Law on the Prevention of Juvenile Delinquency acts as the reference. This principle is made up of three main elements: (1) when custody is applicable during criminal litigation, juveniles should be held separately from adult suspects; (2) when dealing with cases involving both juvenile and adult accomplices, judicial diversion should be applied provided that it does not interfere with the trial; (3) the implementation stage: juveniles and adults should not share the same prison cells. The principle of judicial diversion attaches great importance to the adequate protection of juveniles during criminal litigation and prevents adult criminals having an adverse impact on juveniles.

The third principle is to protect the rights of the child. The Constitution and relevant laws give children a number of rights and place great emphasis on ensuring the realization of these rights. For example, all criminal suspects and defendants enjoy basic rights, and additional special rights are given to juvenile suspects and defendants. For instance, juveniles have the right to be interrogated in the presence of a legal representative, and those who are unable to hire a lawyer have the right to designated defense support. The judicial organs guarantee that children are able to exercise their special rights in the litigation process.

The fourth principle is that trials of juvenile delinquents should not be open trials. This principle is based on the article 153 of the Criminal Procedure Law and the article 45 of the Law on the Prevention of Juvenile Delinquency. The courts should ensure that juvenile cases are not heard in public and prohibit correspondents from reporting these cases. The news media is not allowed to publicize the name, age, occupation, living address, or photos of a juvenile defendant. The trial process is not open, but the verdict is proclaimed in public. The reasons for not hearing the trial in public are to safeguard the reputations of the juveniles and to avoid any resulting trauma which may then have a negative impact on their educational correction.

The fifth principle is a comprehensive investigation (see article 11 of the Interpretations on Certain Issues about Applying Laws on the Hearing of Juvenile Criminal Cases and No.4 of article 16 of the Regulations on Handling Criminal Cases of Children in Conflict with the Law by People's Procuratorate). When handling juvenile cases, judicial organs are required to carry out an investigation into the physiological and psychological characteristics, personalities, and living conditions of juveniles as well as their reasons for committing the criminal offences, and, if necessary, a juvenile defendant may be required to undergo a medical check and a psychological or pathological analysis. The purposes of this principle are to formulate a proper educational correction plan and to achieve an outstanding reeducation outcome through an investigative analysis of the personality, qualities, and life experiences of juveniles and the circumstances under which they committed criminal offences.

In recent years, against the background of constructing a harmonious society, the suggestions on lenient, strict, and complementary policies for criminal crimes have laid a solid foundation for a more practical policy for handling juvenile criminal cases. The policy is extremely significant as it enlarges the scope of delinquency prevention and reduction, and aims to safeguarding social harmony and stability. The Supreme People's Court and the Supreme People's Procuratorate promulgated judicial interpretations as a response to the lenient, strict, and complementary policies on criminal crimes. [21] According to the interpretations issued by these two bodies, they are more inclined to be lenient when dealing with juvenile delinquency. In order to handle juvenile cases leniently, the basic principles of "education, persuasion, and redemption" and the principle of making education the priority and punishment a subsidiary concern should be adhered to. In practice, lenient decision could be made based on consideration into different factors, such as the motives and objectives of juveniles when committing a crime, the nature of the crime, the circumstances and the severity of the social consequences of the crime, whether the defendants are first-time offenders, whether any remorse is shown after arrest, and the personal development and general performance of the defendants.

[21] The Supreme People's Court (2010). *Several opinions on implementing lenient, strict, and complementary policy on criminal crimes*; The Supreme People's Procuratorate (2006). *Several opinions on implementing lenient, strict, and complementary policy on criminal crimes during prosecution.*

Child Protection System and Implications for Juvenile Justice in China

Generally speaking, China has so far basically created a distinctive and comprehensive legal and regulatory framework that differentiates children in conflict with the law from adult criminals, focuses on the protection of the rights of juveniles, and provides special treatment for children both in law and within society. Furthermore, China has developed a series of fundamental principles for handling juvenile criminal cases under the principle of education, persuasion, and redemption.

With the rapid socioeconomic development of China, juvenile justice faces a number of new challenges (e.g., judicial diversion for juveniles, correction within society and education, and supervision and guarding the migrant juvenile criminals). A response to these new challenges is an absolute necessity and can be achieved at the legislative and judicial practice levels. In addition, China's existing laws and regulations remain insufficient compared to the CRC and other international standards. For example, a specialized litigation procedure, a diversified judicial referral mechanism, the combination legal protection systems of judicial organs and social powers have not yet been developed. Provisions under the CRC and other international standards shed light on how to improve compliance with state obligations in relation to China's juvenile justice reform.

Also, viewing from the angle of prevention, community correction, and social reintegration, the current shortage in China's community-based child protection systems reveals a challenge to launch an in-depth reform of juvenile justice in China. For example, due to a shortfall of professional social workers and a lack of integrated child protection systems at all levels, there is a lack of systematic response and management mechanisms to respond to the needs of children in communities; for children in conflict with the law, this also means that after returning to the community under judicial diversion, there would be insufficient support, monitoring, and protection for them. Migrant children in conflict with the law are particularly vulnerable when returning to the community; they face more difficulties, including the lack of effective community support and supervision.

In 2010, the Leading Group of Prevention on Juvenile Delinquency under the Central Committee of Integrated Administration, the Supreme People's Court, the Supreme People's Procuratorate, the Ministry of Public Security, the Ministry of Justice, and the Communist Youth League of China jointly released *Several Opinions on Further Establishing and Perfectly Handling the Supplementary Working Systems of Juvenile Criminal Cases*. These opinions basically followed the relevant regulations set out by the CRC and other international standards; they suggested the further establishment and improvement of specialized organs to deal with juvenile criminal cases and strengthening the protection of the legal rights of children in conflict with the law. More importantly, these opinions proposed a comprehensive supplementary working mechanism for juvenile justice, emphasizing the interconnection of various justice departments and the importance of social support systems in educational correction and giving the first concise definitions of the term *appropriate adults* and the features of other professional social work sectors described in the country's regulatory documents.

Meanwhile, the National People's Congress of the People's Republic of China has formally launched a revision program to amend "mature" legislation such as the Criminal Procedure Law. The first deliberation on Amendment (VIII) to the Criminal Procedure Law (Draft) was conducted during the 22nd Session of the *11th* National People's Congress in

August 2011. The further amendments to the Criminal Procedure Law demonstrated the legislators' mounting concerns over the reform of the juvenile justice system and the establishment of a consensus on the principles, mechanism, and litigation procedure of juvenile justice: for example, by (a) insisting on the principle of making education the priority and punishment a subsidiary concern whereby the rights of children in litigation can be guaranteed, (b) enlarging the scope of legal aid for juveniles, (c) strictly limiting the use of custodial measures on juveniles, and (d) enforcing the separate treatment principle for juveniles by using different forms of detention, management, and education. The amendments also improved the system for legal representative attendance during interrogations and court hearings: Other relevant persons can be notified to attend provided that it would be difficult to ensure the attendance of legal representatives. Others amendments included the establishment of non-charging systems and supplementary conditions for juveniles, a clarification of the issue of no public disclosure of juvenile case hearings, a regularization of the content of the social background investigation for juveniles on trial, and systems for the elimination of previous criminal records.

It should be stated that if further improvements were made to the legal framework of China's juvenile justice system to make it more comprehensive, it would bring the system more in line with the requirements of the CRC and other international standards. In addition, China's judicial reform faces a systematic challenge. On one hand, the society in transition presents new requests for judicial intervention, such as migrant issues in cities, and on another hand, the law and practice are out-of-date. How to make the reform rightly responding to such challenge is a mission to be completed including those concerning juvenile justice.

Analysis of the Major Challenges and Pilot Responses to Juvenile Justice Reform in China[22]

Overview

China is undergoing a transition period, and the whole country is facing much more developing pressures from each aspects of society. Using juvenile crime as an example, according to the research findings conducted by Chinese Society for Juvenile Delinquency Prevention Research, there was a rapid increase in the total number of juvenile offences initially, but since 2008, the number has fallen. Having made up quite a large proportion of criminal offences, there has been a gradual decrease in the number of juveniles committing criminal crimes for five consecutive years since 2006.[23] However, when the severity of the risk and personal danger posed by juvenile offenders is taken into account, the situation seems more pessimistic.[24] The contradiction between the insufficiency of existing laws and regulations and the demands of law enforcement has gradually become more prominent,

---

[22] The content of this section is sourced from the project of "Research on the Reformation of Juvenile Criminal Justice in China" chaired by Professor Song Yinghui, Beijing Normal University.

[23] F. Li. *Survey indication: The total number of juvenile delinquency has begun to decrease since 2008 in China*. Available at "Preventing Juveniles from Committing Crimes in China": http://www.yffz.org/E_Read News.asp?NewsId=1588, last visited on August 5, 2011.

[24] Y. H. Zhang. & B. Yao (2009). Analysis of the execution of the criminal policy of tempering justice with mercy in cases of crimes committed by minors. Law Science Magazine, 30(11).

resulting in many problems in practice. Hence, the need to further address the rights and protection of juveniles at both legislative and judicial practice level, especially in terms of giving extra care to, and tangibly protecting the rights of, juveniles in legal proceedings remains a critical issue for the Chinese government.

In recent years, having reflected on the realistic circumstances related to the protection of children's rights, some local regions have actively conducted pilot projects involving the reform of juvenile justice treatment and the protection of juveniles' rights. These pilot schemes have resulted in the accumulation of rich experiences, and yet some problems still remain. As a response to this situation, we adopted an integrated research approach, including questionnaires, face-to-face interviews, field visits, and desk research analysis, with the intention of analyzing the challenges of juvenile justice reform and relevant innovations in enforcement from an empirical perspective.

Child Rights Challenges in the Police Interrogation Stage

Statement of Problem

With a view to ensuring children's rights to access to justice and to be free from violence, threat, and confession by inducement, the laws in most countries and the relevant international conventions stipulate that legal representatives, guardians, or other appropriate adults should be present when a juvenile is interrogated by the police in order to ensure better protection of the rights of juveniles. In China, the Criminal Procedure Law clearly stipulates that when interrogating juveniles under 18, the interrogator can notify his/her legal representatives to be present. However, the law uses the word "can" instead of "shall," which greatly undermines its mandatory effects. Later, a revision was made to the Law on the Protection of Minors and relevant judicial interpretations which replaced "can" with "shall" and requested the interrogator to notify the guardian of the interrogated juvenile to be present at the interrogation. The "shall" stipulation made great help to regularize the practices.

Nevertheless, problems may still occur when it actually comes into practice. A large number of children in conflict with the law are from migrant populations. In some cases, the interrogators are unable to make contact with the legal representatives or guardians of the juvenile suspects in time. For some cases in which notification is sent, the actual participation of guardians or legal representatives in the interrogation becomes impossible due to the long distances involved or some other reasons. The Six Departmental Opinions issued in 2010 widened the choice of adults who could be present for interrogations through the regulation that stated "if legal representatives are inappropriate adults or are unable to be present, other closely related appropriate adults, including relatives and friends, social workers, teachers, lawyers, etc., can be present following the authorization of the juvenile suspects or defendants." However, these opinions are not law and the wording is limited to "can"; as a result, in practice, it is more appropriate to use them as guidance.

Although the concept of appropriate adults has been adopted, the Six Departmental Opinions and other relevant documents on juvenile justice reform do not precisely stipulate on how the concept is to be operated (e.g., the duties, qualifications, selection requirements, training, and supervision of the appropriate adults). The actual practice of this concept still depends on the different doings of exploration in each region.

Case study – Juvenile Judicial Pilot Project in Panlong District, Kunming City, Yunnan Province

Since 2002, Save the Children and Panlong district government have been conducting the Juvenile Judicial Pilot Project in Panlong District, Kunming City, Yunnan Province (hereinafter, the "Panlong Project").[25] The key focus of this project is on the attendance of an appropriate adult (hereinafter, "AA") during the interrogation of a juvenile. Our survey indicated that in the Panlong Project, the following guidelines are followed:

(1) The AA should be a full-time worker recruited through social recruitment examination. He or she is required to undergo on-the-job training in psychology, education, sociology, law, and other professional knowledge.
(2) The AA should act as a third party during the interrogation; he/she is not a replacement for a legal representative. The two roles are different and hold different responsibilities, and the AA and the legal representative can participate in the interrogation together at the same time.
(3) For all juvenile crimes committed in Panlong District, the AA should be present during the interrogation regardless of the local or nonlocal status of the juvenile.
(4) Upon the arrival of the juvenile suspect, police officers shall notify the AA to be present in addition to notifying other persons who are required by law to be present, or the interrogation should not take place. Upon notification, the AA shall get to the police station within the specified time limit, which is usually 30 minutes in an urban area and 1 hour in a rural area, even if the case takes place at midnight. The interrogation notes prepared by the police should be signed off by the AA. Notes without the AA's signature will otherwise be regarded as flawed evidence and remedial action will have to be taken.
(5) The duties of the AA include supervision, communication, comfort, and so on. The AA shall explain his/her role and the suspect's rights and obligations during the interrogation; facilitate communication; stop police officers from using inappropriate interrogation approaches; and provide assistance to juveniles under interrogation so that the rights of juveniles can be exercised legally.

In addition, the AA's presence during interrogation marks the first intervention step in individual cases. The value of the AA's support is further demonstrated in the follow-up stage and throughout the entire judicial procedure and in the efforts made to achieve one of the final objectives, which is to actively pursue judicial diversion and help children in conflict with the law to return to society.

During the implementation of the Panlong Project, the AA's presence during interrogations was gradually increased. According to the statistics, during the period January 2005 to February 2009, 1,160 of the 1,720 suspects obtained the services of the AA during police interrogations, and this coverage rate has been increasing over the years. In both 2007 and 2008, the rate was around 87%.

[25] The collaboration between the Palong District Government and Save the Children came to an end in January 2010. Since then, Palong District Government has continued to independently initiate appropriate adult participation mechanisms.

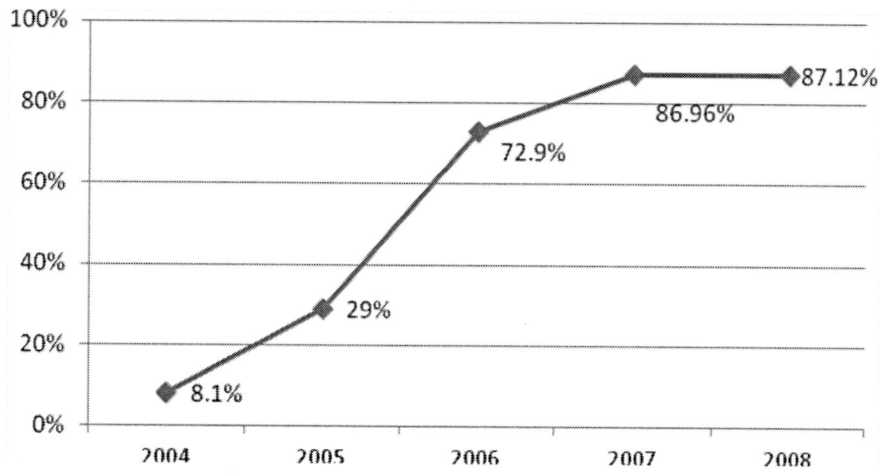

Chart 1. Coverage rate of AA's presence during interrogation[26].

The survey indicated that in the Panlong project, AAs perform more than just their neutral third-party role when they give more weight to safeguarding the legitimate rights of children. Among the 11 AAs who took part in the survey, all displayed the following behaviors: explaining the AA's role of helping juveniles; asking the juveniles whether they were physically unwell and whether they needed food or water; and explaining their rights and obligations. 10 out of 11 AAs helped juveniles on one occasion to understand their own behavior and it subsequent consequences; 9 AAs once explained the objectives of the interrogation and 7 once explained the nature of measures, including interrogation and detention.

In addition, the survey found that the presence of an AA during interrogation resulted in a positive outcomes in terms of improving the interrogation approaches of police officers and ensuring a smooth interrogation procedure. The survey showed that 15 juvenile suspects experienced situations both with and without the presence of an AA. Among these 15 juveniles, 14 (93.3%) stated that police officers had a more courteous attitude while the AA was present, 12 (80%) stated that police officers stressed the protection of the child's legitimate rights more when the AA was present, and 6 (40%) felt that the duration of interrogation was shorter when the AA was present.

Although the attendance of an AA may delay the start of the interrogation, 90% of police respondents stated that the presence of an AA was not an obstacle to the interrogation, but rather an advantage in ensuring the smooth running of the interrogation.

Remarks

Overall, the interrogation approaches adopted by AAs in Palong District achieve the expected outcomes and confirm that the presence of an AA during interrogations can protect the rights of juveniles better.

---

[26] Research Group of Research on the Modes of Judicial Protection, Community Education and Correction for Juvenile in Conflicts with the Law. *Exploration and practice of juvenile justice protection work: Developmental manual of juvenile judicial pilot project in Panlong District, Kunming City, Yunnan Province* (p. 9).

Some regions, such as Shanghai, are beginning their own initiatives to introduce the presence of an AA during interrogation into the practice of justice. The main difference between these initiatives and the Panlong Project is that the Palong Project accepts the simultaneous participation of both the AA and legal representatives whereas other regions regard the presence of the AA as a replacement or a remedy measure for the nonattendance of legal representatives or guardians, and permission to attend is only issued to an AA in the absence of legal representatives or guardians. In spite of the fact that different regions have adopted different approaches to the AA's presence during interrogation, these approaches share the same objectives: to safeguard the legitimate rights of children in conflict with the law and to promote the functions of AAs in terms of supervision, communication, and providing comfort.

In practice, some problems exist in relation to the use of AAs during interrogations: no unified standard for the selection of AAs; description of the rights and obligations of AAs is unclear; the multiple responsibilities of AA; whether interrogation notes made when the AA is not present can still be used as legitimate evidence; and so on. However, the underlying objectives of establishing the system of AA presence during interrogations are to better safeguard the legitimate rights of children and to enhance the establishment of judicial diversion and the development of similar systems.[27]

For this reason, the role of the AA should be determined by the basic responsibilities of the role, the main one being the protection of children's legitimate rights. In the meantime, ensuring the role of the AA as a neutral third party, and the AA shall not stand by judicial organs or each parties. An outstanding AA interrogation mechanism should be able to create a good balance between the protection of the rights of children and the smooth running of the interrogation procedure; it should also act as a solid foundation for the system of having an AA present during interrogation.

Social Background Investigation and Risk Assessment Mechanism

Statement of Problem

The Criminal Procedure Law of the People's Republic of China does not strictly request judicial organs to carry out research on the social background of juveniles. However, the Supreme People's Court and the Supreme People's Procuratorate do have relevant regulations on this, but in these regulations, the wording is limited to "can" in relation to regularizing social background investigations and no legal consequences are laid down for those who fail to conduct these investigations.

In practice, the judicial organs usually initiate some kind of social background investigation and appropriate risk assessment for children in conflict with the law, but whether this work is done is mostly determined by the judicial organs; in some regions, it is done by lawyers. Due to the limitations of time and energy, judicial investigators do not normally have enough time to carry out a detailed investigation into the background of juveniles, such as their living conditions, personal development, and previous experience.

[27] L. D. G. Thomson, V. Galt, & R. Darjee (2007). Professionalizing the role of appropriate adults. *The Journal of Forensic Psychiatry & Psychology*, *18*(1), 99-119; Harriet Pierpoint (2008), Quickening the PACE? The use of volunteers as appropriate adults in England and Wales. *Policing and Society: An International Journal*, 18(4), 397-410.

Lawyers, who have to take both the person's interests and defense into account, usually shift the focus onto collecting useful evidence when conducting social background investigations; this evidence then becomes the juvenile suspects' or defendants' best advantage and can positively influence the judicial organs in the case investigations. For this reason, it is absolutely essential to have a neutral third party carry out social background investigations on juveniles.

Case Study – Juvenile Judicial Pilot Project in Panlong District, Kunming City, Yunnan Province

In the Panlong Project, as well as conducting social background investigations on children in conflict with the law, the AAs are also in charge of the basic duties required during the interrogation process. A social background investigation involves making contact with parents, relatives, neighbors, teachers, and friends and collecting in-depth information from them on the personal and family background of a juvenile and offence-related matters, including the juvenile's age, origin of residence permit (hukou), current residence, educational background, family structure, social networks, past performance, feelings of remorse, conditions of guardianship, and so forth. In light of the information collected, the AA assesses all of the relevant information and carries out a written risk assessment of the risk to society posed by the juvenile, the possibility of the juvenile reoffending, and the chance of correction. The assessment acts as a reference for the judicial investigators to make decisions regarding arrest, charges, and sentence.

A survey showed that a social background investigation and risk assessment can reduce pretrial detention to some extent and widen the use of noncustodial punishment. For example, compared with the situation before the pilot project, the use of noncustodial measures for juveniles by the police stations that participated in the project at the early stage increased by up to 15% a year after the launch of the Panlong Project, and this trend has continued year after year.

Remarks

Social background investigations form an important basis for the judicial protection service for children in conflict with the law. Social background investigations for juvenile suspects appear to have achieved recognition within the communities covered by the Panlong Project, and yet issues such as the legal status of social background investigations and determining the person in charge of these investigations still trouble the investigation departments and organizations who participate in the Panlong Project.

During the implementation of the Panlong project, the participation of social workers provided a better option for the launch of social background investigations and risk assessments. In the project, the AAs conduct detailed social background investigations and detailed reports on these investigations and risk assessments are submitted to judicial organs within a specified time. Time and energy savings in handling cases are therefore achieved for judicial investigators and organs. More importantly, given the neutral third-party status of the AAs, social background investigations and risk assessment reports are more readily accepted by the judicial organs and provide reference points for them to handle cases appropriately.

Community-Based Supervision, Correction, and Reintegration

Statement of Problem

Convicted juveniles experience many psychological and physical pressures from society or even from themselves. Psychological disorders are common among juvenile offenders due to the negative feelings they experience, such as low self-esteem and depression, and their worsening relationships with their families. Juvenile offenders are more likely to be dismissed by schools and employers, and it becomes difficult for them to seek a career or resume their education. They become, through no choice of their own, isolated in society. Given that children in conflict with the law will fail to reintegrate into society without proper supervision and support from family and society, being isolated within society can pose a potential threat to the stability of society and cause harm to juveniles and their families.

Case Study – Juvenile Judicial Pilot Project in Panlong District, Kunming City, Yunnan Province

The Panlong Project is dedicated to providing effective supervision and correction for juveniles that helps them to reintegrate into society. A survey revealed that community-based supervision, correction, and reintegration provide a better way for children in conflict with the law to be reintegrated into society, as explained below.

First, AAs provide support to juveniles through home visits or casual conversations; they also conduct psychological assessments in light of the juvenile's family background, cognition, personality, and emotions.

Second, AAs are responsible for organizing and planning social activities. The aims of these activities are to nurture the juvenile's autonomous abilities, living skills, and team spirit and to tackle psychological disorders in a timely manner. The survey indicated that some juveniles who were judicially diverted entered the voluntary sector and were given "Outstanding Volunteer" awards; some joined the Communist Youth League of China; and some actively participated in different training activities hosted by the Panlong Project (e.g., national or regional children's forums, tea art training, etc.).

Third, through the participation of both the community and the AAs, a communication bridge has been built to improve the deteriorating relationships between parents and juveniles. An interview conducted for the evaluation report of the Panlong Project revealed that among the 49 juveniles who were interviewed, 26 (53.1%) indicated that their relationship with their parents was improving, 20 (40.8%) stated that the situation between them and their parents was unchanged, and 3 (6.1%) said that their relationship with their parents had worsened. Similar findings were obtained from the interviews with parents.

Fourth, as a response to the education, employment, and family issues faced by juveniles, the Panlong Project provides children and families with recommendations through community activity centers and from the data collected by the AAs; the project also uses coordination and reflection procedures to call on relevant organs to offer support. Resolving these issues could not only make a considerable difference to the promotion of normal family functioning, but could also help to improve the administration of the education and supervision to juveniles. Approaches such as contacting schools and introducing work opportunities can help the reintegration of children in conflict with the law into normal social life, work, and education. During an interview with 49 juveniles who had been in conflict with the law, 87.7% of the children stated that they were reentering the education and career sectors following judicial diversion; 28 of them (57.1%) were continuing their education, 15 (30.6%) were in employment, and only 6 (12.3%) were still unemployed.

Lastly, the Panlong Project draws up individual supervision and correction plans. The intention of these plans is to eliminate the links through which juveniles can come into contact with poor friends and their bad habits can be developed, which might trigger reoffending. At the time they were interviewed, none of the 49 juveniles had engaged in reoffending; most of them stated that they had returned to work or school and that their relationship with their family was improving.

In addition, a downward trend in the number of crimes committed by juveniles has been reported in Panlong District in recent years, from 590 in 2005 to 264 in 2008, representing a 55.25% reduction for four consecutive years. This also showcased the achievements of the Panlong Project in relation to the prevention of reoffending by juveniles.

Remarks

Juveniles are a special group. They are not yet mentally mature, and some aspects of their behavior are subject to evolution and development. Our survey showed that juveniles are inclined to have a positive attitude toward social reintegration provided that timely and effective supervision and correction takes place following criminal behavior. In summary, adopting the approaches of supervision and correction for children in conflict with the law should not be limited to the internal activities of judicial systems; rather, this should be seen a social systems engineering project, and it should be the responsibility of the state and society to seek collaborative support from the whole of society to accomplish the project.

Issues of Noncustodial Measures for Migrant Children

Statement of problem

In recent years, there has been a growing problem among migrant populations who commit crimes in China. Migrant juveniles are responsible for a vast majority of juvenile crimes (over 80% in some regions).[28]

According to article 53 of the Criminal Procedure Law, a criminal suspect or defendant who meets certain conditions can either provide a guarantor or pay guaranty money to apply for release on bail while awaiting trial. Compared with local juveniles, most migrant juveniles who are involved in criminal cases have no definite residence and/or have low incomes; this makes it difficult for them to provide an appropriate guarantor or sufficient guaranty money. As a result, custody becomes almost inevitable for these juveniles. This not only violates the fundamental principle of everyone being equal before the law, but also has a harmful impact on the juvenile detainees. The Supreme People's Procuratorate called for a noncustodial mandatory measure to be imposed on juveniles in judicial interpretations.

In practice, some regions have begun to explore the possibility of establishing social support mechanisms for appropriate noncustodial measures for migrant juveniles who are

[28] Supra. Note 19.

involved in criminal cases, the intention being to provide more options in terms of appropriate measures for these juveniles.

Case Study

In practice, some regions, such as Shanghai City, Wuxi City in Jiangsu Province, and Changzhou City, have begun to explore the idea of establishing a noncustodial social support mechanism for children in conflict with the law. The practical operation of the mechanism varies between regions, but the basic approach is to use a "correctional base" for the supervision and protection of children in conflict with the law in collaboration with local corporations, schools, nursery homes, and communities where a specialist is designated to be in charge of supervising, managing, helping, and educating juveniles who qualify for noncustodial measures.

A survey found out that some regions ask juveniles to go through a risk assessment before joining the correctional base. In other words, a qualitative test has to be conducted to assess to the appropriateness of using noncustodial measures with a juvenile or the possibility of him or her entering the correctional base. Risk assessment consists of a social background investigation and a legal assessment. Only after this assessment will the judicial organs determine whether a juvenile qualifies to enter the correctional base and whether it is appropriate to adopt a noncustodial measure for him or her.

The correctional base is, in fact, a kind of supplement to the guarantee approach of guarantors. A legal department of corporations or security departments are usually put in charge of supervising and educating children in conflict with the law. If the correctional base is located in a school, the counselors of the convicted students would be the guarantors. During the period of supervision, the following activities take place in the correctional base:

(1) *Supervision*. Upon the request of the criminal procedure law, judicial interpretations, and judicial organs, children in conflict with the law will be supervised and managed. If a convicted juvenile violates the agreed regulations, the matter must be reported immediately to the judicial organs.
(2) *Communication*, including casual chats, written reports on thoughts, etc.
(3) *Psychological counseling*. Hire professional counselors to teach lessons and provide one-to-one counseling for individual juveniles.
(4) *Legal education*. Enhance the legal knowledge of convicted juveniles.
(5) *Vocational skills training*. Arrange appropriate vocational training to juveniles, taking their age, gender, and other personal factors into account. The correctional base has to complete a written assessment on the performance of a convicted juvenile at the time of supervision and submit it to the judicial organs for their reference.

A survey indicated that the use of a correctional base can effectively increase the percentage of convicted juveniles that can be dealt with through noncustodial measures. In one example of 12 juveniles in a city, only 1 was sentenced to criminal detention; the remaining 11 juveniles were convicted without sentence, punished by fines or suspended sentences, or not charged. The proportion of noncustodial cases was 91.67%. The correctional base has a beneficial impact in terms of enhancing the ability of juveniles to survive and work, helping them to be rehabilitated and reintegrated into society successfully, and increasing the pressure for change in the investigative approach of judicial investigators.

Remarks

To date, the use of correctional bases is still an ongoing explorative process, thus leaving room for further regularization and improvement. For example, at present, the imbalance between the rights and obligations of a correctional base makes it difficult to trace who or what is responsibility for the faults of juveniles under guardianships. During interviews with judicial investigators, the respondents stated that no one person has been identified as bearing the responsibility for any accidents, reoffending, or escapes that occur when juvenile suspects are on bail. Moreover, problems occur when a risk assessment has to be carried out at the time of a bail application: Who is the appropriate person to carry out the risk assessment? What are the appropriate standards for a risk assessment? How can a fair and objective risk assessment be ensured?

In spite of this, it is undoubtedly true that the social empowerment created by corporations, schools, and communities can increase the use of noncustodial measures so as to achieve equal protection for migrant juveniles and help juvenile criminals to reintegrate into society.

Elimination of Criminal Records

Statement of Problem

In practice, individuals with criminal records tend not to be recognized and accepted by society, and this imposes limitations on them in terms of job hunting and continuing their education. Such individuals are easily susceptible to criticism and isolation, doubling the difficulties they face when trying to lead a new life in society. The impossibility of social reintegration makes them more inclined to label themselves as criminals, thus increasing the possibility of reoffending. Previous criminal records can therefore have a very harmful impact on juveniles.

As a result, many countries have set up systems to eliminate criminal records or to permit only limited disclosure of criminal records for juveniles. In China, the promulgation of Amendment (VIII) to the Criminal Law that entered into force on May 1, 2011 stipulates that a convicted person who was sentenced to less than 5-years fixed-term imprisonment and was under 18 at the time of offending can be exempted from the corresponding rights and obligations associated with criminal records. This provision includes destroying some parts of previous criminal records. When this came into force, some regions initiated useful investigations into implementing this amendment.

Case Study

In China, many regions, such as Shanghai City, Qingdao City in Shangdong Province, Taiyuan City in Shangxi Province, and the Siming District of Xiamen City, Fujian Province, have been exploring the practice of eliminating criminal records in recent years in order to minimize the negative impact of previous records on juveniles, to better protect the legitimate rights of children, and to target children who may be involved in crimes.

A survey discovered that the approaches adopted varied from region to region but could be divided into two main types: (1) eliminating the records of juveniles who commit petty crimes and (2) limiting the disclosure of juvenile offences for which no charges were made.

The former targets juveniles who were put on trial and punished; the courts determine whether the elimination of a juvenile's criminal record can be authorized, provided that he/she meets certain conditions. The latter approach depends on the decision of prosecuting organs following their decision not to issue charges against a juvenile; in such cases, the juvenile was neither judged nor punished.

In practice, the elimination of criminal records or the limited disclosure of offences for which no charges were made can lead to the following legal consequences:

(1) No public disclosure of the criminal acts of the person concerned.
(2) No impact on the employment and education of the person concerned.
(3) Judicial organs should keep the criminal records of juveniles confidential. Exceptional circumstances under the law can result in an exemption to this rule. Otherwise, reading, copying, or abstract copying of the criminal records of juveniles is not permitted.

A survey indicated that the elimination of previous criminal records can effectively diminish a juvenile's stereotype of himself/herself based on his/her previous criminal status; thus, juveniles can regain their confidence and strength and better prepare themselves for social reintegration. It also helps to prevent reoffending and effectively promotes harmonious relationships within families.

According to the surveys conducted by the authors in a few pilot areas, none of the 169 interviewed juveniles whose previous criminal records were eliminated have committed further crimes; at least 30 juveniles have resumed their schooling or pursued further education, and 5 of these 30 juveniles have gone to university. Furthermore, most of these juveniles' relationships with their families and friends improved after the elimination of their previous criminal records. For most of them, their low self-esteem diminished to a great extent or, at least, to some extent. They also felt "satisfied" or "more satisfied" with their current lives and had an optimistic attitude toward life.

Remarks

To some extent, criminal records can help in crime prevention. Nevertheless, a criminal record can also have a "stereotype effect," subjecting the children in conflict with the law to negative comments from the judicial system and society over a long period of time, thus resulting in unequal treatment which makes it difficult to achieve the objectives of judicial correction and social reintegration. This is, in fact a kind of "systematic discrimination". Moreover, the disclosure of previous criminal records is associated with the issue of the protection of a citizen's privacy. Controversies remain with regard to whether the disclosure of criminal records amounts to illegal intrusion on the grounds that it breaches the citizen's constitutional right to privacy.

As a response to the above issues, the elimination of criminal records could be an effective solution. A number of positive outcomes could emerge as a result of limiting the disclosure of juveniles' criminal records, such as ensuring that juveniles are treated fairly when they exercise their rights and opportunities, creating a good atmosphere for juveniles returning to society, and better safeguarding every aspect of children's rights. Amendment (VIII) to the Criminal Law stipulates the exemptions from disclosing criminal records, but, as yet, no real provision has been made for the elimination of criminal records. A mechanism for the elimination of criminal records that stipulates the appropriate conditions and procedures for this process, legal consequences, and the organs that have the authority to make decisions needs to be formally established.

CONCLUSION

First of all, the basic objective of the reform of China's juvenile justice system is to move toward the establishment of sound, complete legal systems within China. This involves strengthening the implementation and effectiveness of policies, a commitment to deal with the contradiction arising from the weaknesses of laws and regulations and the growing demands for the implementation of laws whereby the justice systems designed for juveniles can be placed in a better position to meet the requirements of international standards, and satisfying the need to put Chinese laws into practice.

With these requirements in mind, the policies and laws shall insist on the basic principles of distinctive treatment of juveniles and the guiding line of education, persuasion, and redemption. Working in the best interests of children should be the basis for emphasizing the protection of child rights and reeducation for change and strictly abiding by the basic principles of juvenile justice. Juvenile policies, laws, and regulations should be detailed and more practical and should safeguard the legitimate rights of children. This can be achieved in a number of ways through the establishment of a comprehensive juvenile justice system, procedures, and working mechanisms; for example, a system involving the presence of AAs during interrogations, social background investigations, a risk assessment mechanism, a community supervision and correction mechanism, the elimination of criminal records, and appropriate noncustodial measures for migrant juveniles. In reality, juvenile justice reform will develop and improve gradually rather than be accomplished successfully in a short time. Therefore, following the process of piloting in the regions, expanding to the nation, and then obtaining a legal confirmation is workable.

Second, the success of juvenile justice reform will not solely rely on the actions taken within the legislative and judicial bodies. The challenges and issues facing children in conflict with the law largely reflect the challenges and problems within the broader child protection system. As mentioned at the beginning of this paper, the CRC's stand on juvenile justice issues calls for a positive approach to children by the judicial system; often, it is the system that fails children, and so a comprehensive look at the state's obligations in relation to child protection is needed in order to ensure that juvenile justice reform has a lasting impact.

China has made massive progress toward ensuring better protection of the rights of children in conflict with the law, including local practical experiments to identify juvenile justice issues within the broader context of building a child protection system. Nonetheless, there is still a long way to go in China before a comprehensive child protection system with clearly mandated administrative organs and enforceable coordinated working mechanism among responsible agencies is established. Practices have demonstrated that the prime objective of a juvenile justice system is to be preventive, rehabilitative, and restorative, and this requires efforts to be made right from the beginning of the reform process. In another words, juvenile justice reform has to go hand in hand with the building of a child protection system, through which an enabling social environment and policy response can be developed to ensure a nonviolent childhood for children in China.

Lastly, China is undergoing large-scale legal reform. The amendment to the Criminal Procedure Law is still being revised in an orderly way, with particular attention being paid to important juvenile justice issues. Some regions are actively exploring ways of integrating social empowerment into the juvenile justice system; through these measures, the legitimate rights of children can be protected and juvenile cases can be handled properly and more easily. In the pilot project areas where reforms have taken place, central government has recognized these reforms and has even promulgated relevant documents to confirm and guide the practice of laws. Such practice provides support for and evidence of the beneficial influence of social empowerment on the functions of legal systems. A judicial system should not operate in a "closed-door" manner, but rather should develop within a free and open society. Justice is, in fact, a tactic for implementing social management. It not only needs a "source of nutrition" from society in order to absorb "nutrition"; it also needs to work continuously in a mature manner and to maintain close contacts with other social mechanisms in order to offer mutual assistance, to work together, and to develop a systematic and scientific social management mechanism.

References

Lin., W. (2001). *Review of recent juvenile delinquency statistics in China: Analysis from judicial and legislative perspectives. Vol. 29*(3).

Save the Children. (2004). *Juvenile justice: Modern concept of working with children in conflict with the law.* London, England: Save the Children.

Save the Children. (2005). *The right not to lose hope: Children in conflict with the law - A policy analysis and examples of good practice.* London, England: Save the Children.

Save the Children. (2007). *For tomorrow: An integrated collection of forums on juvenile protection and juvenile delinquency.* Beijing: China Prosecuting Publisher.

Save the Children. (2008). *Child protection system in emergencies: A review of current thinking and experiences.* London, England: Save the Children.

Thomson, L. D. G., Galt, V., and Darjee, R. (2007). Professionalizing the role of appropriate adults. *The Journal of Forensic Psychiatry and Psychology, 18*(1), 99-119.

UN General Assembly. (2006). *Report of the independent expert for the United Nations study on violence against children.*

UNICEF, UNHCR, Save the Children, and Chapin Hall. (2010). *Adapting a system approach to child protection: Key concepts and considerations.* New York, NY: UNICEF.

Zhang, Y. H., and Yao, B. (2009). Analysis about execution of the criminal policy of tempering justice with mercy in cases of crimes committed by minors. *Law Science Magazine, 30*(11).

In: Child Protection in Chinese Societies
Editor: Ko Ling Chan

ISBN: 978-1-61942-879-9

Chapter 7

CYBERBULLYING IN HONG KONG, TAIWAN, AND MAINLAND CHINA: IN SEARCH OF A REGULATORY FRAMEWORK

Anne S. Y. Cheung
Faculty of Law, University of Hong Kong, Beijing, P. R. China

ABSTRACT

Cyberbullying is a global and alarming problem, and this has led to calls for regulation at the national, regional and international level. Yet, the resort to direct and sole legal means to tackle cyberbullying has remained controversial. The alternative model of co-regulation combining legal intervention, education, and regulation from the telecommunications industry has been adopted, in various degrees, in Europe and North America. Drawing from their lessons, this chapter first maps out the problem of cyberbullying in Hong Kong, Taiwan and Mainland China, then explains why the current legal regimes in the three jurisdictions have failed to address adequately the problem of cyberbullying. This is followed by discussion on current attempts on anti-bullying policies made by the education authorities in Hong Kong and Taiwan. Finally, it argues why a co-regulatory and integrated approach involving all stakeholders should be implemented to tackle the problem.

Keywords: Cyberbullying, Law, Co-Regulation, Policy, Education

INTRODUCTION

Modern information communication technology (ICT) has connected us in unprecedented ways. We send e-mails, play games, check Facebook, tweet, and text almost every day. Yet, not all of us may enjoy the convenience and freedom that technology has brought. In particular, for victims of bullying, ICT has only opened up another new avenue for harassment.

Despite the lack of a universal definition of cyberbullying, it generally refers to situations where a child is threatened, humiliated, embarrassed, or otherwise targeted by another child or children through electronic means, including interactive and digital technologies, the Internet, and mobile phones (WiredSafety, 2011). It often takes the form of mockery, insults, gossip, harassment, or exposing someone else's personal information on the Internet.

Cyberbullying has become a global and alarming problem, and this has led to calls for regulation. At the international level, in 2007, the Rapporteur's Report to the United Nations General Assembly condemned all forms of violence, including bullying (Baleseng, 2007). At the regional level, in 2009, the Stockholm Call for Action statement to the European member states at the L'Europe de L'Enfance meeting listed cyberbullying as a form of violence that warrants the development of state intervention and national strategies (The Stockholm Call for Action, 2009).[1] Indeed, in Annex II of the same document, it was stated that violence against children, including bullying, was one of the primary concerns mentioned by children themselves. Since 1999, the European Commission Safer Internet Programme has involved 30 state governments and 20 social networking companies in efforts to combat cyberbullying in Europe (European Commission Information Society). The European Union sponsored a study on Internet safety and children's interests; this study was carried out between 2006 and 2009 in 21 member states, and it reported that 20% of teenagers in Europe had been cyber-bullied (Livingston and Haddon, 2009).[2]

At the national level, a 2010 study in the United States revealed that 20% of students aged between 10 to 18 years had experienced cyberbullying (Hinduja and Patchin, 2010).[3] As of July 2011, 46 states in the United States have legislation criminalizing acts of bullying, 32 states have laws on electronic harassment, and 7 states have legislation specifically on cyberbullying (Hinduja and Patchin, 2011).[4]

Yet, the resort to direct and sole legal means to tackle cyberbullying and to check on the unbridled freedom that some children have abused remains controversial. Other than the fact that legal actions are lengthy and costly, many may be hesitant to punish the abusers who are also children. Existing psychological research on bullying has shown that the social and psychological development of the bullies, the bystanders, and the victims are adversely affected in this hostile, abusive, and violent form of interaction (Ivarsson, Broberg, Arvidsson, and Gillberg, 2005; Gradinger, Strohmeier and Spiel, 2009). In other words, the bullies and the bystanders who join in are also, in the broader sense, victims themselves. Elsewhere, I have argued for a co-regulatory framework involving a coherent and integrated

1 This was an NGO statement, signed by 46 groups across Europe, to L'Europe de l'Enfance, a ministerial group among European Union member states that was set up to protect children's rights in Europe (This intergovernmental group was set up in 2000; information available at http://www.childoneurope.org/ee/history.htm).

2 It was reported that 10% of teenagers in Germany, Ireland, and Portugal had received unwanted sexual comments online, while 25% to 30% of teenagers in Iceland, Norway, the United Kingdom, and Sweden had a similar experience. The most serious problem was in Poland, where 50% of teenagers had had this unpleasant experience.

3 The most common form of cyberbullying was carried out via mobile phone (83%), while the most popular means of cyberbullying on the Internet was through Facebook (50%). However, this figure actually represented a significant drop (50%) in cyberbullying since 2004. The survey covered 4,441 students aged between 10 and 18.

4 The United States has a federal law banning harassment but not cyberbullying. While 39 states rely on the school sanctions method, 44 states require schools to have anti-cyberbullying policies.

approach which combines legal intervention, education, and regulation from the telecommunications industry (including Internet service providers) (Cheung, 2012).[5] Writing on children's rights, Eva Lievens defined co-regulation as a regulatory strategy which consists of elements of both direct state regulation and self-regulation (Lievens, 2010). This implies that states should take actions to protect children from cyberbullying through laws and policies which coordinate efforts between the stakeholders, including parents, schools, industries, and the children themselves. Such an approach would produce a responsive and adaptive model that requires stakeholders to develop their codes of practice, and enable policy makers to overcome the hurdle of legislation that is lagging behind technological advancement.

Here, I advocate that the above approach is equally apt for Hong Kong, Taiwan, and Mainland China, where there is a growing awareness of the need to tackle the rising problem of cyberbullying. Despite the fact that Hong Kong inherited a common law system while Taiwan and the Mainland have continental civil law systems, all three places share a lot culturally. In addition, none of these places has any legislation specifically on cyberbullying. This, however, does not mean that cyberbullying is not regulated. Arguably, depending on the context, cyberbullying is covered by various pieces of legislation under criminal and civil law, such as legislation relating to defamation and intimidation. Hence, it would be worthwhile to examine whether the current legal regimes in the three jurisdictions have addressed adequately the problem of cyberbullying. Other than analyzing legal measures, anti-bullying policies in the education systems of Hong Kong and Taiwan will also be discussed.

While the Hong Kong Education Bureau is at the early stage of experimenting with this approach, the Taiwan Ministry of Education has implemented anti-bullying school policies in concrete terms. In contrast, the Government of the People's Republic of China (PRC) has no education policy on cyberbullying.

In order to provide a critical analysis of the anti-bullying approaches in Hong Kong, Taiwan, and Mainland China, this chapter begins (Part I) by discussing the nature of cyberbullying and its prevalence in the three jurisdictions. Part II will then map out the legal regimes governing cyberbullying (in its common forms of defamation, intimidation, and the unauthorized disclosure of personal information) in these places. I will then explain why the current legal response in all three places is inadequate to tackle the problem of cyberbullying. A better alternative would be to combat the problem of cyberbullying through the education system, an approach which is being explored by the Hong Kong and Taiwan education authorities.

Yet, this should not be seen as the only solution or as a replacement for a legal solution. Instead, in the final part of this chapter (Part III), I will argue why an integrated and co-regulatory approach involving schools and the industries should be adopted. Although the major concern here is peer-to-peer bullying among minors, references will also be made to cyberbullying among university students and other relevant issues. The terms *child* and *minor* are used interchangeably in this chapter.

---

[5] Part of the content of this chapter can also be found in my other work.

CyberBullying and its Prevalence in Hong Kong, Taiwan, and Mainland China

The Nature and Manifestation of CyberBullying

Shariff and Hoff asserted that cyberbullying is a "psychologically devastating form of social cruelty among adolescents" (2007, p.80). According to them, cyberbullying is an extension of traditional bullying, which customarily manifests itself in overt physical aggression such as beating and shoving; however, covert bullying, which aims to exclude its victims through gossip, verbal threats, or harassment, exists side by side with overt bullying. A case of cyberbullying is often a variation of covert bullying through electronic media, not only crossing various electronic media (mobile phone and Internet) but also blurring the boundaries between the online and offline worlds. Unlike traditional bullies, cyberbullies are less inhibited about restraining their behavior because bullying of this kind can be carried out in an anonymous, impersonal way (Hinduja and Patchin, 2009). Technological advances have also provided the bullies with the ability to infiltrate the private spaces of their victims beyond the schoolyard, making it impossible for the victims to seek refuge at home. Moreover, bullying can also easily take place regardless of whether or not the perpetrators have a strong physical build. In other words, in the context of this information age, bullying is no longer confined to face-to-face confrontations. Rather, it is now the combination of online and offline harassment—24 hours a day, 7 days a week—involving multiple aggressors (up to hundreds or even millions) against a single victim. These victims, therefore, often feel helpless, unable either to trace the initial perpetrator or to secure the cooperation of the telecommunications companies or Internet service providers (ISPs) in filtering, blocking, or removing the offending messages or photos. As a result, studies in the United States have shown that victims of cyberbullying often suffer from depression, not to mention the definite link between cyberbullying and teenage suicide (Hinduja and Patchin, 2010).

In their report to the Anti-Bullying Alliance in the United Kingdom, Peter Smith and his colleagues identified seven types of cyberbullying, including sending abusive text messages, instant messages, e-mails, and phone calls to the victims and their social circle; taking pictures or video clips of the victim without his/her consent and posting them online; and bullying in online chat rooms and on social networking sites (Smith, Mahdavi, Carvalho, and Tippett, 2006).

The content of cyberbullying includes harassment, threats of physical or sexual violence, and sending damaging statements about victims to other students. It can also take the form of technological attacks, for example, shutting down the victims' blogs or hacking into their accounts and sending offensive messages in their names to others. Another strategy involves setting up Internet polling or rating sites targeting the victims. Examples of rating sites include "Pick the Hottie" or "Hot or Not" (Hinduja and Patchin, 2009, p. 38).

Furthermore, a deeply disturbing practice of cyberbullying is ironically known as "happy slapping," which involves videotaping (often using mobile phones) a physical attack and posting it online. For instance, in 2011, Taiwan society was shocked by a video clip on YouTube showing a group of four to five female students bullying another female student in a park in Hsinchu (Hou, 2011). The victim was forced to kneel on the ground; not only was she kicked, slapped, and beaten, but attempts were made by the group to burn her hair. The event was recorded somehow and uploaded onto YouTube. This prompted a call for police, legislative, and educational intervention. A petition was posted on the Facebook page of President Ma Ying-jeou urging him to take action.

The above mentioned forms of cyberbullying have demonstrated that technological advancement unfortunately now has the capacity to bring out, in an unprecedented altered and amplified form, a greater cruelty and violence in human nature than that demonstrated in William Golding's classic novel *Lord of the Flies* (Shariff, 2009).

The Prevalence of Cyberbullying

The multiple forms of cyberbullying have become a serious global and cross-cultural problem (Hanley, 2010). Hong Kong, Taiwan, and Mainland China are not exempt from this worrying phenomenon.

In Hong Kong, a survey conducted between November 2009 and February 2010 on Primary 5 and Primary 6 students revealed that 50% of them had been victims of cyberbullying, while 30% had been perpetrators of such behavior (SingTao News, 2010a).[6] Another study conducted during the same period on secondary school students showed that 30% had been victims of cyberbullying (SingTao News, 2010b).[7] More recently, in 2011, a study conducted among 1,818 secondary students revealed that 32% had been perpetrators of cyberbullying (Ming Pao News , 2011).[8] The same study showed that the most common forms of bullying were making fun of others, giving them nicknames, and spreading rumors about them (50.5%), followed by insulting others (44.4%).

Perhaps, the most comprehensive survey and set of data on cyberbullying in our study came from Taiwan. A study conducted in 2007 covering nearly 2,000 primary and junior high school students in Taiwan revealed that 24% of the student respondents had been perpetrators of cyberbullying (The Child Welfare League Foundation, 2007).[9] Out of these, 66% were high school students and 34% were primary students, and 57% were male and 43% were female. The common forms of cyberbullying reported in this study were spreading rumors about the victims and insulting or teasing them online. Another study conducted by Huang and Chou on junior high school students in Taiwan revealed a similar trend (Huang and Chou , 2010). Out of 545 participants from eight junior high schools, their survey found that 20.4% had cyber-bullied others, 34.9% had been victims, and 63.4% admitted having witnessed or having been aware of cyberbullying. The same study showed that the most common types of cyberbullying were threatening and harassing others (20.4%); making jokes about and making fun of others (18.2%); and spreading rumors about others (12.2%).

Unfortunately, there is no nationwide statistical data on the prevalence of cyberbullying in Mainland China. What is available is a study conducted by Li on 202 seventh-grade students in a large city in southern China, which revealed that 33% of the respondents were

---

[6] The survey was conducted by The Chinese University between November 2009 and February 2010; 626 primary school students were interviewed.

[7] The study was conducted by the Hong Kong Family Welfare Society and The Chinese University: 1,800 secondary school students were interviewed for this study.

[8] The study was conducted by Dr. Annis Lai-chu Fung of City University, Hong Kong.

[9] The study was conducted in June of 2007 and covered nine primary schools and eight high schools. The target respondents ranged from primary four and five students to form one and two students. In total, 2,120 questionnaires were sent, of which 1,919 were completed successfully.

victims of cyberbullying, but only 7% admitted to being cyberbullies (Li , 2008). An interesting finding from this study was that 66% of the Chinese respondents indicated that they had reported incidents of cyberbullying to adults when they were victims and 75% of them believed that adult intervention would be effective. This is in marked contrast to Canadian respondents in the same age group. In the same study, less than 9% of the Canadian student participants reported the matter to adults when they were cyberbullied, while 67% believed that adult intervention was effective. Another study worth noting was carried out by Su and Holt; they examined cyberbullying in Chinese web forums (Su and Holt , 2010). In their study of 374 threads from web forums in 21 schools in 21 regions from China, they found that the most common form of cyberbullying was denigration (i.e., individuals making negative, harsh, or insulting comments about the character or behavior of others).

THE LEGAL LANDSCAPE AND EFFORTS BY EDUCATION AUTHORITIES

Overall, as we have seen, about 25-50% of primary and secondary students in the three regions have either been victims, perpetrators, or bystanders of cyberbullying. Indeed, the figure is alarming to warrant state intervention. Yet, the question remains: what type of state intervention is the most appropriate? A plausible answer is legal intervention.

Available Legal Remedies

Given the fact that there is no specific law governing cyberbullying in any of the three jurisdictions under discussion, recourse has to be made to existing legal remedies.[10] Due to the various manifestations of cyberbullying, this discussion will focus on its most common forms in the three regions: defamation and intimidation. Furthermore, due to the increasing popularity of sharing information on the Internet, unauthorized disclosure of personal information will also be discussed.

Defamation

In the common form of cyberbullying which involves spreading rumors, gossip, or slander, one can rely on the remedy of defamation. Although the elements of a defamation action vary slightly in each of the jurisdictions in our study, the common feature among them is that a plaintiff has to prove that a defamatory statement has been published about him/her (Fenwick and Phillipson, 2006; Wang 2009; Fu and Cullen, 1996).[11] A defamatory statement

[10] The Ministry of Education in Taiwan has listed the relevant legal provisions concerning various aspects of cyberbullying on its website (Ministry of Education of Taiwan 2011).

[11] For the common law position which is applicable to Hong Kong, *see* Helen Fenwick & Gavin Phillipson, *Media Freedom under the Human Rights Act* (Oxford, 2006) 1043. For the position in Taiwan, *see* Wang Zejian, *Tort Law* (Taipei: Wang Muhua fa xing, 2009) (in Chinese). With regard to the position in Mainland China, Fu and Cullen have pointed out that to launch a legal action for reputational harm in China is akin to establishing a defamation action in common law. The Supreme People's Court, in a 1993 explanation on reputation rights, delivered the opinion that four issues must be addressed: whether (a) the reputation of the victim has been harmed; (b) the act of the defendant was unlawful; (c) the unlawful act caused damage to the victim's reputation; and (d) the defendant was at fault. Fu and Cullen observed that in actual practice, the Chinese courts have essentially adopted the common law analysis on defamation.

is one that is "calculated to injure the reputation of another by exposing him or her to hatred, contempt, or ridicule or a tendency to lower the plaintiff in the estimation of right-thinking members of society generally." (Fenwick and Phillipson, 2006, p. 1043) The alleged statement is presumed to be false by the court, and so it is for the defendant to raise the defence of truth. Defamation is further divided into slander and libel. The difference between them is that slander is a statement uttered in a non-permanent form while libel is the publication of a defamatory statement in a permanent form, such as in a painting or a printed work (Carey, 2010, p. 33).

In Hong Kong, defamation is essentially a civil action between parties in their private capacities. Despite the fact that defamation is a criminal offence under the Defamation Ordinance,[12] this is rarely invoked by the Hong Kong government. The last prosecution for defamation in Hong Kong was back in 1952.[13] Unlike the position in Hong Kong, defamation can be both a criminal and a civil action in Taiwan and Mainland China.

In Taiwan, one's reputation and dignity are protected under article 195(1) of the Civil Code[14] and article 310 of the Criminal Code.[15] Under the latter provision, slander carries a maximum sentence of 1 year, while libel carries a maximum sentence of 2 years. In addition, under article 309 of the Criminal Code, it is an offence to publicly insult another person. The difference between an insult and defamation is that the latter has an alleged factual basis.

In Mainland China, one's reputation is an enshrined right in the PRC Constitution. Article 38 of the PRC Constitution states that "the personal dignity of citizens is inviolable. Insult, libel, false charge or frame-up directed against citizens by any means is prohibited."[16] In addition, under article 101 of the General Principles of the Civil Law of the People's Republic of China (GPCL), "citizens and legal persons shall enjoy the right of reputation. The personality of citizens shall be protected by law, and the use of insults, libel or other means to damage the reputation of citizens or legal persons shall be prohibited."[17] Serious cases of slander or insult also constitute criminal offences in China.[18] The police have the power to detain a person for up to 10 days for insulting or slandering another person.[19]

The Challenge to Defamation Action

The above test of defamation may not be easily satisfied if a website makes it explicit that its intention is to make fun of someone. This poses a peculiar difficulty for common law jurisdictions because a court would have been likely to hold that, given the context, it would

[12] Section 5 of the Defamation Ordinance, Laws of Hong Kong (Cap. 21).

[13] Fei Yi Ming and Lee Tsung Ying v. The Crown, 36 *Hong Kong Law Reports* 133 (1952). The Hong Kong colonial government prosecuted Wen Wei Pao, a pro-Communist Party press at that time.

[14] Civil Code of the Republic of China, (26 May 2011) at http://law.moj.gov.tw/Eng/LawClass/LawContent.aspx?PCODE=B0000001

[15] Criminal Code of the Republic of China, (26 January 2011), at http://law.moj.gov.tw/LawClass/LawAll.aspx?PCode=C0000001(in Chinese).

[16] The Constitution of the People's Republic of China (1993), available at http://english.gov.cn/2005-08/05/content_20813.htm.

[17] General Principles of the Civil Law of P.R.C. (promulgated by the President of P.R.C., April 12, 1986, effective Jan. 1, 1987) art. 101, LAWINFOCHINA.

[18] Criminal Law of the P.R.C. (adopted at the Second Session of the Fifth National People's Congress, July 1, 1979, promulgated by Order No. 5 of the Chairman of the Standing Comm. National People's Congress, July 6, 1979, effective January 1, 1980), art. 145, LAWINFOCHINA.

[19] Administrative Regulations on Penalties for Public Security, art. 25 (promulgated by the Standing Committee of the Tenth National People's Congress, August 28, 2005, effective March 1, 2006).

not satisfy the legal test of being a defamatory statement which lowers the reputation of the plaintiff in the mind of right-thinking members of the community.

For example, in Canada, a high school student named David Knight was falsely described as a homosexual, a pedophile, and a rapist on a website called "Welcome to the Page that Makes Fun of Dave Knight" (Leishman, 2005). Not only did the site attack Knight, but it also attacked all of the members of his family. However, all that Knight knew was that the website had been set up in Thailand. In order to start a legal battle, he had to discover the identity of the defamers and to overcome the jurisdictional problem. It took the Knight family 6 months to get the ISP company to remove the site. Moreover, arguably, Knight could have lost a defamation lawsuit because the title of the website suggested that it was meant to be a joke, despite that fact that it was a cruel and crude joke.

Along the same line of legal logic, defamation action may not be able to help victims who have been targeted in polling or rating sites, such as sites that pose questions such as "Who is the ugliest?", "Who is the most promiscuous?", or "Who should be the next to die?"[20] This is because the above examples are merely invitations to express opinions, and, as such, they may not be considered to pass the legal test of factual allegation under defamation law. The position that value judgment is a protected form of speech has been accepted by the US Court and the European Court of Human Rights (Young, 2000).[21] Furthermore, offensive or insulting words sent directly to a victim's mobile phone or e-mail account would not constitute defamation because there has been no publication to a third party.

Arguably, victims in a similar position to David Knight may fare better in a legal battle in Taiwan or Mainland China because the law in these places protects one's dignity against insult. However, the victims of cyberbullying have yet to identify the exact culprits and to overcome the problem of jurisdiction in cyberspace. The challenges associated with pursuing litigation in the courts are well illustrated in the case of Zhang Ying. The story of Peking University graduate Zhang Ying was one of the biggest Internet scandals of 2007. Zhang Ying allegedly appeared nude in order to raise money while studying overseas (Wang, 2007). The story, along with supposedly naked photos of Zhang, first appeared in March 2007 on a North American website designed for Chinese persons travelling overseas (Wang and Shi, 2007). Within a week, various websites had widely distributed the story in China. In early April 2007, a Chinese website called Xinmin.cn issued reports that the story was in fact false and the photos were fakes (Wang, 2007). In the same month, Zhang learned about the allegations against her while she was living as a student in Canada. Infuriated and embarrassed, Zhang returned to China in early July 2007 to explore the possibility of suing the various ISPs.[22] She formally complained to the police, hoping that they would commence

---

[20] The US case of *Emmett v. Kent School District No. 415,* 92F. Supp. 2d 1088 (W. D. Wash, 2000) concerned a senior student who had set up a website on mock obituaries that allowed visitors to vote on who should be the next to die in the school. The student was suspended, but then successfully brought an action under the free speech clause of the First Amendment. The court found that the school had failed to demonstrate there was any threat or violence intended by the plaintiff.

[21] The position that value judgment is a protected form of speech has been accepted by the US Court and the European Court of Human Rights. The English position is not entirely clear at this stage. For the position in the US, see American Law Institute, Restatement of the Law - Torts (1977, current through August 2010) § 566.

[22] *Bei da nü liu xue sheng bei wu "luo ben" an, nü zhu jue yi wei se qing mo te [The Heroine Appears To Be An AV Model In The Case Where A Female Peking University Graduate Studying Abroad Was Alleged To Have Gone Naked],* August 1, 2007, http://news.xinhuanet.com/edu/2007-08/01/content_6458564.htm.

a legal action.[23] Zhang also requested that the ISPs concerned delete the defamatory content, restore her reputation, apologize, and compensate her for the damages she suffered, but her efforts were to no avail. The managers of the various websites explained to Zhang that they did not know who first posted the photos and story (Wang and Shi). At the time of writing this article, alleged naked photos of Zhang could still be found on the Web. Despite the seemingly comprehensive legal remedies available under both civil and criminal laws in Mainland China, Zhang was completely helpless.

Intimidation

A second common form of cyberbullying in all three jurisdictions is intimidation. In fact, the Internet has been described as the "high tech playgrounds for intimidation" (Chaffin, 2008, p.773). Examples of intimidation include sending e-mail messages or SMS messages to the victims with threatening remarks such as "You will be beaten up in school tomorrow" or "You will be dead tomorrow."

In Hong Kong, under s.24 of the Crimes Ordinance, a person may be guilty of criminal intimidation if he/she threatens another with injury to his/her person, reputation, or property.[24] Such a threat is deemed sufficient if the other person is alarmed that such a threat might be carried out or if the accused intended the threat to be taken seriously and not as an empty threat.[25] Intimidation can also be a civil law action under common law. Under the classic rule laid down in *Wilkinson v Downtown* back in 1897, any word said or act done, whether directly or indirectly, with the intention of inflicting harm incurs tortious liability as long as harm is actually caused,[26] and this harm refers both to bodily and recognized psychiatric illnesses, meaning that a victim suffering from mere distress is highly unlikely to make a successful claim.

In Taiwan, intimidation is an offence under article 305 of the Criminal Code, whereas in the PRC, it is governed by article 293 of the Criminal Law. In addition, threatening the personal safety of others by means of letters or other methods is punishable under article 42 of the Law on Public Security Administrative Provisions in the PRC.[27] The police can detain the accused for up to 10 days.

Other than fearing for one's physical safety, females may have to face the additional threats of sexual assault. In the Hong Kong case of *HKSAR v. Ko Kam Fai*, two female university students received rape threats from the accused (a university hall-mate) (Hong Kong SAR Court of Appeal, 2001). Their e-mail accounts were also hacked by the accused and flooded with obscene photos, with their data on their computer was altered. The judge did not accept the accused's explanation that all of the above mentioned acts were meant to be a

[23] *Bei da nü sheng "luo ben" tu pian zai xian, jing fang zheng ju bu zu zan wei shou li [The Pictures of The Female Graduate of Peking University "Going Naked" Reoccur, But Police Refuse To Investigate Due to Lack Of Sufficient Evidence]*, July 27, 2007, http://news.xinhuanet.com/edu/2007-07/27/content_6438702.htm.

[24] Crimes Ordinance, Laws of Hong Kong (Cap 200).

[25] Section 24(c)(i) of the Crimes Ordinance. See discussion, *Halsbury's Laws of Hong Kong*, para. 130.408 (Sweet & Maxwell 2003).

[26] *Wilkinson v. Downtown* (1897) 2 QB 67.

[27] The Law of the People's Republic of China on Public Security Administration Punishments, Order of the President (No. 38), adopted on August 28, 2005 at the 17th session of the Standing Committee of the Tenth National People's Congress of the People's Republic of China on August 28, 2005, promulgated and implemented on March 1, 2006, at www.lawinfochina.com.

joke as the victims had been placed in a position of extreme fear. Instead, the judge sentenced the accused to 12 months imprisonment for criminal intimidation and criminal damage.

Unauthorized Disclosure of Personal Information

With the increasing use of mobile phones and cameras, the unauthorized publication of photos, use of images, and dissemination of personal contact information or other information has become an easy form of cyberbullying. Other than the problem of happy slapping, which was mentioned earlier in the chapter, there is a phenomenon known as "renrou sousuo," literally meaning "the search for human flesh." The term originated in Mainland China, but it is now used in both Mainland China and Taiwan. In Hong Kong, its equivalent is known as "qidi". What happens is that a call is made to identify a particular individual through mobilizing others on the Internet with the single aim of digging out facts and exposing the target to the baleful glare of publicity (Bai and Ji, 2008). Netizens are asked to provide information on a particular individual until a full picture emerges in this cyber relay. Very often, personal contact information, including names, phone numbers, and addresses, is circulated wildly on the Internet, beyond the control of the targeted individuals. Although this may be more often used to expose corrupt officials or to punish those who have violated social norms, children and minors can also be victims of this form of cyberbullying.

For instance, one innocent victim was Zhang Shufan in Mainland China. In 2007, Zhang was a 13-year-old high school girl who, in a television interview, had condemned the use of the Internet as a means of promoting violence and disseminating pornography.[28] Because of her statement, angry netizens immediately attacked her, mobilized public opinion, and utilized the human search engine to track her down. Within 5 days, 1,200 postings with her personal information existed on the Internet, running to 12 full web pages on the bulletin discussion board commonly known in China as BBS or Baidu. Her picture was posted, information about her was requested, and stories demonstrating how she was not as pure and wholesome as presented flooded the Internet. Baidu intervened after 8 days of Internet frenzy by netizens (Yang, 2008). The web company decided to freeze postings for 8 days, although it continued to allow the viewing of existing material (Baidu, 2008). Baidu explained that it did this to protect the interests of the girl and "to maintain healthy discussion" on its site.

With their present sets of legal regulations, none of the three jurisdictions would have been well equipped to handle the above situation satisfactorily. Although Hong Kong has the Personal Data (Privacy) Ordinance, this legislation only binds a data user, defined as "a person who, either alone or jointly or in common with other persons, controls the collection, holding, processing or use of the data" (section 2). However, in the context of a human flesh search or qidi, in which hundreds of anonymous individuals can easily become involved in exposing a subject's personal data, it is uncertain who the data user is: is it the person who called for the search and builds the profile of the target victim? Or is it anyone who has contributed to the personal information on the victim? Or is it the web master of a particular web forum? Hong Kong law is silent on the duty of ISPs in such situations. Although the prohibition on unauthorized disclosures of personal data that causes psychological harm is being included in the proposed Personal Data (Privacy) Amendment Bill 2011, it is unlikely

[28] The account was from *Xiao xue sheng: Wang ye hen huang hen bao li [Pupil: Web Pages Are Very Pornographic and Very Violent]*, http://epaper.xkb.com.cn/view.php?id=184695, posted on January 7, 2008.

to be effective in regulating behavior related to human flesh search or qidi unless the role and responsibilities of ISPs are defined.[29]

In Taiwan, the Personal Information Protection Act was enacted in May 2010, but it has yet to come into effect pending Executive Yuan's announcement. (Ministry of Justice, Republic of China, 2010) [30] This Act would cover both the public and private sectors, but it excludes the collection, processing, or use of personal information "in the course of personal activity of a domestic nature" (clause 51). Moreover, seeking prior consent from data subjects is not required for the posting of information, group photos, or videos onto electronic social networking sites, as long as the information or materials are acquired at "public places or open activities" and do not reveal other personal information (Clause 51). Thus, taking pictures of individuals during public activities and posting them on blogs or other similar types of Web content without revealing other personal data is unlikely to be a violation. Hence, it is uncertain whether and how human flesh search activities would be regulated. In comparison, there have been legal efforts at the local level in Mainland China to halt this type of cyberbullying and harassment, as witnessed in the below case of Wang Fei.[31]

Sadly, this case started as a family tragedy in Beijing. The facts themselves may have little relevance to cyberbullying, but their legal implications for privacy protection are significant. In 2007, an aggrieved wife in Beijing jumped to her death after discovering that her husband, Wang Fei, had been unfaithful. Before her suicide, the wife disclosed her frustration and her reason for committing suicide on her blogs, placing the blame on Wang. After her death, many netizens were so angry with Wang that they searched for, collected, and eventually disclosed the personal contact information of Wang, his family, and the third party who allegedly broke up the marriage. Death threats were left outside the home of Wang and his parents, and Wang resigned from his job in the face of social pressure. Since the death of his estranged wife at the end of 2007 to the time of trial at the end of 2008, Wang had not been able to find work as a designer. Eventually, he successfully brought a claim against one blog writer and one ISP before the Beijing District Court to protect his privacy. Another ISPs involved was found not liable because it had removed the objectionable materials and information within a reasonable time.

For the first time, a Chinese court had addressed the issue of cyber violence, specifically with reference to the alarming trend of using the human flesh search engine to hunt down individuals. In addition, the court also addressed the issue of privacy directly. It called for privacy protection reform from the Ministry of Information Industry shortly after delivering its judgment.[32] In its decision, the court explained that privacy refers generally to a person's private interests and personal relations, including his/her personal life, personal information, personal space, secrets, and any aspect of life that he/she would not like to share with the world. Hence, any unauthorized disclosure or dissemination constitutes a violation of a person's privacy interests. On this uncertain note, legislative intervention maybe the best solution to clear the present legal ambiguity. While in 2010, the Tort Liability Law was

---

[29] Clause 22(2)(b) of the Personal Data (Privacy) Amendment Bill 2011, (8 July 2011) at http://legco.gov.hk/yr10-11/english/bills/b201107081.pdf.

[30] Personal Information Protection Act of the Republic of China, (26 May 2010) at http://law.moj.gov.tw/Eng/LawClass/LawAll.aspx?PCode=I0050021.

[31] *Wang Fei v. Zhang Leyi, Daqi.com and Tianya.com,* No. 10930, (Beijing Chaoyang Dist. People's Ct., Dec. 18, 2008) http://www.chinacourt.org:80/html/article/200812/18/336418.shtml.

[32] Beijing to Ministry of Information Industry, Proposal for Stricter Supervision of the Internet, (Beijing Chaoyang Dist. People's Ct., Dec. 18, 2008) Chinalaw@hermes.gwu.edu discussion board (P.R.C.).

amended to include a right to privacy in its list of protected civil rights and interests,[33] the exact scope of this right and its implications for halting acts of cyberbullying or human flesh searches is not known, particularly as article 36 of the same piece of legislation states that an ISP may incur liability for failing to remove objectionable content once notice of a tortuous infringement has been received.

The Legal Challenge and Criminal Responsibility

Although I have cited successful cases of litigation, the use of the above laws will be confined inevitably to relatively straightforward cases in which there are identifiable offenders within the specific jurisdiction. This is far from adequate given the multifaceted nature of cyberbullying, the anonymity of most perpetrators, the huge numbers of people involved, and the borderless nature of cyberspace.

Above all, the option of resorting to the legal system would necessarily mean that the child perpetrators, often teenagers, have to face criminal sanctions. Critics have expressed grave concerns about the appropriateness of adopting a purely punitive approach to deal with "kiddie crimes" (Brenner and Rehberg, 2009). Notwithstanding the effectiveness of this method, others have reminded us that those who have committed criminal offences or wrongs are also children that need help. (Shariff and Churchill, 2010). To a certain extent, the concern to protect child offenders and to give them a second chance is also reflected in the age of criminal culpability in all three jurisdictions in our study.

In Hong Kong, there is a conclusive presumption that no child under the age of 10 can be guilty of an offence under s.3 of the Juvenile Offence Ordinance.[34] For a child aged between 10 and 14 years old, there is a rebuttable presumption of criminal responsibility under common law if it is proven that the child was aware that his act was seriously wrong and not merely naughty or mischievous. For young person aged 14 years old or above but under 16 years old, a judge can sentence him/her to a place of detention (s.14 of the same Ordinance).

In Taiwan, under article 18 of the Criminal Law, the age of criminal responsibility is 14.[35] For child offenders who are under 14, an order can be made under article 86 for a minor to be sent to a rehabilitation center. A person over 14 but under 18 years of age is criminally responsible for the crime committed but will receive a reduced sentence.

In Mainland China, a child under 14 years of age is exempt from criminal responsibility. Under article 17 of Chapter 2 of the Criminal Law of the PRC, a person who has attained the age of 16 is held criminally responsible for the crime committed.[36] A person who has attained the age of 14 but is under 16 years of age would only be held responsible for serious offences

---

[33] Article 2 of The Tort Law of the People's Republic of China, Decree of the President of the People's Republic of China (No. 21), adopted at the 12th session of the Standing Committee of the Eleventh National People's Congress on December 26, 2009, promulgated and came into force on July 1, 2010.

[34] Juvenile Offenders Ordinance, Laws of Hong Kong, Cap. 226.

[35] Criminal Law of the Republic of China (amended version 26 January 2011) at http://lis.ly.gov.tw/lgcgi/lglaw?@43:1804289383:f:NO%3DC704536*%20OR%20NO%3DC004536%20OR%20NO%3DC104536$$4$$$NO (in Chinese).

[36] Criminal Law of the People's Republic of China. Adopted by the Second Session of the Fifth National People's Congress on July 1, 1979 and amended by the 19th meeting of the Standing Committee of the Eleventh National People's Congress of the People's Republic of China on February 25, 2011, effective on May 1, 2011 at www.lawinfochina.com.

committed.[37] However, a person who has attained the age of 14 but is under 18 years of age is given a lesser punishment or a mitigated punishment for the crime committed. Under the same article, where a person is not criminally punished because he/she has not reached 16 years of age, the head of his/her family or his/her guardian will be ordered to subject the person to discipline. Shelter and rehabilitation will be provided by the government on a needs basis.

The different standards of criminal culpability for children or young persons may explain why there is no specific criminal legal provision on cyberbullying in the three jurisdictions under study. As an alternative, efforts have been made by the Education Bureau in Hong Kong and the Ministry of Education in Taiwan to combat the problem.

Efforts through Education Policies

Hong Kong

The Hong Kong Education Bureau has set up a website on anti-bullying policies and campaigns in schools in which the only reference to the law is article 3 of the United Nations Convention on the Rights of the Child (UNCRC) (Education Bureau, Hong Kong Special Administrative Region, 2011). The said provision of the UNCRC sets out the international and legal standards and guidelines for the protection of children and emphasizes that "the best interests of the child" should be the primary consideration for its state parties. Under article 19 of the UNCRC, state parties have the obligation to protect children from all forms of physical or mental violence.[38] It also obliges a state party to enact preventive measures to ensure that all child victims of violence receive the support and assistance they require. The Hong Kong Education Bureau's website makes it clear that it is the duty of schools to ensure a safe environment in which their students can learn. Such an approach is both preventive and educational. In 2011, a pilot project_with a target of about 100 schools (including both primary and secondary schools) will be involved in the development of anti-bullying awareness campaigns.[39]

The Hong Kong police force has also been working with schools to combat the problem of bullying. However, it has no specific policy on cyberbullying, and the emphasis of the police is on crime prevention and detection (HKSAR Police, 2011). This means that unless an act has violated the criminal law of Hong Kong, there may not be justifiable grounds for police intervention. Obviously, this approach would cover acts of assault or intimidation, but

[37] Serious offences include the following crimes: the intentional killing of another; the intentional injuring of another; causing serious injury or death; rape; robbery; drug trafficking; arson; causing an explosion; and poisoning.

[38] The full text of article 19 reads: 1. States Parties shall take all appropriate legislative, administrative, social and educational measures to protect the child from all forms of physical or mental violence, injury or abuse, neglect or negligent treatment, maltreatment or exploitation, including sexual abuse, while in the care of parent(s), legal guardian(s) or any other person who has the care of the child. 2. Such protective measures should, as appropriate, include effective procedures for the establishment of social programs to provide necessary support for the child and for those who have the care of the child, as well as for other forms of prevention and for identification, reporting, referral, investigation, treatment and follow-up of instances of child maltreatment described heretofore, and, as appropriate, for judicial involvement.

[39] Information courtesy of Ms Pearl Chan, Senior School Development Officer, Hong Kong SAR Education Bureau, 23 September 2011.

it would not cover the common forms of cyberbullying such as spreading rumors and taunting or insulting others.

Taiwan

More interestingly, Taiwan comes closest to having a legal regime that addresses specifically the problem of cyberbullying. In June 2011, a bill was tabled before the Legislative Yuan to amend the Education Fundamental Law.[40] Under the proposed amendment, all schools would be required to implement anti-bullying policies, including the setting up of preventive measures and handling procedures and the provision of counseling service for students affected by bullying. As the current bill has completed only its first reading,[41] it is uncertain at the time of writing whether and when this will be enacted into law. Despite the lack of an official legal endorsement, in February 2011, the Ministry of Education in Taiwan issued a strong statement condemning any acts of bullying, including cyberbullying.[42] It called for schools to implement appropriate policies and to submit proposals for anti-bullying policies, and it has set up a 24 hour hotline service for anyone seeking help.

Mainland China

Although we have yet to see any formal policy from the education authorities in Mainland China, some schools have formulated their own set of policies on campus and online safety. As previously mentioned, Su and Holt studied Chinese web forums in 21 schools in China. They found that 9 of the 21 schools had posted their policy concerning on how students should behave on campus on the Internet. In addition, one school had specific policy related to unacceptable behavior of bullying, including cyberbullying, for its students (Su and Holt, 2010, p. 681). Certainly, these are laudable efforts by schools in China.

Considering that bullying and cyberbullying are forms of violence inflicted on children by other children, together with the health factors related to the social and psychological development of the younger generation, a purely legal approach of holding children, as defendants, either liable in civil actions or culpable in criminal prosecutions may not be the best solution.

The Alternative Co-Regulation Model

This chapter therefore advocates an alternative approach of co-regulation based on children's rights. According to the UNCRC, which has been ratified by 140 states, including China and Hong Kong, states have a duty to prevent violence and harm being inflicted on

[40] Proposed Amendment to Article 8 of the Education Fundamental Law by the Executive Yuan to Legislative Yuan, Taiwan, Bill No. 1263, 26 May 2011 at http://lis.ly.gov.tw/lgcgi/lgmeetimage?cfc8cfc8cec8c8cdc5cbceccd2cbceca (in Chinese).

[41] Parliamentary Library Legislative Yuan, Taiwan, Legislative Process of the Proposed Amendment to Article 8 of the Education Fundamental Law, 10 June 2011 at http://lis.ly.gov.tw/lgcgi/dispg?@351:1724997181:ttsweb:2:dispg@@1596558875 (in Chinese).

[42] Ministry of Education, Essential Points on the Implementation of Protecting School Safety, 23 February 2011, Taijun (2), 1000018469 C at http://140.111.1.88/rule/detail/12 (in Chinese).

children.[43] It is important to note that this international human rights approach based on a children's rights perspective is no longer grounded on a traditional vertical relationship between the state and individuals with largely negative obligations incumbent on the state to refrain from human rights violations such as torture or degrading treatment (Wouter Vandenhole, 2010). Rather, it is based on a horizontal relationship with obligations on the state to enforce rights between individuals and to offer adequate protection to them. This would require the state to implement protective and preventive measures against cyberbullying for the welfare and best interests of children regardless of who the perpetrators are and how many. As we discussed in the introductory section, the children's rights based approach differs from the traditional form of legal intervention and calls for a proactive response from the states. Under this approach, as advocated in the Stockholm Call for Action, national strategies should include a reporting system that is accessible to the children themselves and a mandatory action plan in each school to prevent and to handle bullying and cyberbullying (Stockholm Call for Action, 2009, para. 32 and 33).

Here, I would further advocate a similar mandatory action plan for reporting, handling, and preventing cyberbullying being imposed on ISPs under a co-regulation governance regime. Indeed, the existence of a children's rights based approach necessarily entails a co-regulatory model of governance simply because such an approach requires the various parties to share responsibility for the care of our future generation. Another reason for co-regulation is that the law struggles to keep pace with technological advances, and the problem of cyberbullying is no exception. To tackle the problem of cyberbullying effectively, co-operation from ISPs and telecommunications industry is essential. In addition, as mentioned earlier, there are multiple stakeholders involved, and it is in the nature of cyberbullying to be often anonymous with multiple aggressors involved. Therefore, a co-regulation model offers a workable solution with key building blocks, such as parental control tools, awareness action, a reporting system, a code of conduct on the part of the industry, and cooperation across borders Lievens, 2010, p.105). The stakeholders involved should include children, parents, non-governmental organizations (NGOs), the government, and the industry. The closest model that we have so far is the European Commission's Safer Internet Programme, which was launched in 1999, with 30 countries participating, and with three major aims: to promote the safer use of the Internet and other communication technologies, particularly by children and young people; to educate users, particularly children, parents, carers, teachers, and educators, in this regard; and to fight against illegal content and harmful conduct online (Europe's Information Society, 1999). This Programme includes an education campaign to raise awareness, to involve parents, to conduct a study on the issue of cyberbullying, and to involve ISPs as one of the main key actors (Europe's Information Society, 2009a). During 2010, 20 major social networks companies joined this program, including Bebop (America Online), Facebook, MySpace, and Google/YouTube (Europe's Information Society, 2009b). While this model has provided a significant reference for governance, the present European Commission's framework is not a co-regulatory model because it is wholly dependent on the voluntary participation of the industry and has no monitoring mechanism or sanctioning

[43] Article 19 of the UNCRC stipulates that States Parties shall take all appropriate legislative, administrative, social and educational measures to protect the child from all forms of violence. By October 2010, 140 out of 193 states had ratified the treaty. United Nations Treaty Collection at http://treaties.un.org/Pages/ViewDetails.aspx?src=TREATY&mtdsg_no=IV-11&chapter=4&lang=en.

power. The shortcoming of this model will be evident in our later discussion on the role of ISPs.

Role of Schools

It is not difficult to understand the role of schools in the co-regulatory model. In fact, the participation of schools in tackling the problem of cyberbullying is indispensable because most bullying takes place in schools, and so cyberbullying and bullying often go together hand in hand. Many of the victims of cyberbullying and bullying in schools find it a form of unbearable pressure and are forced to withdraw from their studies. As a result, a child's right to education, which is guaranteed under articles 28 and 29 of the UNCRC, is indirectly compromised.

While it is important to have anti-bullying policies in schools, this may not be an adequate remedy if the scope of the policies is based on a strict division between on-campus and off-campus activities being contingent upon whether school resources (e.g., school computers, web-based system) have been employed. This deficiency is illustrated in the situation in the United States. Critics have pointed out that victims of cyberbullying have to face the huge obstacle of proving that online bullying has caused substantial and material interference or disruption to their learning at school. Short of satisfying this legal standard, First Amendment free speech rights will prevail in most situations. Yet, it is not clear whether the learning of the whole class has to be adversely affected in order to satisfy the "substantial and material interference" to learning test or whether it is adequate to prove that the learning of one or two children has been substantially and materially disrupted (Servance, 2003). On top of this, although 44 states in the United States require schools to have an anti-bullying policy, many have not defined the meaning of bullying or even alluded to cyberbullying For instance, Arizona, Michigan, and Mississippi only mention the concept of bullying, not cyberbullying(Hinduja and Patchin, 2011, p. 7).

In comparison, the United Kingdom has provided an alternative, although the effectiveness of this alternative is hard to predict or judge as it is still in its experimental stage. As far as we can tell, consistent with the children's rights approach, in 2004, the United Kingdom Government formulated the *Every Child Matters* policy. The aim of this policy is for every child and young person aged from 0-19 years to achieve the following: be healthy; stay safe; enjoy and achieve; make a positive contribution; and achieve economic well-being (The Department for Children, Schools and Families, UK, 2004). Schools in the United Kingdom have a statutory responsibility to ensure that they have in place an anti-bullying policy and behavior management practices that satisfy current UK legislation on children's rights. For instance, s.89(1) of the Education and Inspections Act of 2006 requires all schools to have anti-bullying measures and empowers schools to have their jurisdiction extended to related off-campus activities under s.89(1) and s.89(5).[44] Likewise, the School Standards and Framework Act requires head teachers to have measures in place to prevent all forms of bullying among pupils under s.61(4).[45] In addition to its statutory duties, the UK government's guidance of 2007 requires schools to adopt a comprehensive anti-bullying

[44] Education and Inspections Act of 2006, Ch. 40 (UK).
[45] School Standards and Framework Act of 1998, Ch. 31 (UK).

policy that includes staff training as well as disciplinary sanctions against students who bully (Department for Children, Schools and Families, 2007). Moreover, the school curriculum is required to cover the issues of Internet safety and the handling of cyberbullying. The new primary curriculum came into force in September 2011, while the secondary curriculum in England has, in fact, included these aspects since 2008 (Byron, 2010). In other words, the United Kingdom has adopted a combined approach of empowerment (awareness-raising, protection, and prevention) and punishment as part of the education of all children.

The United Kingdom's experience will provide invaluable lessons for designing anti-bullying schemes in Taiwan and Hong Kong, and it will also act as a future reference for Mainland China.

The Role of Internet Service Providers

While legal duties have been imposed directly on schools, with teachers and school principals willingly embracing the measures described above, the telecommunications industry has so far been exempt from direct legal intervention regarding their role in combating cyberbullying. One may also question the basis and justification for imposing such a responsibility on ISPs because, after all, they are neither educators nor child carers. Attempts have been made to hold the ISPs accountable as they are usually more resourceful than individual perpetrators and are more effective at removing, blocking, and filtering materials. Lichtman and Posner have also argued convincingly that ISPs should be held responsible for the malicious acts of their users based on the common law doctrine of the indirect liability of those who are in a position to control the "bad actors" or to mitigate the harm generated by them (Licthman and Posner, 2006). Also, the ISPs are indirectly deriving benefits from their users by attracting advertisers' sponsorship on their sites. The imposition of liabilities on third parties who are in a position to control and mitigate the harm done is actually consistent with the underlying principles of tort law.

In addition, private telecommunications companies have created a public space which plays a key role in contemporary youth culture. By July 2011, Facebook, the most popular social networking site, had reached 750 million registered members (Facebook, 2011). According to the International Telecommunications Union Report in 2010, 55% of Facebook users were aged between 13 and 17 (International Telecommunications Union, 2010). By October 2011, 13% of Facebook users in Hong Kong and Taiwan and 10% of Facebook users in the Mainland were aged between 13 and 17.[46]

Although Facebook is one of the members of Europe's Safe Internet Programme, the mechanism under this program is based on a voluntary and self-regulatory model. According to the evaluation report released in early 2010, it has been commented that the principles which the ISPs had signed have remained to be aspirational rather than legal. Despite the fact that major social networking sites have to make a self-declaration of their intentions to conform with the principles of self-regulation (Europe's Information Society, 2010), and 20 companies have pledged to introduce a "report misuse" button for their users and to alert local

[46] In October 2011, there were more than 3.8 million Facebook users in Hong Kong, nearly 11 million users in Taiwan, and 468, 000 users in Mainland China. Statistics were from Socialbakers Statistics at http://www.socialbakers.com/facebook-statistics/.

authorities to inappropriate contact from or conduct by another user, on closer inspection, this situation is far from ideal. For example, on Facebook, there is no report mechanism for wall posts and comments; the report mechanism is only available for photos, videos, and notes. After a user has reported an abuse, an administrator will look into the complaint, but the user will not be notified of any action taken (Lobe and Starksrud, 2010). It was reported in 2011 that only two of the social networking sites participating in the European Commission scheme had made minors' profiles private by default (Baker, 2011). This illustrates the shortcomings of a voluntary, self-regulatory model, and so if a co-regulatory model is to be effective, mandatory reporting and handling systems must be implemented by the ISPs and enforced by the regulators. Although legal regulations would not be able to spell out every regulation detail due to the ever-changing and flexible technological infrastructure, the industry cannot be given an entirely free hand because this, of course, would be unlikely to solve the problem of cyberbullying.

Regardless of whether or not the ISPs are able to implement a fully filtered mechanism after complaints have been made, their role in the control of cyberbullying is crucial, as witnessed in the aforementioned case of Zhang Shufan. On the other side of the globe, in 2010, the Italian Court convicted Google and handed a suspended sentence to the giant company for violating the Italian Privacy Code by failing to act promptly to a happy slapping complaint (Donadio, 2010). The incident occurred in 2006, when an autistic boy was beaten and insulted by four high school students. The attack was recorded using a mobile phone and then uploaded onto YouTube. The clip was available on YouTube for more than 2 months before Google took it down after receiving a formal police complaint.

At this point, one might question whether the duty imposed on the ISPs would be too onerous. Are we not asking them to be both censors and arbitrators? Bearing in mind the European model of the E-Commerce Directive, ISPs are exempt from liability when acting as mere conduits or just hosting or caching information from third parties unless they have actual knowledge of the unlawful information.[47] A children's rights based model is consistent with the existing legal regime for it only requires a minimum standard of compliance with a reporting mechanism, an effective action plan, a support mechanism for victims, and a notice and take-down system upon complaint. Lievens (2010) proposed a system of benchmarks with indicators on when ISP action is needed to remove material. Obvious illegal material or information would include child pornography (including doctored photos of a victim, or estranged boyfriends sending intimate photos of their girlfriends after their relationship has turned sour), the dissemination of sensitive personal information without consent, and video clips of happy slapping. In the light of the above, a framework with a number of clear indicators could also be designed for less clear cases (e.g. defamation or intimidation). In this way, the role of ISPs can be easily clarified.

CONCLUSION

With ever-changing technology and the explosive growth of mobile phone usage and social networking sites, we are living in a global culture of interconnectedness where it has

[47] Directive on Electronic Commerce, 2000/31/EC of June 2000 [2000] OJ L178/1, articles 12-15, available at http://eur-lex.europa.eu.

become the norm for the younger generation to hang out in the cyber world as a daily pastime. Yet, our fascination with interactive media and the cyber world should not blind us to the dark side of human nature and the abusive power of information communication technology. The increasing ability to connect with one another carries with it the equal menacing potential to disrupt and tear apart the life of another human being.

As we have seen in our discussion, the Internet is filled with tales of cyberbullying of various kinds, where victims are often at the mercy of an anonymous crowd regardless of time and space. This phenomenon is indeed worrying and alarming and makes the call for state intervention justifiable, but the aim of our search for a regulatory regime is not to ask for tougher penalties against the cyberbullies. Despite the fact that we are living in a cyber age, the phenomenon of bullying has a long history with complex roots, and it reflects a pervasive form of violence in our society (Rivers, Chesney and Coyne, 2011, p. 212). From this broader perspective, it makes it more urgent for us to look for a co-regulatory and integrated model that can address the problem. It is essential for the law to set mandatory legal standards for a compliance and regulatory regime for schools, industries, and other stakeholders. The Taiwan government has taken an important step in tackling the issue, asking all schools to shoulder the important responsibility of prevention, education, and punishment related to cyberbullying. If they do not implement such measures, schools would, in effect, be tacitly condoning bullying behavior. What is yet to be seen are efforts from ISPs. In particular, ISPs should develop a code of practice within a model of compliance; they should have a mechanism for reporting harmful material and for following up on such reports and a notice and take-down system for dealing with these materials.

The Internet is now more than 20 years old. Many of us might once have thought that cyber space would realize the utopian dream of the free flow of speech and ideas in a global communal village. Perhaps, it is time to instill a sense of civility in both the real and the cyber world.

REFERENCES

Bai, X., and Ji, S. (2008, July 4). Human flesh engine: An Internet lynching? *Xinhua News.* Available at: http://news.xinhuanet.com/english/2008-07/04/content_8491087.htm.

Baidu (2008, January 8). *Notice: Declaration on protecting Zhang Shufan.* http://tieba.baidu.com/f?kz=308107848.

Baker, J. (2011, June 21). Social networking self-regulation isn't working says EU. *PCWorld.* http://www.pcworld.com/article/230788/social_networking_selfregulation_isnt_working_says_eu.html.

Beijing Chaoyang District People's Court. (2008, December 18). *Wang Fei v. Zhang Leyi, Daqi.com and Tianya.com*, No. 10930. http://www.chinacourt.org:80/html/article/200812/18/336418.shtml.

Brenner, S.W., and Rehberg, M. (2009). Kiddie crime? The utility of criminal law in controlling cyberbullying. *First Amendment Law Review 8,* 1-85.

Byron, T. (2010). *Do we have safer children in a digital world? A review of progress since the 2008 Byron Review.* http://www.dcsf.gov.uk/byronreview/pdfs/do%20we%20have%20safer%20children%20in%20a%20digital%20world-WEB.pdf.

Carey, P, (2010). *Media Law.* Sweet and Maxwell.

Chaffin, S. (2008). *The new playground bullies of cyberspace: Online peer sexual harassment. Howard Law Journal 51,* 773.

Cheung, A.S.Y. (2012). Tackling cyber-bullying from a children's right's perspective. In M. Freeman (Ed.), *Law and Childhood Studies.* Oxford University Press.

Civil Code of the Republic of China (2011, May 26). http://law.moj.gov.tw/Eng/LawClass/LawContent.aspx?PCODE=B0000001.

Criminal Code of the Republic of China (2011, January 26). http://law.moj.gov.tw/LawClass/LawAll.aspx?PCode=C0000001.

Donadio, R. (2010, February 24). Larger threat is seen in Google case. *New York Times.* http://www.nytimes.com/2010/02/25/technology/companies/25google.html.

Education Bureau, Hong Kong Special Administrative Region. *Creating harmonious schools, zero tolerance to bullying.* http://peace2.edb.hkedcity.net/preface.htm.

European Commission Information Society. *Safer Internet programme: The main framework for European policy.* http://ec.europa.eu/information_society/activities/sip/policy/programme/index_en.htm.

Europe's Information Society. *Policy: Making the Internet safer for Europe's children.* http://ec.europa.eu/information_society/activities/sip/policy/index_en.htm#programme.

Europe's Information Society (2010, February 9). *Implementation of the safer social networking principles for the EU.*
http://ec.europa.eu/information_society/activities/social_networking/eu_action/implementation_princip/index_en.htm.

Europe's Information Society (2009, February 10). *Safer Internet Day 2009: Commission starts campaign against cyber-bullying.* http://europa.eu/rapid/pressReleasesAction.do?reference=MEMO/09/58.

Europe's Information Society (2009, February 10). *Social networking: Commission brokers agreement among major web companies.* http://ec.europa.eu/information_society/newsroom/cf/itemlongdetail.cfm?item_id=4672

Facebook. *Timeline.* http://www.facebook.com/press/info.php?timeline.

Fenwick, H., and Phillipson, G. (2006). *Media freedom under the human rights Act.* Oxford.

Fu, H.L., and Cullen, R. (1996). *Media Law in the PRC.* Asia Law and Practice Publishing.

Gradinger, P., Strohmeier, D., and Spiel, C. (2009). Traditional bullying and cyberbullying: Identification of risk groups for adjustment problems. *Journal of Psychology 217*(4), 205-213.

Halsbury's Laws of Hong Kong. (2003) Butterworth.

Hanley, J.A. (2010) *Cyberbullying – A global concern: Family online safety institute report.* http://www.fosi.org/downloads/resources/Cyberbullying.pdf.

Hinduja, S., and Patchin, J.W. (2009). *Bullying beyond the schoolyard: Preventing and responding to cyberbullying.* California: Thousand Oaks.

Hinduja, S., and Patchin, J.W. (2010). Bullying, cyberbullying, and suicide. 12(3) *Archives of Suicide Research 12*(3), 206. Retrieved from http://www.cyberbullying.us/cyberbullying_and_suicide_research_fact_sheet.pdf.

Hinduja, S., and Patchin, J.W. (2010). *Cyberbullying: Identification, prevention and response.* http://www.cyberbullying.us/Cyberbullying_Identification_Prevention_Response_Fact_Sheet.pdf.

Hinduja, S., and Patchin, J.W. *State cyberbullying law: A brief review of state cyberbullying laws and policies*. Cyberbullying Research Centre 1.

http://www.cyberbullying.us/Bullying_and_Cyberbullying_Laws_20110701.pdf.

HKSAR Police (Wanchai Branch). (2011). *News on crime prevention*. http://hkuspace.hku.hk/wchpol-schlink/anticrimeif7.html.

Hong Kong Government. (2011, July 8). *Personal data (privacy) Amendment Bill 2011*. http://legco.gov.hk/yr10-11/english/bills/b201107081.pdf.

Hong Kong SAR Court of Appeal (2001, June 20). *Criminal Appeal No. 83 of 2001, CACC 83/2001*. http://legalref.judiciary.gov.hk/lrs/common/ju/judgment.jsp.

Hou, L. (2011, March 27). President Ma expressed concerns, bullying against young girl, school principal apologized. *TVBS News*. http://www.tvbs.com.tw/NEWS/NEWS_LIST.asp?no=yehmin20110327121209.

Huang, Y.Y., and Chou, C. (2010). An analysis of multiple factors of cyberbullying among junior high school students in Taiwan. *Computers in Human Behavior 26,* 1581-1590.

International Telecommunications Union (2010, June 7). *Child online protection statistics framework and indicators*, (Draft). http://www.itu.int/council/groups/wg-cop/second-meeting-june-2010/COP_Stat_Framework_7%20June_2010.pdf.

Ivarsson, T., Broberg, A.G., Arvidsson, T., and Gillberg, C. (2005). Bullying in adolescence: psychiatric problems in victims and bullies as measured by the Youth Self Report (YSR) and the Depression Self-Rating Scale (DSRS). *Nordic Journal of Psychiatry 59,* 365-373.

Leishman, J. (2005, March). Cyber-bullying. *CBC News*. http://www.cbc.ca/news/background/bullying/cyber_bullying.html.

Li, Q. (2008). A cross-cultural comparison of adolescents' experience related to cyberbullying. *Educational Research 50,* 223-234.

Licthman, D., and Posner, E. (2006). Holding Internet service providers accountable. *Supreme Court Economic Review 14,* 221.

Lievens, E. (2010). *Protecting children in the digital era: The use of alternative regulatory instruments.* Leiden.

Livingston, S., and Haddon, L (2009). *EU kids online: Final report*. http://eprints.lse.ac.uk/24372/1/D6.5_EU-Kids-Online-Final-Report.pdf.

Lobe, B., and Starksrud, E. (2010, January). *Evaluation of the implementation of the safer social networking principles for the EU Part II: Testing of 20 providers of social networking services in Europe*. European Commission Safer Internet Programme. http://ec.europa.eu/information_society/activities/social_networking/docs/final_report/sec_part.pdf.

Ming Pao News. (2011, April 3). *Cyberbullying among Hong Kong students is more serious than Europe and the US.*

Ministry of Education of Taiwan. *If a student has committed acts of cyber-bullying, what is his potential legal responsibility?* 140.11.1.88/download.

Ministry of Justice, Republic of China. *Comparison table on the computer processed Personal Information Protection Act and the newly enacted Personal Information Protection Act.* http://www.moj.gov.tw/ct.asp?xItem=197182andctNode= 28156 andmp=001.

PRC Government. (2010, May 26). Personal Information Protection Act of the Republic of China. http://law.moj.gov.tw/Eng/LawClass/LawAll.aspx?PCode=I0050021.

Rivers, I., Chesney, T., and Coyne, I. (2011). Cyberbullying. In C. P. Monks and I. Coyne (Eds), *Bullying in Different Contexts*. Cambridge University Press.

Servance, R.L. (2003). Cyberbullying, cyber-harassment, and the conflict between schools and the first amendment. *Wisconsin Law Review,* 1213.

Shariff, S. (2009). *Confronting cyber-bullying.* New York.

Shariff, S., and Churchill, A.H. (2010). Appreciating complexity: Detangling the web of stakeholder influence and responsibility. In S. Shariff, and A.H. Churchill (Eds.), *Truths and Myths of Cyber-Bullying: International Perspectives on Stakeholder Responsibility and Children's Safety*. US Peter Lang Publishing.

Shariff, S., and Hoff, D.L. (2007). Cyber bullying: Clarifying legal boundaries for school supervision in cyberspace. *International Journal of Cyber Criminology 1,* 76.

SingTao News. (2010, July 3). *Survey revealed 30% of secondary school students had been cyberbullied*. http://hk.news.yahoo.com/article/100703/3/iz26.html.

SingTao News. (2010, August 24). *30% of senior primary school students had cyberbullied others*. http://hk.news.yahoo.com/article/100823/3/jumh.html.

Smith, P., Mahdavi, J., Carvalho, M., and Tippett, N. (2006, July). An investigation into cyberbullying, Its forms, awareness and impact, and the relationship between age and gender in cyberbullying: A Report to the Anti-Bullying Alliance. http://www.education.gov.uk/research/data/uploadfiles/RBX03-06.pdf.

Su, C., and Holt, T.J. (2010). Cyber bullying in Chinese web forums: An examination of nature and extent. *International Journal of Cyber Criminology 4,* 672-684.

Tebatso Future Baleseng (2007). *Promotion and protection of the rights of children.* Report of the Third Committee to the United Nations General Assembly, 66 Session, 3 December 2007 (A/62/435). http://www.ohchr.org/documents/press/a.62.435.pdf.

The Child Welfare League Foundation (2007). *A survey report on cyber-bullies in the Children schoolyards*. http://www.children.org.tw.

The Constitution of the People's Republic of China (1993). http://english.gov.cn/2005-08/05/content_20813.htm.

The Department for Children, Schools and Families. *Every child matters outcome framework.* http://www.dcsf.gov.uk/childrensplan/downloads/ECM%20outcomes%20framework.pdf.

The Department for Children, Schools and Families (2007, September 21). No hiding place for bullies – Ed Balls. *DFES News.* http://www.dcsf.gov.uk/pns/DisplayPN.cgi?pn_id=2007_0168.

The Stockholm Call for Action (2009). NGO statement to the EU member states at the meeting of the Permanent Intergovernmental Group. *L'Europe de L'Enfance.* http://www.tfal.org.mt/MediaCenter/PDFs/1_The%20Stockholm%20Call%20for%20Action.pdf.

Vandenhole, W. (2010, May 26). Cyber bullying from a children's rights perspective. *The Legal Aspects of Cyberbullying: Cost Action ISO0801 Workshop Abstract* 37. http://sites.google.com/site/costis0801/.

Wang, P., and Shi, Y. (2007, July 27). *Female graduate of Peking University alleged to have gone naked abroad was obliged to Interrupt her study and return to China to defend Her rights*. http://news.xinhua.com/edu/2007-07/24/content_6420749.htm.

Wang, Y. (2007, April 6). *Elite student from Peking University was falsely alleged to have gone naked to raise funds*. http://news.qq.com/a/20070406/001809.htm.

Wang, Z. (2009). *Tort Law.* Taipei:Wang Muhua fa xing.

WiredSafety (2011). *What is cyberbullying, exactly?* http://www.stopcyberbullying.org/what_is_cyberbullying_exactly.html.

Yang, X. (2008, January 8). What does this Egao incident show? *People's Daily*. http://paper.people.com.cn/rmrb/html/2008-01/11/content_38069275.htm.

Young, A.L. (2000). Fact, opinion, and the Human Rights Act 1998: Does English Law need to modify its definition of "Statements of Opinion" to ensure compliance with Article 10 of the European Convention on Human Rights?. *Oxford Journal of Legal Studies 20(1)*, 89.

(2000, June). Directive on electronic commerce, 2000/31/EC of June 2000 [2000] OJ L178/1, articles 12-15. http://eur-lex.europa.eu.

(2007, July 27). The pictures of The female graduate of Peking University "going naked" reoccur, but police refuse to investigate due to lack of sufficient evidence. http://news.xinhuanet.com/edu/2007-07/27/content_6438702.htm.

(2007, August 1). The heroine appears to be an AV model in the case where a female Peking University graduate studying abroad was alleged to have gone naked. http://news.xinhuanet.com/edu/2007-08/01/content_6458564.htm.

(2008, January 7). Xiao xue sheng: Wang ye hen huang hen bao li. *[Pupil: Web Pages Are Very Pornographic and Very Violent]*. http://epaper.xkb.com.cn/view.php?id=184695.

(2011, January 26). Criminal Law of the Republic of China. http://lis.ly.gov.tw/lgcgi/lglaw?@43:1804289383:f:NO%3DC704536*%20OR%20NO%3DC004536%20OR%20NO%3DC104536$$4$$$NO.

(2011, February 23). Ministry of Education, Essential Points on the Implementation of Protecting School Safety, 23 February 2011, Taijun (2), 1000018469 C. http://140.111.1.88/rule/detail/12.

(2011, May 26). Proposed amendment to Article 8 of the Education Fundamental Law by the Executive Yuan to Legislative Yuan, Taiwan, Bill No. 1263. http://lis.ly.gov.tw/lgcgi/lgmeetimage?cfc8cfc8cec8c8cdc5cbceccd2cbceca.

(2011, June 10). Parliamentary Library Legislative Yuan, Taiwan, Legislative Process of the Proposed Amendment to Article 8 of the Education Fundamental Law. http://lis.ly.gov.tw/lgcgi/dispg?@351:1724997181:ttsweb:2:dispg@@1596558875.

SECTION 3.
HEALTH AND SOCIAL SERVICES IN CHILD PROTECTION AND RELATED ISSUES

Section 3 focuses on the health and social services related to child protection in Mainland China and Hong Kong. In particular, details about the general child welfare and protection systems and policies are provided, and information about several specific programs or systems is presented.

In Chapter 8, the author reviews the child welfare and protection policies, educational and social services by focusing on the impact of traditional Chinese cultural background on the perspectives and behaviors of Chinese people. Relevant issues concerning child welfare and protection in Mainland China are also discussed in Chapter 9, where the authors put a special emphasis on how UNICEF supports the Chinese government to strengthen social welfare system for children and to move forward the establishment of an effective child protection system. Chapter 10, on the other hand, focuses primarily on the related systems in Hong Kong. The author reviews the progress and milestones in child protection in the past three decades, and later in the chapter suggests ten strategies to improve child protection in Hong Kong.

Chapter 11 and Chapter 12 describe more specific issues related to health and social services in child protection in Chinese societies. Chapter 11 leads us to the HIV/AIDS-related issues and their impact on children in Mainland China. It first examines the situations faced by children affected by the problem, then analyzes the needs of these children, and finally provides different suggestions for a more effective social support system for them.

More related to the health systems, Chapter 12 gives a picture of a hospital-based education program for the prevention of child accidental injury in Shanghai, China. Strategies used to organize as well as the ways to launch the program are discussed. At the end of the chapter, suggestions to for improving child protection in the country are also provided.

In: Child Protection in Chinese Societies
Editor: Ko Ling Chan
ISBN: 978-1-61942-879-9

Chapter 8

Policies and Social Services Related to Child Protection in Mainland China and Hong Kong

Ko Ling Chan
Department of Social Work and Social Administration
University of Hong Kong, Pokfulam, Hong Kong

Abstract

The policies and social services related to child welfare and child protection in Mainland China and Hong Kong are examined. The traditional Chinese cultural characteristics of filial piety and familism have a great influence on the perspectives and behaviors of the Chinese. The legal and social service delivery systems in Mainland China and Hong Kong are quite different. Hong Kong is relatively more mature in terms of the development of a child protection system, although there is still much room for improvement. The development of child protection services in Mainland China can use the experiences of Hong Kong as reference points, while the new initiative in Mainland China can, in turn, create a positive force to push Hong Kong to further improve its system.

Keywords: Social policy, Social services, Chinese Culture

Introduction

In this chapter, the policies and social services related to child welfare and child protection in Mainland China and Hong Kong are examined. The first section focuses on China. I first discuss the traditional Chinese cultural characteristics of filial piety and familism, which have a great influence on the perspectives and behaviors of the Chinese. I then review the laws and regulations in China, particularly those related to child welfare and child maltreatment, and the social welfare services in China, including nongovernmental organizations (NGOs) at the international, national, and provincial level. I also look at child abuse education, the specialized services available for promoting the prevention of child abuse and neglect, and the issues of child abandonment and child trafficking in China.

The second section of this chapter focuses on the legislative and social welfare areas in Hong Kong; these are compared to the corresponding areas in China. First, I examine the laws and policies that are implemented for the purpose of protecting the victims of child abuse and their family members. I also identify the various medical and social welfare services that have been developed for the same purpose. I then examine some important effects of child abuse education and child awareness projects on child care and child trafficking in society.

SITUATIONS IN CHINA

Background

Traditional Chinese Culture: Filial Piety

Chinese parents have very definitive views on the discipline and education of children, and these are mostly influenced by traditional Confucian beliefs. First, the ethic of *xiao (hsiao孝)*, or filial piety, prescribes that children should always obey the commands of their parents without question and should respect their parents at all times. The underlying principle of this ethic is that children are the property of their parents; thus, their parents can deal with them with little or no interference from others (Tang, 2002; Tang and Yan, 2004). The child is not so much an individual with an independent personality and human rights but a subordinate of a larger social unit, the family, and, in turn, a subordinate of the clan. Central to these requirements is the duty to fulfill one's filial obligations and to live up to parental expectations (O'Brian and Lau, 1995).

To develop their children's filiality, Chinese parents often adopt childrearing practices such as the inducement of physical and emotional closeness to foster a lifelong parent-child bond and the use of strict discipline to maintain parental authority and children's obedience (Tang, 2002). A child is the passive recipient of the teaching of the adults around him/her who has to show absolute obedience no matter how unreasonable the parents' demands or how harsh the treatment inflicted by them. Accordingly, the education of the young is a matter of strict discipline, which includes shaming children and physical punishment. As the Chinese proverb goes, "Filial sons are produced from the club" (O'Brian and Lau, 1995). In addition, Chinese parenting is characterized by other features consistent with the notion of psychological aggression, such as scolding, shaming behaviors, threats of abandonment, and derogatory comments. In Chinese culture, the use of shame or *chih* (耻) is commonly found in the socialization process used to control children's behavior. Chinese parents believe that "when punishment is not properly administered, the people do not know how to move hand and foot; to rule a family strictly should be the same as ruling a nation" (Lieh-Mak, Luk, and Chung, 1985). Thus, child maltreatment, including the use of physical abuse and psychological aggression, is generally considered acceptable among Chinese families.

Traditional Chinese Culture: Familism

Familism is another important cultural theme that has emerged from the literature. The importance of the family system outweighs individualism (Hong and Hong, 1991). There are rules and regulations governing interpersonal relations that leave little room for individuality. In the end, one's own self or *xiao wo* (small me,小我) should be regulated and sacrificed for the good of the *da wo* (big me,大我), such as family and society (Lau, 1996). Individual achievement or conduct is also linked to the gain or loss of family status (Stevenson and Lee, 1996). A poor performance is not only associated with a loss of prestige for the individual but also with a loss of family status. The belief that "if a child fails in school, the entire family is shamed" signifies that children's behaviors are highly relevant to the family's face or fame. This attitude from social networks and the community may create a great burden on parents and thus lead them to inflict corporal punishment on their children. In addition, the Chinese tend to refuse external interventions, including assistance, in affairs that they believe to be internal to the family, such as the parenting of children (Hong and Hong, 1991). Therefore, there is also a lot of pressure within Chinese families to protect the family from shame, and this leads to a reluctance on the part of the victims of child abuse, especially sexual abuse, and their family members to report the abuse or to support the victims (Tang, 2002).

Laws and Regulations

Based on the current status of the socioeconomic development of China, even though child welfare is still underdeveloped, the current laws of China have made provision for the prohibition of child maltreatment. In general, all policies and laws can be categorized into three levels: international, national, and provincial. Two of the major international documents related to children's rights that the Chinese government has signed and ratified are the United Nations Declaration of the Rights of the Child (hereinafter, "the Declaration") and the Convention on the Rights of the Child (hereinafter, "the Convention").

The Declaration, proclaimed by a General Assembly Resolution in 1959, was the basis of the Convention, which was adopted by the UN General Assembly 30 years later in 1989. It proclaimed that "everyone is entitled to all the rights and freedoms set forth therein, without distinction of any kind" and that "the child, by reason of his physical and mental immaturity, needs special safeguards and care, including appropriate legal protection, before as well as after birth" provided by parents and by specialized agencies and international organizations concerned with the welfare of children (United Nations, 1959). It contains 10 principles aimed at protecting the rights and serving the best interests of the child.

The Convention was the first legally binding international instrument aimed at providing special care and protection for children and achieving world recognition of children's human rights. It sets out these rights in 54 articles. The articles of the Convention can be grouped into four categories of rights (nondiscrimination; devotion to the best interests of the child; the right to life, survival, and development; and respect for the views of the child) and a set of guiding principles. The Convention spells out the basic human rights that children everywhere have: the right to (a) survival; (b) develop to the fullest; (c) protection from harmful influences, abuse, and exploitation; and (d) participate fully in family, cultural, and social life (United Nations, 1989).

By agreeing to undertake the obligations laid down in the Declaration and the Convention (by ratifying or acceding to them), national governments agree to "respect and ensure" the rights identified by the Convention. By ratifying the Convention, states parties are also obliged to "undertake all appropriate legislative, administrative and other measures for the implementation" in the light of the best interests of the child (United Nations, 1989)

On March 2, 1992, China ratified the Convention, thereby agreeing to commit itself to protect and ensure children's rights and to develop and undertake all actions and policies in the light of the best interests of the child. However, China has exploited one of the major weaknesses of the Convention in terms of compliance: reservations. A reservation is a "unilateral statement, however phrased or named, made by a State when signing, ratifying, accepting, approving or acceding to a treaty, that purports to exclude or to modify the legal effect of certain provisions of the treaty in their application to that State" (Schabas, 1997). For example, with respect to Article 6 of the Convention, which states that "every child has the inherent right to life and the State Party will insure to the maximum extent possible the survival and development of the child" (United Nations, 1989), China's reservation states that the Convention must be subordinate to China's family planning policy. The effect of China's reservation allows China to implement its one-child policy, which has resulted in sterilizations, forced abortions, and killing "out-of-plan" babies, without violating Article 6 (Fitzgibbon, 1998). Moreover, China's one-child policy, which punishes the out-of-plan child by disqualifying them from education, health care, day care and housing, breaches numerous enumerated rights in the Convention. For instance, Article 24 specifically states that "State Parties recognize the right of the child to the enjoyment of the highest attainable standard of health" and "State Parties shall strive to ensure that no child is deprived of his or her right of access to such health care services" (United Nations, 1989). By denying out-of-plan children access to the health care or family assistance that they would normally receive, China is clearly violating Article 24 of the Convention. The reservations illustrate that the substantive rights of the Convention will not be recognized unless the State has validated and implemented its articles with proper enforcement mechanisms (Fitzgibbon, 1998). The Chinese government should improve its efforts to comply with the Convention in order to provide better protection of the rights of the child in the country.

On the national level, the 2001-2010 National Program of Action for the Development of Children outlines the national action to be taken to further promote healthy and sustainable child development in China. In addition, the primary law governing child protection is the Law of the People's Republic of China (PRC) on the Protection of Minors, which was originally passed in 1991 and then revised in 2006. The newly revised Minors Protection Law was enacted on June 1, 2007. This law lists the responsibilities of families, schools, and the government with regard to the protection of children's rights and the judicial protection of these rights. In addition, the Protection of the Rights of Women and Children within the PRC Law, the Law on the Protection of Children, Article 49 of the Constitutional Law of the PRC, and Article 3 of the Marriage Law are important laws that state that child maltreatment is prohibited in China (Qiao and Chan, 2005). The Adoption Law of the PRC, the Memoranda on Help for Orphans, and the Foster Policy for Orphans and Disabled Children are ordinances that protect the rights of orphans and prohibit illegal adoption.

Furthermore, there are different regulations and policies at the provincial level that further promote the work and importance of child protection within the country. In general, Mainland China declares that it protects a wide range of children's rights through domestic legislation and by ratifying and joining relevant international conventions and treaties. However, the reality is still debatable; in particular, the enforcement of laws and policies remains a huge problem.

Social Welfare Services

International NGOs in Mainland China

UNICEF. UNICEF (www.unicef.org/china) works in partnership with the Chinese government to save children's lives and improve their chances of becoming productive members of society, primarily by supporting the provision of basic services such as health care and education. UNICEF has five priorities in relation to improving the daily lives of the children. The first priority is early childhood care, which UNICEF supports through a wide range of programs that ensure that children in their early childhood benefit from good health care and nutrition, clean water, decent sanitation and hygiene, and proper maternal care. The second is immunization: UNICEF purchases and provides vaccines in all developing countries, especially to prevent the spread of HIV/AIDS among children, which is UNICEF's fourth priority. The third priority is education, especially for girls who do not have a chance to study; by giving them equal access to education, UNICEF improves their chances of survival and development. Last but not least , UNICEF allocates roughly 10 per cent of its resources to protecting children from sexual exploitation, illegal child labor, and military service (UNICEF, n. d.)

Since there is a relative lack of NGOs in China, UNICEF works more closely with the Chinese government in carrying out its work for children. It makes suggestions to the government on policies that concern children. It also cooperates with other social service agencies, such as the China Association for Science and Technology (CAST), the Chinese National Committee for the Care of Children (CNCCC), and the China National Center for Children (CNCC), to provide child care services (UNICEF, n. d.).

Save the Children China Programme. Save the Children is the leading independent organization that inspires the way the world treats children. It aims to achieve immediate and lasting change for children in need around the world by improving their health, education, and economic opportunities. Its programs aimed at ensuring the well-being of children and transforming children's lives to break the cycle of poverty operate in more than 120 countries. In partnership with individuals, foundations, corporations, governments, and national and international agencies, Save the Children focuses on results and proven solutions in promoting the rights of every child (Save the Children, 2010).

The Save the Children China Programme (www.savethechildren.org.cn) works in over 10 provinces, cities, and regions across China. The head office for the program is in Beijing, and there are program offices in Yunnan, Tibet, Xinjiang, Sichuan, and Shanghai. Since the earthquake in the southwest Sichuan province of China, Save the Children has been working over the past few years to provide for the protection, education, and health needs of children affected by the earthquake, especially those who have been living in temporary housing. Its lasting services help communities to rebuild through long-term recovery programs. It aims at resolving the immediate struggles that children face every day and replacing them with hope for the future (Save the Children, 2010).

SOS Children's International Village. SOS Children's International Village (www.soschina.org.cn) is an independent, nongovernmental international development organization that has been working to meet the needs and protect the interests and rights of children in more than 100 countries. The China SOS Children's International Village was first established in 1984 with the cooperation and support of the Chinese government. Since then, its villages have been established in nine districts—Tianjin, Nanchang, Chengdu, Kaifeng, Yantai, Qiqihar, Putian, Ürümqi, and Lhasa—to provide childcare services for children, especially children without parental care and families in difficult circumstances. There are also nine SOS youth facilities, 10 SOS kindergartens, one SOS Hermann Gmeiner school, two social centers, and three SOS vocational training centers in China providing education and accommodation for children without parents (SOS Children's Village International, 2009).

In each village, there are 12 to 18 families with 7 to 8 children in each family. SOS Children's Village focuses on family-based long-term care of children so that children can experience reliable relationships and love once again and thus recover from what they have experienced, which has often been traumatic. They grow up in a stable family environment and are supported individually until they become independent young adults. The aim of SOS Children's Village is to respect, promote, and stand up for children's rights and, at the same time, encourage children to actively take part in the decision-making processes that affect their lives and, if possible, to actually represent themselves (China SOS Children's Village, n. d.)

International China Concern. International China Concern (http://english.chinaconcern.org) was established in 1993. It is a Christian development organization that brings love, hope, and opportunity to China's abandoned and disabled children. Its main centers are located in Changsha and Hengyang, and these centers provide care for babies, children, and young adults who have been abandoned and/or have special needs. The belief of International China Concern is that every child is precious and has the right to be loved, to have hope for the future, and to have the opportunity to realize their dreams. It works in partnership with the Chinese government to develop social welfare for the abandoned and disabled which not only provides services and homes for life, but also empowers and trains Chinese nationals to save lives, support families, transform communities, and change attitudes (International China Concern, 2010).

Plan China. Plan China (http://plan-international.org.cn/) started working in China in 1995. The first projects began in Yanqing County northwest of Beijing; these projects helped to improve agriculture, health, school buildings and infrastructure, sanitation, and environmental protection. In 1999, Plan China established a partnership with the Shaanxi Women's Federation, a branch of the All China Women's Federation. Over the years, the programs have expanded to improve the lives of children and their communities throughout China. Their work has benefited children in 16 provinces and administrative regions in the areas of health, water and environmental sanitation, rights and protection, education, and livelihood.

National Level Government Departments

National Working Committee on Children and Women (NWCCW). The National Working Committee on Children and Women (NWCCW) is a coordinating organization that is responsible for giving advice to government departments on the prevention of domestic violence. It operates under the State Council, which consists of ministers from 33 ministries and commissions[1] (National Working Committee on Children and Women, 2008).

The NWCCW aims at coordinating and promoting various government departments' work on protection and development programs related to the rights and interests of children and women. It also provides guidance in relation to examining and monitoring the work of the working committees on children and women in various provinces, autonomous regions, and municipalities that are directly controlled by the Central Government (National Working Committee on Children and Women, 2008).

Social Welfare and Affairs Department. In China, a wide range of social welfare services for children and youths are provided by the Chinese government and by subsidized and nonsubsidized NGOs. The objectives of welfare services are to improve and promote family education, serve the best interests of children and youths, allocate resources for related research, and provide procedural guidelines for the implementation of social work. The Social Welfare and Affairs Department (SWAD) is a division of the government department responsible for drafting national social welfare policies and programs; mapping out protection policies for minorities, including the elderly, orphans, and the disabled; and managing the administration and distribution of charity work at the national level. With regard to the welfare of children, SWAD supports the provision of basic services such as health care and education, protects the rights of the orphans, and prevents the spread of HIV/AIDS among children. It aims to serve the best interests of children in China.

Other departments. Owing to the large area and population of China, unlike the social welfare services in Hong Kong, the Chinese government has established special departments or organizations focusing on different groups of minors: children and youths. With regard to children, the Women and Children Special Group of the Internal and Judicial Affairs Committee of the National People's Congress was set up to protect the legitimate rights of women and children. Organizations such as the Anti-Domestic Violence Network of the China Law Society, the Children and Family Department of the Women's Federation, the China Next Generation Caring Commission Expert Committee, the China Children and Teenagers' Fund, and the National Children and Teenagers' Supplies Association provide safe environments, child care, education, and supplies for children in China. The Chinese government has also established the China Center of Adoption Affairs, which specializes in nurturing children living in social welfare institutions and handling the work of intercountry and domestic child adoption.

Regarding the development of the youth of China, the China Juvenile Delinquency Research Society was set up to handle the issue of juvenile delinquency and also to develop associated strategies for coping with and preventing youth crime. Organizations such as the

---

[1] The ministries and commissions include: the Publicity Department of the Central Committee of the Communist Party of China, the State Development and Reform Commission, the Ministry of Foreign Affairs, the Ministry of Education, the Ministry of Science and Technology, the State Ethnic Affairs Commission, the Ministry of Public Security, the Ministry of Civil Affairs, the Ministry of Justice, the Ministry of Finance, the Ministry of Personnel, the Ministry of Labor and Social Security, the Ministry of Construction, the Ministry of Water Resources, the Ministry of Agriculture, the Ministry of Commerce, the Ministry of Culture, the Ministry of Health, the State Family Planning Commission, the State Bureau of Industry and Commerce, the State Bureau of Quality Supervision, the State Environmental Protection Administration, the State Administration of Radio, Film and Television, the State Press and Publication Administration, the State General Administration of Sport, the National Bureau of Statistics, the State Forestry Administration, the Legislative Affairs Office of the State Council, the China Federation of the Disabled, the All-China Federation of Trade Unions, the All-China Youth Federation, the All-China Women's Federation, and the China Association for Science and Technology.

Youth Special Group of the Internal and Judicial Affairs Committee of the National People's Congress and the All-China Youth Federation mainly work on the protection of the legitimate rights of youths. The aims of education and social services, including the China Youth Development Foundation, the Juvenile Out-of-School Education Subcommission of the Chinese Society of Education, and the Children Department of the China Communist Youth League Committee, are to advocate the spirit of national culture, provide youth protection and research services at the provincial level, and improve the quality of education in schools. By doing so, they aim to create a healthy environment for youth development, promote patriotic education, and improve the chances of youths becoming productive members of society.

It is not only children and youths who are protected. Disabled children are also served by associations such as the China Deaf Children Rehabilitation and Research Center, which is a center providing rehabilitation, medical treatment, and scientific research services as well as resources and administrative assistance. The multifarious needs of children and youths in China will be served through these different kinds of service agencies.

Provincial Level NGOs

Furthermore, there are different social services agencies and organizations at the provincial level; these have been established to facilitate child protection and to further promote the work and importance of child protection within the country.

Women and Children Activities Centers have been established in many provinces of China, such as Suzhou, Jinan, Jiangsu, and Fujian, to serve the best interests of the children and women in the assigned districts. The services provided by these centers include education, training, and activities in the areas of science, culture, arts, and sports. Education programs are also provided; the aim of these programs is to create happy and healthy families, communities, and schools for women and children. In addition, services for orphans are provided in many provinces through the Children's Welfare Homes organization. Its service centers can be found in cities such as Beijing and Tianjing. The Children's Welfare Homes organization has the most complete contact information about national child welfare services, orphanage agencies, donations, and activities.

Disabled children are also served by associations such as the Deaf Children's Rehabilitation Centers, which can be found in provinces such as Hubei, Guizhou, Zhejiang, Shanghai, and Jiangsu. A comprehensive rehabilitation package focused on education, research, and treatment for deaf children and their families is provided in these centers.

Education

Education in China is a state-run system of public education run by the Ministry of Education. However, for a country as huge as China, it is not an easy task to reform its education system. The importance of the school setting in relation to identifying incidents of child sexual abuse (CSA) has been documented in the literature. Education in schools can demystify CSA, which is still viewed as a taboo topic in many Chinese communities (Tang, 2002). It can also change attitudes by getting people to see that protecting children from abuse is a societal responsibility rather than a private domestic matter (Ma, Yau, Ng, and Tong, 2004). Research shows that abuse often begins at early puberty (i.e., when children are in primary school), but most children keep the abuse secret; thus, prevention programs that provide knowledge about abuse, sexuality, and self-protection skills should be targeted on these children through the concerted efforts of parents and schools (Rhind, Leung, and Choi, 1999; Tang, 2002).

Recently, primary and secondary schools have been involved in providing education agendas and prevention programs to students and their parents to increase their awareness of child abuse, particularly sexual abuse against children. There is very substantial support from parents for the introduction of school-based programs for young children to reduce the risk of sexual abuse (Chen, Dunne, and Han, 2007). Positive community attitudes toward education programs for the promotion of sexual health are also evident in China. Furthermore, researchers have also stressed the importance of targeting adults (Tang and Yan, 2004). Parents lack knowledge about the nature of CSA, with many saying they were unaware that boys can be sexually abused or that females can be perpetrators. The majority of parents appear not to believe that children are most often sexually molested by familiar people. Therefore, CSA education programs can be beneficial for parents, helping them to learn about CSA and, at the same time, helping them to identify CSA and intervene early in CSA situations and enabling them to educate their children on CSA prevention (Tang and Yan, 2004; Tsun and Lui-Tsang, 2005). Through school education on CSA, professionals, participating children, and parents can play an active role in the prevention of CSA.

Specialized Services at District Level

Child Abuse and Neglect Prevention in Xi'an. Xi'an is the capital of Shaanxi province and a subprovincial city in the People's Republic of China. As one of the oldest cities in China, with more than 3,100 years of history, Xi'an held an important position throughout the dynasties of Chinese history. After the economic revival of the interior of China especially in the central and northwest regions, Xi'an re-emerged as an important cultural, industrial, and educational center of the central-northwest region with facilities for research and development, government infrastructure, and welfare services.

To improve the living environment of children, especially in relation to child protection, the Xi'an Philanthropic Child Abuse Prevention and Treatment Center (CAPTC, *西安博爱儿童虐待预防救助中心*), sponsored by the International Society for the Prevention of Child Abuse and Neglect (ISPCAN) and the Shaanxi Friendship Hospital, was established in 2006. It is Mainland China's first ever nongovernmental institution to provide free medical treatment and counseling for abused children. The center has a team of pediatricians, nurses, and counselors drawn from local hospitals and recruits volunteers from China and abroad to help nurse the children or edit the center's publications. With funding and professional guidance from ISPCAN, it provides free diagnosis, medical treatment, counseling, and therapies to abused children and their family members. It also carries out field studies on child abuse and neglect and promotes child protection education and training for schools and teachers. Through its activities, it aims to prevent child abuse and neglect and to arouse public concern at the community level (Child Abuse Prevention and Treatment Centre, 2008).

In addition, the center also acts as a medium for the detection of child abuse. If domestic violence is suspected, the center's agents gather information from neighbors or relatives and take action. In some serious cases, the organization calls the police and someone else will be given custody of the child. Since opening in 2006, the center has treated more than 90 victims of physical, emotional, and sexual harassment (Child Abuse Prevention and Treatment Centre, 2008).

The Xi'an Prevention of Child Abuse and Neglect Association (*陕西省防止虐待与忽视儿童协会) is another organization working on the prevention of child abuse and neglect in Xi'an. It aims at protecting the welfare of children through assessments, counseling, therapies, and education.* It performs an investigatory role by conducting a general assessment and interview regarding the alleged abuse. If the victims of abuse and other forms of sexual violence present symptoms of psychopathology, they are provided with treatment services and counseling. Based on the information gathered during the assessment, a team of pediatricians, clinical psychologists, nurses, and counselors from local hospitals and volunteers recruited from China and abroad provide consultations on the management of victims. Psychotherapy or psychological intervention, which is based on psychological theories, clinical judgment, and research evidence, is carried out in various ways, such as family therapy, group psychotherapy, play therapy, cognitive-behavioral therapy, and psychoanalytic psychotherapy. The aims of the psychotherapy are to help victims change the framework of their perceptions, to alter their emotional responses, to ameliorate psychological symptoms, and to reduce psychological disturbances.

In addition, legal aid is also provided to victims of child abuse to help them to institute civil legal proceedings for an injunction order or to use other legal remedies. With the support of legal aid, the legitimate rights of children can be guaranteed. Furthermore, it also works with the Chinese government in child protection work. The Xi'an Prevention of Child Abuse and Neglect Association provides advice and suggestions on formulating child policies and regulations to create a healthy and safe environment for child development. It also participates and encourages international exchange programs on child abuse prevention between other social agencies within and outside states.

Many nongovernmental institutions also play an active role in the protection of children's interests. For example, Plan China and World Vision are international development NGOs working in China that specialize in child-focused integrated community development. They help poor children access their rights to health, education, livelihood, and protection, and their aim is to build a caring and safe society. Other organizations, such as Xi'an Children's Village, Xi'an Children's Welfare Institution, and Xi'an Help Center, look after orphans in the area. The Xi'an Children's Village is designated especially for orphans or children whose parents are criminals. These children are often discriminated against, isolated, or even abused by the public. By providing child care to these children, Xi'an Children's Village aims to respect, promote, and stand up for children's rights and, at the same time, to encourage children to actively take part in the decision-making processes that affect their lives and, if possible, to actually represent themselves.

Child Abandonment. China has undergone rapid changes over the last three decades, transforming itself from an isolated country into the world's second largest economy. While China is celebrating her roaring economy, her citizens are paying the costs of economic development. To alleviate social, economic, and environmental problems in China, the Chinese government implemented the one-child policy in 1979. This policy is controversial because of the subsequent negative economic and social impacts it has had on Chinese society. Restricting families to one child and the gender preference for male children have led to large numbers of female infants being abandoned, and it has been suggested that these are two of the reasons for the gender imbalance in Chinese society (Ren, 1995). In addition, the one-child policy also reinforces the gender-differentiated expectations for boys and girls and gender role behavior among parents (Liang, 2007).

Accordingly, China has promulgated the Adoption Law of the PRC, memoranda on help for orphans and fostering policy for orphans, and disabled children ordinances to protect the rights of orphans and to tackle the problem of illegal adoption. The state has taken over all welfare institutions, assuming full responsibility for financial and service provisions to orphaned and abandoned children in cities. The state allocates resources to local governments for the establishment of institutions to look after orphans and abandoned children. The main role of the state is to make regulations that protect the interests of vulnerable children throughout the adoption process and monitor the relevant institutions in each district.

With regard to local government, different campaigns have been carried out to provide social support and assistance to orphaned children. For example, in Chenzhou, there are three minimum living security (MLS) projects aimed at providing formal social assistance and basic living assistance to orphans in both urban and rural areas. The aims of these projects are to recognize the rights of orphans to a regular social life and to secure a basic living standard for them (Shang, 2008). Other local districts, such as Nanchang, encourage adoption, foster care, and the reunion of children with their birth parents by providing subsidies. These subsidies are designed to (1) give 1-year's relief supply of grain to a family who adopts one child from the orphanage; (2) provide 9 months of relief for households in poverty to help them look after their own children at home (thus preventing abandonment); (3) provide subsidies for 1 year to foster parents who look after weak babies at home; and (4) provide subsidies for 5 years to families who foster sick or disabled children from the orphanage (Shang and Wu, 2003a).

Other than these provisions, kinship foster care, which acts as a permanent care arrangement for orphaned children, is another important way of solving the issue of child abandonment (Shang, 2008; Shang and Wu, 2003b). Three forms of kinship foster care have been identified according to the blood relationship between the fostered children and their foster carers: paternal grandparents, aunts and uncles, and maternal grandparents (Shang, 2008). Kinship foster families not only provide children with care, but also with their basic living requirements and the costs of their education and health services, thus solving immediate problems such as starvation and homelessness (Shang, 2008).

NGOs, especially international NGOs, have also played important roles in the protection of orphans. NGOs such as the SOS Children's International Village China Center of Adoption Affairs and the Children's Welfare Homes specialize in providing services for orphans and managing the arrangement of adoptions. Their services include the provision of funds to complement those provided by the state and others for child welfare initiatives, the introduction of new management methods for foster care, and the facilitation of arrangements for potential international adoptive families (Shang and Wu, 2003a).

In China, where population control is a major problem and where sons enjoy preference over daughters, masses of abandoned and stigmatized female babies end up in state-run orphanages with harsh regimes. Through cooperation between the state, the extended families, and NGOs or other forces, these orphans can experience reliable relationships and love once again, meaning that they can recover from their often traumatic experiences. They can grow up in a supportive environment, in which protection and physical and emotional care are provided, until they become independent young adults.

Child Trafficking. There is a great demand for trafficked children as cheap labor or for sexual exploitation in China. China's one-child policy denies many out-of-plan children public education, thus forcing these children to engage in income-earning activities. It is estimated that children make up twenty per cent of China's workforce (Fitzgibbon, 1998). Without the government's assistance and subsidies, families with out-of-plan children, especially those in rural areas, face a heavy financial burden. In order to alleviate the burden of these families, most child victims are taken from poor rural western parts of China and trafficked to more affluent areas, such as the coastal provinces. However, children and their families are often unaware of the dangers of trafficking; instead, they believe that better employment and better lives lie in other countries (UNICEF, n. d.). Trafficking crimes always violate a child's right to grow up in a family environment. In addition, trafficked children face a range of dangers, such as violence and sexual abuse; they can even end up being arrested and detained as illegal aliens. As such, trafficking causes a series of social problems, thus seriously affecting social harmony and stability.

Other than domestic child trafficking, cross-border trafficking appears to be on the increase. If current trends continue, China could soon become Asia's trafficking hub. Some studies have indicated that the majority of all regional trafficking cases are China-related. Victims are trafficked into China from Vietnam, Myanmar, Mongolia, Russia, and Nepal and trafficked out of China to regions such as Thailand, Malaysia, Taiwan, Japan, Singapore, Hong Kong, and Macau (UNICEF, n. d.). More concerted efforts by the government and local communities and increasing social awareness in the country have led to a gradual decline in child trafficking.

The Chinese government has consistently paid attention to child trafficking prevention work. In recent years, China has promulgated and revised laws such as the Criminal Law of the PRC, the Law on the Protection of the Rights and Interests of Women of the PRC, the Labor Law of the PRC, the Law on the Protection of Minors of the PRC, the Law of the PRC on the Prevention of Juvenile Delinquency, the Marriage Law of the PRC, and the Adoption Law of the PRC (State Council of China, 2007). In accordance with related regulations and other international documents that the Chinese government has signed, China's National Plan of Action on Combating Trafficking in Women and Children (2008-2012) (hereinafter, the "Plan of Action") has been developed with the aim of preventing, prosecuting, and reducing trafficking and other such criminal activities that violate the legal rights and interests of children (State Council of China, 2007). In the Plan of Action, procedural guidelines and suggested actions on handling child trafficking are provided for each relevant department.

Led by the government, various cooperation mechanisms involving the participation of civil groups and relevant departments and agencies have been established to introduce practical methods of coping with child trafficking (State Council of China, 2007). Public security agencies have actively developed specialized campaigns to combat the criminal activities of child trafficking, and these campaigns have led to the successful rescue of a large number of trafficked children. Welfare services for the provision of assistance, recovery, and aftercare services for rescued children and the expansion of publicity and educational activities have also been carried out in related rehabilitation centers. A large number of pilot projects aimed at preventing child trafficking and assisting rescued children have been implemented in partnership with relevant international organization. For example, UNICEF has been working with the Chinese government to combat cross-border trafficking by piloting community-based prevention models and advocating for policy improvements to provide more efficient cooperation in law enforcement in relation to human trafficking crimes and the repatriation and reintegration of victims (UNICEF, n. d.). In summary, under the leadership of various levels of the government and through cooperation with various spheres of society and relevant agencies, child trafficking is expected to decline and vanish.

Situations in Hong Kong

Policies and Laws

Policy Address

The Policy Address is an annual document announced by the Chief Executive at the first meeting of each session of the Legislative Council, and it outlines the policy objectives of the government for the following year.

In recent times, the Hong Kong government has taken special measures and devoted resources to support families in need and to resolve family crises. These measures include providing more social service staff; enhancing cooperation among the police, the Social Welfare Department (SWD), and NGOs; improving the planning and coordination systems in the districts; and increasing publicity, education, and staff training (Tung, 2005). Counseling for domestic violence offenders and providing protection through the law for victims of domestic violence have also been proposed. Additional resources have been provided to strengthen district welfare planning and coordination in order to (a) utilize community capital to set up community support networks and (b) reach out to families that have not sought help so as to address their problems at an early stage (Tsang, 2006; Tung, 2005). Partnership between the government and the business community has been encouraged in order to create a family-friendly and community environment in the workplace. Assistance, such as child care services, is provided for working parents to enable them to achieve a better family-work balance so that they can improve the quality of their family life.

In addition, the establishment of a Family Council chaired by the Chief Secretary for Administration was announced in 2007. The Family Council has implemented policies and initiatives related to family support (Tsang, 2007). It has launched a Happy Family Campaign, which includes liaising with stakeholders to establish an interdisciplinary and interactive information and support network to promote family core values (Tsang, 2009). Furthermore, the Neighborhood Support Child Care Project started in 2009 has been a success. The government has proposed to extend the coverage of the project from the current 11 districts to all 18 districts in order to benefit more families in need. The Comprehensive Child Development Service, which enables the early identification of pregnant women, mothers, and children in need and their referral to suitable health or welfare service units for follow-up and support services, has also been extended to all 18 districts.

Legal Protection: Ordinances

Domestic violence is intolerable. The Hong Kong government endeavors to pursue the perpetrators of violence and bring them to justice. Various legislative provisions are in place to protect the welfare of children, and these set out the responsibilities of parents and carers.

Child abuse is a general term used to describe different abusive acts committed against children. Specific abusive acts are dealt with under a number of ordinances, such as the Crimes Ordinance (CAP 200) and the Offences Against the Person Ordinance (Cap 212).

The primary law that governs child protection is the Protection of Children and Juveniles Ordinance (CAP 213), and this law should be discharged by a police officer or a social worker authorized by the Director of Social Work whenever a situation warrants the protection of a child or juvenile who is in need of protection from assault, ill-treatment, neglect, sexual abuse, or harm. As far as sexual abuse is concerned, the Crimes Ordinance (CAP 200) and the Prevention of Child Pornography Ordinance (CAP 579) cover offenses such as incest, rape, abduction, trafficking, and child pornography. In addition, there is a list of ordinances and offences which can be referred to as and when necessary and appropriate.

The ordinances related to child protection and child abuse are as follows:

a) Evidence Ordinance, CAP 8.
b) Employment Ordinance, CAP 57 (Employment of Children Regulations, CAP 57B, Employment of Young Persons Regulations, CAP 57C).
c) Crimes Ordinance, CAP 200.
d) Offenses Against the Person Ordinance, CAP 212.
e) Protection of Children and Juveniles Ordinance, CAP 213.
f) Criminal Procedure Ordinance, CAP 221.
g) Live Television Link and Video Recorded Evidence Rules, CAP 221J.
h) Education Ordinance, CAP 279.
i) Adoption Ordinance, CAP 290.
j) Child Abduction and Custody Ordinance, CAP 512.
k) Prevention of Child Pornography Ordinance, CAP 579.

Procedural Guide for Handling Child Abuse Cases

The Procedural Guide for Handling Child Abuse Cases (hereinafter, the "Procedural Code") was developed and revised to promote multidisciplinary cooperation to serve the best interests of the victims. Since suspected child abuse cases or victims may come to the attention of different organizations (e.g., schools, police, medical social services units, hospitals and clinics, and child centers), all parties concerned should maintain communication about the progress of individual cases in the interests of the welfare of the children and their families. The Procedural Guide acts as a reference for the concerned sectors on how to work together as a team to protect victims and provide welfare services to their families. The key concept of the Procedural Guide is that effective action is built on the multidisciplinary approach of working together and trusting each other and working for the welfare of children (Procedural Guide for Handling Child Abuse Cases, 2007).

Under the Procedural Guide, approximately 15 relevant government departments or organizations play a role in handing child abuse cases. A multidisciplinary case conference (MDCC) on child abuse is held after a case of child abuse has been referred by the concerned units to allow the departments and organizations to work together in the handling and investigating of the case. The MDCC is an important mechanism for handling suspected child abuse cases as it provides a forum for professionals to share their professional knowledge, information, and concerns and, most importantly, to analyze risks and to recommend actions to be taken in formulating a welfare plan for the child and his/her family (Procedural Guide for Handling Child Abuse Cases, 2007).

In accordance with the Procedural Guide, child abuse is defined as any act of commission or omission that endangers or impairs the physical/psychological health and development of an individual under the age of 18. An "act" includes behaviors such as physical abuse, sexual abuse, neglect (physical neglect, medical neglect, educational neglect, and emotional neglect), and psychological abuse. If a child suspected of being abused comes to the attention of any concerned unit, each service unit should handle the report/referral seriously regardless of the source of referral, give paramount concern to the immediate safety of the child, assure the confidentiality of the victim's identity and personal data, and refer the suspected case to the appropriate unit as soon as possible if the current unit is not responsible for conducting the social investigation. The definition of child abuse and the principles in handing child abuse cases are provided to facilitate relevant professionals or personnel to safeguard the welfare of children being abused or at risk of abuse. The definition of child abuse is not a legal definition (Procedural Guide for Handling Child Abuse Cases, 2007).

Child Protection Registry (CPR)

The Child Protection Registry (CPR) is a computerized record system, administered by the Family and Child Welfare Branch of the SWD, for case registration and case-checking and facilitating statistical research (Social Welfare Department, 2005).

Police Force Intervention

The Hong Kong Police Force is one of the best-trained and most highly motivated and dedicated police forces in the world. It is devoted to ensuring the safety of Hong Kong citizens and the stability of the community. It handles and investigates all complaints or reports of child abuse and sexual violence cases.

The Child Protection Policy Unit (CPPU), which specializes in the formulation and implementation of policies and other matters pertaining to child abuse, domestic violence, sexual violence, and juvenile crimes, was formally established in October 1997 (Hong Kong Police Force, n.d.). It also provides support to regional child abuse investigation units (CAIUs) and other crime units investigating cases involving children. In order to improve the police service for victims and to cope with any changing patterns in child abuse cases, the CPPU monitors local and overseas trends in child abuse, sexual violence, and child pornography cases and coordinates with the SWD to provide training for suitable police officers on the basic skills of child protection special investigation and the video recording of interviews with vulnerable witnesses. The CPPU also works closely with individual government departments, NGOs, and other related agencies on multidisciplinary procedures, interagency cooperation, training, and coordination related to these areas (Hong Kong Police Force, n.d.). The CPPU maintains regular contact with overseas law enforcement agencies on new initiatives and practices in child protection, especially in relation to combating the commercial sexual exploitation of children. The experience gained in this field has been used to help the Hong Kong government draft legislation relating to the prevention of child pornography that will go before the Legislative Council in due course. In addition, police officers in the CPPU regularly attend meetings of Interpol's Specialist Group on Crimes Against Children, which is an international forum where law enforcement agencies and NGOs from many countries work together. The purpose of these meetings is to exchange information and experiences so as to facilitate cooperation between member countries and international NGOs in combating crimes against children (Hong Kong Police Force, n.d.).

In handling child abuse cases, the police officers of CAIUs and the social workers of the family and child protective services units (FCPSUs) of the SWD form a Child Protection Special Investigation Team (CPSIT) to conduct joint investigations into serious child abuse cases that fall within the charter of the CAIUs. Investigations of child abuse cases that fall outside the charter of the CAIUs are undertaken by police divisional/district crime units (Social Welfare Department, 2003). Due to the sensitivity of child abuse cases, a review of police procedures, as stipulated in Chapter 24 of the Procedures for Handling Child Abuse Cases - Revised 2007, has been launched to help officers to understand the problem and to provide a quality service for victims and their families.

To reduce the anxiety of child victims, video-recorded interviews with child victims are conducted in private in specially designed video interview suites. In cases of sexual abuse, police investigations are conducted in such a way that the victims are not further traumatized; the victims are not questioned or asked to describe the abuse incident(s) repeatedly (Procedural Guide for Handling Child Abuse Cases, 2007). Victims are furnished with a copy of the Victims of Crime Charter published by the Department of Justice and/or the Rights of Victims and Witnesses of Crime leaflet published by the police which explain the rights of victims in relation to the police investigation to ensure that they understand their rights (Hong Kong Police Force, n.d.). If child witnesses have to give evidence in court proceedings, they are provided with a Witness in Court leaflet for their information; if necessary, a live television link and support persons are arranged (Procedural Guide for Handling Child Abuse Cases, 2007). Serving the best interests of the child is the prime concern. Thus, victims in need of counseling or services are referred to the relevant SWD units and other NGOs (Hong Kong Police Force, n.d.).

Legal Aid Department (LAD)

Victims of child abuse or sexual violence may apply for legal aid at the Legal Aid Department (LAD) in order to institute civil legal proceedings. A victim of child abuse or sexual violence may institute civil legal proceedings for an injunction order, other legal remedies, and/or damages, where appropriate (Social Welfare Department, 2003). If an application for legal aid is approved, the LAD provides eligible applicants with legal representation by a solicitor or, if necessary, with a barrister in civil or criminal proceedings to provide advice (Legal Aid Department, 2005). The assigned solicitor or barrister will take appropriate action to protect the victim's legal rights. Eligible applicants have to satisfy the statutory criteria as to their financial eligibility and the merits for taking or defending legal proceedings (Legal Aid Department, 2005).

Medical Services

Clinical Psychological Services

The clinical psychologists of the five clinical psychology units of the SWD perform an investigatory role in child abuse cases by conducting a general assessment and an interview. Treatment services and counseling are provided to abusers and the victims of abuse and other sexual violence if they present symptoms of psychopathology. Based on the information gathered during the assessment, the clinical psychologists provide consultations on the management of victims and abusers to other professionals within the hospital and to social workers of the SWD (Procedural Guide for Handling Child Abuse Cases, 2007). If warranted, a treatment plan is formulated and psychotherapy is provided. Psychotherapy or psychological intervention, which is based on psychological theories, clinical judgment, and research evidence, is carried out in the form of family therapy, group psychotherapy, play therapy, cognitive-behavioral therapy, and psychoanalytic psychotherapy. The aims of the psychotherapy are to help victims change the framework of their perceptions, to alter their emotional responses, to ameliorate psychological symptoms, and to reduce psychological disturbances. When necessary, the clinical psychologists may make referrals to an FCPSU or a CAIU for further action (Social Welfare Department, 2005).

Medical Social Services

Child abuse and sexual violence cases may come to the notice of the medical social services units (MSSUs) in public hospitals and specialist out-patient clinics via hospital personnel, the police, or other organizations or through direct approaches by patients or their families.

In such circumstances, the medical social workers in the MSSUs conduct an initial social assessment during an interview; they then provide support services or counseling, implement a child protection plan, arrange referrals for rehabilitation, liaise with community services and so forth to help the victims of child abuse and sexual violence cases and their family members. When necessary, the medical social workers communicate with or refer cases to the appropriate SWD or NGO unit for follow-up services (Social Welfare Department, 2003).

Hospital Authority (HA)

Victims of family violence, sexual violence, or child abuse may approach a hospital/clinic in person or through a referral from various sources, such as the police, a social worker, and other organizations. With reference to the Procedural Guide, the Hospital Authority (HA) adopts the multidisciplinary guidelines and a multidisciplinary approach and collaborates with various organizations and agencies to provide holistic care to victims (Hospital Authority, 1990). There are two departments under the HA that specifically provide services to the victims of child abuse, namely the accident and emergency (AandE) and the pediatrics departments of hospitals.

Accident and Emergency (AandE) departments of hospitals. There are 16 public hospitals under the HA that provide AandE services. The mission of AandE departments is to provide a high standard of emergency care to those in the community who perceive the need for, or are in need of, acute care (Hospital Authority, 1990). They are the departments that victims of child abuse or sexual abuse, because of their obvious physical injuries, first come into contact with when they seek help.

For victims of sexual violence, AandE departments provide urgent medical services and assign a member of the nursing staff as the contact person for the case whenever possible. The member of the nursing staff assists with the arrangements for the medical examination or for the interview with the victim in a place that ensures privacy; he/she also coordinates arrangements within the hospital and interagency communication. Follow-up medical services are provided to victims by the designated clinics of the HA (Social Welfare Department,

2003). For victims of child abuse, AandE departments provide immediate medical examination and treatment. Victims are recommended for admittance to a pediatric department for comprehensive in-patient services such as a more detailed medical examination and continual care. An MCCA from the hospital takes care of the victims (Social Welfare Department, 2003).

Besides medical treatment, AandE departments introduce victims to the social services that are available to them so that they can receive social assistance as soon as possible. Victims with special needs may also be referred to clinical psychologists or psychiatrists for continual care (Social Welfare Department, 2003).

Pediatrics departments. Research has shown that children suspected of being abused are often brought to the pediatric departments of public hospitals during the initial management stage because of the accessibility of these departments and the comprehensive services, led by well-qualified specialists, that they provide (Lee, Li, and So, 2006). Therefore, these departments serve as temporary safe havens for suspected victims and provide early detection of abuse during medical examinations (Lee et al., 2006).

In hospitals, MCCAs work under the pediatrics department to handle child abuse cases. The MCCAs are consulted at the strategy planning stage to determine the need for a medical examination. A thorough pediatric health assessment, with special attention to the injuries and to factors that may determine any continuing risk, is carried out. To ensure that their physical, emotional, and developmental needs are understood, counseling, tangible services, and arrangements for hospitalization or referrals for rehabilitation, community services, and so forth are provided for suspected child victims of abuse (Social Welfare Department, 2005).

By working closely with medical social workers, nurses, clinical psychologists, psychiatrists, and other related personnel and using their expertise in child protection, the MCCAs coordinate and facilitate intra-agency and interagency communication and investigation and plan the further handling of the case in order to provide a healthier environment for the child. They have become the pivotal persons within their own institutions in terms of strengthening the clinical management of maltreated children (Lee et al., 2006).

Social Welfare Services

In Hong Kong, a wide range of social welfare services for victims of child abuse, spouse battering/intimate partner violence, and sexual violence are provided by the SWD and subsidized and nonsubsidized NGOs. The objectives of family and child welfare services are to preserve and strengthen the family as a unit, to develop caring interpersonal relationships, to enable individuals and family members to prevent personal and family problems and to deal with them when they arise, and to provide suitable services to meet needs that cannot be adequately met from within the family. (Social Welfare Department, 2005)

Family and Child Protective Services Units (FCPSUs)

FCPSUs are specialized units operated by the SWD to assist families with the problems of child abuse and spouse battering to restore normal functioning and to safeguard the interests of the children affected by custody/guardianship disputes and referred by the courts (Social Welfare Department, 2005).

There are 11 FCPSUs distributed over the different districts of Hong Kong. Any direct application or referral made by any organization to FCPSUs for services relating to child abuse cases is accepted. FCPSUs provide a coordinated package of one-stop services, including outreach, social investigation, crisis intervention, statutory protection, casework, and group work services, for victims of child abuse and spouse battering, batterers, and other vulnerable family members. The concept of the one-stop service aims to avoid the further trauma and stress that can be caused to the victim by having to repeatedly describe and relive the abusive experience. Thus, a multidisciplinary approach is adopted to encourage communication, joint investigation, and cooperation between different professional services (Chan and Lam, 2005).

Supportive services or referrals to various services (e.g., legal aid, school placement, residential placement, and clinical psychological services) can also be arranged whenever necessary. The FCPSUs also provide public education programs to raise public awareness of and promote action for the prevention of child abuse (Social Welfare Department, 2008).

Integrated Family Service Centres (IFSCs)/Integrated Services Centres (ISCs)

While FCPSU social workers take up child abuse cases known to the SWD, Integrated Family Service Centres (IFSCs)/Integrated Services Centres (ISCs) operated by the SWD and subvented by NGOs also deliver family services in Hong Kong (Social Welfare Department, 2003). There is an extensive network of 63 IFSCs across different districts of Hong Kong to meet the need of child victims and their family members. An IFSC/ISC aims to provide comprehensive, holistic, and one-stop services to help victims of child abuse in the community. An IFSC consists of a family resource unit, a family support unit, and a family counseling unit and provides a continuum of preventive, supportive, and remedial services that are child-centered, family-focused, and community-based (Social Welfare Department, 2005).

When IFSC/ISC social workers come across a suspected child abuse case, they conduct an initial social assessment during their enquiries in accordance with their governing principles and general procedures. The intake worker of an IFSC/ISC makes a preliminary assessment from the point of view of the child's welfare if a child is left unattended, neglected, or in any abuse or risk situation. For children left unattended at home or abandoned, IFSC/ISC workers provide an outreach service for initial assessment. If a new case of suspected child abuse is identified as requiring services after investigation, the IFSC/ISC workers will provide associated services such as family life education, therapeutic services especially for sexually abused child, an enquiry service, crisis intervention, and counseling for the victim and his/her families (Social Welfare Department, 2003). When necessary, they also arrange referrals to other services, including clinical psychological services, financial assistance, legal services, schooling arrangements, job placements, housing assistance (e.g., compassionate rehousing, conditional tenancy), and other community resources, in the place of residence of the child's parent/guardian with their consent (Procedural Guide for Handling Child Abuse Cases, 2007).

Family Crisis Support Centre (FCSC)

The Family Crisis Support Centre (FCSC) operated by Caritas-Hong Kong is a center that delivers services and support to families in risks. It aims to provide a time-out facility and a 24-hour integrated package of services to help people under extreme stress or facing a crisis, trauma, or sudden change to (a) remediate their distress; (b) seek a positive solution to family problems, such as domestic violence or child abuse; and (c) prevent future crises (Caritas Family Crisis Support Centre, 2002). Its services include a shelter for people in need, counseling, hotline services, voluntary services, therapeutic assessment, and community activities to meet the multifarious needs of individuals and their family members (Caritas Family Crisis Support Centre, 2002).

Multipurpose Crisis Intervention and Support Centre (CEASE Crisis Centre)

The CEASE Crisis Centre operated by the Tung Wah Group of Hospitals provides comprehensive support to victims, especially sexual violence victims, of individuals/families facing domestic violence or in crisis regardless of their age, ethnicity, or gender. Its services include counseling, a 24-hour hotline, an immediate outreach service, and a short-term accommodation service. It aims to help families seek a solution to the immediate danger and crisis and to coordinate with associated agencies or social services as soon as possible to prevent the deterioration of the problem. It also arranges referrals to other services, including clinical psychological services, legal services, housing assistance (e.g., compassionate rehousing, conditional tenancy), and other community resources.

In providing services for victims, the CEASE Crisis Centre follows five principles: Confidentiality, Empowerment, Advocacy, Self-determination and Safety, and Early Identification and Community Education. In handling abuse cases, the paramount concern is the welfare and safety of the victim. During the assessment/interview, the confidentiality of the information provided by the victim is guaranteed, and in order to avoid further traumatization, he/she is not asked to repeat details of the abuse experience. Social workers encourage the victim to seek help and increase his/her ability to handle the abuse. Yet, the rights of the victim, including the right to decide whether or not to report the abuse to the police or to investigate, are respected. Community activities and public education advocating the intolerance of violence and encouraging help-seeking actions are also carried out to raise public concern (Tung Wah Group of Hospitals CEASE Crisis Centre, 2007).

Child Care Services

The SWD provides practical assistance, such as child care services, to families and children affected by custody/guardianship disputes. The child care services deal with cases referred by the courts, the Department of Justice, and other concerned authorities in accordance with the relevant ordinances. The aims of these services are to support and strengthen the family and to enhance the physical, intellectual, language, social, and emotional development of children under the age of 3 years (Social Welfare Department, 2003). Different types of child care centers (such as child care centers, kindergarten-cum-child care centers, residential child care centers, occasional child care services, extended hours services, special child care centers, and mutual help child care centers) have been established to provide various services to meet the emotional needs and safety of children.

All child care centers are registered and monitored by the Joint Office for Preprimary Services of the Education Bureau and are operated by trained staff who are qualified and recognized by the SWD and the Education Bureau. The staff members in the centers have been trained to be alert to signs and symptoms of child abuse among the children under their care. Under the concept of a multidisciplinary approach, in a child abuse case, the supervisor or caseworker of the child care services center should attend an MDCC to formulate a welfare plan and to report on the child's behavior and emotional state in the center whenever necessary. When necessary, child care center staff consult with the social workers of the FCPSU or the responsible caseworker on how to handle the case and who should handle the case (Procedural Guide for Handling Child Abuse Cases, 2007).

Against Child Abuse (ACA)

Against Child Abuse (ACA) is a specialized NGO providing services solely in the area of child protection with a strong emphasis on advocacy. In the past 20 years, ACA has demonstrated the importance of four significant roles—child protection agent, counselor/therapist, educator/trainer, and child advocate—in creating a caring and nonviolent environment for the optimal growth and development of children. The objectives of ACA are (a) to strive for the removal of all forms of child abuse and/or child neglect in Hong Kong; (b) to establish, maintain, and support a professional service for the assistance of abused or neglected children and their parents; (c) to arouse the awareness of the general public in Hong Kong to the need to prevent child abuse; and (d) to take all appropriate lawful and necessary action to facilitate the attainment of quality child protection that is both remedial and preventive in nature. In applying these objectives, ACA gives equal treatment to all children regardless of race, ethnicity, gender, or age (Against Child Abuse, 1993).

The existing services of ACA include (a) hotline services which encourage the public to call and report suspected cases of child abuse/neglect so that social workers can investigate and provide professional assistance; (b) casework services—appointed social workers take appropriate action, such as counseling, home visits, and collateral interviews, in relation to the cases they handle; (c) group work services, including a wide range of educational, therapeutic, developmental, recreational, and networking activities which help abused children, abusive parents, and families to explore communication patterns and develop their strengths and potential; and (d) other services, including drop-in consultations, publicity, talks and seminars, volunteer services, and training programs for social work students and volunteers (Against Child Abuse, 1993).

The End Child Sexual Abuse Foundation (ECSAF)

The End Child Sexual Abuse Foundation (ECSAF) was founded in 1998 by Ms. Shao Fong Fong, an internationally renowned actress and a qualified clinical psychologist; its mission is to protect youngsters under 18 from sexual abuse (End Child Sexual Abuse Foundation, 2009).

ECSAF provides services such as a hotline for public enquiries. Social workers are available to provide information on CSA to the public, to offer callers an opportunity to vent their stress, and to give referrals to four psychologists offering counseling services to victims, abusers, and their families. ECSAF also provides workshops for parents and teachers and a library containing CSA-related literature. It commissions academic research/surveys on the incidences and causes of CSA in the local context to raise public awareness of the problem in Hong Kong (End Child Sexual Abuse Foundation, 2009).

ECSAF's sex education programs are implemented in local primary and secondary schools in Hong Kong; the focus of these programs is on developing proper attitudes toward sex and providing information and instruction on protection from sexual abuse through interactive activities. Its education outreach programs, which use a variety of multimedia equipment and games, provide interesting learning experiences for young children. In particular, two mobile classrooms tour local primary schools to deliver sexual abuse prevention programs (End Child Sexual Abuse Foundation, 2009).

Harmony House

Harmony House is a nonprofit NGO that aims to create a harmonious and stable community based on the sound family values of harmony, care, mutual respect, and responsibility. It provides a wide range of services, such as shelter and a crisis intervention team for victims, the Third Path Man Service for batterers, children and youth services, and community education and a resource center for the public (Harmony House, 2006).

Shelter for victims. Harmony House was perhaps the first organization to provide a shelter for the victims of wife battering and their children. It accepts both direct applications and referrals by social workers or other professionals for its shelter services. The shelter provides an immediate refuge and safe retreat for women and children. In the shelter, social workers protect and address the needs of children and help abused women to regain their dignity and establish a harmonious relationship. A one-stop integrated package of services, including individual and group counseling, educational and developmental activities, aftercare services, and collaboration and outreach services, are provided in the shelter, which aims at empowering abused women and their children (Harmony House, 2006).

Crisis intervention teams on family violence. Harmony House has set up crisis intervention teams on family violence in the AandE departments of public hospitals to render immediate crisis intervention and support to battered spouses. To meet the needs of the victims of family violence, the team provides services such as crisis risk assessment and intervention, supportive counseling, safety planning, referrals to community resources, and short-term follow-up services (Harmony House, 2006).

Third path man service. To effectively help CSA victims and families, the treatment of offenders is as important as the therapies and counseling provided to the victims (Ma, Yau, Ng, and Tong, 2004). The Third Path Man Service operated by Harmony House is a program designed to address the needs of male batterers. The services it provides include a hotline, individual counseling, a psycho-educational treatment group, an aftercare service, and professional training to counsel and give guidance to batterers in order to stop the cycle of violence and help families affected by domestic violence re-establish harmonious relationships (Harmony House, 2006).

Children and youth services. The children and youth services provided by Harmony House aim to offer an early identification and counseling service to children and youths affected by domestic violence and to educate the affected children and youths on how to establish harmonious interpersonal relationships through individual and therapeutic group counseling, the "Harmony Express" mobile classroom, outreach services, and resilience building programs. Community education and professional training are also provided for parents and schools to raise public awareness of the impact of domestic violence on children (Harmony House, 2006).

Community Education and Resource Center. In an attempt to raise public awareness and knowledge of family violence, Harmony House provides a community education and resource center for professionals, the general public, and schools. Through education and training, social workers and other professionals can, with the assistance of the general public, support victims and their family members in a community context which protects the abused and provides an environment that nurtures emotionally strong individuals who can contribute to society (Harmony House, 2006).

Education

Primary, secondary, and special care schools. Research has pointed out the importance of the school setting in relation to identifying incidents of CSA. Throughout their preteen and teenage years, children are very vulnerable to sexual abuse, and yet most children keep such abuse secret, not knowing what to do (Rhind, Leung, and Choi, 1999; Tang, 2002). Schools, the places where children spend most of their time, can act as a medium for the early detection, sensitive handling and reporting, and prevention of CSA.

Education in schools is important in promoting the sensitivity, awareness, and knowledge of the public and related professionals with regard to CSA; various sexually abusive behaviors should be discussed publicly to demystify CSA, which is still viewed as a taboo topic in many Chinese communities (Tang, 2002). Education programs can change attitudes and make people realize that protecting children from abuse is a societal responsibility rather than a private domestic matter (Ma et al., 2004). Continuous public education on CSA that addresses competency enhancement in sexually abusive situations can help children to develop appropriate values, attitudes, and knowledge related to respect for others and self-protective skills (Procedural Guide for Handling Child Abuse Cases, 2007; Tang and Lee, 1999). The efficacy of these education programs in effectively improving professionals' and participating children's knowledge of CSA and social and sexual skills has been documented in several research studies (Tang and Lee, 1999; Tsun and Lui-Tsang, 2005).

Schools are more than education centers for children; they also facilitate parents to serve as coworkers and partners of the school in the prevention of child abuse by educating them on child protection and building harmonious family relationships for the healthy development of children. Parents can identify and intervene early in CSA situations, and they can also educate their children about CSA prevention by participating in CSA prevention programs (Tang and Yan, 2004). Through the concerted efforts of parents and schools, the welfare of the children can be safeguarded.

Projects

Neighborhood Support Child Care Project (NSCCP). The Neighborhood Support Child Care Project (NSCCP) is a 3-year project, launched in 2008 on a pilot basis, which aims to provide needy parents with a more flexible child day care service as well as regular services for children under 6 and, at the same, to foster mutual help and care in the community. Its services include a home-based child care service that provides child care services for children under 6 in the carer's own residence or in a suitable place approved by the operator and a center-based care group that organizes interesting creative and social group activities for children aged 3 to 6 (Social Welfare Department, 2005).

In 2008, the NSCCP was launched in six districts (Tung Chung, Sham Shui Po, Kwai Chung, Tuen Mun, Yuen Long, and Kwun Tong) where the demand for child care services was high. In March 2009, it was extended to Wong Tai Sin/Sai Kung, Kowloon City/Yau Tsim Mong, Tai Po/North, Sha Tin, and Eastern/Wan Chai, thereby covering all of the 11 administrative districts of the SWD. At present, the NSCCP is run by 11 different service operators in their respective districts.

In the past few years, the NSCCP has successfully achieved the objectives of fostering mutual help in the neighborhood and providing flexible child care services. The Hong Kong government has therefore decided to extend the coverage of the project from the current 11 districts to all 18 districts in order to benefit more families in need (Tsang, 2010).

'Stop Sex Trafficking of Children and Young People' Campaign. Human trafficking is the third largest and the fastest growing criminal activity in the world. It is estimated that approximately 1.8 million children are exploited in the global commercial sex trade, although this figure could be an underestimate. Despite the alarming number of children exposed to this crime in the world, public awareness of the problem appears to be extremely low. In order to arouse public awareness and concern about this serious crime and abuse, ECPAT and The Body Shop formed a unique partnership to launch a 3-year global campaign called "Stop Sex Trafficking of Children and Young People" in August 2009 (The Body Shop, 2009). This campaign aims to arouse public concern about the issue and to raise funds for the victims. During the campaign, the proceeds from every Soft Hands Kind Heart Hand Cream sold in The Body Shop will be donated to ECPAT to fund work on preventing the trafficking and sexual exploitation of children and young people around the world. By 2012, the results of the campaign will be reported to the UN Human Rights Council and, in particular, to the relevant UN Special Rapporteurs in order to review the efficacy of this project (The Body Shop, 2009).

Conclusion

This chapter has provided a brief overview of the policies and social services related to child protection in Mainland China and Hong Kong. Although Hong Kong is a part of China, it has a very different legal and social welfare system for child protection. Hong Kong is relatively more mature in terms of the development of a child protection system, although there is still much room for improvement. The development of child protection services in Mainland China can use the experiences of Hong Kong as reference points, while the new initiative in Mainland China can, in turn, create a positive force to push Hong Kong to further improve its system. I believe that this mutual learning process will make the two systems develop their child protection services.

References

Against Child Abuse. (1993). *The agency.* Retrieved from http://www.aca.org.hk/menu/ef_menu.html?5.

Caritas Family Crisis Support Centre. (2002). *Services and aims.* Retrieved from http://fcsc.caritas.org.hk/.

Chan, Y. C., and Lam, G. L. T. (2005). Unraveling the rationale for a one-stop service under the family and child protection services units in Hong Kong. *International Social Work, 48*(4), 419-428.

Chen, J. Q., Dunne, M. P., and Han, P. (2007). Prevention of child sexual abuse in China: Knowledge, attitudes, and communication practices of parents of elementary school children. *Child Abuse and Neglect, 31,* 747-755.

Child Abuse Prevention and Treatment Centre. (2008). *The Xi'an Philanthropic Child Abuse Prevention and Treatment Centre - Introduction.* Retrieved from http://www.cnspcan.org/ABOUTUS/84.html.

China SOS Children's Village. (n. d.). *Introduction of China SOS Children's Village.* Retrieved from http://sos.mca.gov.cn/article/gjsos/.

End Child Sexual Abuse Foundation. (2009). *Our work: "Hugline" and counseling, workshops, education programs, library, research.* Retrieved from http://www.ecsaf.org/English/index.php.

Fitzgibbon, T. J. (1998). The United Nations Convention on the Rights of the Child: Are children really protected? A case study of China's implementation. *Loyola of Los Angeles International and Comparative Law Journal, 20,* 325-360.

Harmony House. (2006). *Our services.* Retrieved from http://www.harmonyhousehk.org/eng/serviceimage/service7_eng.htm.

Hong, G., and Hong, L. K. (1991). Comparative perspectives on child abuse and neglect: Chinese versus Hispanics and Whites. *Child Welfare, 70*(4), 463-475.

Hong Kong Hospital Authority. (1990). *Services guides.* Retrieved from http://www.ha.org.hk/visitor/ha_index.asp?Content_ID=0andLang=ENGandDimension=100andVer=HTML.

Hong Kong Police Force. (n.d.). *Child protection and domestic violence.* Retrieved from http://www.police.gov.hk/ppp_en/04_crime_matters/child/index.html.

International China Concern. (2010). *Love, hope and opportunity for every disabled child.* Retrieved from http://english.chinaconcern.org/.

Lau, S. (1996). Self-concept development: Is there a concept of self in Chinese culture? In S. Lau (Ed.), *Growing up the Chinese way: Chinese child and adolescent development* (pp. 357-374). Hong Kong: The Chinese University Press.

Lee, A. C. W., Li, C. H., and So, K. T. (2006). The impact of a management protocol on the outcomes of child abuse in hosptialized children in Hong Kong. *Child Abuse and Neglect, 30,* 909-917.

Legal Aid Department. (2005). *Legal aid schemes.* Retrieved from http://www.lad.gov.hk/english/home/home.htm.

Liang, Y. (2007). Parental expectations of only child boys and only child girls in urban China. *Dissertation Abstracts International, A: The Humanities and Social Sciences, 68*(2), 0479.

Lieh-Mak, F., Luk, S. L., and Chung, S. Y. (1985). Child abuse: A review. *Journal of the Hong Kong Psychology Association, 5,* 18-25.

Ma, E. Y., Yau, D. C., Ng, W., and Tong, S. (2004). Characteristics of child sexual abuse cases referred for psychological services in Hong Kong: A comparison between multiple incident versus single incident cases. *Journal of Child Sexual Abuse, 13*(2), 21-39.

National Working Committee on Children and Women. (2008). *Introduction of the NWCCW.* Retrieved from http://www.nwccw.gov.cn/html/35/category-catid-135.html.

O'Brian, C., and Lau, L. S. W. (1995). Defining child abuse in Hong Kong. *Child Abuse Review, 4,* 38-46.

Qiao, D. P., and Chan, Y. C. (2005). Child abuse in China: A yet-to-be-acknowledged 'social problem' in the Chinese Mainland. *Child and Family Social Work, 10,* 21-27.

Ren, X. S. (1995). Sex differences in infant and child mortality in three provinces in China. *Social Science and Medicine, 40*(9), 1259-1269.

Rhind, N., Leung, T., and Choi, F. (1999). Child sexual abuse in Hong Kong: Double victimization? *Child Abuse and Neglect, 23*(5), 511-517.

Save the Children. (2010). *Save the Children's presence in Asia.* Retrieved from http://www.savethechildren.org/site/c.8rKLIXMGIpI4E/b.6115947/k.8D6E/Official_Site.htm

Schabas, W. A. (1997). Reservations to the Convention on the Elimination of All Forms of Discrimination against Women and the Convention on the Rights of the Child. *William and Mary Journal of Women and the Law, 3,* 79-112.

Shang, X. (2008). The role of extended families in childcare and protection: The case of rural China. *International Journal of Social Welfare, 17,* 204-215.

Shang, X., and Wu, X. (2003a). The changing role of the state in child protection: The case of Nanchang. *Social Service Review, 77,* 523-540.

Shang, X., and Wu, X. (2003b). Protecting children under financial constraints: 'Foster mother villages' in Datong. *Journal of Social Policy, 32*(4), 549-570.

Social Welfare Department, The Government of Hong Kong SAR. (2003). *Services on victim support.* Retrieved from http://www.swd.gov.hk/vs/english/intro.html.

Social Welfare Department, The Government of Hong Kong SAR. (2005). *Family and child welfare: List of services.* Retrieved from http://www.swd.gov.hk/en/index/.

Social Welfare Department, The Government of Hong Kong SAR. (2007). *Procedural guide for handling child abuse cases.* Retrieved from http://www.swd.gov.hk/en/index/site_pubsvc/page_family/sub_fcwprocedure/id_childabuse1998/.

Social Welfare Department, The Government of Hong Kong SAR. (2008). *Family and child protective services unit.* Retrieved from http://www.swd.gov.hk/doc/fcw/FCPSUs.pdf.

SOS Children's Village International. (2009). *What we do.*

State Council of China. (2007). *China national plan of action on combating trafficking in women and children.*

Stevenson, H. W., and Lee, S.-y. (1996). *The academic achievement of Chinese students.* (1st ed.). Hong Kong: Oxford University Press (China) Ltd.

Tang, C. S. (2002). Childhood experience of sexual abuse among Hong Kong Chinese college students. *Child Abuse and Neglect, 26,* 23-37.

Tang, C. S., and Lee, Y. K. (1999). Knowledge on sexual abuse and self-protection skills: A study on female Chinese adolescents with mild mental retardation. *Child Abuse and Neglect, 23*(3), 269-279.

Tang, C. S., and Yan, E. C. (2004). Intention to participate in child sexual abuse prevention programs: A study of Chinese adults in Hong Kong. *Child Abuse and Neglect, 28,* 1187-1197.

The Body Shop. (2009). *Values and campaigns: Living our values.* Retrieved from http://www.thebodyshop.com.hk/en/vc_trafficking.aspx.

Tsang, D. Y. K. (2006). *Policy address.* Retrieved from http://www.policyaddress.gov.hk/06-07/eng/policy.html.

Tsang, D. Y. K. (2007). *Policy address.* Retrieved from http://www.policyaddress.gov.hk/07-08/eng/policy.html.

Tsang, D. Y. K. (2009). *Policy address*. Retrieved from http://www.policyaddress.gov.hk/08-09/eng/policy.html.

Tsang, D. Y. K. (2010). *Policy address*. Retrieved from http://www.policyaddress.gov.hk/10-11/eng/index.html.

Tsun, A. O., and Lui-Tsang, P. (2005). Violence against wives and children in Hong Kong. *Journal of Family and Economic Issues, 26*(4), 465-486.

Tung, C. H. (2005). *Policy address*. Retrieved from http://www.policyaddress.gov.hk/2005/eng/index.htm.

Tung Wah Group of Hospitals CEASE Crisis Centre. (2007). *Crisis intervention and support services*. Retrieved from http://ceasecrisis.tungwahcsd.org/intro.html.

UNICEF. (n. d.). *About UNICEF in China*. from http://www.unicef.org/china/.

United Nations. (1959). *Declaration of the Rights of the Child* [A-RES-1386 (XIV). 14 U.N. GAOR Supp. (No.16) 19, U.N. Doc. A/4354 C.F.R.]. Geneva, Switzerland: United Nations.

United Nations. (1989). *Convention on the Rights of the Child* [A/RES/44/25 C.F.R.]. Geneva, Switzerland: United Nations.

In: Child Protection in Chinese Societies
Editor: Ko Ling Chan
ISBN: 978-1-61942-879-9

Chapter 9

DEVELOPING A CHILD WELFARE AND CHILD PROTECTION SYSTEM IN CHINA: UNICEF SUPPORT TO THE GOVERNMENT OF CHINA

Lisa Ng Bow
UNICEF-China, Beijing, China

ABSTRACT

China faces many complex new challenges in light of the current trends of rapid economic growth, urbanization, massive domestic migration, dislocation and separation of family members, changing family structures, increasing cost of basic social services, rising disparities, and increasing frequency of natural disasters. In this current context, children and their families are increasingly exposed to new social welfare and child protection risks, with poverty acting as a contributing factor to the risk of child protection violations. As it has become more difficult for the Chinese government to manage these risks and vulnerabilities through vertical social protection programs, China is beginning to shift from an issues-based approach to social welfare and child protection toward a more comprehensive, multisectoral child welfare and child protection system as the most effective way to address new challenges. This new system comprises a social welfare system that provides (a) universal benefits to support social protection and services for all children and their families, and within this, (b) a child protection system that targets the most vulnerable children.

UNICEF is supporting the Chinese government to strengthen its social welfare system for children at three basic levels: (a) at the upstream and national level, supporting the development of child-sensitive national social protection, social assistance and child protection policies, laws, and frameworks; (b) at the intermediate or provincial level, developing strategies, mechanisms, and plans that facilitate the implementation of national child welfare and child protection laws and policies; and (c) at the community level, piloting and demonstrating effective, affordable, and sustainable intersectoral child welfare and child protection packages and models within diverse local settings for possible government replication (this component also feeds into policy development).

Within this social welfare framework, UNICEF is supporting China to move toward the establishment of a child protection system; this involves policy and legal reforms aimed at a strengthening a systems approach to child protection which is integrally linked with the social welfare and justice systems. Support is also being provided to demonstrate and develop community-based child protection service models that prevent and respond to violence, abuse, exploitation, and neglect.

Keywords: China, UNICEF, Child welfare, Child protection, Social work, Social welfare, Social protection, Children without caregivers, Orphans, Abandoned children, Children with disabilities, Children living in poverty, Street children, Children in conflict with the law, Trafficked children, Migrant children, Left-behind children

I. Current Social Economic Context and Trends in China: Implications for Children

Since initiating economic reforms in the late 1970s, China has achieved remarkable economic growth and advances in poverty reduction. Based on the international poverty line of US$1.25 a day, the proportion of China's population living in income poverty declined from 81.6% in 1981 to 10.4% in 2005 (Chen and Ravallion, 2008). Based on China's national poverty line of 1,196 RMB per capita, the country's rural poor population dropped dramatically from 250 million in 1978 to about 36 million in 2009 (Ministry of Foreign Affairs and UN-China, 2010). China's progress in terms of poverty alleviation and efforts to bolster social protection has, in turn, led to substantial improvements in the quality of life for the vast majority of the population.

These developments have also resulted in significant progress in relation to the survival, development, and protection of children. Between 1991 and 2009, the under-five mortality rate declined from 61 to 17 per 1,000 live births (MOH, 2009). From 1990 to 2005, the prevalence of underweight among children under five decreased from 19% to 7% (China Center for Disease Control, 2005). Nationally, the net enrolment rate for primary education reached 99.4% in 2009 (NBS, 2010), while the gross enrolment rate for junior secondary education rose from 67% in 1991 to 98.5% in 2008 (MOE, 2009).

Alongside these achievements, however, China faces many new challenges in the current development context. Despite the national economic boom that has occurred over the past three decades, the absolute number of people living in income poverty across the country - 135.4 million people - remains extremely high and poverty in many areas remains deeply entrenched. Given current trends, including continued rapid economic growth, increasing inequalities among regions and population groups, accelerated urbanization, massive internal migration, frequent dislocation and separation of family members, and the greater frequency of natural disasters, the Chinese government faces a complex set of new challenges.

In the context of these trends, children and their families, especially the poorest and most disadvantaged, are increasingly exposed to social welfare and child protection risks. Moreover, almost a fifth of the rural population remains highly vulnerable to falling into poverty due to income shocks, loss of employment, illness or accidents, natural disasters, and other adverse economic and social conditions (World Bank, 2009). As a result, it has become increasingly difficult to ensure that all children throughout the country in need of support, especially those most vulnerable to violence, abuse, exploitation and neglect, are able to benefit from the existing child welfare and child protection programs.

Increasing Burden of Health Care and Education Costs on Families

While China's economic reforms have lifted over 200 million people out of poverty, economic restructuring and the transition to a market economy have also generated some negative outcomes. With the dismantling of the commune system and publicly financed social welfare provisions and the subsequent marketization and introduction of user fees for social services, the affordability of and access to basic social services have declined substantially (World Bank, 2009). In addition, financial responsibilities for the provision of public social services have been decentralized from central level to lower administrative levels. This has meant that social services provision has become highly dependent on the fiscal capacity of local governments. Local fiscal capacity is, in turn, strongly correlated with the level of economic development of a particular province or administrative area. While mandated to provide social services to the local population, many poorer provinces, counties, and villages lack the resources to do so (Dollar, 2007). Moreover, field research has indicated that the general decline in public goods and services provision over the past few decades is not only a result of fiscal decentralization, but also of weak accountability frameworks and incentive structures at the village level that have led public officials to prioritize investment in economic growth over social public goods and services (Tsai, 2007).

Thus, families living below or near the poverty line continue to struggle to pay for the rising costs of health care services and education, and consequently, some are forced to limit or sometimes forego these services. A World Bank study estimated that between 1980 and 2004, out-of-pocket household expenditure on health care increased 40-fold (World Bank, 2006). A different study found that educational expenses for a year of primary school and a year of secondary school constituted 40% and 70%, respectively, of the official poverty line (World Bank, 2009). Respondents from yet another survey in 2006 indicated that the main causes for poverty were rising health expenditure, the cost of children's education, and insufficient agricultural income (China Development Research Foundation, 2007).

Central-level fiscal transfers provide a basic level of support to provincial and local governments, and total government expenditure on education and health has increased in recent years. Following the launch of health sector reforms in 2009, government health expenditure rose to 1.4% of GDP and health insurance coverage increased significantly (MOH, 2010). In 2009, total government expenditure on education was 3.6% of GDP (MOE, 2010). However, there are concerns that these new investments in health and education will not translate into reduced disparities at the subnational level. The overwhelming burden of financing social services falls on provincial and lower level governments, and the subnational administration of social services is prone to operational inefficiencies (Brixi et al., 2011). Tsai's (2007) findings on weak accountability and distorted incentive frameworks at village level also point to additional barriers to the equitable provision of public social services. This has resulted in negative outcomes and increased vulnerability for children and their families, especially in poor counties.

Massive Rural-to-Urban Migration

In 2009, an estimated 211 million migrants in China moved from mainly rural areas to cities (National Population and Family Planning Commission, 2010). Among this "floating population", there were approximately 27.25 million children who had migrated to the cities with their parents in 2008 (NBS, 2008). In addition, about 55 million children were left behind in rural areas by one or both migrating parents (Office of Migrant Workers and ACWF, 2008).

Under the household registration system in China, social benefits and access to services are tied to a person's urban or rural household registration or *hukou*.[1] Benefits allowed under rural social assistance and social protection programs are not portable across provincial and municipal borders. Migrants with a rural *hukou* living in urban areas are often only provided with temporary urban residence status, and therefore they do not enjoy the same rights, social services, and protection as registered urban populations. To access public services or social protection, migrants need to return to their place of official rural *hukou* residence, which clearly is not practical. As a result, in terms of access to public health care and public schools in the cities where they live, migrant children do not have the same rights as their urban counterparts. This has resulted in higher rates of mortality and morbidity (such as vaccine-preventable diseases) among migrant children, which in turn, may threaten the health of urban residents. Similarly, the parents of migrant children do not benefit equally from social services and social protection programs, such as unemployment insurance and a pension. This leaves migrant families extremely vulnerable and considerably disadvantaged.

For the children left in rural areas, the loss of direct parental care and protection can have long-term negative effects on their physical, educational, and psychological development and well-being. Substitute caregivers, often illiterate grandparents, frequently do not have up-to-date knowledge on parenting or child-rearing skills and are unable to adequately supervise the health, nutrition, education, care, and protection of these children (Duan, 2005).[2] Children left in rural areas by migrating parents also tend to spend an increasing amount of time on family agricultural work in order to fill the labor gap left by migrating parents; this leaves less time for school and other activities. While not all left-behind children are vulnerable, the lack of sufficient adult supervision raises serious child protection concerns. In recent years, there have been increasing reports of criminal networks and trafficking agents targeting both left-behind children and migrant children, whose parents are often unable to provide adequate supervision as they struggle to earn a living.

In addition, with the easing of restrictions on migration, large population movements, and more developed transportation routes, children in general are more exposed to the risk of trafficking as well as to HIV/AIDS. Young, poor, or socially isolated segments of the rural population, who often do not have adequate knowledge, life skills, or negotiating power to protect themselves, are also at a higher risk of exploitation and abuse, such as trafficking for child labor, sexual exploitation, illegal marriages, and various forms of violence.

---

[1] The government *hukou* system, introduced in 1958 to regulate urbanization, requires household members to register as legal residents with their local public security offices. In 1984, rural laborers were permitted to move to the cities to seek jobs, and this led to a massive migration to more economically developed urban areas.

[2] A UNICEF project baseline study showed that more than 50% of children left in rural areas grow up with a single parent and 47% are entrusted to the care of grandparents, other relatives, or, in some cases, their siblings. About 40% of all left-behind children below the age of 5 years live with their grandparents.

With the total migrant population anticipated to rise to 350 million by 2050 (NPFPC, 2010), a well-developed and comprehensive social welfare and child protection system that includes specific new elements for urban migrants is critical to ensuring universal and equitable access to social services, prevention services and protection for all children.

Demographic Shifts

The demographic profile of China is changing. Following the introduction of China's family planning policy in 1979 (known as the "One Child Policy") and changing social attitudes on family size, the total fertility rate declined from about 5 to 1.77 births per woman between 1970 and 2010 (UNFPA, 2010). With the declining number of births and an increasing life span in China, the country has an aging population. Without an adequate social security system, younger generations are faced with increasing pressure to financially support both their parents and grandparents in old age.

At the same time, within the Chinese context of declining total fertility rates, the increased availability of affordable sex-selection technology, and son preference, the number of boys born compared to girls has also risen. While the global demographic norm for the sex ratio at birth ranges between 103 and 107 male births to every 100 female births, China's sex ratio at birth increased from a relatively normal rate of 108.5 male births to every 100 female births in 1982 to 120.5 male births to every 100 female births in 2005 (NBS, 2005, 2007). There are currently 23.77 million more males than females under the age of 19 in China (Xinhua, 2011). By 2020, it is estimated that males of this age will outnumber their female counterparts by 30 to 40 million (The Economist, 2010).

This large sex imbalance has social implications. Experts suggest that the rising violence and crime rates in the past decade are associated with the increasing number of men unable to marry, and moreover, they anticipate that the overall level of crime and societal violence will be further exacerbated in the coming decades as those born under the family planning policies initiated in 1979 reach marrying age (Edlund et al., 2009). Sexual violence and exploitation in particular are anticipated to rise. A 2005 UNICEF-supported Peking University survey carried out in six provinces and municipalities found the existing prevalence rate of sexual violence to be almost 29% for girls before the age of 16 and 22% for boys (Peking University, 2005). The sex ratio imbalance is already presumed to be a contributing factor in the rising incidence of abductions and trafficking of young women and girls for forced early marriages, prostitution, and sexual exploitation (Waldmeir, 2011).

In the context of Chinese social norms and attitudes, lower total fertility rates have been accompanied by other social consequences. In China, there is tradition of son preference, and this has contributed to the increased trafficking in infant boys for illegal adoption. Lower fertility rates combined with negative social attitudes about children with disabilities and the lack of support services for families with disabled children are believed to be linked to the disproportionately high number of children with disabilities being abandoned in child welfare institutions (CWIs). In 2008, research undertaken with families and CWIs in major cities across China found that over 90% of children living in CWIs were children with disabilities (Shang et al., 2010).

Rising Inequalities

Finally, in the context of rapid growth, China has experienced rising income and human development disparities among different geographical regions of the country and population groups, especially between western, remote, or rural regions and urban areas and between migrating and resident populations. Infant and child mortality in western regions is almost 2.7 times higher than in eastern regions and 2.4 times higher in rural areas compared to urban areas (UNICEF, 2009). More dramatically, the highest provincial under-five mortality rate is eight times the lowest. There are lower rates of access to public health care and education among migrant children. Based on a 2004 survey, only 37% of migrant children received full vaccination coverage. A study on maternal mortality in Ningbo, Zhejiang Province found an estimated maternal mortality ratio of 128 per 100,000 live births for migrant women in these areas compared to 9.5 among women who were permanent residents (China Health Economics Institute, 2006).

The Gini coefficient (a measure of a country's income inequality) in China rose from 0.27 in 1984 to about 0.44 in 2006, reflecting the increasingly uneven development across the country (Chen et al., 2010). Higher Gini coefficients are often associated with increases in social instability. As China continues on its path of rapid economic growth, it will be important to develop a more comprehensive child welfare and social protection system to ensure that the needs of different population groups are met and their vulnerabilities effectively addressed. This will help guard against the further widening of disparities and support social stability.

II. UNICEF's Approach to a Comprehensive Child Welfare and Protection System

A. Supporting a Systems-Based Approach to Child Welfare

Globally, social welfare systems not only aim to reduce income poverty but also to address issues of risk, vulnerability, and social exclusion. The most effective social welfare policies are those that provide universal support as well as specific policies and support for the most vulnerable. Interventions targeting the risks associated with vulnerable groups, such as the poor, elderly, disabled persons, unemployed, children, and families, are therefore one way of achieving universal access to assistance and social protection. Thus, UNICEF's approach to child welfare and child protection in China and across the world has been to support government efforts to promote universal benefits and to strengthen integrated policies and services in order to prevent child protection problems and to respond to the specific needs of children and families who are at risk of significant harm. Significant harm refers to harm to a child causing a long-term or lifelong negative impact.

While low-income countries tend to focus on developing a minimum package of child welfare and protection services with supporting policies and capacities, middle-income countries often work on reforming existing social and legal systems, with attention focused on improving multisectoral coordination, social protection, the rule of law, and gender equality (UNICEF, 2008). As a middle-income country that is undergoing rapid economic development and that has already established social assistance and protection programs, China is well positioned to strengthen its national child welfare and child protection system. Indeed, China is keen to develop a child welfare system that corresponds to its level of economic development. In recent years, the Chinese government has taken the initial steps toward developing a comprehensive child welfare and child protection system, one which has begun to build universal benefits alongside targeted interventions for vulnerable groups.

B. Child Protection as Part of the Broader Social Welfare System

The child protection system is an essential part of the larger national social welfare system for children. While social welfare systems are different in every country and are best determined by the countries themselves according to local conditions, they often encompass a wide range of policies, including social assistance, social insurance, social services, livelihood and employment policy, and child protection and family support policies. In light of the complex development challenges faced by China, the government would greatly benefit from developing a comprehensive child protection system as part of the country's overall social welfare system.

C. Rationale for UNICEF's Systems-Based Approach to Child Protection

Globally, the aim of UNICEF's child protection work is to help develop a protective environment where girls and boys are free from violence, abuse, exploitation, and unnecessary separation from family. To promote this aim, UNICEF supports the development of laws, services, behaviors, and practices designed to minimize children's vulnerability, address known risk factors, and strengthen children's personal resilience (UNICEF, 2008).

UNICEF works closely with governments across the world to achieve this goal in accordance with international child rights frameworks, norms, and standards. Article 19 of the Convention on the Rights of the Child, which reflects government obligations in relation to child protection, states:

> "State parties shall take all appropriate legislative, administrative, social and educational measures to protect the child from all forms of physical or mental violence, injury or abuse, neglect and negligent treatment, maltreatment or exploitation, including sexual abuse, while in the care of parent(s), legal guardian(s) or any other person who has the care of the child" (United Nations, 1989).

Many countries tend to approach child protection through interventions addressing specific categories of children, such as street children, trafficked children, and orphaned children. In parallel, government agencies often carry out interventions focused on a single child protection issue without sufficient collaboration with other government sectors. This occurs for various reasons, including vertically organized institutional arrangements, donor or government resources directed toward one category of vulnerable children, and new initiatives emerging from sudden media attention on a specific issue. The resulting gap in terms of the coverage of child protection areas and the necessary linkages between them results in a less strategic and less efficient and effective use of resources for child protection (UNICEF, 2008).

Most children in need of protection have multiple vulnerabilities and face various risks at the same time or over a period of time; therefore, they cannot all be categorized within one vulnerable group or another. For example, unsupervised children left behind in poor rural areas by migrating parents are more vulnerable to trafficking and may be trafficked into child labor or sold for illegal adoption. A child physically abused by her family may run away from home and become a child living on the streets; under traditional single-issue interventions, authorities might return the street child to her abusive family without addressing the underlying issue of abuse in the family or facilitating the provision of essential services or support. Ultimately, the specific needs of the individual child, which are likely to be multifaceted, must be met. Responding to these needs and preventing a broad range of vulnerabilities, rather than providing narrow services associated with one category of abuse or exploitation, should be the focus of child protection services.

The prevention and response services needed by an abused child should involve cooperation between community workers spread across many different sectors, such as health care workers and teachers to report suspected cases of child abuse, community-based social workers to investigate cases and provide monitoring and case management, and support families to change abusive behaviors and identify alternative care as needed. Thus, fragmented child protection responses may respond to one issue, but in most child protection cases, coordination among many sectors is necessary to meet the multidimensional needs of the child in a sustainable, meaningful way.

The interlinked nature of child protection issues underscores the need for a comprehensive, integrated child protection system that addresses the different vulnerabilities of children. International experiences and lessons have shown that a systems-based approach to child protection in which laws, social services, behaviors, and practices work together to reduce children's vulnerability and risk factors is the most effective way to prevent and respond to the interrelated risk factors and vulnerabilities associated with violence, abuse, exploitation, and neglect.

D. Key Components of a Child Protection System (UNICEF EAPRO, 2009)

Worldwide, UNICEF defines a child protection system as a set of laws, policies, regulations, and services needed across all social sectors to support prevention and responses to protection-related risks and safeguard children against all forms of abuse, exploitation, violence, and neglect. The social sectors that have particularly important roles to play are social welfare, education, health, security, and justice. Child protection systems should be readily accessible, including during emergencies and conflicts.

An effective child protection system consists of three key components—a legal and regulatory system, a social welfare system, and a social behavior change component—which work together to reduce children's vulnerability.

The *legal and regulatory framework* provides the laws and policies that set out the legal basis for preventing and responding to child violence, abuse, exploitation, and neglect. Effective enforcement mechanisms also form a key part of this component, helping to ensure that laws and policies are followed and regulated. The justice sector is also essential in strengthening accountability and the rule of law and denying impunity for violations.

The *social welfare system* provides a range of family support and child protection services operationalized at community level that help to prevent and respond to violence, abuse, exploitation, and neglect involving children. This system encompasses prevention services that help to reduce social exclusion, risk, and vulnerability. It also provides identification, investigation, referral, and response services; family support services; recovery and reintegration services; and counseling and psychosocial support mechanisms. These services need to be readily accessible at the community level, sufficiently financed, and adequately staffed by qualified social workers.

The *social behavior change component* aims to promote attitudes, beliefs, values, and behaviors that support children's well-being and protection. This involves raising public awareness of the social and cultural behaviors, norms, and practices that can have a negative or positive impact on a child's development. This is commonly done through national and provincial public awareness campaigns, as well as through local community and family education services. Such services are critical to reinforcing good behavioral norms (e.g., positive parenting practices or zero tolerance of corporal punishment) within different settings (e.g., households, schools, institutions).

These three components also require meaningful interaction. Laws and policy frameworks delineate what is formally permitted by governments, which then guides and influences social behavior and norms. Conversely, prevailing cultural beliefs and social norms influence what is actually practiced at the local level and the extent to which child protection laws and policies are implemented. For example, if child abuse is widely tolerated as a socially acceptable practice, a law prohibiting child abuse may have limited effect and behavior change communication and advocacy may be needed to alter social and cultural attitudes in order to reduce child abuse.

Similarly, although child protection laws and policies may outline the framework for a child protection system and the social services to be provided, if services are not available to support implementation (e.g., due to the lack of well-trained social workers or a lack of funding for community-level services) or if the justice system does not respond effectively to enforce the law or guard against impunity, then child protection initiatives will be much less effective. By the same token, if social services are widely available but community uptake is low due to a lack of awareness of the services, to poor quality services, or to prevailing negative attitudes of service providers, then child protection interventions will not be successful, thus resulting in negative outcomes for children. Therefore, all three components are vital to an effective children protection system.

III. The Existing Child Welfare and Child Protection System in China

In China, as in many parts of the world, child welfare and protection were traditionally considered to be family matters to be addressed within the private domain. Thus, the Chinese government initially adopted a traditional issues-based approach to child welfare and child protection, focusing primarily on protecting and supporting children without parental care, especially street children, abandoned children, and orphans. As new developments and child protection challenges emerged, the government introduced various new social assistance schemes, and these schemes have had a positive impact on the lives of poor and vulnerable children.

However, the social and economic costs of inadequate child protection systems and the impact of violence against children and the abuse, exploitation, and neglect of children on both the children themselves and on society are gradually being recognized. These costs range from poor educational achievement and human capacity loss to rising public sector expenditures on medical treatment as a result of child injuries and increased criminality stemming from childhood violence and abuse. Thus, the protection of children is being increasingly understood as a government responsibility and a public policy issue.

The Chinese government is also starting to recognize the limitations of narrow social assistance schemes vertical government structures, and programs targeting specific categories of children in addressing child welfare and protection problems. It is therefore beginning to move toward a more integrated approach to addressing these issues. This approach includes supporting interventions to reduce poverty and providing basic social services on a more universal basis, as well as providing an increasingly multisectoral approach to preventing and responding to children at risk of significant harm from violence, abuse, exploitation, and neglect (Di Martino, Shi, and Chen, 2010).

The effectiveness and benefits of this comprehensive approach were evidenced in UNICEF-supported child welfare demonstration pilots for children affected by HIV/AIDS and children in need of special protection. Public social service provision in these pilots prioritized first and foremost children's access to basic essential services, such as health care, education, and social protection, as something that all children need. However, given their special vulnerability, children affected by HIV/AIDS and children in need of special protection also require access to specialized child protection services to prevent stigma, discrimination, violence, abuse, and exploitation.

The sections below discuss the current social welfare system and highlight the child protection components within it.

A. Social Welfare and Child Protection Policy Frameworks

In light of the development challenges described in Part I, China has accelerated its efforts in relation to poverty alleviation and social economic development and has been strengthening its social welfare and protection system, particularly over the past decade.

National Development and Social Welfare Policy Frameworks

Over the past 15 years, the Chinese government has adopted several major poverty reduction strategies and policies for rural areas that have significantly contributed to reducing the poverty risks for vulnerable populations. These measures have included China's Western Region Development Strategy (2000), area-based poverty programs (2001), and policies supporting farmers, such as the elimination of agricultural taxes in 2006 and the provision of agricultural subsidies and training for farmers in 2004 (World Bank, 2009).

In 2004, in response to rising inequalities and social tensions, China adopted the Resolution on Major Issues Regarding the Building of a Harmonious Socialist Society. This resolution called for more balanced, equitable growth; greater attention to social equity and justice; and increased emphasis on resolving social conflicts underpinned by improved public administration and social welfare services. The goal of developing a harmonious society (*he xie she hui)* continues to guide social economic policies and policy implementation in China today.

In 2011, the Government finalized its 12th National Five-Year Plan for Social and Economic Development (2011–2015). This plan, which outlines a shift in strategy from export-oriented economic growth toward domestic demand-driven growth, reflects a parallel need to increase the incomes of poor families and to strengthen social security and protection systems in order to encourage sustainable domestic consumption. China also issued its Ten-year Poverty Reduction Strategy (2011-2020) in 2011; this includes measures to strengthen child-sensitive investments and policies and reflects the key dimensions of the child poverty issue.

International Treaties Related to Children

China has ratified many international treaties and rights instruments to support the protection and promotion of the well-being of children in China. These instruments have presented China with guiding frameworks, international standards, and norms that have contributed to the development of domestic child welfare and protection policies, laws, and national plans of action.

As an early signatory to the 1989 United Nations Convention on the Rights of the Child (CRC), the Chinese government in 1992 pledged to meet its commitment to respect, promote, and fulfill the social, educational, economic, cultural, civil, and political rights of children. China also ratified the two optional protocols of the CRC—the Optional Protocol on the Involvement of Children in Armed Conflict in 2008 and the Optional Protocol on the Sale of Children, Child Prostitution and Child Pornography in 2002— and two other important treaties: the Convention on the Elimination of All Forms of Discrimination against Women in 1981 and the ILO Convention on the Worst Forms of Child Labor in 2002.

To strengthen antitrafficking measures across countries, China acceded to the UN Protocol to Prevent, Suppress and Punish Trafficking in Persons, Especially Women and Children (known as the Palermo Protocol) in 2010, ratified the Hague Convention on the Protection of Children and Cooperation in Respect of Intercountry Adoption in 2005, and signed two bilateral memorandums of understanding (MOUs), one with Myanmar (in 2009) and one with Vietnam (in 2010), to increase cooperation in preventing and responding to human trafficking. China is now in the process of discussing antitrafficking MOUs with other bordering countries.

National Child Welfare and Child Protection Policy Frameworks

China has developed several national plans of action (NPAs) to mobilize and coordinate the implementation of child welfare and protection measures across sectors. Foremost is China's National Plan of Action for Children's Development, which provides the main policy framework for implementing the CRC. In mid-2011, China formally released its new NPA for 2011-2020. Importantly, for the first time, the new NPA has child welfare as one of its five main pillars. This has set the stage for building a more comprehensive, systemic approach to child welfare work in the future, an approach aimed at developing more universal community-based, family-focused child welfare services. This NPA also identified child protection as another major pillar, highlighting the need to strengthen the protection of children at risk and to establish a community-based system to report, identify, and respond to violence against children (NPA for Children's Development, 2011).[3]

China is also in process of developing several key child-welfare-specific policy frameworks, including the 12th National Plan of Action for Child Welfare (2011-2015), the Child Welfare Act, and the Five-year National Plan on the Development of Social Work for Children.

The Law on the Protection of Minors is one of the main laws governing child protection in China. The Chinese government expanded protection for children under a 2006 revision of this law by further delineating the responsibilities of families, schools, and government in relation to child and judicial protection.

With regard to the child protection categories of trafficking, street children, and migrant children, China has been developing multisectoral frameworks to improve coordination. With regard to antitrafficking work, China is in the process of developing its second National Plan of Action on Combating Trafficking in Women and Children (2013-2017) to better coordinate national efforts. The first trafficking NPA (2008-2012) helped to improve antitrafficking coordination and security mechanisms, clarify the different responsibilities of relevant government departments, and establish longer term antitrafficking mechanisms focused on prevention, assistance, and rehabilitation. Related to this, the government also revised the national Penal Code, outlining harsher penalties for trafficking criminals.

To better protect children living on the street, the State Council released the Opinion on Strengthening the Protection and Assistance to Street Children in August 2011, which authorized the establishment of a national interministerial working mechanism to protect street children. This document underscored the need to strengthen prevention and reintegration measures, family support, and access to formal or nonformal education for street children. It also allows courts to remove the custodial rights of parents or legal guardians who allow their children to beg or steal on the streets.

With respect to children affected by migration, the State Council issued an opinion in 2006 which called on the government to reduce discrimination against migrant children and improve their right to education and to improve interministerial coordination to support left-behind children (State Council, 2006). Since then, a number of municipal governments have introduced policies to improve access to compulsory education for migrant children (Shang and Wang, 2011).

For children without parental care, China has developed several government policies on adoption and on family-like, kinship, and foster care for children without caregivers. These policies include the 1992 Adoption Law, guiding frameworks for domestic and international adoptions, and policies managing family-like foster care. Regulations establishing parameters for the institutional care of children without caregivers have also been issued; among other items, the basic requirements for food, care, rehabilitation services for children with disabilities, psychosocial support, education, and physical facilities were outlined (Shang and Wang, 2011).

These new child welfare and multisectoral child protection frameworks are significant in that they provide the broad policy frameworks and the initial basis for a systems approach.

---

[3] The children at risk and in need of protection include abandoned and orphaned children; street children; children affected by natural disasters, migration, and HIV/AIDS; and children whose parents are serving prison sentences.

However, the next set of challenges will include implementing these frameworks at provincial and lower level and departing from sectoral activities aggregated around traditional child protection issues toward more deeply integrated policies, and a continuum of services that benefits from active intersectoral engagement and a primary focus on prevention of risk and vulnerability.

B. Social Assistance Schemes, Social Insurance, Fee Waivers, and Services

In addition to laws and policy frameworks, China has introduced a wide range of social assistance schemes, social insurance, fee waivers, and child welfare and protection services for vulnerable groups. These measures have improved the social and economic security of families, providing a first line of protection for children. As a result, the child welfare and protection system has been strengthened. Other developments include substantial improvements in child nutrition, universal access to 9 years of compulsory education, and improved access to basic public health care services (UNICEF-China, 2010).

Social Assistance Schemes

The various social assistance schemes that have been adopted in China have helped to assist the poorest segments of the population to have the basic minimum living standards, and defend against further impoverishment. The *Tekun* scheme provides subsistence living assistance to extremely poor families living under the poverty line in rural areas. Recipients often have no means of supporting themselves due to illness, disability, injury, or disasters. Under the *Wubao* scheme (or five guarantees program), very poor households receive five basic items: food, clothing, housing, medical care, and funeral costs. This scheme, which is financed by local governments, serves three segments of the poor and vulnerable population—the elderly, people with disabilities, and children under 16—if they are unable to work, have no means of earning an income, and have no other form of support; this includes orphans and poor children with disabilities (Shang and Wang, 2011).

One of the most important and far reaching forms of social assistance is the *dibao* scheme. The urban *dibao* scheme (or minimum subsistence allowance program), with eligibility based on household per capita income, was set up in 1999 to support poor urban residents. A parallel rural *dibao* scheme was initiated in 2007, expanding this basic subsistence allowance nationally to rural residents. By the end of 2010, the *dibao* scheme was reported to have benefitted more than 75 million people: 23 million urban residents and over 52 million rural residents (Shang and Wang, 2011). This program, supported by local and central level funding, has helped to improve basic child nutrition and the uptake of health and education services by the poorest people in society.

The Medical Financial Assistance (MFA) scheme was initiated in rural areas in 2003 and in urban areas in 2005, and aims to offset the heavy financial burden of health care costs for poor households. This scheme, administered by the Ministry of Civil Affairs (MCA), provides support to cover health insurance premiums and copayments for impoverished households, as well as some out-of-pocket medical expenses for poor uninsured households. By 2007, the scheme had been established in all rural counties and 86% of cities; however, problems have been identified with regard to the targeting of beneficiaries (World Bank, 2009).

China, as a disaster-prone country, provides disaster relief assistance to affected populations, usually through a central fund providing cash transfers, food, clothing, reconstruction, and medical care. The Chinese government has increased disaster assistance in recent years, from 5.1 billion RMB in 2004 to 11.34 billion RMB in 2010 (MCA, 2009/2010). The scale of assistance varies with the severity of the disaster. After the devastating 2008 Wenchuan earthquake, for example, China provided almost 61 billion RMB to assist those affected, including a 600 RMB monthly subsidy for each child orphaned after the earthquake (World Bank, 2009).

China has also developed targeted social assistance programs for specific vulnerable groups, including children affected by HIV/AIDS and orphans. In 2003, China's introduced the "Four Frees and One Care" HIV/AIDS policy, which supports the provision of free prevention of mother-to-child transmission services and antiretroviral treatment as well as living support and education for children orphaned by AIDS. The pilot work of UNICEF and the MCA supported the implementation of this policy and produced four demonstration models of community-based care for children affected by AIDS. The care given since 2004 to orphans who have lost both parents was extended to all children affected by AIDS in 2009 following the issuance of China's 2009 Opinion on Enhanced Efforts in Welfare Protection for Children Affected by AIDS.

In October 2010, the State Council issued an important new policy in its Opinion on Strengthening Social Protection for Orphans, outlining government provisions to ensure a basic standard of living for orphans, as advocated through the joint MCA-UNICEF child welfare demonstration pilots. This policy states that all orphans should receive a monthly cash transfer: 1,000 RMB for orphans raised in institutional care and 600 RMB for orphans raised by kin or in foster care;[4] the latter is significant in that the government, for the first time, is providing a subsidy for care by kin and for foster care. The central government also allocated 2.5 billion RMB (about US$367 million) to provincial departments to support the implementation of this policy.

Social Insurance

Given the increasing vulnerability of families and children to poverty due to various shocks, China has introduced different social insurance schemes in rural and urban areas, and these have helped to improve social protection for families and the well-being of children.

Rural areas. The new Rural Cooperative Medical Scheme (RCMS), initially developed in the 1960s but then dismantled during the economic reform period, was relaunched in 2003. The RCMS is a major voluntary health insurance scheme for the rural population which is financed by central and local governments and individual contributions. The scheme aims to provide universal health insurance coverage in rural areas, and in 2009, it covered over 94% of the rural population (NBS, 2010). However, since the benefits mainly cover catastrophic illnesses and in-patient medical services and offer relatively low reimbursement rates, estimated at around 44% in 2008 (WHO, 2009), out-of-pocket costs remain prohibitively high, especially for the poor. Coverage and benefits are improving as funding of the scheme

[4] Central-level funds are allocated to Chinese provinces by region, with the eastern Chinese provinces receiving 180 RMB per month per child; central Chinese provinces 270 RMB per month per child; and Western Chinese provinces 360 RMB per month per child. While the total central-level contribution is significant, provincial- and county-level authorities still need to provide supplementary funding to meet the minimum living standard criteria outlined, and this poses difficulties for poorer counties.

grows, but many poor households continue to forego certain basic health services due to the high out-of-pocket costs. In addition, rural families who migrate to cities for work cannot benefit from the RCMS.

The Basic Rural Pension Scheme, which was introduced in the late 1990s, covers rural residents between 20 and 60 years of age and is funded by individual contributions with some government support. Pension benefits are provided after participants reach the age of 60. However, actual coverage under this pension scheme remains low, with only about 72.8 million rural residents qualifying for the basic pension in 2009, and no system exists to allow the portability of benefits for internal migrants (World Bank, 2009).

Urban areas. In urban areas, the Chinese government has strengthened social security by providing five types of protection under its Social Insurance Fund: basic medical insurance, unemployment insurance, work injury insurance, maternity insurance, and a pension.

China introduced basic medical insurance (BMI) in 1998 in order to provide health insurance coverage for urban workers in the formal sector. In 2009, this insurance scheme covered over 219 million workers and about 55 million retirees. Building on the BMI, the government introduced Urban Resident Basic Medical Insurance (URBMI) in 2007, offering voluntary basic health insurance for the unemployed urban population, including students and children not covered by the BMI. In 2009, the URBMI covered more than 182 million people (NBS, 2010). Like the RCMS, these two schemes are financed by central government, local funds, and individual contributions.

Unemployment insurance was made more widely available in 1999 as large numbers of workers in state-owned enterprises were being laid off due to economic restructuring. Under certain criteria, this scheme provides a maximum of 2 years of unemployment allowance, with medical subsidies in cases of illness. By 2009, this scheme covered over 127 million urban enterprise employees and government workers.

Work injury insurance, which is funded by employers, insures enterprise and business employees against medical expenses for work-related injuries and diseases. Benefits provide allowances for disability and injury and nursing fees, but these vary according to the sector and the level of occupational hazard. Recently, the government expanded coverage to rural migrant workers employed in high-risk jobs such as construction. In 2009, almost 149 million workers participated in this scheme.

Maternity insurance provides female enterprise employees and female urban workers in government agencies and other public organizations with 90 days of paid maternity leave and covers the cost of medical expenses during pregnancy. There were 108.75 million workers covered by maternity insurance in 2009.

The social insurance fund also supports the Basic Urban Pension scheme; in 2009, this scheme covered nearly 235.5 million people.

Fee Waivers or Fee Reductions

Health care services. China's 1995 Law on Maternal and Infant Health formally assigned the state with the responsibility to ensure that women and infants receive basic maternal and child health care services. In support of primary health care, the government supports the basic management of childhood diseases through the provision of health care services supporting disease prevention in children under five. In 2001, the State Council introduced Implementation Rules for the Maternal and Infant Health Law; these rules provide more practical guidance on implementing the law and outline the various responsibilities of different government and medical institutions for maternal and child health services. Neither law, however, requires services to be provided free of charge.

However, the government has since outlined various fee waivers, fee reductions, subsidies, and free services to promote access to maternal and child health care services, including immunization, maternal supplements, and maternal and newborn screening. Under the National Plan of Action on the Expanded Programme on Immunization (EPI) issued by the Ministry of Health (MOH) in 2007, China has supported universal access to vaccinations by waiving immunization service fees and has expanded the number of diseases covered under the EPI to 15. The government has also allocated 2,720 million RMB for vaccines, syringes, and health worker allowances to facilitate vaccinations in poor areas.

In 2000, China began to provide subsidies for poor rural women to deliver babies in hospital; this scheme was expanded to all rural counties in 2009. In addition, free folic acid supplements and breast and cervical cancer screenings for rural women were initiated in 2009. The government also introduced new measures for screening for diseases in newborns. In 2010, the MOH and the MCA issued an opinion to initiate work on increasing health care coverage and protection for rural children with serious diseases (Shang and Wang, 2011). Free treatment for certain communicable diseases (such as AIDS, tuberculosis, and schistosomiasis) has also been provided. To support children with intellectual disabilities, the MCA issued a policy statement in 2009 which focused on accelerating access to services for these children and set a target of reaching 5,000 children a year from 2009 to 2011. This policy was introduced in the context of the finding of a 2006 survey that 61% of children with disabilities never received the services intended for them.[5]

Education services. The 1998 Compulsory Education Law outlines the right of all children in China to receive 9 years of compulsory education: 6 years of primary school and 3 years of junior secondary education. In 2006, in an effort to increase universal access to 9 years of compulsory education, the government abolished tuition, textbook, and miscellaneous fees and provided boarding school subsistence for poor rural families; these benefits were extended to urban areas in 2007. Fiscal transfers from central to provincial and local governments help schools to offset the losses incurred as a result of the abolition of tuition and other fees, while county governments bear the cost of boarding subsidies.

More recently, in 2010, the State Council, in its Opinion on the Development of Preschool Education, outlined government plans to increase expenditure on early childhood development (ECD). The Chinese government will finance the construction of new preschool facilities, support private centers, improve training and benefits for teachers, and provide educational subsidies to rural areas. The government has also committed itself to making 1 year of preschool education universal by 2020. Over the past decade, the Ministry of Education (MOE) has piloted ECD initiatives in less developed rural areas, and these have demonstrated the tremendous benefits of ECD.

With regard to children with disabilities, a 1994 policy issued by the China Disabled Persons' Federation (CDPF) and the MOE formally established the right of children with disabilities to enter public schools. The Compulsory Education Law reinforces this right by

[5] The Second National Sample Survey on Disability conducted in 2006 by the China Disabled Persons' Federation found that 61% of children with disabilities never receive any of the services intended for those with disabilities (e.g., medical services, rehabilitation services, subsidies or exemptions for education fees, vocational training, employment placement and support, legal assistance, barrier-free facilities, and access to information and cultural services).

emphasizing the responsibility of public schools to enroll children with disabilities. Subsequent policies have promoted the increased enrolment rate of disabled children into public schools. However, in terms of educational access, major gaps remain (Shang and Wang, 2011). With regard to other barriers to school enrolment, the MOH, the MOE, and the Ministry of Human Resources and Social Security jointly issued a circular in 2010 cancelling hepatitis B tests during health checks for school enrollment.

Child Welfare and Protection Services

The Chinese government's care and protection services for children originally focused on orphans, abandoned children, and street children, and thus existing institutional child protection structures reflect this focus. Across China, there are 303 CWIs and 800 social welfare institutions (SWIs) that provide alternative care for orphaned and abandoned children (Shang and Wang, 2011). According to the government, as of 2009, these institutions had supported over 115,000 children without parental care. There are also 1,400 relief centers, including 116 street children protection centers (SCPCs); as of 2009, these centers had provided temporary care and protection for about 145,000 street children. China has started to expand the services of CWIs and SWIs to include the facilitation of alternative care options, such as family-like foster care.

Diversifying Child Welfare and Child Protection Services

However, because the existing system of SWIs, CWIs, and SCPCs is unable to address the emerging complex and vast needs of all at-risk and vulnerable children, the Chinese government has begun to adopt a new strategy of diversifying the services provided by these institutions. The 2011-2020 NPA for Children's Development calls for (a) each urban and rural community to be staffed with at least one qualified child welfare professional and (b) one shelter for street children in each county and every city above prefecture level.

UNICEF has supported several CWIs and SCPCs in China[6] in diversifying their services in order to offer family support and community-based child welfare and protection services. The services these institutions provide to the children they serve include foster care, small-group family care for children under state care, rehabilitation services, parent education programs, social work support services, and outreach services to vulnerable children and their families.

Zhengzhou model for children living on the street. In 2001, the MCA, supported by UNICEF, began diversifying the child-friendly services available to children living on the streets in Zhengzhou City, Henan Province. The additional services offered by the Zhengzhou SCPC included outreach activities, street kiosks near bus terminals and train stations providing basic information and support, a drop-in center offering temporary shelter, rehabilitation services, referral services, a community-based residential center, facilitated foster care, informal education, vocational training for older children, and follow-up support for children returning home to their families.

The model has helped to provide temporary safe shelter to street children and to build their skills and capacity for independent living and decision making. It has also provided community-based family-like support, assistance with longer term living arrangements, and

---

[6] Diversified services were piloted in CWIs in Qingdao (Shandong), Yibin (Sichuan), and Urumqi (Xinjiang) and in SCPCs in Chengdu (Sichuan) and Panjin (Liaoning) with UNICEF support.

reintegration into mainstream society support. The expansion to more comprehensive services has helped to significantly reduce the number of street children returning to live on the streets and has opened the doors to the provision of services for all vulnerable urban children – not just street children. The Chinese government has recognized the value of this pilot, now referred to as the Zhengzhou model, and has since replicated this model successfully in 15 cities across China.

Child Protection Units. In 2006, child protection units (CPUs), piloted by the MCA and other partners with UNICEF support, developed a community-based mechanism focused on child protection. The CPUs aim to provide multisectoral prevention, identification, assessment, reporting, referral, and response services to children and families needing support, particularly in cases of violence against children and the abuse, exploitation, and neglect of children. A community-level database and monitoring system for vulnerable children has been set up to support the identification of at-risk, vulnerable families and children and case management by local social workers. To ensure collaboration from various sectors, CPUs involve the police, civil affairs workers, health workers, teachers, volunteers, parents, and children. The CPU model has helped to inform national strategies and local policies on developing a child protection system.

Child Friendly Spaces. Following the 2008 Wenchuan earthquake (Sichuan) and the 2010 Yushu earthquake (Qinghai), the National Working Committee for Children and Women (NWCCW) piloted a global UNICEF model called child friendly spaces (CFSs) and developed community-based CFSs in China. The CFSs established in Sichuan provided a safe community-based space for children to gather and engage in interactive group play activities aimed at helping children and their families to support each other and to obtain any other support needed to recover from the trauma of the earthquake. Other CFS services included registering vulnerable children and providing psychosocial support and counseling for children and their families. Similar sites were set up in Yushu. To help children and families in post-disaster settings in the future, a Five-year Plan of Action on Social Work in Disaster Reconstruction and a Manual on Children and Social Work in Emergencies were developed. The CFS model and accompanying tools have improved government capacity to provide social work services in post-emergency settings.

In addition, the CFS model was adapted and replicated to provide community-based services to vulnerable migrant and left-behind children in rural areas. Services include registration, facilitated access to health and education services, family education for parents and caregivers, and psychosocial support. The CFS model, which is considered to be highly effective by government partners,[7] was included in the NPA for Children's Development (2011-2020) as a model for further replication.

Child welfare demonstration pilots. Child Welfare Demonstration Pilots, launched by the MCA in 2010 with UNICEF support, is a 6-year initiative supporting 120 villages within five provinces (Yunnan, Sichuan, Shanxi, Henan, and Xinjiang) with large numbers of vulnerable children. In these areas, many of the highly vulnerable are children affected by HIV/AIDS. The pilots are aimed at showing the value of a child welfare system approach by developing an essential package of child welfare services available to all children determining the cost of

[7] The 2010 midterm evaluation of CFSs in Sichuan by Peking University found that the CFSs established within quake-hit areas provide both a wide coverage of services and effective targeted services for vulnerable children and children with special needs which are "indisputably conducive for (the children's) sound development" and contribute to a rich culture of community.

providing this service package and assessing its feasibility for wider replication. With the critical support of community-level child welfare directors, the community centers identify and monitor vulnerable families and children and support their to access social services, including birth registration, family care and support, education, vocational training, health care, and income-generating activities.

Widening the Range of Social Work Service Providers, Including the Nonprofit Sector

Alongside these child welfare and child protection models, China is beginning to experiment with different models for government procurement of social work services through pilot "incubators" (*fu hua qi*). The models include incorporating the services of nongovernmental and voluntary groups into existing government social work service institutions, as well as government outsourcing social work services to registered nonprofit organizations. Experimentation with these models has been initiated in major cities such as Shanghai, Guangzhou, and Shenzhen. Given the immense need for child welfare and protection services at community level, the potential services and outreach provided by expanding the nonprofit sector could greatly assist in filling the current gap in social services. In the coming years, the government also plans to develop social welfare services in rural western and central areas through a human resource exchange program, in which a corps of qualified and experienced social workers from eastern coastal regions will train workers in these areas.

IV. Remaining Challenges for Developing a Child Welfare and Protection System

China has made progress in developing a more comprehensive child welfare and child protection system in the past three decades, reforming policy and legislative frameworks and expanding social welfare and child protection schemes and services to cover the most vulnerable families. China has achieved almost universal access to basic education and has greatly improved access to basic public health services. The new policy of providing cash transfers to orphans is also a positive step forward and opens the door to more universal approaches to social assistance for vulnerable children. However, some constraints remain.

Social Protection Coverage Has Expanded, but Average Benefits Are Low

While coverage in terms of social assistance, social insurance, fee waivers, and social services has expanded and increased considerably in both urban and rural areas in recent years, the average social benefits provided remain low in comparison to the poverty line and do not meet basic living standards for poor and vulnerable populations. According to a National Bureau of Statistics-World Bank study, in 2004, the village *dibao* scheme provided 65 RMB per person per year, representing a very small proportion of the 931 RMB per person per year poverty line (World Bank, 2009). Similarly, while the RCMS now provides almost universal rural health insurance coverage, RCMS benefits are often limited to catastrophic illnesses and in-patient medical services and reimbursement rates are low (NCMS Evaluation

Task Force, 2006). Many people remain underinsured, face high out-of-pocket costs, and remain highly exposed to the risk of long-term poverty as a result of enormous health expenditure (UNICEF-China, 2008).

In addition, the coverage provided by the various health insurance programs in China varies over 60-fold between the RCMS and that available to workers in the state sector. Access to many publicly subsidized services, including antenatal care, basic and comprehensive emergency obstetric and newborn care, postnatal care, and infant screening, is below 50% in the rural areas of most western counties of China. Thus, poor families continue to struggle to meet basic living needs, secure adequate social protection, and obtain the essential services they require.

Implementation of Policy Frameworks at the Lower Level Remains Weak

At the policy level, the numerous legislative and policy frameworks for social welfare and child protection elaborated by the Chinese government provide a strong foundation for further developing a comprehensive child welfare system in China. However, for the reasons discussed in Part I, local implementation and enforcement—from provincial to village and community level—remain relatively weak. Weak upward and downward accountability mechanisms and distorted incentive structures at local level hamper the effectiveness of implementation. A 2006 citizen scorecard survey examining people's opinions and experiences with public service delivery demonstrated the value of citizen feedback for policy development and implementation and offers some promising possibilities (Brixi, 2009). In the absence of an effective coordination body and stronger accountability, monitoring, and enforcement mechanisms, the implementation of a system-based approach at various administrative levels remains a major challenge.

Inadequate Financial Resources and a Decentralized Fiscal System Impede Social Service Provision

Weak policy implementation is also related to current financing levels and mechanisms. For poor populations, the financial resources allocated for child welfare and child protection assistance are currently insufficient to meet their basic living standards. Also, as discussed above, China's highly decentralized fiscal system obliges local governments to supplement central-level fiscal transfers and to pay for basic social services and assistance at local levels, such as cash transfers for *dibao* or medical financial assistance payments. The lack of financial resources at lower administrative levels, especially poor counties and villages, is a major barrier to the universal provision of basic social services at community level. Since the level of social assistance is highly dependent on the local government's fiscal capacity, there are significant variations and inequalities across the country in terms of access to social services. Poor households in impoverished areas are therefore less likely to receive basic assistance or social services to meet minimum living standards (Dollar, 2007).

Sustainability of Protection Systems in an Economic Downturn

The Chinese government has greatly increased its spending on social services, including those for children, in recent years. This has occurred in an environment in which the economy and the government's overall fiscal resources have been expanding rapidly, meaning that these expenditures have been made without having to cut back on other government programs. At present, there are increasing concerns about the sustainability of China's rapid growth due to both international uncertainty and domestic risks. It is not clear that the current social protection programs will function as an effective social safety net if the economy enters a downturn and government revenues are affected. Social protection and social services are most urgently needed by poor households during a period of economic decline, and yet this has to be set against the great pressure placed on government to direct funds and support productive economic sectors. Thus, the sustainability of social services and social protection in a downturn would require a degree of advanced institutionalization and rules-driven budget allocations, both of which need further development in China.

Fragmented Systems and Vertical Institutional Structures Undermine Necessary Coordination

Given the legacy of the single-issue approach to social welfare and child protection programs in China, the social welfare, child protection, and justice systems and corresponding programs remain fragmented, with a continued reactive focus on issues or categories of children. Current child protection interventions also focus more on response than on prevention. Moving beyond individual schemes and vertical programs and increasing the focus of interventions on the prevention and the reduction of risks for children would greatly support better outcomes for children, and a more integrated, cost-effective child welfare and protection system and interventions.

In addition, there is a continued absence of integrated, coordinated linkages between sectors, particularly between the health, education, and child protection sectors, at various levels, including national, provincial, and community levels. In many countries, for example, health workers and teachers at the community level are required to screen for disability, abuse, neglect, or families at risk and report any findings to community social workers. Social workers then go on to investigate and provide appropriate services, family support, and referrals for more specialized services, as required. Social welfare support to families would be greatly enhanced by first establishing a national coordination body with an authoritative mandate to facilitate multisectoral cooperation and then developing mechanisms to support policy implementation at various levels, such as public financing allocations and governance systems regulating local intersectoral implementation.

Tendency to Expand Institutions for Children without Parental Care

The Chinese government's issues-based approach to child protection is also manifested in associated institutions for children without caregivers. SWIs, CWIs, and SCPCs provide long-term support and residential care for orphaned children, including children affected by HIV/AIDS, abandoned children (including many children with disabilities), street children, and others without parental care. Based on international experience, placing children into residential institutions is considered to be a measure of last resort. The ideal forms of alternative care are kinship care, foster care, and community-based family-like care, which have been shown globally to be cost effective where effectively resourced, and to result in better outcomes in terms of the social, emotional, and healthy development of the child. While CWIs recognize that kinship and foster care are better options than institutional care, there is a tendency in China to build and expand CWIs.

While the new 2011-2020 National Plan of Action for Children's Development positively calls for a minimum of one qualified child welfare professional in each community and a shelter for street children in each county and city, it also calls for the establishment of one CWI in each of these locales. It will be important for the government to discuss and determine the appropriate roles and responsibilities of these welfare institutions and SCPCs prior to expansion; this process should give some consideration to global lessons showing that institutional care is best used as a measure of last resort and for the shortest time possible. It will also be important to orient and incentivize institutions to support social work services that encourage family support, monitoring and case management; provide referral services; and facilitate alternative community-based care over institutionalization.

In parallel, it will be important to work with existing CWIs, SWIs, and SCPCs in order to diversify their services, moving away from residential care and toward building systems for foster care and community-based solutions and placing children in alternative care in the best interests of each child. It will also be essential to tailor social welfare policies and lower level implementation guidelines in the same vein in order to support community-based alternative care. For example, the new orphan subsidy supports kinship and foster care. However, the subsidy for institutions (1,000 RMB) is greater than that for kinship and foster care (600 RMB), and this may have the unintended effect of creating incentives to institutionalize orphaned children rather than to seek alternative care options for them. The implementing regulations, for example, would benefit from a delineation of the role of CWIs and clearer guidelines on how the orphan subsidy to institutions can be used to facilitate alternative community-based care.

Nascent Child Welfare and Child Protection System in China

In addition, the child welfare system in China is still in its early stages of development. Current trends—rapid economic growth, large-scale migration, urbanization, changing family structures—will increase children's vulnerability to new risks, and the existing social welfare and protection system will not be able to prevent and respond to these risks completely. Social security and child protection systems will need to be significantly bolstered. In particular, the low availability and unequal access to community-based public social services, especially family support and child protection for the most vulnerable, will need to be addressed.

Social Work System in Early Stages of Development

The social work field is still a nascent profession in China, and the number of qualified social workers is currently very low. In 2009, only 8,418 people were certified as professional social workers and about 27,000 people were certified as social worker assistants. Moreover, the majority of these professionals have not yet had the opportunity to gain social work experience. With a population of over 1.3 billion, China needs an estimated 10 million social workers. According the government's national human resources development plan, China aims to have 2 million social workers by 2015 (State Council, 2010). However, it will be many years before a professional corps of qualified social workers is established and operational to meet welfare needs in China.

Underdeveloped Nonprofit Sector for Providing Community-Based Social Services

Across the world, social welfare provision often encompasses a mix of interventions provided by the public, private, and nonprofit sectors. Each country needs to determine what mix is best for it at different stages of its development. As mentioned above, in a positive move, the Chinese government plans to expand the number of social work positions in the public sector and is experimenting with government procurement of nonprofit social work services. However, China's nonprofit sector could be further developed given the enormous potential of this sector to help meet the significant need for community-level social welfare services and to alleviate social problems at their root. Exploring further avenues for expanding nonprofit-sector social welfare services will be important for the development of more effective overall social service provision in the country, particularly in rural areas where the needs are greatest. At the same time, it will be important to ensure adequate registration, regulation and inspection, supported by national standards, training and guidance materials.

Specifically, it will be essential to provide an enabling environment for the development of the nonprofit sector. This would include simplifying the registration process and reducing the registration requirements for nonprofit organizations. At the same time, for both the nonprofit sectors and the public and private sectors, it will be important to establish adequate regulatory frameworks to support accountability and transparency in the management and use of donated funds and to develop monitoring and evaluation frameworks for social work service standards and implementation. These measures will be critical to supporting the effective management of social services and positive social welfare outcomes for children.

Unequal Access to Public Social Services for Children

Despite national efforts to increase social protection and service access, ensuring good coverage and equitable access to services for all remains a challenge; for the 211 million migrants in China, in particular, significant barriers exist. Access to social welfare provision is still hampered by policy and structural constraints intrinsic to the provision of social benefits under the existing *hukou* system. For example, RCMS benefits, among many others, are still not transferrable to urban areas, and so many poor migrants are still unable to afford health care and have to forego some primary health care services due to cost. Despite guarantees of 9 years of free compulsory education, a large percentage of migrant children do not attend public school. Vulnerable children left in rural areas by migrating parents are exposed to increased risks of trafficking, abuse, and exploitation. As previously mentioned, a UNICEF-supported CDPF survey showed that 61% of children with disabilities had not received the benefits aimed for them, including medical assistance, rehabilitation, educational subsidies or fee reductions, and vocational training (China Disabled Persons' Federation, 2006). There is a great need to support universal coverage of essential services in policy as well as in practice.

Large Number of Unregistered Children Without Access to Social Services

Beyond those who do have access to public social services, it is likely that a significant number of children in China are unregistered and therefore do not have access to public services and protection. In order to access basic rights to health, education, social welfare, assistance, and protection under the law in China, a child must have a birth registration and a *hukou* (household registration). There are no current birth registration statistics in China. The most recent statistics available are from 1991 to 1999, and these show that during this period, only 60 to 80 per cent of children were registered within a year of their birth (Plan, 2011). There are over 340 million children in China. If between 20 to 40 per cent of births are unregistered, this would imply that an extremely large number of children are unable to access basic social services and social protection. Other research has indicated that the birth registration rate is low, particularly in poor and remote areas, for girls, migrant children, adopted children, and children born outside of locally sanctioned family planning limits, with some overlap among these categories (Li, 2009). Unregistered children are therefore especially vulnerable.

V. UNICEF Support to Strengthen China's Child Welfare and Child Protection System

Child-friendly poverty reduction programs, labor and employment policies, and an essential package of health and education services are critical to preventing income poverty, meeting the essential needs of families and children, and reducing social protection risks. Over the past 30 years in China, UNICEF's Health, Nutrition, Education, Water and Environmental Sanitation, HIV/AIDS and Social Policy Programmes have been providing significant assistance to the Chinese government in these areas, promoting the healthy survival and development of children and helping the government to meet the essential needs of all children with equity. Toward this end, UNICEF assistance has helped to support child welfare policies and services that address the social inequalities, disadvantages, risks, and vulnerabilities of children and families in the general population. These interventions constitute primary prevention.

Equally critical are child welfare and child protection policies and services that reduce the risk of children experiencing violence, abuse, exploitation, and neglect. Children whose families are poor, who experience social exclusion due to discrimination or stigma, or who do not have parental care are more vulnerable to significant harm than their wealthier and more socially integrated peers. Vulnerable children include children living in poverty, children without caregivers, children with disabilities, children affected by HIV/AIDS, children whose parents are serving prison terms, children living on the streets, children in conflict with the law, child trafficking victims, children of migrant workers, children left behind in rural areas by migrating parents, and children with any combination of these or other difficult circumstances. Policies, services, and interventions targeted at reducing the risks associated with these vulnerable groups, families, and children are central to child protection work. UNICEF's Child Protection Programme has provided international experience and technical assistance to support these initiatives in China. These interventions focus on secondary and tertiary prevention (UNICEF-China, 2010).

The key UNICEF policy objectives for child welfare policy are therefore to 1) offset poverty, deprivation, vulnerability, social exclusion, and other risk factors that can lead to lifelong disadvantage; 2) promote and protect children's rights and healthy development; and 3) prevent and respond to abuse, neglect, exploitation, and violence (i.e., child protection) (UNICEF-China, 2010).

To help strengthen the child protection system, the key UNICEF goals over the next 5 years are first to strengthen upstream policy, legislative, and institutional frameworks for child protection system development, implementation, and monitoring; and second, to improve the availability and delivery of family support and community-based child protection services (UNICEF-China, 2010). Public awareness raising campaigns at national and local levels to promote positive social attitudes and behavior change will also be a significant feature of child protection programming.

To support the development of the child welfare and protection system in China, three main levels of support will be provided to the government: 1) strengthening child welfare and child protection system policies, laws, and frameworks at the upstream and national level; 2) implementing national policies and laws at the intermediate and provincial level; and 3) piloting integrated child welfare and child protection models at the community level (feeding into upstream policies and intermediate implementation). This includes supporting the development of social work capacity.

A. Policies and Laws at the Upstream National Level

Upstream Child Welfare System Support

At the upstream level, it will be important to support China in improving its national strategies, laws, legal frameworks, policies, and plans and moving toward the provision of a comprehensive child welfare system. This will not only include providing policy analysis and technical input to assist the development of child welfare policies, laws, and frameworks (e.g., the Child Welfare Act), but also providing support for the development of systems to ensure effective implementation, such as a financing strategy to fund public functions and services, a human resources strategy (particularly for the social work system), multisectoral coordination mechanisms and networks, a service delivery system, a monitoring and evaluation mechanism, a cross-sectoral information system, a governance and accountability framework, and systems for implementing national standards and strategies.

National-level work also entails defining norms, standards, and costs for key aspects within the system, such as identifying the scope of public functions, defining a minimum package of services, costing minimum services across sectors, developing national child welfare standards, and supporting national-level advocacy and public awareness campaigns.

Foremost among China's child welfare policy frameworks are the 2011-2015 National Plan of Action for Child Welfare and the Child Welfare Act. Together, these are anticipated to outline the institutional, organizational, human resource, and financial aspects of the child welfare system, along with the scope of the expanded child welfare services.[8] The National Plan of Action for Child Welfare is expected to set out a broad vision for developing a child welfare system in China with a focus on strengthening family support and community-based services and diversifying and improving the services provided by CWIs (including daycare, respite care, outreach services, and the monitoring of children in kinship and foster care). The Child Welfare Act will (a) outline a broad legal framework for universal child welfare programs and assistance that goes beyond the current narrow focus on categories of vulnerable children and (b) aim to define the scope of diversified child welfare services (Institute of Social Development and Public Policy, 2008). It will be crucial to develop these frameworks with good technical support; UNICEF will support the Chinese government in this regard.

Over the past several years, UNICEF has supported various technical reviews and policy analyses that have contributed to the development of child welfare policy and legislative frameworks, strategies, national plans of actions, and implementation strategies. This assistance has included providing a comparative analysis of international and Chinese child welfare laws and policies, along with other technical social and economic policy analyses, and an analysis of child protection policies. In the future, UNICEF will support additional policy analysis and technical assistance for the above frameworks. Importantly, UNICEF's experiences and evidence from empirical pilot work at various levels will also be analyzed and documented to inform upstream policymaking; for example, pilot experiences and feasibility analyses of implementing child welfare services at the community level in poor counties will be provided to inform policy development.

A multisectoral National Experts Group on Child Welfare System Policy and Legislative Development was established in 2010 to improve cross-sectoral coordination, initially for child welfare policy development. This group provides technical policy advice to the MCA on child welfare system development, and it will provide advice during the development of the new Five-year Plan of Action on Child Welfare (2011-2015) and the Child Welfare Act. It will also provide advisory inputs on the development of a minimum package of services and service standards. UNICEF will provide support by introducing international standards, norms, and experiences, and the MCA child welfare and protection pilots will support policy development with empirical evidence and data.

In support of a child welfare financing strategy, UNICEF is supporting the Ministry of Finance to undertake several studies to evaluate effective ways for financing the child welfare

[8] This will include the legislative, regulatory, and policy frameworks; the effective enforcement of laws and regulations to protect children; adequately staffed and funded child protection services; intersectoral coordination and referral mechanisms to ensure that child welfare is supported by all public services; and public awareness and family education services to support positive social behaviors and good parenting practices.

system. Research topics include improving financing for the rural and urban *dibao* systems, a policy study on financing early childhood development and equitable compulsory education for all, and research on government financing to support equalized public health services. UNICEF is also supporting the MCA in its efforts to define a minimum package of child welfare services and the scope of services and to undertake a costing for community-based services in different socioeconomic settings. These will feed into the larger child welfare financing strategy.

According to a 2010 State Council Personnel Development Plan, China aims to have 2 million qualified social workers by 2015 (State Council, 2010) and to place one qualified social worker in every community at the rural township and urban subdistrict level. Given China's incipient social work system, the MCA will develop a new Five-year Plan for the Development of Social Work for Children which will help to develop a human resources strategy for a comprehensive child welfare system. In the coming years, UNICEF will provide technical assistance to help the MCA to develop (a) social worker positions in the public and nonprofit sectors, (b) national social work guidelines and standards for the professional qualification of social workers, (c) methodologies for evaluating social work services for children, (d) a national policy on government purchase of nonprofit social work services, and (e) related guidelines for nonprofit social welfare organizations.

To facilitate improved national monitoring and evaluation systems, the MCA and UNICEF are working together to develop a child vulnerability monitoring mechanism to provide timely identification, prevention, and response support to at-risk children. The MCA is also developing a case management database on social assistance and a system for carrying out periodic analyses of urban and rural medical financial assistance.

In addition, monitoring and evaluating the effectiveness of implementation mechanisms for social assistance policies will be another key area of support. A study on the implementation mechanism for disbursing the new cash transfer to orphans and for assessing the impact of the subsidy on recipients was initiated. The MCA is also working with UNICEF to examine the feasibility of incorporating a child poverty component into the current *dibao* scheme and to undertake policy research on (a) the intergenerational transmission of poverty in urban *dibao* families, (b) improved modalities to link child social assistance recipients with social work services, and (c) stronger linkages between the basic medical insurance and medical financial assistance to increase health coverage and social protection.

In support of increasing public awareness on child welfare issues, government partners will conduct various national information campaigns, ranging from high-profile advocacy events to sustained education and communication initiatives on child welfare related issues.

Upstream Child Protection System Support

UNICEF will be providing support to the various national government partners on the aspects of children protection policy described below.

To support cross-sectoral collaboration in the child protection system in China, several reference documents were developed for the government, including an international review outlining of the social and economic costs of child maltreatment and the comparative benefits of a national child protection system and a study on the legal and policy framework of China's child protection system. In the future, the government will convene meetings for key child protection system actors at national and local level to discuss and develop a vision for a comprehensive national child protection system across sectors. To lay the groundwork for these discussions, the NWCCW is undertaking a mapping and an analysis of child protection laws, policies, and services in China and the key responsibilities among various governmental departments. This mapping will help to identify gaps and areas where intersectoral linkages could be strengthened and to develop a continuum of policies and services for vulnerable children. A needs and cost analysis on the provision of child protection services will also be conducted by China's National Development and Reform Commission to guide strategic planning for developing the child welfare and protection system.

In addition, UNICEF will support the government to initiate child protection bodies to improve (a) the development, implementation, and enforcement of child protection policies and laws and (b) multisectoral coordination for child protection services delivery. Supporting government reforms in the justice system to improve the protection of child victims, witnesses, and offenders; to promote restorative justice models; and to strengthen data collection and knowledge management for evidence-based systems development are also key programming areas.

Violence against children. To improve the laws protecting children from violence and abuse, UNICEF is sharing international standards and best practices, supporting data collection, and facilitating multisectoral discussion on violence against children. UNICEF's work includes providing support to the National People's Congress and the All-China Women's Federation to study and promote the development of a new Law on Family Violence. Under this proposed legislation, key areas of advocacy will include a multisectoral approach to preventing and responding to violence (including mandatory reporting by professionals such as health workers, teachers, and social workers) and defining family violence to include children witnessing domestic violence. The government is also developing working procedures with clearly defined responsibilities and cooperation mechanisms across sectors to assist child victims of various forms of violence.

Trafficking. With respect to antitrafficking efforts, the government is developing its next National Plan of Action on Combating Trafficking in Women and Children (2013-2017), the aim of which is to improve coordination across government sectors. The government will also undertake a comparative legal analysis and review to identify gaps between national legislation and the Palermo Protocol. UNICEF will provide technical assistance during the development of the NPA and the legal analysis. China signed MOUs with Myanmar in 2009 and with Vietnam in 2010 in order to prevent and combat cross-border trafficking. In the coming years, UNICEF will further support the development of additional antitrafficking MOUs between China and neighboring countries.

China plans to conduct a technical legislative review of the Criminal Code to review the definition of child trafficking, including the age of the child and exemptions from criminal liability for victims of trafficking. In addition, the government will develop child-friendly national service guidelines to assist victims of trafficking and improve investigation procedures for child trafficking victims and working procedures for assisting child victims of violence. Good practices from the ACWF-UNICEF pilot initiative on the prevention of trafficking will feed into policy development for further prevention work.

Juvenile Justice. After the government revised the Law on the Protection of Minors and the Criminal Law, China adopted policies and regulations to protect children and youths in conflict with the law, established specialized departments and juvenile courts to handle juvenile cases, and began piloting noncustodial practices and child-friendly investigation and court procedures. To support a more child-centered juvenile justice system, UNICEF will provide assistance in three key areas over the next several years: (1) research to contribute to evidence-based policy and legislative development, including research on child-friendly trial procedures to protect child victims, witnesses, and offenders; (2) promotion of restorative justice models and community-based rehabilitation for children in conflict with the law to divert child offenders from the formal judicial system; and (3) introduction of international standards and best practices into juvenile justice, including the dissemination of internationally developed juvenile justice indicators to guide lawyers, judges, and juvenile justice workers.

Data and research. Over the next year, in order to improve the availability of data and analysis on key child protection areas, UNICEF is supporting the development of a national data monitoring system for children with disabilities; research on violence against children; a study on the psychosocial support needs of vulnerable children; and research to identify the major barriers to implementing child protection laws and policies. Data analysis will help support the government in its efforts to improve policies and program interventions, particularly those designed to prevent violence against children and the abuse and exploitation of children.

B. Implementation of Policies and Laws at the Intermediate or Provincial Level

Given China's large population and multilayered, financially decentralized structure, it is essential to provide support to ensure effective policy implementation and service delivery at lower levels. Thus, at the intermediate level, UNICEF assistance focuses on supporting provincial-level and midlevel implementation of national strategies, policies, laws, standards, rules, and regulations on child welfare and child protection and on building the capacity at provincial level to improve family and community care services for poor and vulnerable children. This includes supporting the development of (a) provincial-level financing strategies covering both provincial budget allocations and payment mechanisms, (b) a provincial human resources strategy for social workers, (c) monitoring and accountability systems, (d) integrated information systems, (e) planning and management tools, and (f) public awareness campaigns on child welfare.

With the launch of China's new 2011-2011 National Plan of Action for Children's Development, UNICEF will support the government to implement the NPA at lower administrative levels in the coming years, particularly the child welfare and child protection components, along with various aspects of the policies and laws discussed in the section above. More immediately, UNICEF will support the MCA's efforts to design and pilot the implementation of a medical financial assistance policy to support poor segments of the population suffering from severe diseases. UNICEF will also support the government to conduct training workshops on the design and implementation of child-sensitive social assistance programs. To increase awareness at the intermediate level, provincial public awareness campaigns supporting a child-friendly child welfare and protection system will be carried out.

C. Piloting Child Welfare and Child Protection Models at the Community Level

Over the next 5 years, UNICEF will be assisting the government to pilot community-based child welfare and child protection service models targeting the poorest and the most vulnerable children. At the community level, key aspects of an effective service model include a package of public services, a well-developed network of family support and community-based child protection services to protect children from significant harm, and strong social work services to identify and protect the most vulnerable children and families. In general, a well-developed child-friendly social protection system should provide a range of social and child welfare services, including family and social support services, child protection services, and alternative care.

The main goal of developing these models is to demonstrate cost-effective, and sustainable child welfare and child protection models for potential government replication. The lessons and insights gained from empirical pilot experiences will be documented and will contribute to the development of both upstream policy frameworks and downstream service guidelines, standards, and inspection mechanisms. Together, they will help to improve national child welfare policies and systems development and support effective service delivery in communities.

One model being piloted includes the development of child-sensitive approaches to social protection. UNICEF is currently collaborating with the MCA to pilot categorized social assistance schemes for children under the *dibao* system in urban areas and cash transfer models linking vulnerable child recipients to community-based social services such as health and education services. This approach involves UNICEF support to help the MCA study the implementation and monitoring mechanisms of the new orphan subsidy policy.

Another model being piloted is the Child Welfare Demonstration Pilots currently being carried out in counties with large numbers of children affected by AIDS (as described in Part III). The empirical evidence gained from developing and implementing both a universal package of child welfare services for all children at risk and a package of child protection services aimed at protecting children from discrimination, stigma, and significant harm will make an important contribution to policy development.

In a different model being piloted, UNICEF is working closely with the MCA to pilot and develop an integrated model for community-based child welfare services in vulnerable rural communities. In light of the vulnerability of children left behind in rural areas by migrating parents, this model is being piloted in areas with large numbers of such children, although services are available to all vulnerable children.

UNICEF is also supporting the government to develop a model for comprehensive community-based child protection services. This model will focus on establishing effective family support and community-based mechanisms and services to prevent children being subjected to violence, abuse, neglect and exploitation, including trafficking, sexual exploitation, and labor exploitation, and to monitor, identify, report, refer, and assist those children who are at risk of or have suffered these forms of harm. Associated social work services include monitoring poor and vulnerable children in the community, case management, home visits, counseling, referrals, and the facilitation of alternative care options as needed. The CPUs being piloted in four counties and the 30 CFS models in Sichuan (discussed in Part III) demonstrate aspects of this model.

Given the current institutional childcare structures in China, the support provided to the MCA to diversify the range of services offered in CWIs and SCPCs is important. Therefore, the MCA is beginning to diversify and expand the services offered by SCPCs in urban areas, as illustrated earlier by the Zhengzhou Model, and to pilot temporary shelter services for vulnerable children.

The MCA is also beginning to expand community-based alternative care options. Thus, UNICEF is supporting the MCA to pilot alternative care practices for vulnerable children, including foster care and community-based family-like care (e.g., daycare centers, family-based long-term care) for children without parental care and children with disabilities. At the same time, UNICEF will support programs to prevent family separation. The intention of the alternative care model is to meet the needs of all vulnerable children requiring such care, including children affected by HIV/AIDS, children with disabilities, orphaned and abandoned children, children living on the streets, and children without parental care. A key goal of the alternative care pilot schemes is to demonstrate that community-based care is not only better for the survival and the lifelong development of these children, as shown by international experience, but also that alternative care is cost effective and more sustainable in comparison to institutional care.

To support the effective implementation of all of these models, technical assistance is being provided to build the capacity of child protection professionals and community workers. UNICEF is also supporting the development of service guidelines and modules for daycare centers, positive discipline, and psychosocial support training for community workers and school teachers. These models will also be strengthened by more clearly defined institutional frameworks, including goals, roles, and responsibilities; institutional arrangements; provisions for supporting sustainability; and government financing.

To promote positive social attitudes and behaviors that support the realization of children's rights and contribute to their healthy development, UNICEF will work with government partners to support public awareness, social mobilization, and advocacy campaigns. These campaigns will help to increase awareness and knowledge of practices that are harmful and practices that are beneficial to children. They will highlight the issues faced by particularly vulnerable children (such as street children, orphans, children with disabilities, trafficked children), violence against children, and the value of family support and community-based services and care. To monitor the impact of these campaigns and changes in terms of awareness and knowledge of, and social attitudes and behaviors toward, children, UNICEF will undertake surveys on knowledge, practices, and attitudes in the coming years.

CONCLUSION

Having taken the initial steps to reforming its social welfare system policies and services, China is making progress toward developing a more integrated child welfare and child protection system. The Chinese government is moving toward more universalist approaches to social welfare for families and children, for example, by expanding social assistance programs such as *dibao* and medical financial assistance support, widening health insurance coverage and medical financial assistance, and supporting free compulsory education. While there is a continued tendency to focus on categories of children, the government is also encouraging more multisectoral approaches to specific child protection issues (e.g., by developing intersectoral NPAs to combat trafficking and to assist street children). To meet the emerging child welfare and protection challenges and to better protect children from significant harm from violence, abuse, exploitation, and neglect, the government will need to further strengthen and deepen the integration of the child welfare and protection system.

Specifically, the government will need to overcome various factors constraining the development of an effective child welfare and protection system. Supporting universal benefits for basic child welfare provisions will be instrumental in reducing unequal access to public social services for children and their families.

Increased central-level financial inputs for child welfare and child protection into areas with lower fiscal capacity, combined with more effective and efficient financing mechanisms for the use of funds, are greatly needed. In particular, improving enforcement measures and strengthening local-level accountability frameworks for public officials to provide public social services would significantly enhance actual access to services for vulnerable children and greatly improve policy implementation.

Vertical government structures and institutional arrangements will need to be further integrated. A national coordination body and improved intersectoral coordination mechanisms at different levels that help to promote a continuum of policies and services addressing the needs of vulnerable children would greatly facilitate meaningful integration.

Social workers have a critical role to play. To meet the current large gap in social work provision, the government will need to accelerate the development of the social work system and increase the number of trained social workers available at the national, provincial and community level. Importantly, facilitating the expansion of the nonprofit sector and other private social work agencies to contribute to the provision of social work services would help to relieve the great demand and need for social work services.

While the child welfare and child protection system in China is still developing, the government has already demonstrated its commitment to promoting child rights and has begun to address some of the barriers mentioned above. In the coming years, UNICEF will continue to support the government to develop a more comprehensive child welfare and protection system by providing policy and legislative inputs for child welfare and child protection systems development, strengthening capacity at national, provincial, and local levels, piloting approaches for evidence-based policy development and legislative reform, and undertaking communication campaigns for positive social change for children. UNICEF will continue to play a supporting role by introducing international best practices, standards, and norms for the government to consider and adapt as appropriate to the Chinese context.

ACKNOWLEDGMENTS

I am grateful to David Hipgrave, William Bikales, Etienne Poirot, Chen Xuemei, and Diane Swales for their insightful reviews. I would also like to express my appreciation to the Social Policy, Child Protection, and HIV/AIDS Teams of UNICEF-China for developing the initial UNICEF conceptual program frameworks to support child welfare and child protection systems in China, particularly Hana Brixi, Chen Xuemei, Kirsten Di Martino, Huang Jinxia,

Mu Yan, Etienne Poirot, Shi Weilin, Wang Daming, Xu Wenqing, Yang Haiyu, and Zhang Lei.

APPENDIX

Acronyms

ACWF	All-China Women's Federation
BMI	Basic Medical Insurance
CDPF	China Disabled Persons' Federation
CFS	Child friendly space
CPU	Child protection unit
CRC	Convention on the Rights of the Child
CWI	Child welfare institution
EAPRO	East Asia and the Pacific Regional Office (UNICEF)
ECD	Early childhood development
EPI	Expanded Programme on Immunization
GDP	Gross domestic product
MCA	Ministry of Civil Affairs
MFA	Medical Financial Assistance
MOE	Ministry of Education
MOH	Ministry of Health
MOU	Memorandums of understanding
NBS	National Bureau of Statistics
NCMS	New Cooperative Medical Scheme
NPFPC	National Population and Family Planning Commission
NPA	National Plan of Action
NWCCW	National Working Committee on Women and Children
RCMS	Rural Cooperative Medical Scheme
RMB	Ren min bi (official currency of China)
SWI	Social welfare institution
SCPC	Street children protection center
UNICEF	United Nations Children's Fund
UNFPA	United Nations Population Fund
URBMI	Urban Resident Basic Medical Insurance
WHO	World Health Organization

REFERENCES

Brixi, H. (2009). *China: Urban services and governance*. China: UNICEF.

Brixi, H., Mu, Y., Targa, B., and Hipgrave, D. (2011). *Equity and public governance in health system reform: Challenges and opportunities for China*. (Forthcoming publication.).

Chen, J., Dai, D., Pu, M., Hou, W., and Feng, Q. (2010). *The trend of the Gini coefficient in China*. BWPI Working Paper 109, Brooks World Poverty Institute, University of Manchester. Retrieved from http://www.bwpi.manchester.ac.uk/resources/Working-Papers/bwpi-wp-10910.pdf.

Chen, S., and Ravallion, M. (2008). *China is poorer than we thought, but no less successful in the fight against poverty,* World Bank Policy Research Working Paper 4621. Washington DC: World Bank.

China Development Research Foundation. (2007). *China development report 2007: Eliminating poverty in development*. Beijing.

China Disabled Persons' Federation. (2006). *Second national sample survey of disability*. Beijing.

China Health Economics Institute. (2006). *China national health account report*. China.

Chinese Center for Disease Control and Prevention. (2005). *China food and nutrition surveillance report*. China.

Di Martino, K., Weilin, S., and Xuemei, C. (2010). *Developing a comprehensive child welfare system in China*. UNICEF background paper for the 2010 High-Level Meeting on International Cooperation for Child Rights.

Dollar, D. (2007). *Poverty, inequality and social disparities during China's economic reform*. China: World Bank.

Duan, C., and Zhou, F. (2005). Research on China's left-behind children. *Population Research, 29:29-36*.

The Economist. (2010, March 4). Gendercide: The worldwide war on baby girls: Technology, declining fertility and ancient prejudice are combining to unbalance societies. Retrieved from http://www.economist.com/node/15636231.

Edlund, L., Li, H., Yi, J., and Zhang, J. (2007). *Sex ratios and crime: Evidence from China's one-child policy*. IZA Discussion Paper Series 3214, Institute for the Study of Labor. Berlin.

Evaluation Task Force for NCMS. (2006). *Evaluation report on NCMS piloting counties*. Beijing: People's Health Publishing House.

Institute of Social Development and Public Policies, Beijing Normal University. (2008). *Study on the child welfare system in China*. Beijing: Child Welfare Centre.

Li, S., Zhang, Y., and Feldman, M. (2009). Birth registration in China: Practices, problems and policies. *Population Research and Policy Review, 29,* 297-317.

Ministry of Civil Affairs. (2009 and 2010). *China civil affairs statistical yearbook 2009 and 2010*. Retrieved from http://www.mca.gov.cn/article/zwgk/mzyw/ 201106/20110600 161364.shtml.

Ministry of Education, National Bureau of Statistics, Ministry of Finance. (2010). *The 2009 statistical notice on national education expenditure*. Beijing.

Ministry of Education of China. (2009). *Essential statistics of education in China*. China.

Ministry of Foreign Affairs of the People's Republic of China and the UN System in China. (2010). *China's progress towards the millennium development goals: 2010 report*. Retrieved from http://www.un.org.cn/cms/p/resources/30/1539/content.html.

Ministry of Health. (2009). *China health statistical yearbook*. China.

Ministry of Health. (2010). *China health statistical yearbook*. Beijing: China Union Medical University Press.

National Bureau of Statistics. (2005). *2008 China population*. China.

National Bureau of Statistics. (2007). *One per cent population sample survey*. China (2005 data).

National Bureau of Statistics of China. (2008). *National sample survey on population.* China: China Statistics Press.

National Bureau of Statistics of China. (2010). *2010 China statistical yearbook.* China.

National Population and Family Planning Commission. (2010). *The 2010 report on the development of China's floating population.* China.

Office of Migrant Workers of the State Council and All China Women's Federation. (February 2008). *Research report on rural left-behind children in China.* China.

Peking University. (2005). *Retrospective survey on childhood violence experiences among young people in China.* Beijing.

Plan International. (2011). *Universal birth registration: Country case studies: China.* Retrieved from http://plan-international.org/birthregistration/resources/country-case-studies/china.

Shang, X., and Xiaolin, W. (2011). *China's child welfare update, discovery report: Emerging issues and findings for child welfare and protection in China.* China: Social Sciences Academic Press.

Shang X., Xiaolin, W., and Jing, T. C. (2010). *Survival children, discovery report: Emerging issues and findings for child welfare and protection in China. Research on the reform of state child welfare institutions*. China: Social Science Academic Press.

State Council of the People's Republic of China. (2006). *Some opinions to address the issues of rural migrant workers.* China.

State Council of the People's Republic of China. (2010). *Outline of the national medium and long term program for personnel development (2010-2020)*. Beijing: State Council of the People's Republic of China.

State Council of the People's Republic of China. (2011). *National plan of action for children's development, 2011-2020.*

Tsai, L. (2007). *Accountability without democracy: Solidarity groups and public good provision in rural China.* Cambridge and New York: Cambridge University Press.

UNFPA. (2010). *State of the world's population 2010, from conflict and crisis to renewal: Generations of change*. New York.

UNICEF. (2008). *Child protection strategy*. New York.

UNICEF. (2009). *2009 State of the world's children.*

UNICEF-China. (2008). *Mid-term review of UNICEF contribution towards health and nutrition improvement strategies in China, 2006-2008.* Beijing, China.

UNICEF-China. (2010). *China Country Programme Document (2011-2015).* Beijing.

UNICEF-China (2010). *Conceptual framework for the development of a child welfare system in China*. Beijing. (Internal UNICEF working document).

UNICEF East Asia and the Pacific Regional Office. (2009). *East Asia and the Pacific child protection programme strategy toolkit*. Bangkok: UNICEF EAPRO.

United Nations. (1989). Convention on the Rights of the Child. Retrieved 15 November 2011 from http://www2.ohchr.org/english/law/crc.htm#art19.

Waldmeir, P. (2011, July 27). China cracks down on child kidnappings. *Financial Times.* Retrieved from http://www.ft.com/intl/cms/s/0/3909b53e-b857-11e0-8d23-00144feabdc0. html#axzz1Z2SAasCT.

World Bank (2006). *Health reform in rural China: Where next?* Washington, DC: World Bank.

World Bank. (2009). *From poor areas to poor people: China's evolving poverty reduction agenda: An assessment of poverty and inequality in China.* Washington, DC: World Bank.

World Health Organization. (2009). *Global health observatory data repository.* Geneva, Switzerland.

Xinhua News Agency. (2011, August 17). Millions of Chinese men without brides by 2020 due to gender imbalance: Experts warn. Retrieved from http://news.xinhuanet.com/english2010/china/2011-08/17/c_131056376.html.

In: Child Protection in Chinese Societies
Editor: Ko Ling Chan

ISBN: 978-1-61942-879-9

Chapter 10

CHILD PROTECTION IN HONG KONG

Jessica Oi Chu Ho
Director, Against Child Abuse, Hong Kong, China

ABSTRACT

News about child abuse is reported almost daily. It has been recognized as a social problem and not just a family matter of child discipline. Different professionals need to work together for the prevention of child abuse. This chapter reviews the milestones in child protection and examines what has been done and achieved in the past three decades. The World Health Organization (2002) recommends a public health approach to the early identification of child abuse. To improve the system in Hong Kong, it will be necessary to conduct research and strategic evaluations, strengthen professional development, and build bridges between sectors. On the issue of the ways ahead, the following strategies are suggested in this chapter: 1) develop a data link system and conduct a prevalence study so as to inform policies and practices; 2) ensure a home visitation to each family, including cross-border families with newborn children; 3) put effective preventive services into the mainstream; 4) establish a review mechanism for cases of serious and fatal child abuse; 5) show concern for the child victims of psychological abuse and for children who are emotionally disturbed; 6) impose a total ban on corporal punishment as it is a form of violence and an infringement of children's rights; 7) set up a mandatory sex offenders registry; 8) conduct a review of sentencing options and require every convict to receive therapy and treatment; 9) put in place laws and ways to protect unattended children; and 10) establish an independent child commission to look into all child-related issues. Every child is precious. It is everyone's responsibility to ensure that each child is protected and develops in a safe environment. What our society will be like depends on how determined we are to provide a nonviolent environment at home and in society for our children today.

Keywords: Public health approach, Multidisciplinary collaboration, Home visitation, Fatality review, Sex offenders registry, Child commission

INTRODUCTION

News about child abuse is reported almost daily. It took the Hong Kong community a long time to recognize that child abuse is not just a family matter but also a social problem. It also took some time to get different professionals to work together for the prevention of child abuse and to adopt the notion that the child's best interest should be the paramount concern. Before exploring what can be improved and the ways ahead, I will briefly outline the significant milestones in the field of child protection in Hong Kong.

HOW DID CHILD ABUSE COME TO BE RECOGNIZED AS A PROBLEM IN HONG KONG?

In 1951, the Protection of Women and Juveniles Ordinance was enacted, but it contained no mention of child abuse. This suggests that child abuse was not seen as a problem at that time, although behaviors that would now be defined as abusive may well have been present and, indeed, common. It was not until 1978 that Hong Kong society first began to react against the harsh treatment of children. This concern was aroused by the case of a 10-year-old girl called Lai Shuk-mei, whose situation featured prominently in the news after she was found to have bruises all over her body; during a physical examination, she was also found to have bone fractures. She had been abused by her emotionally disturbed mother. Although physical, sexual, and psychological abuse and neglect of children has always existed, publicly, its existence always used to be denied. Lai Shuk-mei's case aroused such grave concerns within the Hong Kong community that the existence of child abuse was publicly acknowledged for the first time. People started to think about how to protect children and what services should be provided to prevent their families from harming them. Following the practice in other countries, the social work profession was the obvious candidate for taking on the new child protection responsibilities. A nongovernment child protection organization, Against Child Abuse, was established in 1979, the International Year of the Child, to provide a hotline service, crisis intervention and preventive services. The government's Social Welfare Department set up a general enquiry hotline in 1982 to deal with, among other things, concerns about child abuse.

In 1983, a young girl, Chow Pui-man, one of twin sisters, died due to inadequate care. This case again aroused public concern about the need to protect children. A multidisciplinary Working Group on Child Abuse was formed to look into child protection policies and systems. The name of this working group was changed to the Committee on Child Abuse in 2000, and this committee was chaired by the Director of Social Welfare.

In 1983, the government formally established a specialized Child Protective Services Unit (CPSU) under the Social Welfare Department to handle statutory child abuse cases. The name of the unit was later changed to the Family and Child Protective Services Unit (FCPSU) in 2000 when battered spouse cases were included in the unit's service provision. In 2002, the FCPSU's responsibilities were further enlarged to include child custody cases.

In 1986, a Child Protection Registry (CPR) was established under the Social Welfare Department to record child abuse and children at risk cases. The CPR was computerized in 1994. This body could have served the purpose of monitoring trends and characteristics in child abuse for planning prevention services; however, few resources have been put into improving the system. Thus, it serves merely to record cases.

In 1986, the same year as the CPR was established, another child abuse case came to prominence and aroused much concern. A 6-year-old girl, Kwok Ah-nui, came to the attention of social workers after she was reported for dropping water bombs on the heads of passersby from the window of a flat. She was routinely left on her own for most of the day by her mentally disturbed mother. She did not attend school and had no contact with the outside world. There was no legal provision at that time for social workers to gain access to places where children were left unattended and thought to be in danger. Following this case, social workers from the Social Welfare Department were granted the statutory power to enter private premises when there was a suspicion of serious child abuse (Lui, 2003).

During the 1980s and the first half of the 1990s, many professionals still considered beating children to be an acceptable means of child discipline and would not classify it as abuse. The traditional Chinese view, namely, that children are the property of their parents who can do what they like with them and that outsiders should not interfere, was strong. I have past experience of spending hours in an accident and emergency department until well past midnight trying to convince the medical officer on duty that a child who was covered in welts made by a rattan cane had been abused and needed to be hospitalized. The process was very frustrating.

In 1995, the Criminal Procedure Ordinance was amended to allow video-recorded evidence to be admissible in court so that vulnerable witnesses, including victims of child abuse, did not have to face the ordeal of a public courtroom. The Working Group on Child Abuse appointed a multidisciplinary task group in 1995 to examine the handling procedures in cases of child abuse and, as a result, a new set of Procedures for Handling Child Sexual Abuse Cases was implemented in 1996. A special investigation team comprising the police and the CPSU was formed in 1995 to investigate and handle child sexual abuse cases. In the same year, the Hospital Authority appointed medical coordinators for each major public hospital. The task group then reviewed and combined the Procedures for Handling Child Abuse Cases 1993 and the Procedures for Handling Child Sexual Abuse Cases 1996 into a comprehensive set of Procedures for Handling Child Abuse Cases – Revised 1998 encompassing all forms of child abuse. After accumulating practice experience for almost 10 years, the guidelines were revised again in 2007.

The number of child abuse cases has increased every year over the past 30 years. The Hong Kong community can no longer deny that this is a family problem as well as a social problem. To the grave concern of the community, shocking and traumatic child abuse cases continue to hit the headlines, despite the efforts made by government and nongovernment organizations (NGOs). The following statistics from the CPR show the increase in the number of reported child abuse cases from 2001 to 2010.

The increase may be partly due to people becoming more aware of the severity of the problem and being willing to admit that child abuse affects family harmony as well as social stability. However, there are many cases that are hidden or have gone unreported. The most commonly reported cases over the years have been those involving physical abuse. Sexual abuse cases have the second highest report rate. The statistics for neglect and psychological abuse remain very low. However, for a child, just one act of neglect can be fatal and one act of psychological abuse can have a long-term negative psychological impact. Can our child protection system effectively prevent child abuse and help families dealing with multiple and complex problems?

Table 1. Child Abuse Statistics in Hong Kong

Case	Year									
	2001	2002	2003	2004	2005	2006	2007	2008	2009	2010
Physical Abuse	306	292	277	345	413	438	499	483	503	488
Sexual Abuse	152	179	150	189	234	233	270	277	331	334
Neglect	29	17	20	40	41	77	114	78	102	113
Psychological Abuse	17	11	4	9	23	12	20	15	15	18
Multiple Abuse	31	21	30	39	52	46	41	29	42	48
Total	535	520	481	622	763	806	944	882	993	1001

(SWD Child Protection Registry Statistical Report 2001-2010).

A Public Health Approach

The World Health Organization (2002) recommends that health professionals take a public health approach to the early identification of child abuse. It regards child protection as a primary care service for child health and development that begins with good prenatal care and involves many disciplines working together to safeguard children. A public health approach looks at populations, not individual cases. For example, in relation to a problem such as SARS, we have to work outside the walls of hospitals; service in hospitals is only a part of the strategies needed to tackle the problem. To address SARS, we need to have extensive public education programs to remind people to wash their hands and wear masks in order to prevent the spreading of germs. We have to train the public to recognize the early signs, such as having a fever. The main focus is on the population and to prevent its occurrence (Scott, 2009).

In the case of child abuse and neglect, we have to establish the prevalence of the problem. The number of reported cases is the incidence, but we know very little about the prevalence of child abuse and the extent of the problem at the community level. A public health approach requires an understanding of the prevalence of the problem, clear classification and definitions, and clarity regarding the risk factors and the protective factors so that effective strategies, involving a combination of disciplines and methods, can be formulated at different levels of intervention.

Challenges Faced by Families

Families in Hong Kong face many challenges, such as long working hours, parenting stress, worries about children's futures, health, finance, and marital and in-law relationships.

Family problems affect individuals' mental health, and it becomes a vicious cycle as family and individual mental health problems increase the economic burdens of society.

Nowadays, many people travel between Hong Kong and Mainland China for business and work purposes. The family breadwinners, usually the fathers, spend more time out of the home, and this affects family life. The mothers left behind have to shoulder all parenting duties. Without support from their spouses, the stress experienced by these mothers increases. In cases where the fathers are involved in extramarital affairs in China, the family situation worsens.

Another phenomenon requiring attention is cross-border and new arrival families from Mainland China. In 2009, among 82,095 newborns, 7.6% were born to Mainland mothers and Hong Kong fathers (Type 1 babies) and 36.3% were born into families where both parents were from Mainland China (Type 2 babies) (HK Population Projections 2010-2039). The number of Type 2 babies has increased rapidly, from 1,250 in 2002 to 32,653 in 2010. From January to May 2011, 15,513 Type 2 babies were born in Hong Kong (Sing Tao News, June 15, 2011). The majority of these parents took the babies back to Mainland China but have the intention of bringing their children to Hong Kong for education. Around 10,000 young students travel across the border daily from Shen Zhen to Hong Kong to attend school and the number is on the increase; the safety of these children is a great concern. After successfully obtaining a one-way permit to Hong Kong, some mothers have to face adjustments and marital and in-law problems. Also, there is a group of single mothers, between 5,000 and 10,000, from Mainland China who face the problem of not being able to obtain a one-way permit to take care of their young children; these mothers have to travel back and forth frequently to renew their visas, and this seriously affects the care they can give their children, who have to suffer separation from their mothers and interruption to their studies.

Achieving a high level of education and a good academic performance are the main expectations parents have of their children. Although Hong Kong is famous in China for its quality education system and many mainland parents would like to send their children to school in Hong Kong, the whole system is still examination and achievement oriented. Parental pressure on children as a result of study issues is reflected in many child abuse cases.

Multidisciplinary Collaboration

It is everyone's responsibility to protect children from harm. The whole community in Hong Kong should invest in our children, and multiple disciplines should join hands at all levels of prevention to make the home a better and safer place for children to grow, explore, learn, and develop.

Primary Prevention

Child abuse and neglect is everyone's concern and should involve everyone. Intervention should be provided as early as possible; the earlier the intervention, the better the chance of success. To create a solid foundation for violence prevention at the earliest stage, support and knowledge about the developmental needs of children should be provided to new parents. In

1997, a Healthy Start Volunteer Home Visitation Model was developed by Against Child Abuse to provide home visits to support mothers-to-be and mothers in the Tuen Mun area during the prenatal/infancy period. Volunteers are trained to conduct home visits under the supervision of registered social workers in order to support mothers and their families to look after their own physical and psychological needs as well as those of their newborns. This model is as successful as a similar home visiting program provided by nurses in the United States (Chan and Lam, 2000; Olds et al., 1998). The mothers regard the volunteers as friends who share their experience and provide support. However, it is necessary to provide professional backup to the volunteers and professional involvement in risky cases.

There is no consensus with regard to what the problem is and what direction Hong Kong should take in seeking to solve the problem. The government has not committed itself to providing universal Healthy Start home visitation services to all families with newborns, including cross-border families.

We have neither good data linkage systems nor prevalence measures to know whether what we are doing is working or not. The existing CPR reports statistics of new cases without showing the total number of cases handled in the year. What the statistics reveal is the tip of the iceberg of the problem. We need prevalence data, and we also need to have epidemiological research on the causes of child abuse and neglect in order to discover an effective intervention approach to these problems.

Secondary Prevention

Secondary prevention targets the vulnerable and at risk. The government piloted the Comprehensive Child Development Services (CCDS) in 2005 for children aged 0-5 years and their families in four selected areas: Shum Shui Po, Tin Shui Wai, Tuen Mun, and Tseung Kwan O. The CCDS identifies at-risk pregnant women, mothers with postnatal depression, and children and families with psychosocial needs and refers them to the Integrated Family Services Centre (IFSC) for follow-up services. The CCDS services are provided by professionals (CCDS Review of Pilot Implementation, 2007). The additional workload may cause higher stress and lower morale among professionals in both the health and social welfare sectors. The CCDS services do not make home visits to unmotivated families, which are actually those most at risk of child abuse and family violence. It would be preferable to design a model of intervention that includes home visits that focus on the physical and psychological safety of the home and the parent-child relationship. Many unmotivated families will not seek help, but they would share their needs and difficulties if they were approached. While the government plans to extend the CCDS to the whole territory, this will still exclude many at high risk of family violence. Many cross-border families will not benefit from such a service if the mother is not a Hong Kong resident. These cross-border families eventually settle down in Hong Kong. There should be a cross-border mechanism and prevention services in place to support these split families. Against Child Abuse has established good parenting services for these families with newborns in partnership with the United Christian Hospital. The ultimate goal is to prevent child abuse by introducing child safety tips and positive parenting concepts, knowledge, and skills and providing community support. The government should support this kind of prevention project because, in the long run, it is cheaper than providing remedial services to violent and abusive families.

Other vulnerable groups include children injured as a result of being left unattended; children who have become addicted to the Internet world, influenced by its violence, or fallen into its sex traps; children with mental illness; children and families in poverty; single parents; and young mothers.

NGOs have made efforts to develop various projects to support such groups. As a child protection agency, Against Child Abuse initiated projects such as the Child Safe and Friendly Community in Wong Tai Sin Project to prevent children being left unattended; the Good Mother Parenting Project to build mutual help networks; the Good Parenting Project to support cross-border families with newborns; the Cyber Safety Project to strengthen children against falling into cyber traps; A Child's Voice for a Caring Community Project to create a platform for children to voice their views to the government, their families, schools, and the media; the Joyful Heart Project for children with mentally disturbed parents; the Bless My Home Forever Project for deprived families in Shum Shui Po; and the Daylily Project for young and single mothers. The aim of these projects is to support these groups throughout life, especially during difficult periods. Schools, hospitals, IFSCs, and NGOs refer children and families in need to receive services provided by trained volunteers and social workers.

However, there is no stable fund to sustain projects that prove to be effective and helpful in preventing child abuse. The government has set up all sorts of funds, but none of them involves a comprehensive and sustainable plan or a vision to achieve the goals of stopping violence against children and building a safe and friendly society for the optimal growth of children.

Tertiary Prevention

Tertiary prevention aims at the rehabilitation of victims, perpetrators, and significant parties. For over 30 years, both government and nongovernment organizations have been trying to combat the problem of child abuse and neglect. Efforts have been made in relation to multidisciplinary collaboration and handling. According to the Procedural Guide for Handling Child Abuse Cases (Social Welfare Department, 2007), a multidisciplinary child abuse case conference (MDCC) can be held for severe and complex cases. Professionals such as social workers, teachers, pediatricians, police officers, psychologists, and psychiatrists are involved in MDCCs. The purpose of the MDCC is to discuss and define the nature of a case and to formulate a welfare plan for the child and his/her family members. The welfare plan includes consideration of whether a foster home or a small group home should be sought, and whether a Care or Protection Order is required for the child and making a decision on which party will follow up on the child and the family and provide counseling services. Abuse and at-risk cases are registered to the CPR.

Professionals hesitate to define cases where children are badly hurt as abuse cases; rather, they define them as cases of harsh discipline or inadequate parenting because in their view, (a) the suspected abuser had no intention to harm; (b) defining such cases a child abuse means penalizing and labeling the perpetrator and could further ruin the parent-child relationship; and (c) the suspected abusers may have been provoked by the child's misbehavior.

It is usually up to the case worker or his/her supervisor to decide whether a MDCC is required. In fact, many child abuse cases do not require a MDCC if they can be managed at the casework level and do not require the involvement of a variety of professionals. But, what happens after the MDCC? Can the follow-up services help a child recover from the trauma of abuse? Will the abuser change his/her behavior and stop using violence? What kinds of intervention strategy work, and what does not work? What are the criteria for closing a case? Presently, there is no standard policy and system for social services to monitor the progress and effectiveness of follow-up work after the MDCC. It is usually up to the social worker and his/her supervisor to decide which strategies and interventions are employed. There is a great deal of room for improvement.

The safety of the child is always the paramount concern of child protection work. Identification and risk assessment are thus the first steps. To assess the risk, the following key factors must be considered: 1) the child's characteristics, 2) the abuser's characteristics, and 3) the environment's characteristics. Focusing on the rehabilitation of the child is, of course, crucial. However, without change on the part of the abusers, who are, in most cases, the child's parents, abused children are still unsafe if they are under the care of their abusers. Even if the abused children are placed in out-of-home care, such as foster homes or small group homes, the ultimate goal is family union, and no matter how far the parent and the child are apart physically, their emotional bond still strongly ties them together. To stop child abuse, working on and with the parent abusers is necessary.

What Can Be Improved?

Based on my experience of working within the system, I believe that there are various inadequacies in the current system: insufficient resources, lack of research and strategic evaluation, lack of professional development, lack of coordination of interagency collaboration, lack of child-friendly policies and child protection strategies, and inadequate legal protection for children. To improve the system, I suggest that the following areas should be given special attention and adequate resources.

Research and Strategic Evaluation

We do not want to conduct more research studies which are put on the shelf. We would like to see research that informs policy and is put into practice. Research on prevalence measures, identifying risk factors and protective factors, evaluating innovative approaches in service delivery, and doing cost-benefit analyses would help to formulate policies that make interventions to prevent child abuse and neglect more effective.

Professional Development

It is not only professional development in terms of knowledge and skills in child protection that is required. Child protection workers, police officers, teachers, and pediatricians, who all play important roles in identifying, investigating, assessing, and counseling cases of child abuse, have to go beyond procedures to provide individualized and holistic responses to the needy people they encounter. Developing correct professional attitudes is as important as developing knowledge and skills (Scott, 2009).

Building Bridges between Sectors

It is not possible for a single agency to respond to all of the needs of families with multiple and complex needs. There has been surface-level talk about working across sectors, but there has been little in-depth exploration of whether all families receive the support they need. There are differences in perception of a definition of abuse among the disciplines involved in dealing with child abuse. We need to work together and build partnerships to tackle the underlying deep barriers through trust.

THE WAYS AHEAD

Despite the many efforts made in the past, there is still a lot to be done to enhance parents' capacity to take care of their children, to ensure children's safety, and to increase family harmony in the face of rapid social changes. There is an urgent need to improve the system in order to safeguard children from abuse and neglect. We would like to see Hong Kong becomes a child-friendly city where children are well protected and free to participate and develop. To improve child-related legislation and policies, the following 10 strategies are suggested as the ways ahead.

1. Develop a data link system and conduct a prevalence study so as to inform policies and practices
   The number of reported child abuse cases represents the incidence of child abuse, and yet we know very little about the prevalence of child abuse and the extent of the problem. We have adopted a multidisciplinary approach, working together to safeguard children, but we have different data systems. The data in the Social Welfare Department's CPR is different from the data held by the Hospital Authority and the Police Child Protection Unit. We need to develop a data link system to inform policies and to make intervention policies to prevent child abuse and neglect more effective.
2. Ensure a home visitation to each family, including cross-border families with a newborn child
   A primary care service for child health and development begins with good prenatal care. A head start or healthy start with an intensive home visitation approach to each family with a newborn child has been proven effective in the early prevention of child abuse and neglect in many developed countries, and such an approach should be brought into mainstream services in Hong Kong (Old et al., 1998). Additional resources should be provided to form a professional team to follow up on at-risk families identified at CCDSs rather than referring these cases to IFSCs where the workload is already excessive.
3. Put effective preventive services into the mainstream

There are many funds available for NGOs wishing to pilot innovative projects, but the majority of them are one-off and/or short-term projects. Also, it is not certain that these projects, even those that have proved to be successful in supporting vulnerable children and parents, will be able to secure funds to sustain them. The responsibility of sustaining effective services falls on individual NGOs. Without additional manpower and resources, the workload and stress of frontline staff will probably increase, and this may compromise the quality of their work. We suggest that the government should put effective preventive services into the mainstream so that in-depth and appropriate services can be provided to children and families in need.

4. A serious and fatal child abuse cases review mechanism
Among the 209 cases reviewed in the child fatality pilot project review of 2010, 88 children died of non-natural causes: 32 (15.3%) died as a result of accidents, including falls, drowning, drug overdose, and choking; 24 (11.5%) committed suicide; 11 (5.3%) died as a result of assault; and 21 (10.1%) died as a result of miscellaneous other causes (Child Fatality Review, Final Report, 2010). Some of these fatal incidents could have been prevented if signs of their seriousness had been detected and identified at an earlier stage. A mechanism to review serious child abuse cases is required; such reviews could be included in the current Fatality Review Mechanism with the purpose of preventing tragedies. Every child matters. Every child has a right to survival and protection. It is the state's responsibility to ensure that every child is safe and free from abuse.
5. Concern for the psychological abuse of child victims and children who are emotionally disturbed
As a result of the efforts made in the past three decades, the community has become aware that physical abuse is not just a family matter. We have procedures in place for handling complex cases, especially child sexual abuse cases, and more child neglect cases are reported these days. However, psychological abuse is still not easy to identify and handle. The news reports children who are involved in drugs and in bullying and also those who commit suicide. What has been happening to them? Are their voices heard? Are they psychologically wounded? Have they been abused without being identified or defined? Even though, according to the CPR, the number of psychological child abuse cases is not high, the problem may be serious. As we are entering into the fourth decade of child protection work, we should put the focus on, and effort into, identifying and helping children who are psychologically harmed. The psychological well-being of children cannot be ignored.
6. A total ban on corporal punishment
Corporal punishment is a form of violence and an infringement of children's rights. Hong Kong has banned the flogging of convicts in prison and has an Education Ordinance to prohibit corporal punishment in schools. However, Hong Kong has not been determined enough to enforce a policy of zero tolerance toward violence against children by outlawing corporal punishment like 30 countries have done by legislating against corporal punishment in the home and the community. We urge the government to support and educate parents and to ensure that children's rights in this matter are actualized.
7. Mandatory sex offenders registry

The government has launched a voluntary sex conviction record check in December 2011. This is an administrative measure and is only applicable to new employees. We suggest that this check should be extended to all of those involved in child-related work, including all staff and volunteers. Parents should also be given the right to check the private tutors they employ. Ultimately, a mandatory system should be put in place to provide children with overall protection from risk of abuse.

8. A review of sentencing options that requires every convict to receive therapy and treatment

   The existing treatment for offenders provided by the correctional services operates on a voluntary basis. To better safeguard children and minimize the chance of reoffending, we suggest that the sentencing options should be reviewed and that every convict should be required to receive therapy and treatment. The follow-up probation service for prisoners after their discharge from prison should be reviewed and strengthened.

9. Laws and ways to protect unattended children

   In 1991, a government consultation paper concluded that it was not the right time for legislation on the issue of leaving children unattended. Twenty years later, the problem has still not been resolved; we still have children dying as a result of being left unattended. Apart from educating parents/child minders and providing child care support, the government should seriously consider various means and review legislation to protect children from being left unattended. Even a one act of neglect can be fatal.

10. A child commission to represent children

    To ensure that the voices and perspectives of children are heard and considered, an independent child commission should be set up to look into all child-related issues (Committee on the Rights of the Child, United Nations, 2005). Its work should be to centralize relevant data, examine policies and legislation related to children, look into cases and concerns that violate children's rights, educate and share experiences, and so on. Child commissions have been established in many countries, such as Norway, Sweden, Canada, Australia, and the UK, and they have been effective in ensuring that children's needs are attended to and that safe and caring communities are developed. Hong Kong has an Elderly Commission, a Youth Commission, and a Women's Commission; there is no reason for the government to fail our children and delay the establishment of a child commission.

Conclusion

Professional development in relation to knowledge, skills, and especially, correct attitudes is needed. Professionals from different disciplines should actively listen to and share with each other and work in collaboration to keep children physically safe and psychologically secure. Most importantly, we should take our children seriously, listen to their voices, and respond to their needs. What our society will be like depends on how determined we are to provide a safe and nonviolent environment at home and in society for our children today.

The government of the HKSAR submitted a report to the United Nations Committee on the Rights of the Child in 2005. The committee suggested the following: (a) that Hong Kong's legislation and policies on child protection should embody a comprehensive approach to the implementation of the UN Convention on the Rights of the Child and that priority be given to children's issues; (b) that there should be an independent national human rights institution which has a mandate to receive, investigate, and address complaints from the public, including individual children, and that this institution should be provided with adequate financial, human, and material resources (UN concluding observation, 2005). A child commission should be established to address and deal with all issues related to children. The HKSAR government will submit another report to the UN Committee on the Rights of the Child. Let us hope that the government will soon realize the need to set up a child commission in order to really make children's welfare and safety a priority.

REFERENCES

Chan, Y. C., and Lam, G. L. T. (2000). Project research and evaluation. In Part IV, *Healthy start home visiting program report* (pp.32-36). Hong Kong, China: Against Child Abuse.

Committee on the Rights of the Child, United Nations. (2005). *Concluding observations*. Geneva, Switzerland: United Nations.

Family Health Service, Department of Health, HKSAR. (2007). *Comprehensive child development services evaluation report*. Hong Kong, China: Department of Health.

Census and Statistics Department, HKSAR. (2010). Hong Kong Population Projections 2010-2039. Hong Kong, China: Census and Statistics Department.

Olds, D., Henderson, C., Kitzman, H., Eckenrode, J., Cole, R., and Tatelbaum, R. (1998). The promise of home visitations: Results of two randomized trials. *Journal of Community Psychology, 26*, 5-21.

Lui, P. (2003). Important milestones in child protection in Hong Kong. In N. Rhind (Ed.), *Child protection training manual* (2nd edition), Against Child Abuse.

Scott, D. (2009). *A public health approach to child protection*. Seminar report, University of Stirling.

Social Welfare Department. (2007). *Procedural guide for handling child abuse case, revised*. Hong Kong, China: Social Welfare Department.

Social Welfare Department. (2010). *Review panel of the pilot project on child fatality review: Final report*. Hong Kong, China: Social Welfare Department.

Social Welfare Department. (2001-2010). *Child protection registry, statistical report*. Hong Kong, China: Social Welfare Department.

World Health Organization. (2002). World report on violence and health. Geneva, Switzerland: WHO Press.

In: Child Protection in Chinese Societies
Editor: Ko Ling Chan
ISBN: 978-1-61942-879-9

Chapter 11

THE SOCIAL SUPPORT SYSTEM FOR CHILDREN ORPHANED BY HIV/AIDS

Ling Cheng and Deping Xiang
College of Sociology
Central China Normal University, P. R. China

ABSTRACT

With rising public awareness of HIV/AIDS, the living condition of children orphaned by HIV/AIDS has gradually become a focal issue in society. Since the onset of this disease, children orphaned by HIV/AIDS have emerged as a new social group. Struggling with family difficulties, social stigma, and other difficulties, these children have become a typical vulnerable group in society. It is therefore necessary to explore the living condition and unmet basic needs of children orphaned by HIV/AIDS so as to establish a certain social psychological care model and social support system to meet their needs and enable their healthy development. This chapter aims to examine the living condition and social environment of HIV/AIDS orphaned children, to analyze their needs, and to suggest ways to build an effective social support system for them through field investigations.

Keywords: Needs; Children orphaned by HIV; Social support system

INTRODUCTION

The Problem of HIV/AIDS

Since the first HIV case was diagnosed in China in 1985, the HIV pandemic has gone through the afferent phase and the transmission phase followed by the HIV epidemic stage. According to the Ministry of Health of the People's Republic of China, as at October 2010,

HIV had affected over 370,000 people, with about 130,000 patients and about 68,000 deaths.[1] At present, the HIV epidemic in China is still at a critical stage.

Currently, the prevalence of the HIV epidemic in China remains at a low level in general, but it is high among specific subgroups and there are clusters in certain areas. Specifically, the HIV epidemic in China has the following characteristics: the speed at which the disease is spreading is slow; sexual contact is the major means of transmission; vast differences exist across various affected areas; and the disease is spreading from high risk groups to the general population.[2]

The influence of the HIV/AIDS epidemic can be demonstrated at multiple levels. The General Assembly of the United Nations' Declaration of Commitment on HIV/AIDS states that "AIDS will still be a global crisis, a challenge to human dignity, human life, and human rights. AIDS will hinder global societal and economic development, influencing every social class, including nations, communities, families, and individuals." HIV/AIDS not only affects individuals' productivity, leading to financial and life difficulties. The discrimination and aggression prevalent in society means that AID/HIV patients also face various social and societal problems. These problems not only hinder their treatment and recovery, thus affecting their living condition and quality of life; they also disturb the stability and development of society. HIV/AIDS disease control has become a global problem; every country in the world is exploring effective ways to prevent and control the disease.

As HIV/AIDS spreads, the number of children affected by the disease is rising. Living problems, parents' illness, and discrimination and stigmatization by society have irreversible consequences on the physical and mental growth of HIV/AIDS children, making them a doubly vulnerable group. Through an investigation of HIV/AIDS children in Suizhou and Xiangfan cities in Hubei province, we tried to understand their living, learning, and social conditions in order to suggest ways to build a social support network for HIV/AIDS orphaned children based on their conditions and characteristics.

In general, social support can be classified into two categories: (a) objective social support refers to direct material support as well as to the existence and involvement of social networks and communities; and (b) subjective social support means the subjective experience of emotional support, which is the feeling of satisfaction generated by the feeling of being respected, supported, and understood in society. In sociological terms, social support refers to a supportive action provided by a social network to deprived groups through material and psychological assistance. In this chapter, the term *social support* has three connotations. First, the social interactions between an individual and his/her significant others (i.e., family and friends) at times of crisis; an individual receives emotional, instrumental, and informational support from his/her significant others when confronting difficulties. In this chapter, social support primarily refers to the support that children orphaned by HIV/AIDS get from their family and peers. Second, social support refers to the perceived connections with others that make children orphaned by HIV/AIDS feel cared for, encouraged, and accepted. In this chapter, we focus on the support they receive from neighbors, teachers, and people in society. Third, social support refers to actual behaviors expressed by others to the children.

[1] Bai JianFeng (2010). The attenuation of the HIV epidemic. Beijing: The People's Daily Press (in Chinese).

[2] China's News Net, *New Characteristics of China's HIV Epidemic: The production of the second period of immune system*. http://www.chinanews.com/jk/2010/12-01/2691285.shtml.

In this chapter, we report a study conducted using a survey questionnaire and in-depth interviews with HIV/AIDS families and their children. We chose the cities of Suizhou and Xiangfan in Hubei province as the study sites for three reasons. First, these two cities have the largest concentrations of HIV/AIDS patients, and this made it more convenient for participant recruitment. Second, HIV transmission in these two cities involves sexual contact transmission, blood transmission, and mother to infant transmission; hence, the sample would be more representative. Third, the disclosure of HIV/AIDS patients differs significantly in these two cities; thus, the educational systems, social support systems, and the implementation of national policies are different. Therefore, these two cities were selected to facilitate a comparison of social support systems and their impact on the physiological and psychological development of HIV/AIDS orphaned children in order to build an effective support model for them.

In this chapter, an HIV/AIDS orphaned child is regarded as any child who is directly influenced by HIV/AIDS. Specifically, this involves three categories of children: first, orphans whose parents died of HIV/AIDS; second, children from single-parent families in which one parent died of HIV/AIDS; third, children with one parent infected by HIV/AIDS. An important point to note regarding the third category is that despite the fact that both parents are still alive, they can die at any time once they enter the AIDS stage; thus, these children were also included in this study. Among the 152 HIV/AIDS orphaned children in this study, 83 were from Suizhou and 69 were from Xiangfan. The sample consisted of 82 males (53.9%) and 70 females (46.1%). The eldest child was 18 years old and the youngest was 5, the mean age being 14. The group most affected by HIV/AIDS consisted of 79 children (52%): 16 children (10.5%) had lost both parents, 32 children (21.1%) had lost their fathers, and 25 (16.4%) had lost their mothers. Due to the sensitivity of this research topic and the special characteristics of the participants, this chapter omits most of the survey data and the results of the analyses. Nonetheless, all of the discussions and conclusions are based on the data and analyses results.

Social Support Status of HIV/AIDS Orphaned Children

This section mainly analyzes the current social support received by HIV/AIDS orphaned children, including support from family, school, community, society, and government.

Family Support

The family is the basic unit of care in a society. According to the survey, 68.5% and 66.4% of the HIV/AIDS orphaned children were living with their fathers and mothers, respectively. A significant proportion of them were living with their paternal grandfathers, paternal grandmothers, maternal grandfathers, and maternal grandmothers (respectively, 16.8%, 30.9%, 2.7%, and 3.4%). Some were living with their father's or mother's brothers (5.4% and 2%, respectively). These results showed that the major caregivers of these children were single fathers or mothers and grandparents. As for the guardians of these orphans, most were senior members of the paternal family. Thus, in this study, the children orphaned by

HIV/AIDS were generally fostered by kinsfolk; this may be the best alternative way to socialize the children.

Regardless of who they were living with, the HIV/AIDS orphaned children in this study had enough shelter, food, and clothing, and they felt the warmth of their families. Nonetheless, it can be difficult for a family to provide adequate support for a HIV/AIDS child. First, the HIV disease can cause financial difficulties for the family, thus leading to a lack of resources to provide for the child's needs in terms of healthy physical development and basic living. Second, the HIV disease destroys the interpersonal relationships that a child needs for his/her development. HIV/AIDS orphaned children suffer from discrimination, stigmatization, and isolation in society. Third, the basic needs of HIV/AIDS orphaned children are barely satisfied by their guardians due to whose own illness; however, their emotional, educational, competency, cultivation, and moral education needs are hardly met at all. In this study, 31.1% of the HIV/AIDS orphaned children preferred to keep their difficulties to themselves rather than disclose them to their guardians; only 28.8% of the children said that they would talk to their guardians. This illustrated that the children received relatively little emotional/psychological support from their families.

School Support

School is an important place in an individual's socialization process. A child gains acceptance and identity from being a member of groups. The results showed that 72.7% of HIV/AIDS orphaned children were still attending school, while 27.3% were not. A few of the children had dropped out of school due to HIV/AIDS in their families.

In terms of academic performance, 20.6% of the HIV/AIDS children in this study were above average, 43% were average, and 15.8% were below average. The performance of most of the children was average. Concerns about their family members' disease and the real burden of their families were probably the major reasons behind the mediocre grades of the children, but a lack of motivation to study due to the perceived discrimination from teachers and peers might be another reason.

The results also showed that (a) more HIV/AIDS orphaned children liked their teachers (58.1%) than had teachers who liked them (48.3%); (b) only 37.1% of the children and teachers liked each other and 10.5% disliked each other; and (c) 21% of the children liked their teachers but did not receive attention from them, while only 6.7% of them felt that their teachers liked them despite the fact that they did not like their teachers. The level of liking for teachers increased in line with the perceived attention from their teachers. The children returned the same amount of affection if they felt that their teachers liked them. However, the data showed that teachers did not give enough attention to the children or like the children enough. When the children noticed that their teachers did not pay attention to them, or even discriminated against them, they became tired of school life.

Community Support

Community support refers to attitudes toward and acceptance of HIV/AIDS orphaned children within their communities (including community organizations, residents, and peers).

Among all of the child participants in this study, only 5.8% had no friends, while 94.2% had one to six friends. This shows that the HIV/AIDS orphaned children in this study were not rejected by their peers because of their family problems and that they still had their own friends and did not experience much pressure from society. However, the results from the interviews with non-HIV/AIDS families revealed that guardians tried to limit their children's contact with children from HIV/AIDS families in order to avoid infection through blood transmission caused by play injuries. This demonstrated that implicit discrimination against, and isolation of, HIV/AIDS orphaned children still exist.

Regarding visitations, this study found that neighbors and relatives were the most frequent visitors to the HIV/AIDS orphaned children, followed by community physicians. However, community residents still had feelings of fear toward HIV/AIDS. The reason why neighbors were one of the most frequent visitors was because the traditional social network in rural areas emphasizes that "a distant relative is not as good as a near neighbor." The residents therefore sympathized with and cared for the HIV/AIDS families in their communities.

Social Support

Social support refers to support from nongovernmental organizations (NGOs) and the public for the children's financial, medical, educational, and other needs. Since the start of the HIV epidemic, international organizations such as The Globe Fund and Médecins Sans Frontières (MSF), China's AIDS initiatives such as the Women's Federation and the Chinese Communist Youth League, and the general public have all provided aid to HIV/AIDS orphaned children to help with their financial, material, medical, educational, and competence development and other needs. The results of this study showed that the social support received by HIV/AIDS orphaned children was relatively little. There were two problems with the social support provided to these children: (1) nonsustainability—social support organized by international, national, and social agencies is program-based; the HIV/AIDS orphaned children in this study received aid from these programs only when they were operational and lost it soon after a program ended; (2) disparities—international and social sources of aid for HIV/AIDS children are target-specific and have their own purposes, and thus not all HIV/AIDS children are covered.

The social support situation for HIV/AIDS children is related to the development of NGOs in China. NGOs in China have been developing since the country opened up. In terms of quantity, the number of the NGOs has increased by geometric progression, with activities covering each profession. In terms of impact and effects, NGOs have become a force that cannot be ignored. Nonetheless, the NGOs in China still face many problems, such as a lack of legal and social support, premature management, and ambiguous boundaries between NGOs and government organizations. Fully utilizing NGO resources in China is therefore a key step in tackling the problem of HIV/AIDS orphaned children. HIV/AIDS prevention/intervention is a national systematic mission that requires the participation and cooperation of every sector of society. Due to the exceptional nature of this task, some prevention, intervention, and treatment programs are not suitable for the government to organize; the intervention of NGOs and social agencies is therefore of great significance.

Governmental Support

The government is the main force in the provision of aid to HIV/AIDS patients. A government helps by establishing a comprehensive social security and welfare system to ensure the basic survival needs of people with HIV/AIDS. The central government in China has issued a series of policies to provide social support for people living with HIV/AIDS. The issue of HIV/AIDS orphaned children has been raised at a high level. In 2003, the central government issued the "Four Frees and One Care" policy to provide free schooling for children orphaned by AIDS. In the 9-year compulsory education program, school fees and textbook costs are waived for children for families affected by HIV/AIDS, and in further education programs, more financial aid is given to these students to ensure that they complete their studies. Relatives and people in general are encouraged to adopt or foster HIV/AIDS orphaned children, while those who are not adopted are cared for by welfare institutions. These policies tackle the living condition of the children to ensure that, in spite of their financial difficulties, they complete the 9-year education program.

Nonetheless, there are inadequacies in what the government has done. First, the total amount of social support is still insufficient. Although the nation and society has provided a lot of resources, it is still far from adequate to meet the needs of HIV/AIDS orphaned children. Second, the structure of the support is simple. Currently, the social support available is mainly financial and medical; psychological and interpersonal resources are still lacking. Even the financial social support is limited to providing a small amount of money, living necessities, and agricultural materials. Third, the existing social support system lacks specificity. Besides making and enacting the policies, the government and society also need to pay attention to the effectiveness and specificity of the policies; otherwise, a policy loses its meaning if it cannot fulfill its objective when established.

THE NEEDS OF HIV/AIDS ORPHANED CHILDREN

The impacts that HIV/AIDS have on a family include changing the family's resources and structures and the roles of family members. First, since most AIDS patients are in young or mid adulthood, their sickness and death significantly reduces their family's labor force and income. Second, families have to pay the medical expenses and funeral expenses of AIDS patients; these expenses are incurred for any family member if they get sick or die, but they are an additional burden on families. Third, families have to cope with the discrimination, social exclusion, family disintegration, and shrinking social networks brought by HIV/AIDS. Females, in particular, are the carers, and they play a supportive role within the family. Other family members will be significantly affected if the female members of the family are infected with, or die from, HIV/AIDS.

Every change in a family, whether abrupt or gradual, alters the normal life of children orphaned by HIV/AIDS. As a result, they need more help from family, community, school, society, and government in order to survive and develop. The current social support system has not yet been able to provide an adequate survival and developmental environment for these children. Overall, the needs of HIV/AIDS orphaned children include the need for care, mental and psychological support, and acceptance and an equal opportunity to develop.

Need for Care

The need for care is the first need of children orphaned by HIV/AIDS and forms the basis of their survival and development. It includes three needs: the need for survival, safety, and family emotional support.

These children experience financial and material deprivation. The direct impact of HIV/AIDS is the weakening of the family's working capacity and labor force, and this ultimately leads to a loss of income. Second, treatment and funeral costs aggravate the financial difficulties of HIV/AIDS families. The results of this study showed that most HIV/AIDS families only have just enough food and clothing to maintain themselves. The food they can afford is mainly high-grain food, which provides a low level of nutrition. These families also have inadequate resources in other aspects of their lives (e.g., living condition; commuting costs; personal development) due to financial constraints.

In general, the existing social support system cannot guarantee the livelihood of HIV/AIDS orphaned children because of limited social resources, the uneven distribution of these resources, and the instability of social support resources.

The existence of HIV/AIDS in a family also poses a threat to children's health and safety. If HIV/AIDS kills their parents, children will grow up without their parents' protection, and this could jeopardize their health, safety, and security. Economic deprivation and the loss of their carers result in children orphaned by HIV/AIDS having acute care needs.

Mental and Psychological Needs

The family is a child's shelter. Children receive protection, love, and care from their families from birth. However, discrimination, stigmatization, and rejection by society often leave these children feeling sad and hurt. Moreover, family disintegration, parents' separation, living difficulties, and dropping out of school can result in loneliness, depression, anxiety, fear, lack of security, and other emotional disturbances for children orphaned by HIV/AIDS.

One of the main factors that have adverse consequences on these children's mental health is social discrimination and rejection. As a result of this discrimination and rejection, their social networks are broken and they experience internalized stigma; therefore, they automatically choose to leave the mainstream and consequently become isolated, which results in a deterioration in their mental health state.

Another factor that causes these children's mental health issues is the drastic change in the family structure or the need to live with other guardians. Generally, children are moved to their grandparents' house after their parents die. This change and the generational gap between the children and their grandparents often mean that these children refuse to talk to their grandparents about their difficulties. As time passes, loneliness, helplessness, and depression grows. In addition, guardians are often not able to give enough attention to the HIV/AIDS orphaned children living in their household, especially when it comes to their psychological and emotional needs, because there is one more person in their family and so the adults need to put more time and effort into earning income for the family. This issue is especially pertinent in rural areas. Guardians also tend to hesitate when it comes to disciplining the HIV/AIDS orphaned children. Under such conditions, it is hard for

HIV/AIDS orphaned children to integrate into their new family life or to build a sense of belonging. It is therefore likely that such children will suffer from undersupervision or ineffective discipline, which can result in antagonistic behaviors which, in turn, make it more likely that the children will develop mental problems.

Need to Be Interacted with and Accepted

Interaction and acceptance are significant to children orphaned by HIV/AIDS. Peer interaction is a two-way interactive process which allows for the mutual sharing of emotions and acceptance. Through interaction with peers, self-identity is formed, and this can help the children separate themselves from their parents and guardians. Sharing with peers also allows these children to vent their feelings of suppression and dissatisfaction, and this helps them to cope with the difficulties that may arise in real life.

The urgent need of children orphaned by HIV/AIDS is to be accepted and supported by their peers; this need is more pressing for, and is more implicitly expressed by, these children compared to normal children. These children tend to seek support from their peers at the time they lose their parent(s) as a substitute for their own emotional needs. However, the social status of HIV/AIDS also makes these children hesitant when facing their peers. The biggest problem in their peer interactions is the peers' prejudice toward HIV/AIDS. As their peers may lack knowledge about HIV transmission, they may refuse to hang out, communicate, or play with the children from families with HIV. They may not be willing to stay with them, eat at the same dining table, or let them join their activities, thus leaving them isolated. At worst, their peers may even humiliate them; this would cause huge psychological damage to HIV/AIDS orphaned children and result in serious negative consequences in terms of their socialization.

Developmental Needs

For children orphaned by HIV/AIDS, the need to develop refers to the need for education, marriage, employment, and opportunities to obtain certain social adaptation skills. In reality, however, these children are almost in a state of quarantine in terms of political participation, interaction with peers, involvement in social activities, employment, and marriage. One reason for their quarantine status is family financial constraints. If a family is suffering financial difficulties, the most common solution is to let the children enter the labor force early, and this influences negatively on children's development.

The second reason is that the children themselves give up. When some children are faced with a change in their family structure and social discrimination, they choose to withdraw from school to reduce the burden on their families and to avoid social pressure. As they cannot obtain high wages in the labor market, they slip into a more reactive state and their living condition becomes more difficult. Also, if their colleagues discover that they are from a family with HIV/AIDS, they may lose their jobs. Once this information has been disclosed, their career opportunities are destined to be different from those of normal children. Apart from employment, HIV/AIDS orphaned children often fail in marriage because of their partner's ignorance and discrimination. All of the active and passive rejections experienced by HIV/AID orphaned children result in their developmental needs being unmet. Their developmental needs in relation to education, employment, marriage, and so on are the most salient.

Construction of a Social Support System

Children orphaned by HIV/AIDS suffer from the loss of their parents as well as from discrimination by society, thus making them a doubly vulnerable group that requires more urgent care. An integrated social support system is needed. This system should be different from the existing system, which only emphasizes providing aid to cover the basic needs of children (e.g., food, clothing, and shelter); it should also emphasize the all aspects of the development needs of children: education, mental health, interpersonal relationships, and so on. These children should be treated as a unique group of people with special needs. With integrated government policies and the support of society, communities, schools, and families, an integrated social support system can be constructed.

Family-Based Social Support System

The family is the shelter for HIV/AIDS orphaned children. It has significant impacts on the physical and mental growth of these children. An incomplete family structure will cause different problems in relation to the growth of a HIV/AIDS orphaned child, including incomplete personality development, weak academic performance, deviance, and difficulties in interpersonal relationships. To maximize the quality of life of these children, family support and care is needed to help to foster a positive and optimistic attitude toward life in these children and provide developmental resources.

The family-based social support system should include the means to provide the children with survival and developmental resources, thus helping them to plan for future significant life issues, and educate them on HIV infection prevention within the family and palliative care. Through family care, the children's quality of life can be maximized to help them to socialize normally.

In terms of the physical and psychological difficulties of HIV/AIDS orphaned children, the government should provide training and management to their guardians or carers. The purpose of this measure would be to strengthen their social responsibility and awareness and to make them realize that bringing up HIV/AIDS orphaned children is not only a family affair, but also a part of the social support system for these children within society. Moreover, the government should help the guardians or carers to understand the concept of human rights in order to ensure that the human rights of HIV/AIDS orphaned children are protected. The government should also keep track of foster families and provide adequate supervision. More resources should be allocated for children being taken care of by grandparents who are in weak physical health. Guardians and carers should help HIV/AIDS orphaned children to develop self-esteem and self-acceptance in order to ensure that these children will be able to live a normal life in the future.

Community-Based Social Support System

A community can function as a platform to provide social support. In Mainland China, a community is a significant unit in society that impacts on family and personal life. To strengthen social support, comprehensive community building needs to be developed. Community awareness needs to be raised and biases against HIV/AIDS orphaned children need to be eliminated in order to establish a supportive environment. Local activities at the community level should be promoted to sustain the integrated social support system.

When the transmission of HIV/AIDS and relevant knowledge are widely publicized, the misconceptions about HIV/AIDS can be challenged in order to change the general public's negative perception of the disease. Providing help to HIV/AIDS families or to members of these families demonstrates the support given by the public to these particular groups of people and could ultimately reduce the pressure they feel from society and increase their sense of belonging to the community.

Communities and the government should work together hand in hand in mutual trust and interact together to effectively control and prevent HIV/AIDS. While the government provides funding and establishes policies, the community should mobilize volunteers to support the children and provide feedback to the government on the problems and needs of the children and their families.

School-Based Social Support System

Moral education and life skills training are effective means of improving the physical and mental health of children orphaned by HIV/AIDS. A school functions as a base for providing social support and care to these children by offering educational activities to develop their potential and creativity, to increase their self-esteem, tolerance and cooperation; and to enhance their coping ability.

Values education and living skills training are effective ways to improve the mental health status of young people. Intensifying school education is also an effective means of providing a substitute for the lack of family education to HIV/AIDS orphaned children. Through school-based social support programs, these children can be involved in normal interactions with peers and in developing the various psychological resources they need to cope with problems and develop healthily. Such activities can also help them to turn their mourning for their parents into a desire to work harder.

Government-Led Social Support System

The government functions as the main social support for children orphaned by HIV/AIDS. At present, the greatest hardship faced by HIV/AIDS families is poverty, which is primarily due to having lost a member of the family's labor force, and huge medical expenses. The government should therefore include people living with HIV/AIDS in its social security coverage and provide them with certain social welfare, insurance, and assistance benefits to protect their right to survival and improve their quality of life.

Currently, there are social assistance policies for people living with HIV/AIDS but not for children orphaned by the disease. China has gradually established policies on HIV/AIDS related to prevention, intervention, protection, and assistance, but the coverage is limited and the means are oversimplified. Due to financial and material resources constraints, the resources currently available are mostly financial and medical. Policies on the psychological and interpersonal needs of people living with HIV/AIDS and the special needs of HIV/AIDS orphaned children have yet to be developed to foster their healthy development.

To create human resources incentives for HIV/AIDS affected families, apart from providing free education for affected children, the government should also waive fees on education-related materials and facilities and provide additional subsidies to these children to enable them to finish formal education.

Meanwhile, the negative image of people living with HIV/AIDS should be eradicated in order to encourage public tolerance, acceptance, understanding, and trust of them. The ignorance and prejudice toward HIV/AIDS is the source of discrimination against and rejection of people living with HIV/AIDS and the orphans. Therefore, as the primary information channel for the general public, the mass media should take on responsibility for disseminating scientific and accurate HIV/AIDS knowledge and avoiding sensitizing and negative reporting.

Society-Based Social Support

The establishment of a social support system needs the cooperation and support of all sectors of society. In building the system, the key is to establish cooperation between government and nongovernment organizations. NGOs play a significant role in supplying care services and volunteer home-care training. After their professional training, volunteers are equipped with the basic knowledge and skills. In addition, NGOs also function as a medium for providing information, consultations, and policy suggestions to the government to increase the quality of the services it provides to HIV/AIDS orphaned children.

We should mobilize social organizations to help HIV/AIDS orphaned children and rely on professional social services concepts and skills to provide services to these children. These social organizations include enterprises and NGOs, both of which are significant forces in aiding HIV/AIDS orphaned children. Policies to encourage the involvement of social organizations in this cause need to be enacted.

NGOs have volunteering, nonprofit, and self-service characteristics. To establish a social support network for HIV/AIDS orphaned children, these organizations need to be utilized; charitable organizations, fund-raising groups, counseling organizations, and other NGOs can help to expand the social support system in diverse ways. The government should promote the development of NGOs and help them to develop more standardized and centralized forms in order to maximize their effectiveness.

Lastly, families, schools, communities, the government, and the whole of society need to be integrated in order to form a social support system for HIV/AIDS orphaned children; the government should play the lead role while the other actors actively cooperate.

REFERENCES

Ashley, D. F., and Wasserman, S. (2002). Social support and social networks: Synthesis and review. In J. A. Levy and B. A. Pescosolido (Eds.), *Social networks and health* (pp. 29-73). JAI Press:Greenwich,CT.

Barrera, M., and Ainlay, S. L. (1983). The structure of social support: A conceptual and empirical analysis. *Journal of Community Psychology, 11,* 133-143.

Chen, C., and Pan, Z. (2000). The sociological meaning of social support. HuNan Normal University's Sociology Press, 6. (in Chinese).

Huang, C. (2010). The nurturing model of children orphaned by HIV. Journal of Hebei Youth Administrative Cadres College, 1. (in Chinese).

Liu, B. (2005). The assistance and emplacement model for Henan province's children orphaned by HIV. Social Welfare, 10. (in Chinese).

Liu, B. (2011). China's children orphaned by HIV: Retrospect and prospect. China Agriculture University Press (Social Science Edition), 1. (in Chinese).

Liu, N. (2005). HIV, stigma, and social discrimination: Quantitative analysis of both national and local groups of people. Sociology Research, 6. (in Chinese).

Qiu, H. (1998). The transition of the social support construct: from singular to multi. Sociology Research, 4. (in Chinese).

Turner, H., Pearlin, L., and Mullan, J. (1998). Sources and determinants of social support for caregivers of persons with AIDS. *Journal of Health and Social Behavior, 39,* 137-151.

Wang, H., and Yang, S. (2009). "Relation isolated island": Socializing plight of rural AIDS orphans and countermeasures. A social survey from rural AIDS areas in Hubei and Henan. Journal of South-Central University for Nationalities (Humanities and Social Sciences), 29(4) (in Chinese).

Wang, J. (2003). The impoverished social group in China and its social support system. HuNan's Sociology, 5. (in Chinese).

Wellman, B., and Wortley, S. (1989). Brothers' keepers: Situating kinship relations in broader networks of social support. *Sociological Perspectives, 32.*

Xiang, D., and Chen, Q. (2004). The social support of HIV carriers. Academic Forum, 3. (in Chinese).

Xiang D., and Tang, L. (2006). The social discrimination against HIV carriers in rural areas. East China Normal University Press: Philo-social science edition, 6. (in Chinese).

Yang, S. (2006). The problem confronted by China's children orphaned by HIV and its countermeasure. China Society Periodical, 10. (in Chinese).

Zhou, X., and Chang, Y. (2005). The practical application of a social support system in society. China Agriculture University Press (Social Science Edition), 2. (in Chinese).

In: Child Protection in Chinese Societies
Editor: Ko Ling Chan
ISBN: 978-1-61942-879-9

Chapter 12

HOSPITAL-BASED EDUCATION PROGRAM FOR THE PREVENTION OF CHILD ACCIDENTAL INJURY

Qingying Ji
Social Work Department, Shanghai Children's Medical Center, P. R. China

ABSTRACT

As the world's economy has grown, the child mortality rate due to infectious and contagious diseases has dropped significantly. However, while the latest developments in medical research and technologies are improving the health of children, the situation with regard to child injuries and deaths has worsened considerably. Accidental child injury can be fatal, and it has a significant impact on both families and society. It has been recognized as an essential child health issue by international academic communities. This chapter explains the importance and the necessity of child safety education by reviewing the literature and presenting typical cases. It then introduces the strategies used to organize educational programs. It discusses in detail how to cultivate a harmless environment for children and provides accompanying guidance on educating parents and suggestions to the government and society on the protection of children.

Keywords: Child injury, Hospital-based, Prevention education

INTRODUCTION

The Definition and Concept of Accidental Injury

Injury refers to an acute injury to the body as a result of body parts being (a) exposed to damaging energy (kinetic, thermal, chemical, or electrical) or (b) devoid of some material essential for life (e.g., oxygen when drowned; heat when injured in freezing temperatures) (Yang, 2005). Injuries can be categorized into accidental and intentional injuries. The term *accidental injury* means that the injury to the body is caused by an external, abrupt, unintended, and nonillness-related event (WHO, 2008).

The term *child accidental injury* refers to events which (a) happen in daily life, (b) occur suddenly, and (c) cause damage to the safety and health of children due to their unexpected and unpreventable nature (Chen, 2011). Child accidental injury is listed in ICD-9 as a category of illness, and it includes the following: traffic accident, poisoning, falling, bitten or struck by insect or animal, burns/scalds, drowning, chocking/suffocation, crash/squeeze injury, cutting/piercing, and electric shock (Liu, 2005). It can also be categorized according to the characteristics of the event: (1) by the cause of the injury: suffocation, drowning, traffic accident, poisoning, fall, burn/scalding, electric shock, natural disaster (earthquake, flood, debris flow, hurricane, avalanche, landslide, etc.), smash injury, and other injuries, such as injuries caused by firecrackers, machines, or sharp items and animal bites; (2) by the nature of injury: physical (e.g., burn, scalding, electric shock, fall, etc.), chemical (e.g., drug and pesticide poisoning, strong acid and alkaline poisoning, carbon monoxide poisoning, etc.), and biological (e.g., food poisoning, dog/snake bite, bee sting, etc.); and (3) by the location where the injury occurred (e.g., family, kindergarten, school) (Shi, 2005).

There is no standard definition of accidental injury in Mainland China. Researchers have used different definitions for accidental injury, thus making it difficult to draw comparisons between the research findings of different studies. Given this situation, Wang (2001) proposed the following definition of accidental injury: An accidental injury is one that (a) is diagnosed as an injury by a medical care institution; (b) results in an application for more than half a day's leave; or (c) requires the administration of first aid and care by family members, teachers, colleagues, or partners. Although there is no consensus regarding the definition of accidental injury in the world, most of the epidemiology studies on child injury in Mainland China have adopted Wang's definition. Accidental injury is now considered as an "illness" that has a pattern of occurrence which can be traced, understood, assessed, and prevented (Liu, 2005).

Current Studies of National and International Child Accidental Injury

According to WHO's annual report in 1995, 50% of child deaths worldwide were caused by accidental injuries; this figure was higher than the combined death rate from pneumonia, malicious tumors, congenital malformations, and heart disease (Yang, 1996). Worldwide, more than 1 million children under 15 die as a result of accidental injuries annually; this represents 26.1% of the total child death rate, and the figure is still increasing at a rate of 7-10% annually (Miao, 2003). The updated report by WHO and UNICEF in 2008 stated that, every day, more than 2,000 child die of accidental injuries and thousands are hospitalized, and many of these children are left with permanent disabilities (WHO, 2008).

Studies from the United States have shown that the number of children who die as a result of accidental injuries in the United States has surpassed the combined fatality figure for all other illnesses (Rosenbere, 1996), which cause about 12,175 child (under 20 years old) deaths annually (Borse, 2008). Traffic accidents, drowning, and fires are the top three causes of accidental death among children. The main cause of accidental death among children is traffic accidents, with motorcycle accidents causing the highest number of deaths. The highest risks for preschool children are drowning, burns, and scalds (Bass, 1989). Research in the

United Kingdom has also found that accidental injuries are the major cause of death among youths (Roberts, 1998). In European countries, about 190,000 people die of accidental injuries annually (Morrison, 2000).

Research conducted by UNICEF and The Alliance for Safe Children in five countries in South Eastern Asia showed that for every child (under 19 years old) death caused by accidental injury, there are 12 children who require hospitalization or are left with permanent disabilities and 34 children who require medical services or have to suspend their schooling (Linnan and Michael, 2007). Among children, the causes of accidental deaths are different from the causes of nonfatal injuries. In most countries, fatal accidental injuries are caused by traffic accidents and drowning, while more than half of nonfatal injuries are caused by falls. In the United States, 9,200,000 children are treated in emergency rooms for accidental injuries; among these injuries, falls are the most common cause of nonfatal injuries (2,800,000 children) (Borse, 2008).

Research on child accidental injury in Mainland China started after the first international child accidental injury conference in Sweden in 1989. From 1991 to 1994, Liu's epidemiology study team conducted a study on children aged 0-14 among the 2,220,000 population in Hunan, Hubei, Hebei, and Inner Mongolia. In 1995, they reported their findings: the accidental death rate among children was 67.13/100,000; this accounted for 31.3% of the total child death rate and was the main cause of child mortality (Liu et al., 1995). In the same year, Lin et al. (1995) reported the results of a 1991-1993 investigation into the accidental injury death rate in 81 cities/counties among 8,550,000 children under 5: an infant accidental injury death incidence of 502.1/100,000; an accidental injury death incidence among children aged 1-4 years of 70.8/100,000; and a higher incidence in the rural areas than in the cities. In 1999, Lu et al. (1999) analyzed the epidemiological data on accidental injuries among primary and secondary school students in Jiangmen and found the prevalence of injury to be 43.53% for primary school students and 62.3% for secondary school students. In 2003, Yin et al. (2003) conducted an epidemiology study on 9,643 children aged from 0 to 14 in four counties in Jiangsu province and found the injury prevalence for primary school and secondary school students to be 14.26% and 11.94%, respectively. The prevalence of nonfatal injury among children in Beijing was 2.25%; the highest prevalence rate was among children aged 6-9 years, and the rate was higher for boys than for girls. Falls were the main cause of child injury, followed by animal bites and traffic accident injuries (Zeng, 2006). In another study, the prevalence of child nonfatal injury in Jiangxi was 5.66%; the highest prevalence rate was among children aged 1-4 years, the second highest rate was among the 5-9 age group, and the rate was higher for boys than for girls. The top three types of injury were animal bites, falls, and traffic accident injuries. The rate of disability due to accidental injury was 65.1/100,000 (1.15% of all cases). The top two causes of injury were falls and traffic accidents (Research Team of Child Injury Survey in Jiangxi, 2007).

There has, as yet, been no national study or hospital data analysis on the incidence and prevalence of child injury in Mainland China. In recent years, the largest studies in China that most closely conform to international standards have been the child (under 18 years old) injury investigations in Beijing (2003) and Jiangxi (2005) organized by UNICEF and The Alliance for Safe Children. These investigations produced the following findings: (a) accidental injury was the primary cause of child death in Beijing (Zeng, 2006); (b) the incidence of child fatal injury (1-17 years old) in Jiangxi was 53.7/100,000, the highest incidence being among the 1-4 year age group (99.4/100,000) and the incidences for children aged 5-9, 10-14, and 15-17 years being 56.8/100,000, 31.5/100,000, and 21.1/100,000, respectively; (c) the fatal injury incidence rates for boys and girls were 70.8/100,000 and 31.8/100,000, respectively; (d) accidental injury accounted for 69.44% of all causes of death and was the top cause of child death; and (e) the top two causes of accidental death were drowning and traffic accident (Research Team of Child Injury Survey in Jiangxi, 2007).

Child Accidental Injury Prevention and Intervention

From the above information, it can be concluded that child accidental injury is the primary factor that could prevent children from growing up healthily. Death or disability as a result of accidental injuries to children causes incalculable psychological suffering and economic loss to families as well as placing a heavy burden on, and causing instability in, society. Injured children lose their physical health and some develop problem behaviors and psychological disorders, and some family members blame themselves or each other, which can, in turn, lead to family break ups. The research shows that in the United States, the loss caused by child accidental injury is 41,000,000 person years, which amounts to US$8.3 billion (Liu and Liu, 2001). The cost of child accidental injuries in Japan is US$1.2 billion (Liu and Liu, 2001). WHO statistics (1991) have shown that the accidental injury death rate of 1-4 year old children in China is 3.5 times that in Egypt and Chile and 10 times that in Japan and the United Kingdom. Although no statistics are available on the economic loss in China, the cost is incalculable and creates a heavy burden on families, society, and the nation, as a result of the population being large.

Child accidental injury is not just about the physical injury. It is also a serious social problem that creates a great economic burden on society and families and consumes a considerable amount of medical resources. Hu et al. (1999) calculated that the potential life span lost as a result of child accidental injury deaths in Xuzhou in 1998 was 1,442.5 years. The literature on the social and economic loss caused by child accidental injury has estimated that 40,000,000 primary and secondary school students in China suffer various types of injuries, among whom 13,600,000 need clinical or emergency care, 3,400,000 are hospitalized, 1,270,000 suffer impaired normal functioning, and 740,000 are disabled. The economic loss is estimated to be 3.2 billion RMB, and the loss in terms of number of days absent from school is 0.238 billion days (Wang et al., 2000). In addition, the suffering caused to families by child injury deaths and disabilities is incalculable.

Szabo (1997) suggested that to prevent accidental injury, people not only need to understand the damage accidents cause to the body but also, more importantly, how to prevent accidents. Safety education is therefore an important intervention strategy. Research has shown that through education by professionals, children learn this knowledge and modify their behaviors and the incidence of accidental injuries (e.g., traffic accidents) significantly decreases (Bass, 1993). At the same time, making relevant laws and improving safety facilities are also necessary steps to take in order to reduce accidental injuries. Developed countries, especially European countries and the United States, have established accidental injury surveillance systems, such as the Statewide Childhood Injury Prevention Program (SCIPP) in the United States (Guyer et al., 1989). Through these systems, accidental injuries can be better and more fully analyzed and estimated and thus more effectively prevented.

Child accidental injury research in Mainland China started relatively late, and, as yet, no unified and substantial intervention plan and method has been developed (Xiang and Liu, 2003).

The mortality rate of infants and children under 5 is an important measure of a nation's level of economic and social development. Decreasing the child mortality rate is the goal of global child development. Both the UN's report on *A World Fit for Children* produced by the UN Special Session on Children and the *Outlines of Children Development in China 2001-2010* stated that reducing the child mortality rate is an important child development goal (Song, 2006). Both developed and developing countries realize the consequences that injuries bring to a society. Accidental injuries are not unpredictable or unpreventable events. Based on previous studies and practices, we can conclude that accidental injuries to children can be understood, prevented, and controlled. Moreover, accidental injury prevention is not only executable, but also effective (Xiang and Liu, 2003).

Hospital-Based Child Accidental Injury Prevention Program

This section will examine an injury prevention program operating in Shanghai Children's Medical Center (SCMC), Shanghai Jiaotong University School of Medicine, a hospital that integrates medical services, teaching, research, and prevention. The hospital has standard medical departments, admits 1,200,000 patients, performs 15,000 operations annually, and treats children from all over the country. The pediatric intensive care department is a national key department; it also acts as an emergency department in Shanghai and treats many emergency cases. In recent years, the hospital has admitted many accidental injury cases. In one week period, it dealt with the following cases: three children who had fallen from balconies at home and severely injured themselves; a child under 3 who had suffered a pierced cheekbone as a result of falling onto a pair of scissors while playing at home; two children who had fallen into a pool near their home while playing, cases that resulted in one death and one injury; a child poisoned by mistakenly ingesting stramonium fruit; a 2-year-old child who choked on a peanut and died of suffocation; a 4-year-old boy scalded by boiling water at home who suffered 40% burns; a 6-year-old boy whose leg bones were crushed by a compactor at his father's workplace; a 2-year-old girl who suffered severe brain injury as a result of oxygen deprivation caused by choking on jelly; and an 18-month-old boy poisoned as a result of eating candy contaminated with Tetramine[1] that he had picked up in a trash dump. As a result of such accidents, countless parents experience great regrets and many families feel doomed. According to the Intensive Care Unit of the hospital, in the first half of 2011, 38 children were injured in traffic accidents, 8 were injured by falls, 7 were affected by drugs (pesticides), 3 drowned, and 2 other deaths were recorded. These traumatic experiences remind us that many traps surround children and that they face threats all of the time. We need to mobilize all possible resources to create a safe environment for children.

[1] Tetramine: Tetramine is a raticide. Although it has been banned as a raticide in China for many years, illegal usage still occurs. Its toxicity is very strong, damaging the nervous, circulation, and digestive systems, and there is no effective antidote.

Worldwide, the spectrum of child disease has changed significantly. The infectious diseases, contagious diseases, and nutrition problems that used to affect children's health have been replaced by congenital defects, tumors, accidental injuries, chronic diseases, mental and behavioral illnesses, and environment-related diseases (Shen, 2005). From the pediatric point of view, children are the most vulnerable group in society; therefore, they need special care. Children's hospitals should assume responsibility for caring for the physical and psychological needs of their child patients and for illness prevention/treatment. They should also (a) pay attention to family and environmental factors that may endanger children and (b) play the role of health professionals in terms of preventing illness, promoting health, and increasing the professionals' ability to prevent and respond to accidental injuries among children and young people (0-22 years old).

Looking at the characteristics of child development, children are at a special stage of life development. They need special care, and there is a great demand for children to be provided with a safe environment in which to develop. There are two general goals of intervention:

Environmental Change

The healthy development of children has always relied on the provision of suitable natural, living, physical, social, family, and school environments. Children face many disguised risks in their daily lives, such as exposure to sharp items, slippery furniture, reachable taps, boiling water on burning stoves, swimming pools, and busy streets. Each type of childhood injury involves three components: child-related factors, injury-causing items, and the environment in which the injury takes place. The content and types of protection needed at different developmental stages are significantly different for each child. The dangers children face at every stage of their life should be carefully examined and removed. We should focus on the physical environment and objects and design an environment that is free of items that can cause injury (Steven, 2004).

For example, take the example of the case of Yangyang: Yangyang was two and a half, healthy, and lively. He went out for walks with his grandfather every day. One day, as usual, Yangyang's grandfather carried him down the stairs to the doors of the building where they lived. As soon as the doors opened, Yangyang struggled and got down onto the floor, ran outside, and was hit hard by a taxi. He died on the spot. Yangyang lived in an old neighborhood where the buildings had stairs not elevators and the entrance doors were only one meter away from the stairs. Outside the doors were busy streets and vehicles. At the turn in the street, there was a "Slow" sign, but drivers usually did not slow down. There were no speed bumps in the neighborhood. After Yangyang's death, people were sad and full of regrets: Yangyang would have had the chance to grow up if the driver had complied with the "Slow" sign, if his grandfather had not let go of Yangyang's hand, if there had been speed bumps on the roads in the neighborhood, if Yangyang had known there was danger, if everyone had been paying attention to the dangers in the environment, or if there were more laws and regulations regarding child protection.

Age-Specific Intervention

Children are at an early stage of life. Any harmful incidents could have a great impact on their growth. For children, the world is full of wonders, and they actively explore their world. At the infant stage (children aged one month to 2 years), children have already acquired some knowledge about how the world operates, and their behaviors have changed from reflexive to goal-oriented behaviors. Once they start to move, risks will arise: falling out of bed, entering places that they should not enter (e.g., the kitchen), actively seeking things to taste, and so on. The second year after birth is always a dangerous year because, by this time, children's physical abilities have surpassed their understanding of the consequences of their behaviors (Steven, 2004). At this stage, parents or guardians have to pay full attention to caring for and protecting their children and isolating them from sources of danger. At the early childhood stage (children aged 2-5), the main developmental task for children is to gain social skills through playing. Children run, jump, climb, and fall; they enjoy challenging their bodies. However, children at this stage are not fully able to understand the consequences of events or the harmful consequences their behaviors can bring to other people or themselves (Steven, 2004). At the middle childhood stage (6-12 years old), children spend less time with their parents and enjoy more time with their friends. Although they become more like adults at this stage, they still have a lot to learn; they are still developing, physically and psychologically. They always go beyond their capacity for self-protection.

INTEGRATING INJURY PREVENTION INTO SOCIAL WORK INTERVENTION

There are two major approaches to integrating injury prevention into social work intervention: community-based education and hospital-based education.

Community-Based Education

A community-based education approach involves introducing injury prevention education to the community. Community education can change the behaviors and thoughts of residents in the community, the opinions of families and groups, and even social policies and institutions so as to effectively promote the development of community work (Li, 2001). The SCMC is among the few hospitals that have set up a medical social work department. The development of the injury prevention program has mainly involved applying social work concepts and methods, and the working approach is constantly being improved. The SCMC plays the following roles:

Advocacy Role

The hospital uses its academic prestige and influence, real cases, and research data to conduct a major community event every year. It uses the hospital platform to advocate injury prevention to society, parents, and government (e.g., asking the government to make a series of policies, laws, and regulations regarding injury prevention and control); for example, it recommended that the government should (a) introduce a policy requiring all vehicles to be fitted with safety belts and child safety seats; (b) set speed limits; (c) put up warning signs on roads near kindergartens and primary schools; (d) establish specialist child protection organizations; (e) establish community organizations to supervise child safety practices; and (f) unite communities in promoting child protection policies. Every year, the SCMC regularly organizes a "children health day"[2] to teach health knowledge and skills related to injury prevention; the activities and services provided include case analyses, health consultations, life skills training, and the promotion of injury prevention knowledge and first aid knowledge and skills. The SCMC has fully responded to the "Ped FACTs" program of the Shanghai Education Committee[3] and has organized doctors with international first aid qualifications to train local kindergarten teachers in child protection and first aid skills. As part of the Ped FACTs program, the SCMC provides certificated training for over 1,000 teachers in the Pudong area, thus improving the first aid abilities of those who represent the first line of rescue for children. At the same time, it provides consultations to kindergartens and schools to increase safety awareness and improve the activity environment for children; these consultations are well received in the education system.

Organizer Role

According to the statistics of the SCMC, the winter and summer school breaks are the peak seasons for children being admitted to hospital with accidental injuries. During these periods, children are "freed" from tense study activities and become extremely active. Moreover, as the summer break is long, parents do not have enough time to supervise their children, and thus the accidental injury rate in summer is especially high. During the winter break, the most common injuries are scalds, electric shocks, fire cracker injuries, and Carbon Monoxide poisoning; during the summer break, the most common cases are traffic accidents, drowning, poisonings, and falls. Since 1999, the hospital has organized a "children safety month" every year based on the above characteristics,[4] ringing the alarm bell of child safety within society through one month of activities. The education activities of children safety month are carried out both within the hospital and in the community. Inside the hospital, an injury prevention educational exhibition is set up around the lobbies; first aid demonstrations are carried out by medical professionals in the activity rooms; all of the TVs in the hospital play an educational program on child safety; safety education pamphlets are distributed; and safety posters are displayed along the corridors in the wards. Preventing falls, scalding, drowning, fires, and pesticide poisoning are among the topics covered. In the community, the SCMC use community resources to organize groups (e.g., residents, community leaders, and volunteers) to create a safe environment for children and build a safe community. Every children safety month, SCMC workers visit two to three streets and communities, organize

---

[2] Children Health Day: Shanghai Children's Medical Center has organized health education activities on June 1 every year since its establishment in 1998. The medical staff organizes education programs and provides education materials to children and their parents in the communities. It is a traditional activity of the hospital.

[3] "Ped FACTs" program: This program is organized by the education committee of Shanghai. It especially provides training on child first aid and rescue skills to kindergarten and primary school teachers. It covers the whole Shanghai area. The child medical center is a key training location, providing training for about 1,000 people by using doctors with international first aid qualifications as teachers.

[4] Children Safety Month: Research shows that summer is the high season for accidental injuries to children. The hospital conducts theme activities, talks, and community visits for a month in the summer school break each year to provide safety education and training. It is a traditional activity of the hospital.

safety talks, and distribute educational materials. Each year, medical professionals go into schools for migrant workers' children which lack safety education resources.[5] In accordance with the characteristics of the accidental injuries that frequently occur, they conduct safety education on swimming, traffic, and food safety. Parents are encouraged to be role models for their children (e.g., by not swimming in rivers; by not pouring pesticides into empty cola cans or water bottles but instead putting them away in places that are not accessible to children). A traumatic lesson can be learnt from what happened to Shanshan, a 4-year-old girl: Shanshan's parents had just washed their hands and were ready to eat dinner when they saw her lying on the floor unconscious and with foam in her mouth. They suddenly remembered the pesticide in the corner of the room, and they found the bottle open and lying on the floor. During the rescue process, Shanshan had serious convulsions, and although her life saved, her recovery was very slow. Her parents spent all of the savings they had earned from farming to help their child. They deeply regretted not keeping their eyes on their child, but they had put the pesticide in a cola bottle and left it in a place that was accessible to her. However, child pesticide poisoning is not a rare event among farming families and finding a way to prevent it is challenging.

The SCMC conducts a series of experiential learning activities, such as role plays, to improve knowledge and understanding regarding accidental injury prevention. In 10 years' time, it will have served 1,000,000 persons. According to the statistics of the emergency department and intensive care units, the number of incidents of drug (pesticide) poisoning and drowning involving children have decreased significantly.

Empowerment Role

Utilizing the community and residents health education platform in Pudong (the new district in Shanghai), the SCMC promotes the concepts and skills of child accidental injury prevention and brings them to the attention of community residents. At the same time, it provides scientific evidence to enable communities to make and improve relevant laws, regulations, and policies. Through community activities, the SCMC calls for safety awareness, such as setting up speed bumps and road safety signs around schools, kindergartens, residential neighborhoods, and playgrounds to make the dangers visible and setting up traffic control measures such as one-way streets. It also promotes the safety management of water facilities, especially the removal of children from dangerous situations (e.g., setting up railing around pools, effectively reducing the child drowning rate). It has developed community safety education into a long-term self-running community mechanism, for example, by encouraging residents' participation in road safety campaigns in order to increase their knowledge of injury prevention and their awareness of providing a safe environment for children. By improving safety measures, the SCMC has created a safe community environment for children to grow up in.

---

[5] Schools for children of migrant workers: Schools primarily provide education to children of migrant workers. Such schools are usually located in the suburban areas where most migrant workers live. The schools are usually deprived and lack the manpower to run activities.

Hospital-Based Education

The perception of the general public is that education is conducted mainly in schools. However, such a myth has been challenged by the community education and lifelong education promoted by the hospital.

Educators

The SCMC provides large educational events to help children and their cares learn about accidental injury prevention and first aid. These programs increase children's and cares' awareness of child safety and thus reduce the possibility of child accidental injury. The featured services include Sunny Lodge,[6] Patient School,[7] and Buds Library."[8] These services incorporate social work interventions, and they have helped to improve community care and the quality of volunteer services. Physicians are involved in producing and editing safety education pamphlets and conducting first aid training. Ward education provides education for in-patients. According to the needs of different departments, the SCMC educates the parents of children who are newly admitted into the hospital. During the education process, the nurse-in-charge introduces information about the hospital and child care knowledge, teaching parents how to use the hospital facilities appropriately and, more importantly, how to take good care of their children.

Needs Assessors

Before, during, and after the services provided by the SCMC, the hospital conducts needs assessments of the child patients and their cares with regard to child accidental injury prevention knowledge and skills. The SCMC designs and improves activities according to the target population's actual needs in order to increase the effectiveness of the interventions; for example, based on survey results from the nursing department, "Be careful of scalding" and "Caution: Slippery" signs were put up in the kitchen and parents were instructed how to use home utensils such as a microwave oven. On the corridor walls, there are many "No smoking" signs and instructions explaining how to evacuate the building safely. There are also many exhibition boards providing parents with knowledge about the diseases and illnesses their children may have. In the wards, there are notices illustrating how to wash hands to avoid cross infections between parents, visitors, and child patients. On the beds, there are signs reminding parents to put up the side rails of the bed in order to prevent their children from falling out.

---

[6] Sunny Lodge: Sunny Lodge was advocated by the Women's Federation of Shanghai; it provides a place for children with leukemia to receive health education and to participate in delightful activities.

[7] Patient School: Patient School was established in 1998; it was the first facility created in Mainland hospitals to provide a learning place for patients. It provides hospitalized children with cultural, music, and drawing classes run by local school teachers and helps the children to reintegrate into school and society after recovery. The medical staffs also provide child care training, including accidental injury prevention, to parents.

[8] Buds Library: This library was established by the hospital to provide a learning and reading environment for child in-patients. It is also a place where they can receive health education. Its books are chosen by experts according to the characteristics of children of different ages, and these books can be borrowed by the children. It is actually a children's library.

Information Providers

The SCMC provides information on policies and laws to child care groups. During children safety month, it provides accidental injury prevention and emergency handling education and face-to-face consultations between experts and parents on the relevant policies and laws related to the different needs of newborns, infants, young children, preschool children, primary school children, and secondary school children. The SCMC equips parents, teachers, policy makers, and the children themselves with injury prevention knowledge and skills, thus helping to reduce child injury, disability, and death rates.

Mediators

The SCMC integrates social resources, including hospital resources (e.g., participation of medical professionals), community resources (e.g., volunteers, school teachers), and other social resources (e.g., safety and philanthropic organizations). It provides resources to increase the effectiveness of activities, thus drawing society's attention to the prevention of child accidental injury and serving its target population effectively.

CONCLUSION

Multi-Factorial Approach to the Prevention of Child Accidental Injury

The safe growth of children is related to many factors—social, economic, hygiene, family, school, and cultural (Shen, 2005). Children are the treasures of their families, the hope of the nation, and the future of society. Their health is related to the happiness of their families. However, their healthy growth cannot be separated from an affluent economy, a stable society, a harmonious family, and good child welfare policies. Taking care of children is the responsibility of families, society, and the social welfare system, and keeping children healthy has become a major political task for all countries (Liu, 2010).

Modern society is multifaceted. Illness is not only a medical problem but also a social phenomenon. The occurrence of disease is affected by many factors, including biological, natural, social, and psychological factors. Traditional medical sciences usually diagnose and treat from the perspective of biological medicine. However, an important aspect of modern medical science development is the socialization of medicine (Shen, 2005). Hospitals, especially children's hospitals, should take on more social responsibilities in relation to child accidental injury prevention education.

Multidisciplinary Collaboration to Prevent Child Injury

Child accidental injury is not just a medical problem. It concerns children, families, communities, schools, medical service organizations, and children's products and facilities (Song, 2006). To lower the child accidental injury rate is a social and synthetic project that requires multidisciplinary collaboration under government leadership. The government is responsible for public hygiene, public security, education, and traffic; it intervenes through education, legislation, and administration and by setting up multi-organization mechanisms, clarifying responsibilities, and mobilizing all social resources.

Accidental Injury Is a Crisis for Both Children and Their Families

Assessing the impact of child accidental injury on the children and their families is important to providing timely intervention, pacifying the emotions of the families, and getting them to cooperate in the treatment process. Counselors provide a warm, appropriate, and trusting environment in which children and their parents can express their emotions and troubles. To increase the ability of the children and their parents to adjust, educators provide services such as case counseling and child accidental injury prevention training to enable them to learn adjustment skills, accident prevention knowledge, and first aid skills. With regard to injuries that have already occurred, the staff at the SCMC help them to adjust to the hospital environment and to prevent a reoccurrence of injuries. Behavioral modifiers change the problems behaviors of children and parents by using simple and clear behavior modification skills to prevent problem behaviors caused by injuries or hospitalization.

Paying Attention to the Safety Education and Training of Children and Parents and Prompting Behavior Change

It is very important to educate parents about injury prevention. We should increase awareness of injury prevention through propaganda in the public media and intensify the mobilization of parents in injury prevention. Through health education, we should increase parents' awareness of safety in daily life, especially in relation to identifying and eliminating dangerous injury factors in the family in order to prevent accidental injuries to children. Parents and teachers should provide different safety education and training to children at different developmental stages, thus increasing their self-protection ability.

Making and Improving Relevant Laws, Regulations, and Policies

Making and enacting laws, regulations, and policies is the most effective way to prevent injuries. Evidence has shown that legislation increases society's acceptance of preventive measures designed to significantly reduce the rate of child injury, such as requiring vehicles to be fitted with safety belts and child safety seats; introducing speed limits; and requiring factories to consider safety issues when producing toys, home electrical equipment, medicines, and food (Gao, 2006). Since the 1950s, the Chinese government has produced a series of policies, laws, and regulations related to injury prevention and control, but it still needs to add child protection measures into the laws and policies dealing with construction safety, food safety, traffic regulations, and public areas and facilities.

Creating a Safe Environment

Changing the environment to safeguard users is an important way to prevent injuries. Developed countries have developed effective ways to improve road traffic, such as setting up speed limits and marking and treating road surfaces around schools, kindergartens, residential neighborhoods, and playgrounds; increasing the visibility of traffic condition; and creating one-way streets to stabilize the traffic. Improving the management of bodies of water and separating children from dangerous bodies of water (e.g., setting up railings around pools) can effectively reduce the death rate from drowning. Families, communities, schools, and kindergartens are the primary locations of child activities and also the major locations for child injuries. Creating an environment free from dangerous factors is another important way of reducing and preventing child injuries.

Establishing a Complete Surveillance System

A complete and scientific surveillance system is beneficial for effective injury prevention. Through a complete surveillance system, it is possible to obtain reliable data on the nature and location of injuries and to describe the status and trends of injuries so that public health policies can be developed, resources can be located optimally, and intervention measures can be carried out correctly, with the results evaluated to determine the effectiveness of the interventions, thus enabling intervention strategies to be improved and/or adjusted at any time (WHO, 2006). China has not yet established a national child injury surveillance system. Although through the cause of death registration system, the disease surveillance system, the death report system, and the injury surveillance system based on hospitals, public security and traffic police, insurance companies, and schools, it is possible to know the basic situation with regard to injuries (Li, 2005), this information is limited in terms of the description of injuries and its accuracy. At the same time, there is little communication between departments, and this affects the making and enacting of policies by injury control research organizations.

The healthy development of children requires the protection of children from harm. The protection of vulnerable children's health is related to society's development and future. Currently, China has basically solved the problem of child survival. However, in the 21st century, many factors that affect children's health have emerged; to protect children, these factors have to be identified and solutions to problems have to be found.

REFERENCES

Bass, J. L., Mehta, K. A., and Eppes, B. M. (1989). What school children need to learn about injury prevention. *Public Health Report, 104*(4), 385-388.

Borse, N. N., Gilchrist, J., Dellinger, A. M., et al. (2008). *CDC childhood injury report: Patterns of unintentional injuries among 0-19 year olds in the United States, 2000-2006.* Atlanta, GA: Centers for Disease Control and Prevention, National Center for Injury Prevention and Control.

Chen, D. (2011). Accidental injury investigation and harm factor analysis on primary school students in Minghang District, Xinzhuang County. *World Health Digest, 22,* 133-136.

Child Accidental Death Epidemiological Research Group. (1995). Chinese women and children health program county child accidental injury death epidemiological study. *Chinese Journal of Pediatrics, 33,* 206-208.

Department of Health Disease Control Bureau, Department of Health Statistics Information Center, Chinese CDC. (2007). *China injury prevention report.* Beijing: People's Hygiene Press.

Duan, L. L. (2004). *Guidelines on injury surveillance - WHO.* Beijing: People's Hygiene Press.

Gao, J. P. (2006). Research progress on epidemiological studies of child injury in our country. *Chinese School Hygiene, 7,* 555-557.

Gong, L. M. (2010). Current status and intervention of child accidental injuries. *Chinese Journal of Women and Children Hygiene, 1,* 213-216.

Guyer, B., Gallagher, S. S., Chang, B. H., Azzara, C. V., Cupples, L. A., and Colton, T. (1989). Prevention of childhood injuries: Evaluation of Statewide Childhood Injury Prevention Program(SCIPP). *American Journal of Public Health, 79*(11), 1521-1527.

Hu, P. Z., and Li, H. (1999). An analysis on YPLL of injured deaths of 0～9-year-old children in Xuzhou. *Chinese Journal of Disease Control and Prevention, 3,* 320-321.

Li, D. (2005). Current status, strategies and future prediction of injury prevention and control in China. *China Health Education, 21,* 258-261.

Li, T. B. (2001). *Community work.* Shanghai: Electronic Press Ltd.

Lin, L. M., et al. (1995). Surveillance report of 0-4 years old Chinese children accidental deaths from 1991 to 1993. *Chinese Journal of Pediatrics, 33,* 202-205.

Liu, J. T. (2010). *National responsibilities and child welfare*. Beijing, China: China Society Publishing House.

Liu, L., and Liu, X. X. (2001). Accidental injury during childhood and its prevention [In Chinese]. *Medicine and Society [In Chinese]*, *14*(2), 32-34.

Liu, X. Y. (2005). *Child health care*. Jiangsu: Jiangsu Science and Technology Press.

Lu, G. P., et al. (1999). Epidemiological characteristics analysis of primary and secondary school students' injuries in Jiangmen city. *Chinese Journal of Epidemiology, 20,* 170-173.

Miao, X. H. (2003). Child accidental injury prevention measures. *Chinese Journal of Practical Pediatrics, 14**(2),*** 39.

Morrison, A., and Stone, D. H. (2000). Injury mortality in the European Union 1984-1993: An overview. *European Journal of Public Health, 10,* 201-207.

Research Team of Child Injury Survey in Jiangxi. (2007). Epidemiological survey of child injury in Jiangxi province. *China Preventive Medicine, 8,* 521-526.

Roberts, I., Li, L., and Barker, M. (1998). Trends in intentional injury deaths in children and teenagers (1980-1955). *Journal of Public Health Medicine, 20*(4), 463-466.

Rosenbere, H. M., Venttrra, S. J., and Mauter, J. D. （1996）. Births and deaths: United States. *Monthly Vital Statistics Report, 45*(2), 31.

Shelov, S. P. (2001). *Health and safety in child care by the American Academy of Pediatrics.* Beijing, China: China Social Welfare Press.

Shen, X. M. (2005). *Clinical pediatrics*. Beijing: People's Medical Publishing House.

Shi S. H. (2005). *Child health care*. Beijing: People's Medical Publishing House.

Shi, S. H. (2006). Prevention of child accidental injuries. *Chinese Journal of Children Health Protection, 14,* 326-328.

Song, W. Z. (2006). Basic strategies for preventing and controlling child accidental injury. *Chinese Journal of Children Health Care, 14,* 325.

Wang, H. L. (2005). *Human behaviors and social environments: The biological, psychological and sociological perspectives.* Beijing: People's University Press.

Wang, S. Y., et al. (2000). A study on incidence of injury and its socio-economic loss in children and young adults. *Chinese Journal of Preventive Medicine, 34,* 203-205.

Wang, S. Y., and Huang, Q. D. (2001). *Injury prevention and control.* Guangzhou, China: Maps Press.

World Health Organization. (2008). *World report on child injury prevention.*

Xiang, B., and Liu, X. X. (2003). Child accidental injury and its impact factors. *Foreign Medicine - Social Medicine, 20,* 104-108.

Yang, B. S. (1996). Child accidental injury research. *Chinese School Medicine, 4,* 310-313.

Yang, G. H. (2005). *Chinese population death and risk factors prevalence, trends and distribution.* Beijing: Xiehe Medical University Press.

Yin, H., et al. (2003). Epidemiological study on child injuries of 9643 0-14 year old children. *Jiangsu Preventive Medicine, 14,* 55-56.

Zeng, G., et al. (2006). Epidemiological study on children and adolescents injuries in Beijing. *Chinese Journal of Epidemiology, 27,* 1024-1028.

SECTION 4.
CHILD PROTECTION: FUTURE DIRECTIONS

Section 4 outlines the suggestions and recommendations for future development of more effective child protection in the Chinese societies.

The author of Chapter 13 notes the inadequacy of current child protection measures, and urges for a comprehensive approach for the protection of children's rights as laid down in the United Nations Convention on the Rights of the Child (UNCRC). In particular, a human rights institution to monitor children's rights and a timely establishment of children's commission to tackle child victimization are emphasized.

Chapter 14 introduces the first database system to monitor abuse-related hospital admissions in Hong Kong. Regarding the lack of an effective surveillance system to report key epidemiological data on child victimization in Chinese societies, the success of the database in Hong Kong provides supportive evidence for the development of child abuse surveillance system for better child protection in other Chinese societies.

In: Child Protection in Chinese Societies
Editor: Ko Ling Chan
ISBN: 978-1-61942-879-9

Chapter 13

CHILDREN'S COMMISSION: CHILD PROTECTION BEYOND RHETORIC

Patricia L. S. Ip
Department of Paediatrics and Adolescent Medicine,
United Christian Hospital, Hong Kong, P. R. China

ABSTRACT

Hong Kong professes to have zero tolerance toward violence against children, and the government claims that child protection is already built into various policies and systems. Yet, every day, many children still experience different forms of violence, whether at home, in school, in the community, or in the virtual world. Child protection is often viewed in terms of programs targeting different forms of maltreatment, but to tackle the root causes of child abuse, a comprehensive approach that respects and protects the basic rights of the child as laid down in the United Nations Convention on the Rights of the Child (hereinafter, the "Convention") is required. In its concluding observations on the report on the Convention submitted by Hong Kong in 2005, the United Nations Committee on the Rights of the Child urged Hong Kong to establish a human rights institution to monitor children's rights and to implement the Convention. A motion to set up a Commission on Children was passed in the Legislative Council in 2007, but as this was a nonbinding motion, no action has yet been taken. Using examples of recent concerns in Hong Kong, this chapter discusses why no time should be lost in establishing a children's commission if Hong Kong is to turn zero tolerance toward violence against children from a slogan into a reality.

Keywords: Children's commission, Child protection, Child abuse, Child maltreatment

INTRODUCTION

The ratification of the United Nations Convention on the Rights of the Child (hereinafter, the "Convention") (United Nations, 1989) was extended to Hong Kong in 1994. As a result of this ratification, Hong Kong is obliged to realize the obligations placed on it under the Convention. Article 19 of the Convention (below) specifically addresses child abuse and neglect:

> (1) State Parties shall take all appropriate legislative, administrative, social and educational measures to protect the child from all forms of physical or mental violence, injury or abuse, neglect or negligent treatment, maltreatment or exploitation, including sexual abuse, while in the care of parents(s), legal guardian(s) or any other person who has the care of the child.
>
> (2) Such protective measures should, as appropriate, include effective procedures for the establishment of social programmes to provide necessary support of the child and for those who have the care of the child, as well as for other forms of prevention and for identification, reporting, referral, investigation, treatment and follow-up of instances of child maltreatment described heretofore, and, as appropriate, for judicial involvement.

After ratification, state parties have to submit periodic reports on the implementation of the Convention to the United Nations Committee on the Rights of the Child (hereinafter, the "UN Committee"). The UN Committee can seek further information or clarification from the representatives of the state parties on their reports at hearing sessions in Geneva; it then gives feedback and recommendations to the state parties in the form of concluding observations.

It is relatively easy for governments who have ratified the Convention to declare that they have already fulfilled their obligations by listing what they have done. The articles of the Convention are often interpreted at face value. In Hong Kong's initial report on the implementation of the Convention to the UN Committee (Government of Hong Kong, 1996), the government highlighted the multidisciplinary response system for dealing with child abuse, the local legislation related to child protection, and the rehabilitative services that were already in place. The Hong Kong Special Administrative Region government's next report (The Government of Hong Kong SAR, 2003) provided similar information together with an elaboration on educational measures. Unfortunately, the government did not state how well children were actually protected in Hong Kong, what gaps in policy and services existed, what difficulties were encountered in the fulfillment of its obligations under the Convention, or the steps being taken or contemplated to overcome these difficulties (Article 44 of the Convention). The reports gave the impression that the government considered that it had, in general, discharged its duties under the Convention. Its response to the many recommendations in the concluding observations of the UN Committee (1996, 2005) was either that these recommendations had already been carried out or were considered unnecessary. In particular, the call for an independent mechanism specifically to monitor the implementation of government policy on the rights of the child was not heeded.

As the articles of the Convention are written in succinct terms, general comments on specific articles or important issues are published by the UN Committee to guide state parties as to the interpretation of the articles and what is expected of the state parties in the implementation of these articles. The UN Committee published General Comment No. 13 (United Nations Committee on the Rights of the Child, 2011) on article 19. With reference to General Comment No. 13 and using examples related to physical and sexual abuse and neglect, this chapter will discuss why children continue to be at risk of maltreatment due to the lack of a comprehensive approach to the implementation of the letter and the spirit of the Convention through the establishment of a children's commission. For a basic understanding of the child protection system in Hong Kong and Hong Kong's recognition of and response to child sexual abuse, reference could be made to the recent reviews by Ip (2009, 2011).

TOLERANCE OF CORPORAL PUNISHMENT

The United Nations Study on Violence against Children (Pineheiro, 2006) starts with the statement "No violence against children is justifiable; all violence against children is preventable." Violence is taken to have a broad meaning. It includes all forms of physical, sexual, and psychological violence toward children; corporal punishment; children witnessing domestic violence; and child neglect which often lead to increased morbidity and mortality in children.

In Hong Kong, although corporal punishment was prohibited in child care services in 1976, in the penal system in 1990, and in schools in 1991, this is not the case for children in the home. The UN Committee's concluding observations in 1996 stated that there should be a non-acceptance of corporal punishment. In the UN Committee's concluding observations in 2005, the wordings were stronger, stating that corporal punishment should be prohibited by law in all settings, including within the family. In fact, the UN Committee (2006) also published General Comment No. 8 on the issue.

Tolerance of corporal punishment skews the statistics on physical abuse as established in multidisciplinary case conferences on child abuse. In 1997, Ip wrote about multidisciplinary decision making in such conferences. In these conferences, it was argued that abusive acts purported to be "for the child's own good" were cases of "child discipline" or "harsh and excessive physical punishment" rather than abuse. Despite the clear intention to hurt and inflict pain, which is part of corporal punishment, in these cases, professionals used the lack of an intention to harm to differentiate corporal punishment from physical abuse. Such discussions are still present, although to a lesser extent, in case conferences today. It is good that General Comment No. 13 clarified that "all forms of violence against children, however light, are unacceptable" and that "intent to harm" is not a prerequisite for the definition of violence, although decisions on the level of intervention may take this into account. It is hoped that this will guide future deliberations at case conferences.

Against Child Abuse (ACA) (2007), a nongovernmental organization in Hong Kong intent on the removal of all forms of violence toward children, wished to draw attention to the need to ban the corporal punishment of children under any circumstances. In 2005, ACA initiated a signature campaign for a Declaration against Violence toward Children. The then Director of Social Welfare signed the document on behalf of the government, but when it came to prohibiting corporal punishment by law, the government preferred to continue its policy of educating parents, which is only one of the measures recommended in article 19.

How well has parental education worked? In 2010, the Child Protection Registry recorded 488 new cases of physical abuse (Social Welfare Department, Hong Kong SAR, 2011), not a large number considering the child population of over 1 million in Hong Kong. In 1999, Lau, Chan, Lam, Choi, and Lai (2003) surveyed 489 Form Two students in 10 schools in Hong Kong. Among these students, 4.5% reported that corporal punishment had been inflicted on them by a family member in the preceding 6 months. Chan (2011) reported on a household survey conducted 5 years later in Hong Kong among 1,094 children aged 12 to 17 years; 18.1% of these children reported having experienced corporal punishment during the year preceding the survey, while the lifetime experience figure was 39.5%. Corporal punishment has certainly not become a rarity in Hong Kong as a result of parental education.

If Hong Kong had a children's commission to ensure a children's rights approach to child protection, a child would have the right to have his/her human dignity respected in the same way as adults when subjected to what would be considered a physical assault, and the government would have to justify its inaction (apart from parental education) to this commission. Hong Kong would then be closer to the 30 states that protect children from all corporal punishment by law, as reported by the Global Initiative to End All Corporal Punishment of Children (2011).

Children Left Unattended

In the late 1980s, Hong Kong was registering some 30 deaths per year of children left unattended. In 1991, the Social Welfare Department put out a consultation paper on measures to address this problem through legislation and parental education and support. With regard to legislation, the emphasis was on penalties rather than on the educational value of a clear community stand on what is acceptable child-rearing practice. There was a fear in the community that parents would be imprisoned and their right to work undermined. The loss of their children was thought to be a severe enough penalty for parents who left their children unattended. Hence, the conclusion of the consultation paper was that there should be no change in legislation but rather an enhancement of public education and support. Little weight seemed to be given to the right of the child to life.

Two decades on, there appears to be little change in the government's stance. After years of nongovernmental organizations advocating the introduction of a practice that had been implemented overseas in 1978 (The National Center for Child Death Review, 2011), the government finally gave the Social Welfare Department the task of launching a Pilot Project on Child Fatality Review in 2008. A nonstatutory panel was appointment with a general term of reference to look at service delivery systems, if any, before the death of a child and to recommend improvements, identify trends in child deaths, and enhance interdisciplinary and interagency cooperation. The panel certainly put much effort into the pilot project, but unfortunately the design of the project itself meant that there were limitations to what the panel could achieve.

Without a legal mandate, the review had to wait for cases with possible legal proceedings to be settled, which could mean a delay of 2 years or more. The source of information was that provided to the coroner, whose primary interest was to find out the cause of death, which was different from the purpose of a child fatality review. Other information from agencies involved with the child prior to his/her death was submitted to the panel on a voluntary basis. The panel had no power to access the records of these agencies.

In the review panel's final report on the pilot project published in 2010, on the subject of the deaths of children while unattended, the recommendation was little different from the conclusion of the 1991 consultation paper. The recommendation was to "strengthen public education on the possible fatal risk of leaving children unattended." With no indicator as to what "strengthen public education" meant, not surprisingly, the immediate response to the panel from the Department of Health and the Social Welfare Department was that both departments were already conducting a considerable amount of public education.

Had the establishment of the child fatality review been overseen by a children's commission, the approach, and hence the outcome or recommendations, may have been different. A children's commission would have asked why, in the best interests of the child or in the interest of preventing future child deaths, the review system itself does not have legislative backing like many systems in other countries that have proven effectiveness. Such a legal mandate would have pacified concerns about confidentiality and release of information for the purposes of the child fatality review. When the review panel looked into whether the system in Hong Kong had failed our children who had died, the focus may not only have been on the service delivery process of individual agencies but also, in a broader sense, on whether "appropriate legislative, administrative, social and educational measures" had been taken and the "necessary support for the child and for those who have the care of the child" had been provided (Article 19 of the Convention).

In terms of legislation specifically on child neglect, the government has not initiated a debate since the 1991 consultation paper on children left unattended. In discussing the legal response to the issue, a previous Secretary for Justice, Ms Elsie Leung (1997), stated that the Offences Against the Person Ordinance may be "all embracing" in making it a crime to willfully neglect a child in a manner likely to cause unnecessary suffering or injury to his/her health, but this is open to interpretation. Legislation that specifies an age below which carers are not allowed to leave children unsupervised could have a deterrent effect on such behavior. ACA (1991) proposed an upper age limit of 10 years. The age limit can certainly be revisited through consultation with the community, including the children themselves. Unfortunately, reviewing existing legislation was not mentioned at all by the review panel.

As to social support, after the 1991 consultation, there were various initiatives, such as places for occasional child care attached to child care centers, the encouragement of mutual help childcare groups, and, lately, neighborhood support childcare. Each of these projects requires years to assess its effect or lack of effect on the problem of unattended children. A children's commission would also have required data to monitor the situation. The concern should not only be the number of child deaths. Other indicators could include the number of children who need to be rescued by the police or the fire services department. To discover the prevalence of the practice of leaving children unattended in the community, regular surveys using a similar methodology need to be conducted. This information could well form part of the central databank mentioned in the concluding observations (UN Committee, 2005).

Indeed, in the Child Health Survey 2005-2006, Lau et al. (2009) reported on the frequency of children aged 0 to 10 years being left alone at home or being cared for by older children under 16 in the 12 months preceding the survey. Overall, 13.6%, or an estimated 77,400 children, had such an experience sometimes, most of the time, or always. Although this figure included more older children, it also included 3,500 in the 0 to 1 year age group and 18,000 in the 2 to 5 year age group. The 100 or so established cases of child neglect on the Child Protection Registry pales in light of the figures in this survey (Social Welfare Department, Hong Kong SAR, 2011).

Leaving children unattended affects not only their physical safety but also their development and socialization, and it also has a long-term impact. Although parents have primary responsibility for their children, the government needs to render appropriate assistance to parents to enable them to carry out their child-rearing responsibilities. What social policies and measures have been instituted to reduce the risk of parents leaving children unattended, and what effective deterrents are there for negligent behavior? While the introduction of each of the additional social supports mentioned above may serve the needs of some families, they do not make a significant difference to the vast majority of the children left unattended found in community surveys. Strategies to reduce poverty and to enable low-income working parents to earn reasonable wages and not to have to work unduly long hours are important. Regular affordable and accessible childcare provided by trained, appropriately remunerated, and supervised personnel should be available to the full age range of children at risk. Without waiting for parents who ignore the fact that they are putting their children at risk by leaving them unattended to feel regret after their child comes to harm, clear legislation which indicates what constitutes unacceptable behavior and the consequences of such behavior should be introduced. Neighbors should also know the threshold for reporting such behavior as defined by the law. This is what article 18 of the Convention means by "State Parties shall render appropriate assistance to parents and legal guardians in the performance of their child-rearing responsibilities and shall ensure the development of institutions, facilities and services for the care of their children." Unattended children should no longer be an issue to be dealt with in a piecemeal fashion. Our children's right to survival, protection, development, and participation is at stake.

Prevention of Child Sexual Abuse - Sex Offences Record Check for Child-Related Work

Hong Kong's recognition of child sexual abuse has moved on. Prior to the 1990s, barely 2% of cases on the Child Abuse Registry were categorized as child sexual abuse. Following the publicity and training surrounding the amendments of laws to facilitate the video recording of evidence and young children giving evidence in court in 1995, the recognition of child sexual abuse increased. The percentage of such cases on the Child Protection Registry then stabilized at around 30 to 35%, although actual numbers have increased because of the overall increase in cases on the registry (Social Welfare Department, Hong Kong SAR, 2011).

In the early 2000s, reports of repeat offences began to appear, particularly in relation to occupations such as school teachers, private tutors for academic studies and musical instrument tuition, and workers in welfare agencies. The Law Reform Commission of Hong Kong was called upon to review the existing legislation on sexual and related offences. A public consultation was conducted on the establishment of a sex offenders register. Amidst the voices to uphold the rights of offenders (Panel on Security, Legislative Council, 2010), the government eventually decided to adopt the interim proposal of the Law Reform Commission (2010a) to introduce sexual offences record checks for child-related work.

This is possibly one way to prevent child sexual abuse, but had there been a children's commission to oversee the whole exercise, children may be better protected by a more comprehensive approach. It would not be left to the lone voice of the Under Secretary for Security to promote a voluntary administrative scheme for such records checks.

Offenders certainly have rights to privacy, rehabilitation, and employment. A children's commission would point out that the preamble of the Convention stipulated that "the child, by reason of his physical and mental immaturity, needs special safeguards and care, including appropriate legal protection." With the ratification of the Convention, Hong Kong has an obligation to protect children from all forms of sexual abuse and exploitation. Following the principle that "in all actions concerning children... the best interest of the child shall be a primary consideration" (Article 3 of the Convention), the protection of children in vulnerable positions should be accorded higher priority than serious sex offenders' rights to privacy and choice of employment, which may put children at risk. Nevertheless, the children's commission would also point out that in the interests of offenders and, at the same time, for the better protection of children, there should be a holistic scheme including risk assessment, treatment, rehabilitation, and management of offenders. Another measure could be to look into the mandatory treatment of offenders.

Under such an administrative scheme, a more comprehensive approach would also involve educating the community that most sexual abuse against children is committed by their family members or friends (for which such sex offences record checks would not be carried out) and not by pedophiles. There would always be the first offence which this scheme could not have prevented. At present, Hong Kong does not have mandatory reporting of child abuse. Offenders may be dismissed or urged to resign of their own accord without going through an official investigation that could lead to a conviction and an official record of the offence. In Hong Kong's legal system, a conviction may not be registered due to difficulties in collecting evidence or to the defendant being given the benefit of doubt or, through plea bargaining, being convicted of a lesser offence not covered by the scheme. The administrative scheme also does not cover other forms of child abuse, convictions outside Hong Kong, or employees brought in from overseas. Other measures to enhance the ability of adults and organizations to protect children and the ability of children to protect themselves should be introduced. This is an opportune moment to urge organizations involved with child-related work to develop codes of conduct for their employees and volunteers and to have regular audits of their compliance with these codes. Organizations should assess the risk of abuse for the children under their care and have systems in place to avoid such risks while the children are in the company of adults.

The loopholes of a voluntary scheme are many. Child molesters may seek out employers who do not routinely check potential employees; another child would have to be molested and the act discovered before it was recognized that the employer had failed to conduct a record check. A system required by law would protect employers from being accused of discrimination. The confidentiality of the personal data of sexual offenders would also be better protected. When the scheme was debated in the Legislative Council by the Panel on Security (2010), a motion was actually passed requesting the government to "introduce a bill within 12 months to commence the formal process of legislating for the protection of children against sexual abuse as well as the provision of counselling services and assistance for the rehabilitation of sex offenders" and urging the government and the Legislative Council "to complete the enactment of legislation by the end of the current term." Unfortunately, there is, as yet, no time frame for making the scheme mandatory through legislation.

JUVENILE JUSTICE

Juvenile sex offenders are another concern. The Law Reform Commission (2010b) made a recommendation to remove the common law presumption that a boy under 14 is incapable of sexual intercourse, although the separate rebuttable presumption of doli incapax continues to apply between the ages of 10 and 14. This means that for a child within this age group, the prosecution needs to prove beyond reasonable doubt that the child was aware that what he did was seriously wrong, rather than just being naughty or mischievous. The report cited a number of cases whereby because of this presumption, a child under the age of 14 could not be charged with rape. The recommendation was considered to be straightforward. Hence, there was no prior consultation with the public. The Security Bureau has also agreed to introduce a legislative amendment to implement the recommendation.

With regard to the case of the 13-year-old boy mentioned in the report who was eventually sentenced for indecent assault on a 5-year-old child in a hospital ward, the magistrate was most unhappy that harsher sentences were currently not possible, and hospitals were reprimanded for not looking after teenage boys and girls separately in the wards (Cheung and Wong, 2011). The irony was that the 13-year-old boy was himself in hospital because it was suspected that he had been abused, which makes one wonder whether the boy himself was also a victim. Furthermore, would the solution be separating adolescent boys and girls in hospitals when boys can abuse boys and girls can abuse girls?

There is no doubt that boys under 14 are physiologically capable of sexual intercourse, but a children's commission would require a child impact study to be conducted before any change in policy related to children and, in this particular case, would also check that any policy change complied with article 40 of the Convention concerning juvenile justice. The implication of such a change on a child under 14 with respect to his immediate management and his long-term rehabilitation following his conviction for the crime of "rape" when the minimum age of criminal responsibility in Hong Kong remains at 10 needs to be thoroughly reviewed.

The minimum age of criminal responsibility in Hong Kong used to be 7. After the Law Reform Commission report in 2000 on the issue, the minimum age was raised to 10 in 2003 with the rebuttable presumption of doli incapax continuing to apply to children of 10 and below 14 years. In making the change, the government promised to raise the age to 12 when additional supportive measures were in place for unruly children below the minimum age (Legislative Council, 2003). Unfortunately, no such proposal has been put forth since then.

Although the Convention itself does not specify a minimum age of criminal responsibility, the UN Committee issued General Comment No. 10 (2007) on children's rights in juvenile justice. The Committee considered a minimum age below 12 to be not internationally acceptable. If the current minimum age in a country is 12, the Committee encourages the country to continue to raise the minimum age to a higher level of 14 to 16. Having two minimum ages of criminal responsibility within which criminal responsibility is assumed only if the child is deemed mature enough to be held responsible is not recommended as it is considered to be confusing and leaves much to the discretion of the court or the judge.

For children in conflict with the law, although one may feel repugnance toward the act, rehabilitation and restorative justice still take precedence over repression and retribution. With a child's right to participation enshrined by the Convention, a children's commission would ensure that children are consulted and their views taken into account, both from the perspective of a victim and a perpetrator. The good news is that compared with adult offenders, adolescents involved in sexual offences are more likely to benefit from high-quality treatment (Association for the Treatment of Sexual Abusers, 2000). The availability, accessibility, and quality of treatment programs would be another concern of a children's commission.

CHILDREN'S COMMISSION FOR HONG KONG

General Comment No. 13 not only covers article 19 on child abuse and neglect. There are related articles on child labor, sexual exploitation, trafficking, torture, armed conflict, and juvenile justice. There are also other articles important to the implementation of article 19 covering the best interests of the child; the right to life, survival, and development; health and well-being; participation; and nondiscrimination. General Comment No. 13 calls for a national coordinating framework on violence against children based on a child rights rather than a child welfare approach to child protection. This means that the child is a holder of rights entitled to protection and not a recipient of the benevolent acts of adults. The child is overall best protected by fulfilling all the child's rights as laid down in the Convention.

Back in 1991, ACA was very concerned about the deaths of unattended children, and it formed the Concern Group on Children Left Unattended. This evolved into the Hong Kong Committee on Children's Rights (HKCCR). In 1995, the HKCCR submitted an alternate report to the UN Committee on the implementation of the Convention in Hong Kong. In the report, the HKCCR called for the formation of a children's commission. In its concluding observations on the initial report from the Hong Kong government, the UN Committee (1996) recommended "the establishment of an independent mechanism specifically to monitor the implementation of government policy in relation to the rights of the child." The message was even clearer when the UN Committee (2005) remarked on the establishment of a "national human rights institution." In fact, the UN Committee had issued General Comment No. 2 (2002) on the role of such institutions.

Unfortunately, the response from the government (The Government of the Hong Kong SAR, 2006) was that the Convention "covers areas of government that are the responsibility of several different policy bureaux" assisted by different advisory boards, committees, and NGOs. This arrangement was said to allow flexibility. The government was "unconvinced" that a children's commission should be set up. It considered that the best interests of the child were already taken into account as a matter of course. There was therefore no need for a new arrangement involving the assessment of the impact of any policy proposal on children; neither was there a need for a comprehensive plan of action to implement the Convention. Indeed, not having a children's commission gives the government immense flexibility to maintain the status quo.

The HKCCR (2006) even commissioned a report on a children's commission for Hong Kong. To gather more strength for the advocation of children's rights, the Alliance for Children's Commission (HKCCR, 2010) was formed. In 2007, 24 agencies and professional groups joined forces to call on the government to establish a children's commission. The climax was a motion debate in the Legislative Council on June 6, 2007 which moved to establish a Commission on Children in Hong Kong. All representatives of different parties and constituencies gave the proposal a unanimous vote of support. The anticlimax was that the motion was nonbinding, which means that the motion was not intended to have legislative effect. Therefore, the government did not have to take any action, and, indeed, no action was taken.

Hong Kong has a commission for youth, for the elderly, and for women. While the Alliance for Children's Commission called for a children's commission, the government instead set up a Family Council in 2007. The Family Council's role is to advise on family matters and rationalize the work of the other three commissions. A year later, "taking into account the sentiments and strong wish of the stakeholders," it was announced that the three other commissions were to remain. On the other hand, the establishment of a children's commission was considered to be contrary to the government's intention to put "family related commissions under the roof of the Family Council" (Family Council, 2008). The government seems to think that all matters related to children are to do with the family and that there are no occasions when the best interests of the child, the most vulnerable within the family because of his/her age and immaturity, are different from the interests of other family members.

On the other hand, when the Alliance for Children's Commission discussed the function of the proposed commission, the intention was not to have a commission whose role was mainly advisory like the existing commissions mentioned above. The functions of a children's commission should include the ability to advocate and influence policies; research and analyze; coordinate, communicate, and cooperate; educate and promote; conduct enquiries; and speak for children: in short, to monitor child rights and the implementation of the Convention (HKCCR, 2007).

Globally, there are already 32 members in the European Network of Ombudspersons for Children (equivalent to child commissioners) and 17 independent children's rights institutions in Latin America and the Caribbean, 3 in North America, 8 in Australia, and 1 in New Zealand (European Network of Ombudspersons for Children, 2011). While Hong Kong strives to be a world city, it is lagging behind other regions in protecting the rights of children.

CONCLUSION

Few societies, including Hong Kong, will not claim that children are their priority and that protecting children is carried out as a matter of fact. Often, child protection is taken to mean the recognition of injuries caused by abuse and having programs targeting different forms of abuse. When children display undesirable behavior, such as bullying in and out of school and in cyberspace and drug abuse, the response to each manifestation is compartmentalized. The primary cause of failing to provide an environment conducive to the optimal growth and development of children or enabling their carers to provide such an environment seems too difficult to address. There is more and more evidence that adverse childhood experiences will take their toll from before birth through to childhood, adolescence, and adulthood. The effects take the form of chronic physical and mental illnesses, risk-taking behaviors, and even premature death (Centers for Disease Control and Prevention, 2010). In order to examine the root causes of problems and not just simply respond to apparent, urgent cases, there needs to be a change in mindset in Hong Kong.

General Comment No. 13 provides a good basis from which to explain what is meant by article 19 of the Convention, that is, "state parties shall take all appropriate legislative, administrative, social and educational measures to protect the child" from all forms of maltreatment and exploitation including programs of support for the child and carers, programs for prevention, recognition of maltreatment through to that for rehabilitation. The General Comment expands on the relationship of other articles of the Convention to this article on child abuse and neglect. The best means of protecting the child is to take a holistic approach that respects and protects the basic rights of the child as laid down in the Convention. The most expedient way is through the establishment and work of a children's commission.

If Hong Kong firmly believes that any form of violence against children is not to be tolerated and is not just paying lip service to child protection, the establishment of a children's commission is the natural path to take. Community attitudes need to be modified. The child is no longer just a victim who needs protection but a rights holder with a right to protection. The human dignity and the physical and psychological integrity of the child should be respected and promoted. Children have the right to be heard and their views given due weight. Their best interests should be the primary consideration. At the same time, the capacity of duty bearers should be enhanced so that they can meet their obligations to the growing child.

Asking for a children's commission to be set up in Hong Kong is not even asking for a "first call for children," but rather that they should not be discriminated against, as there are already three other commissions for youth, women, and the elderly and a Family Council. Had Hong Kong acted when the UN Committee called for the establishment of a children's commission in 1996, this commission would soon reach "the age of majority." We cannot afford to delay any longer.

References

Against Child Abuse. (1991). In response to consultation paper on measures to prevent children from being left unattended at home. Retrieved from http://www.aca.org.hk/app/posppr/2.2.pdf.

Against Child Abuse. (2007). Response to the day of action for the 1st anniversary of the release of the UN Study on Violence against Children (in Chinese). Retrieved from http://www.aca.org.hk/ofs/ofs20071024/un_vac.pdf.

Association for the Treatment of Sexual Abusers. (2000). The effective management of juvenile sexual offenders. Retrieved from http://www.atsa.com/effective-legal-management-juvenile-sexual-offenders.

Centers for Disease Control and Prevention. (2010). Adverse childhood experiences (ACE) study. Retrieved from http://www.cdc.gov/ace/findings.htm.

Chan, K. L. (2011). Children exposed to child maltreatment and intimate partner violence: A study of co-occurrence among Hong Kong Chinese families. *Child Abuse and Neglect*, 35(7), 632-642.

Cheung, S., and Wong, M. (2011, June 24). Shape-up for juvenile law after sex case. South China Morning Post.

European Network of Ombudspersons for Children. (2011). Global network of children's ombudspersons. Retrieved from http://crin.org/enoc/network/index.asp.

Family Council. 2008. Synergy among the Family Council, the Elderly Commission, the Women's Commission and the Commission on Youth. Retrieved from http://www.familycouncil.gov.hk/english/docs/Family_20080923_4th_Meeting_Notes.pdf.

Global Initiative to End All Corporal Punishment of Children. (2011). States with full abolition. Retrieved from http://www.endcorporalpunishment.org/.

Hong Kong Ordinances. Chapter 212, section 27. Offences against the person ordinance. Retrieved from http://www.hklii.hk/hk/legis/en/ord/212/s27.html.

Ip, P. (1997). Multidisciplinary decision-making. In C. O'Brian, C. Y. L. Cheng, and N. Rhind (Eds.), Responding to child abuse: Procedures and practice for child protection in Hong Kong (pp. 47-62). Hong Kong: Hong Kong University Press.

Ip, P. (2009). Child protection system in Hong Kong. *International Journal of Child Health and Human Development*, 2(3), 349-356.

Ip, P. (2011). Recognition of and response to child sexual abuse in Hong Kong. Gender Studies and Policy Review, 4, 20-32.

Lau, J. T., Chan, K. K., Lam, P. K., Choi, P. Y., and Lai, K. Y. (2003). Psychological correlates of physical abuse in Hong Kong Chinese adolescents. *Child Abuse and Neglect*, 27(1), 63-75.

Lau, Y. L., Lam, T. H., Low, L., Leung, G. M., Cheung, Y. F., Lee, S. L., et al. (2009). Child Health Survey 2005-2006. Surveillance and Epidemiology Branch, Centre for Health Protection, Department of Health, Hong Kong SAR. Retrieved from http://www.chp.gov.hk/files/pdf/chs_0506_eng.pdf.

Legislative Council. (2003). Report of Bills Committee on Juvenile Offenders (Amendment) Bill 2001. Retrieved from http://www.legco.gov.hk/yr01-02/english/bc/bc52/reports/bc520312cb2-rpt-e.pdf.

Leung, E. (1997). The legal response to child abuse. In C. O'Brian, C. Y. L. Cheng, and N. Rhind (Eds.), Responding to child abuse: Procedures and practice for child protection in Hong Kong (pp.78-88). Hong Kong: Hong Kong University Press.

Panel on Security, Legislative Council. (2010). Minutes of special meeting held on Thursday, 8 April 2010 at 9 a.m. in the Chamber of the Legislative Council Building. LC Paper No. CB(2)2254/09-10. Retrieved from http://legco.gov.hk/yr09-10/english/panels/se/minutes/se20100408.pdf.

Pineheiro, P. S. (2006). Report of the independent expert for the UN Study on Violence against Children (A/61/299). Retrieved from http://daccess-dds-ny.un.org/doc/UNDOC/GEN/N06/491/05/PDF/N0649105.pdf?OpenElement.

Review Panel of the Pilot Project on Child Fatality Review. (2010). Final report. Retrieved from http://www.swd.gov.hk/doc/whatsnew/201101/PPCFRFR.pdf.

Social Welfare Department, Hong Kong. (1991). Consultation paper on measures to prevent children from being left unattended at home. Hong Kong: Social Welfare Department.

Social Welfare Department, Hong Kong SAR. (2011). Statistics on child abuse, battered spouse and violence cases. Retrieved from http://www.swd.gov.hk/vs/english/stat.html.

The Government of Hong Kong. (1996). Initial report of the United Kingdom of Great Britain and Northern Ireland in respect of Hong Kong under Article 44 of the Convention on the Rights of the Child. Hong Kong: Government Printer.

The Government of Hong Kong SAR. (2003). Report of the Hong Kong Special Administrative Region under the Convention on the Rights of the Child. Retrieved from http://www.cmab.gov.hk/en/issues/child_report.htm.

The Government of Hong Kong SAR. (2006). Initial report of the Hong Kong Special Administrative Region under the Convention on the Rights of the Child: Response to the concluding observations of the Committee on the Rights of the Child. Retrieved from http://www.cmab.gov.hk/en/issues/child_forum_20060329paper.htm.

The Hong Kong Committee on Children's Rights. (1995). The rights of the child in Hong Kong. Hong Kong: The Hong Kong Committee on Children's Rights.

The Hong Kong Committee on Children's Rights. (2006). A Children's Commission for Hong Kong: Shaping the future. Retrieved from http://www.childrenrights.org.hk/v2/archive/06publications/20061200_ShapingTheFuture.pdf.

The Hong Kong Committee on Children's Rights. (2007). Statement to support the establishment of a commission for children in Hong Kong. Retrieved from http://www.childrenrights.org.hk/v2/archive/04concerns/ChildrenCommission_StatementToSupport_en.pdf.

The Hong Kong Committee on Children's Rights. (2010). About the Alliance for Children's Commission. Retrieved from http://www.childrenrights.org.hk/v2/archive/index/AboutAlliance_Jan2010.pdf.

The Law Reform Commission of Hong Kong. (2000). Report: The age of criminal responsibility in Hong Kong. Retrieved from http://www.hkreform.gov.hk/en/publications/rage.htm.

The Law Reform Commission of Hong Kong. (2010a). Report: Sexual offences records checks of child-related work – interim proposals. Retrieved from http://www.hkreform.gov.hk/en/publications/rsexoff.htm.

The Law Reform Commission of Hong Kong. (2010b). Report: *The common law presumption that a boy under 14 is incapable of sexual intercourse.* Retrieved from http://www.hkreform.gov.hk/en/publications/boy_14.htm.

The National Center for Child Death Review. NCFR and the history of child fatality review. Retrieved from http://www.ican-ncfr.org/auHistory.asp.

United Nations. (1989). Convention on the Rights of the Child. Retrieved from http://www2.ohchr.org/english/law/crc.htm.

United Nations Committee on the Rights of the Child. (1996). Concluding observations of the Committee on the Rights of the Child (Hong Kong): United Kingdom of Great Britain and Northern Ireland. Retrieved from http://www.unhchr.ch/TBS/doc.nsf/0/f2b9c21c3e8badc7c12563f000323553?OpenDocument.

United Nations Committee on the Rights of the Child. (2002). General comment no.2: The role of independent national human rights institutions in the promotion and protection of the rights of the child. Retrieved from http://www2.ohchr.org/english/bodies/crc/comments.htm.

United Nations Committee on the Rights of the Child. (2005). Consideration of reports submitted by state parties under article 44 of the convention. Concluding observations: China (including Hong Kong and Macau Special Administrative Regions). Retrieved from http://www.unhchr.ch/tbs/doc.nsf/898586b1dc7b4043c1256a450044f331/04186f9dc54bc087c12570ec004ef94a/$FILE/G0545139.pdf.

United Nations Committee on the Rights of the Child. (2006). General comment no. 8: The right of the child to protection from corporal punishment and other cruel or degrading forms of punishment. Retrieved from http://www2.ohchr.org/english/bodies/crc/comments.htm.

United Nations Committee on the Rights of the Child. (2007). General Comment no.10: Children's rights in juvenile justice. Retrieved from http://www2.ohchr.org/english/bodies/crc/comments.htm.

United Nations Committee on the Rights of the Child. (2011). General comment no. 13: Article 19: The right of the child to freedom from all forms of violence. Retrieved from http://www2.ohchr.org/english/bodies/crc/comments.htm.

In: Child Protection in Chinese Societies
Editor: Ko Ling Chan

ISBN: 978-1-61942-879-9

Chapter 14

CHILD ABUSE IN HONG KONG AND THE IMPORTANCE OF BUILDING AN EFFECTIVE SURVEILLANCE SYSTEM IN CHINESE SOCIETIES

Patrick Ip, Wilfred Hing Sang Wong and Sophia Ling Li
Community Child Health Unit, Department of Paediatrics and Adolescent Medicine, University of Hong Kong, P. R. China

ABSTRACT

Child maltreatment has been recognized as a major public health problem in Chinese communities and worldwide. Around 50 to 90 children under 18 die of external causes in Hong Kong annually; 5% of these cases are due to "assaults." The Child Fatality Review conducted in Chinese communities elsewhere identified a significant number of child deaths due to unnatural causes that were related to neglect and a lack of proper care. In a review of 494 suspected child abuse cases reported in Hong Kong hospitals from June 1997 to August 1999, 58% were substantiated as child abuse and 1% (5 children) had died from serious head injuries. Child abuse is a prevalent problem worldwide, and in western countries, official statistics from child protection registries or statistics on offenses against children are considered to be important social indicators. However, most Chinese communities lack an effective surveillance system to monitor and report key epidemiological data on child abuse and thus to describe the real situation and address the need for child protection. In 2010, the Hong Kong Child Abuse Collaborative Research Team produced the first database of abuse-related hospital admissions in Chinese. From 2001 to 2008, there were 5,430 admission cases that were later discharged with a diagnosis of child maltreatment syndrome. In contrast to the significant decline in the annual incidence of child maltreatment syndrome in England, there has been an upsurge in maltreatment admissions in Hong Kong. The annual incidence rate has followed a simple linear curve and has increased from 32.5 to 73 per 100,000 (R^2 0.96, $p<0.0001$). The alarming rise in child maltreatment and the unequal distribution of cases in Hong Kong demonstrate the need to recognize child abuse as an important social indicator which warrants further investigation to delineate its underlying causes and to recommend appropriate prevention strategies. There is an obvious need to build up a more effective child abuse surveillance system in order to improve child protection in Chinese communities. Our team is working on an innovative project commissioned by the government to integrate the social service sector's Child Protection Registry (CPR) and the health sector's Child Abuse Database in order to provide a clearer picture and epidemiology of child maltreatment and to explore the feasibility of integrating existing key databases, which could then serve as a child abuse surveillance model in Chinese communities.

Keywords: Child abuse, Surveillance, Chinese, Child development, Safeguarding children

INTRODUCTION

Child abuse has been recognized as a social problem for long time, and, in recent decades, it has also been recognized as a major public health issue. The issue of child maltreatment is critical and touches the hearts of everyone, no matter whether they have children or not. While the physical consequences of child abuse and neglect may not be immediately visualized, it is indeed a phenomenon that destroys families, scars the community, and extends beyond generations. Local statistics in Hong Kong showed that in 2009, nearly 1,000 children were the victims of child abuse or neglect (Child Protection Registry, 2009), almost double the 2003 number (Child Protection Registry, 2003). In 2010, we witnessed an infant dying of starvation at the hands of her abusive parents in Hong Kong, which is regarded as a relatively wealthy city. All of these tragedies point to failings in our child protection system or to actual flaws in our society. There are important lessons that have yet to be learnt from the traumatic events occurring almost every day in Hong Kong, greater China, and the region. Child abuse potentially has serious physical, psychosocial, mental, and behavioral consequences. Research on suicide victims has shown that experiencing child abuse may even alter gene expression in children's brains (McGowan, et al., 2008). Damage to a child's growing brain as a result of abuse can lead to long-term cognitive delays and emotional difficulties. On top of the impact on individuals, the potential social, economic, and legal burden caused to our society may be even more devastating and should not be underestimated.

Child abuse comes in many forms, including neglect and physical, sexual, and emotional abuse, and we must bring this issue out of the shadows and into the light. Health professionals (doctors, nurses, allied health professionals) need to work closely with colleagues from the law, education, social service, community, and government sectors in adopting a new and holistic approach toward child protection, conducting research committed to child protection in Hong Kong and greater China from multiple perspectives, and building a constructive platform to create a synergy among these different disciplines working toward the common goal of safeguarding our children, the future of our society. It is also their responsibility to shape social consciousness in the region by serving as educators to society in the pursuit of social justice.

In order to overcome the barriers and reluctance of the concerned families and the community at large, there is a strong need to develop an evidence-based intervention approach using the best quality research to influence policy makers and to educate society in the pursuit of our common goal. In order to do so, health professionals need to play a critical role and change the outdated perception that the physical, psychological, behavioral, and societal consequences of child abuse and neglect are not a core medical concern. Indeed, such an approach provides a good opportunity to potentially save a family and protect a child at the very moment when a child at risk is seeking professional advice from a medical professional. It is immensely important to note the complexity of child abuse issues, which requires well-coordinated collaboration among health professionals, social scientists, and law and policy-making colleagues and among those on the frontline dealing with these critical social issues.

Given the changing trend in tackling child abuse over the past two decades, the need for the effective and integrated surveillance of child abuse is becoming critical. The accumulated scientific evidence suggests that preventing child maltreatment requires a rights-based approach instead of welfare-driven programs, a public health approach instead of individual management, a community-based instead of a center-based approach, and a child participatory instead of simply a parent-oriented approach. A child abuse surveillance system would be able to inform us about the magnitude of the problem, incidence trends, clustering patterns, underlying risks and protective factors, and distribution in relation to available service provision, information which is critical to facilitating policy formation and service planning as well as actual implementation. This challenging task requires clear coordination and cooperation among colleagues in various sectors, especially those on the frontline in the identification of child abuse cases.

CHILD ABUSE DATA IN HONG KONG

Comprehensive data on child abuse and neglect are lacking in most Chinese societies, including Hong Kong. The Database for Child Protection in Hong Kong includes primary data collected for research projects in the form of household or school surveys, for example, the Hong Kong Violence Household Survey 2005 (Chan, 2005), and secondary data from (a) official databases, including the Child Protection Registry (CPR), which are kept strictly confidential for individual case management purposes, (b) the Hospital Authority database produced by an effective computerized record system capturing abuse cases admitted into the public hospital system, and (c) a domestic violence and child abuse database handled by the Police Taskforce which is only accessible to a restricted number of officials.

The three major databases on child abuse in Hong Kong are discussed below; (A) and (B) are official databases, while (C) is the largest representative survey conducted by a local university.

Public Hospital System - Clinical Data Analysis and Report System (CDARS)

CDARS is an information system for supporting management decisions, clinical audits, and research and analysis in facilities managed by the Hospital Authority (HA) of Hong Kong. The data source for CDARS comes from a multitude of data warehouses, including the Accident and Emergency Information System (AEIS), the Medical Record Abstract System

(MRAS), the Clinical Management System (CMS), the In-Patient Administration System (IPAS), and the Pharmacy Management System (PMS)/Corporate Drug Dispensing History (CDDH). By integrating these information sources, CDARS provides physicians, administrators, and researchers with opportunities to conduct detailed in-patient episodes analyses of admissions and discharges, diagnoses and procedures performed, and prescription drugs data.

Through this effective electronic record system, child abuse cases admitted to all public hospitals can be retrieved by authorized staff searching using the standard diagnostic codes (currently, ICD 9CM version) for child abuse. Detailed information on the perpetrator, complications, and outcomes can also be retrieved and analyzed.

Social Welfare Department – Child Protection Registry

A computerized record system for maintaining the CPR was devised through the joint efforts of the Social Welfare Department (SWD), nongovernmental organizations (NGOs), and the Hong Kong Council of Social Service. The functions of this system, which is administered by the Family and Child Welfare Branch of the SWD, include case registration, case checking, and facilitating statistical research. The registration of individual cases under 18 years old (cases over 18 years old would be inactivated) can be checked by registered social workers and social service units for individual case management purposes. Information on the CPR is kept strictly confidential and is not accessible to academic researchers or the public.

Hong Kong Violence Household Survey (2005, 2010)

The 2005 household survey was a population-representative study commissioned by the SWD that was carried out in Hong Kong between December 2003 and August 2004. This population study was the first of its kind to be conducted in Hong Kong to examine the prevalence and risk factors of spouse battering and child abuse. A total of 4,347 valid quarters were randomly sampled from the Register of Quarters maintained by the Census and Statistics Department of the Government of Hong Kong. This is the most up-to-date and complete sampling frame available in Hong Kong. A stratified random sample design was adopted according to geographical area and the type of quarters. A total of 5,049 adult respondents were successfully interviewed, with an overall response rate of 71% (Chan, 2005).

In 2010, another population-representative household survey, funded by the UBS Optimus Foundation (Switzerland), was conducted. Following a similar stratified random sampling scheme to that used in the previous household survey (2005), this population study also took socioeconomic levels into account by using stratification on housing type (publicly subsidized or private) in addition to geographical regions. A total of 2,949 adult respondents were successfully interviewed; the overall response rate was 70.7%.

Hong Kong's Population Statistics and Linkage to Mainland China

Comparing with other Asian countries, life expectancy at birth in Hong Kong is similar to that in Singapore and Japan and a little higher than it is in Taiwan and China (Agency, 2008; United Nations Children's Fund, 2006). According to the official data provided by the Census and Statistics Department, in 2008, the population of Hong Kong was around 7 million and children made up 20% of its population; around 1.35 million Hong Kong residents were children under the age of 19 (0-4: 220,000; 5-9: 280,000; 10-14: 400,000; 15-19: 450,000). Counterintuitively, although Hong Kong has a large population, the crude birth rate is only around 1%. From the late 1990s onward, Hong Kong's crude birth rate dropped gradually, but in the past few years it has started to slowly increase again (Census and Statistics Department, 2010). During the same period, the proportion of Mainland mothers who gave birth in Hong Kong also increased dramatically, accounting for over 40% of total births in recent years. It is expected that even more Mainland mothers will be giving birth in Hong Kong and that over half of local newborns will be born to Mainland parents in the near future. Hence, it is anticipated that in the coming decades there will be a change in the demographic pattern of the Hong Kong population and also social and economic changes due to the close links between Hong Kong and Mainland China. Although Hong Kong may be seen as being different from Mainland China in terms of political and economic environment, the growing communication and integration between the two has already established common ground for transferring knowledge and informing better policy and practice using evidence arising from both sides. In addition, as suggested in many studies, Mainland China, especially Chinese urban cities, tends to follow the trends observed in Hong Kong. Therefore, the evidence gathered and the experience gained from Hong Kong in relation to building up an effective child abuse surveillance system will not only predict the future situation in the greater China region but will also provide critical information to inform policy, practice, and research that will have an impact on a much larger section of the population.

Importance of Child Protection and the Implications of Child Abuse

In the past two decades, the accumulated scientific evidence supports the biology of adversity and the early childhood roots of learning, behavior, and health impairments. Research has confirmed that early life experiences are built into human bodies and affect development in later life (Shonkoff, Boyce, and McEwen, 2009).

Developmental Delay

Young children (birth to 3 years) have the highest rate of victimization (16.1 per 1,000) and are at highest risk of experiencing maltreatment. There is emerging evidence on how early life experience plays a critical role in the development of a young child's cognitive functions. Scarborough and Lloyd's (2009) study revealed that for children younger than 36 months, those who have been maltreated were at significantly higher risk of experiencing subsequent developmental problems (Scarborough, Lloyd, and Barth, 2009). Among the specific developmental domains that can potentially be affected are the social, cognitive, emotional, and physical health of the child, and there is also the possibility of such children subsequently developing psychopathology. Regardless of the type of maltreatment experienced, negative developmental consequences are consistently found in at least one developmental domain. The effects of maltreatment are often more severe than those of other factors (e.g., poverty or economic disadvantage).

Mental Illness

Depression has been recognized as a major form of morbidity affecting a significant proportion of the population. An adverse event in early life such as child abuse has been found to directly and indirectly cause the development of mental health disorders such as depression (Chapman and Scott, 2001). In situations of prolonged physical or emotional abuse, children are affected by toxic stress if they have no supportive adults in their lives. This could disrupt the architecture of the brain and cause the stress management systems to respond at relatively lower thresholds. As a result, there would be a higher risk of stress-related mental health and physical illness associated with early life adversity.

Epigenetic and Child Abuse

The dynamic between genes and early life experience provides another important perspective from which to understand the adverse impact of child maltreatment. The Dunedin birth cohort in New Zealand generated longitudinal data which provided evidence supporting the function of the serotonin-transporter gene in the hippocampus frontal brain region and its relationship to the risk of developing mental illness (Caspi, et al., 2003). Similar observations have also been provided from studies of rhesus macaque monkeys. The maltreatment of young monkeys or humans can lead to the poor regulation of the sterol pathways and effects on the serotonin pathway. For humans with a short allele for the serotonin transporter gene, their serotonin pathway in adult life would be altered and the risk of depression during adulthood would be much higher if they were maltreated at a young age. If they were not poorly treated when they were young, the risk of depression during adulthood would be the same as for those with a long allele. This evidence delivers a very important message, which is that both early life experience and the interaction between experience and gene activation may alter brain function and subsequently result in mental problems in adult life. Since mental health problems such as depression have a significant cost to individuals and society, it is quite clear that public policy to improve early child development in our society should be much stronger than it is at present. The maltreatment of young children could affect brain development in the early years and lead to long-term adverse effects. Compared to treating depression during adulthood, the use of prevention measures to improve the conditions for early child development (e.g., through early child development and parenting programs) is probably more cost effective.

Physical Health Problems

In addition to the impairment of cognitive development, physical health and social-emotional behaviors are also affected by child abuse in early life. Dong and Giles's (2004) study investigated adults with a history of early adverse childhood experiences in order to determine whether these experiences increased the odds of these adults experiencing alcoholism, drug abuse, and a range of other unhealthy behaviors later in life. Perhaps not unexpectedly, all of these behaviors were substantially more prevalent among adults who had scored higher in the measure of adverse childhood experiences in their early years. These adverse experiences were also found to lead to increased odds of major physical health problems, such as cardiovascular disease (Dong, et al., 2004). An elevated inflammation (e.g., high-sensitivity C - reactive protein of more than 3 mg/L) is associated with adult cardiovascular disease and is also used as an important predictor of cardiovascular disease among healthy individuals. Dong et al.'s study also measured fibrinogen, white blood cell counts, and chronic activation of the inflammatory response system and all showed the same elevated pattern not only in the depressed adults, but also in the nondepressed adults who had suffered maltreatment in early childhood. While depression itself is correlated to heart disease, even without depression, suffering maltreatment as a child has also been proven to be an important risk factor that should not be ignored (Danese, et al., 2008). These associations have also been found for diabetes, hypertension, stroke, obesity, and cancer.

Suicidality is also associated with child maltreatment. A local study conducted by Caritas Social Service Group on a group of 820 students aged 14 to 19 in 2002 found that compared to adolescents who had not been maltreated, adolescents who were maltreated had a higher risk of suicidal ideation, self-harm, and attempted suicide. This study also indicated the association between child maltreatment and other behavioral and social problems, which is consistent with findings in the West.

All of these findings support a possible causal model of how child maltreatment and discrimination can have lifelong impacts on health and development. The most rapid phase of brain growth occurs during the early years of life (0-5 years), which have been found to be the most critical years of human development; these years are crucial in setting the stage for later life and building the foundation for future development. Emerging evidence suggests that nurturing and responsive caregiving in early life is the key to ensuring quality developmental and health outcomes for all children in both the short and long term. Therefore, preventing childhood adversity and modifying the factors that contribute to the childhood roots of disparities in health and development should be the way forward.

HOSPITAL VERSUS SELF-REPORTED CHILD ABUSE DATA

In the past two decades, a network of medical coordinators of child abuse (MCCA) in each of the 14 major hospitals with pediatric units has been built up covering the whole territory of Hong Kong. The MCCA Committee provided the foundation work on child abuse, including a pilot project started in late 1997, which was followed by a longer study on prospective data collection from 1997 to 2002. In the pilot project from June 1997 to August 1999, 494 cases of child abuse were handled by pediatricians in public hospitals and 452 multidisciplinary case conferences (MDCC) were held; 58% of the cases were considered to be established child abuse cases, and 87% of these cases involved physical child abuse. Among the cases of physical child abuse, 5 cases (1%) involved deaths caused by a serious head injury (Medical Coordinators of Child Abuse, 2003). During the subsequent child abuse surveillance conducted by the MCCA during a 5-year observation period, 1,831 cases (903 males, 928 females; mean age: 7.9) were reported; 57% were eventually diagnosed as child abuse, among which 84% were cases of physical child abuse. Among the nine cases of death, eight were due to a head injury and one was due to carbon monoxide poisoning caused by charcoal burning. As shown in Table 1, the pattern of child abuse cases in the official database in Hong Kong is very different from overseas experience. In 2007, the rate of child abuse case investigations was only 0.16%; such cases, especially child neglect and psychological abuse cases, were probably underreported.

Table 1. Prevalence of Child Abuse from Child Protection Registry

	UK	US	Canada	Australia	Hong Kong
Year	2007	2006	2003	2003	2007
Investigated	1.5%	4.78%	3.34%	3.34%	0.16%
Substantiated	0.3%	1.21%	0.68%	0.68%	0.08%
Neglect	11%	60%	38%	34%	12.1%
Physical abuse	15%	10%	23%	28%	52.90%
Multiple	10%	12%			4.3%
Psychological	23%	11%	23%	34%	2.1%
Sexual	7%	7%	9%	10%	29.6%

Table 2. Types of Child abuse – Comparison of different places

Yearly rate	Severe Physical abuse	Psychological abuse	Sexual	Neglect	Witness IPV
UK, US, NZ, Finland, Italy, Portugal	3.7 - 16.3%	10.3% (US) 4-9% (US, Sweden)	Cumulative boys : 5 - 10% girls : 15 - 30%	1.4 - 15.4%	10-20%
Macedonia, Moklova, Latvia, Lithuania	12.2 - 29.7%	12.5 - 33.3%	World wide Any sexual abuse boys : 8.7% girls : 25.3%		
Siberia, Russia and Romania	24 - 29%		Noncontact boys : 3.2% girls : 6.8% Contact boys : 3.7% girls : 13.2%		
Hong Kong	6.1%	57.6%	0.3% sexual harassed 0.1% forced sex	27.4%	Physical violence - 8%, Psy viol 28%

Although there is an increased awareness of child abuse among the general public and professionals in Hong Kong, we still lack reliable surveillance data; the estimated prevalence based on different sources has resulted in divergent pictures of the extent of the problem. As shown in Table 2, the findings of a larger scale territory-wide household survey conducted locally are very different from the official statistics. In the household survey, child abuse as a whole, child neglect, and psychological abuse were found to be far more common in Hong Kong (Chan, 2005). This results of this survey, which is the most representative household survey conducted in Hong Kong so far, revealed that the incidence of self-reported cases were as follows: physical abuse 6.1%, psychological abuse 57.6%, sexual abuse 0.3%, neglect by parents 27.4%, and witnessing domestic violence 30%. Each year, around 70,000 children under 18 years of age in Hong Kong are severely or very severely abused by their adult carers. In contrast, according to the government's official report, the yearly number of cases notified in 2006 was only around 600, giving a notification rate of <1% (Chan, 2005). Such a discrepancy is noteworthy and has also been reported elsewhere in the world (Gilbert, et al., 2009).

The present CPR collated by the SWD focuses mainly on the basic statistics on the number and types of abuse cases and the perpetrator-child relationship and provides little information that can be used for prevention purposes. The guidelines from the World Health Organization and the Centre of Disease Control and Prevention could serve as useful references in any future modifications to surveillance forms (Sethi, et al., 2004); (German, Armstrong, Birkhead, Horan, and Herrera, 2001). The pattern of child abuse has evolved rapidly in modern society. There is an urgent need to establish a robust data collection system that cuts across health, social, education, and judicial services (Al Eissa and Almuneef, 2010). The huge difference between the self-reported incidence of child maltreatment and the number of substantiated cases signifies a gross underrecognition of and underresponse to the issue of child abuse by professionals and the public. Such underreporting may be due to inadequate training, restricted access to qualified social workers, concerns that services cannot meet the demand for support, worries that reporting may not bring any benefit to the child or family, and fears about potentially damaging professional-child relationships.

It is worth noting that official recognition of child abuse and the provision of services are also affected by legislation and policies which govern the recognition of and the response to child abuse. In a study conducted by the Secretariat of the Legislative Council in 2007, the legislation and the provision of services for child protection in Hong Kong compared poorly with the legislation and provision of the United Kingdom, Australia, and Canada (S. K. Wong, 2007). There are two general approaches regarding policies governing responses to child maltreatment, namely the child and family welfare approach and the child-safety approach (Gilbert, et al., 2009); these two approaches overlap to some degree. Hong Kong practices a more child-safety approach, which is more conservative and tends to concentrate on the investigation of maltreatment and the assessment of future maltreatment risk rather than on addressing broad child and family welfare needs.

REQUIREMENTS OF A GOOD SURVEILLANCE SYSTEM

Even though child maltreatment has been recognized as a significant public health problem in both developed and developing countries, surveillance systems are usually fragmented and comprehensive data on child abuse are often lacking. In planning an effective surveillance system for child protection in Hong Kong and other Chinese societies, the following seven dimensions adopted from injury surveillance systems could serve as a useful reference (adapted from WHO Injury Surveillance Guidelines, 2004):

(1) Simplicity – the surveillance system should produce the required data in the most simple way;
(2) Acceptability – the people who are expected to provide information, through interviews and in other ways, should be willing to participate and should be involved in the system design whenever possible;
(3) Flexibility – the system should adapt, at minimal cost, to changes in the operating conditions and data required;
(4) Reliability – the system should have a high sensitivity, specificity, and positive predictive value so as to ensure that end users have confidence in the accuracy of the data;
(5) Utility – the system should be practical and affordable and should increase knowledge about the problem;
(6) Sustainability – the system should be easy to maintain and update, with adequate resources allocated to guarantee continuing operation; and
(7) Timeliness – should generate updated information.

EPIDEMIOLOGY OF CHILD ABUSE – UNITED KINGDOM VERSUS HONG KONG

Child abuse is a prevalent problem worldwide. Official statistics in child protection registers, the number of children referred to child protection services, and statistics on offenses against children are considered to be important social indicators in the United Kingdom and many western countries (May-Chahal and Cawson, 2005). In Hong Kong, there is a lack of comprehensive data on child abuse cases and related medical admissions and only limited studies and publications on local scenarios. In 2005, Chan conducted the first territory-wide household survey on child abuse and spouse battering and reported a very significant prevalence of child abuse and abuse-related issues among Hong Kong families (Chan, 2005). In response to González-Izquierdo et al.'s (2010) detailed analysis of the variation in the recording of child maltreatment admissions in relation to the childhood injury database in United Kingdom (González-Izquierdo, et al., 2010) and the observation of a very stable burden of child abuse throughout the years in the United Kingdom, our research team at the University of Hong Kong reported the first comprehensive review based on an electronic database of child maltreatment hospital admissions in the Chinese population (Ip, et al., 2010). The situation in Hong Kong has been found to be very different from that in the United Kingdom: trends in Hong Kong show a rapid increase in child maltreatment admissions and the increasing burden of child maltreatment syndrome. From January 1, 2001 to December 31, 2008, 5,430 children were admitted to hospital and discharged with a diagnosis of child maltreatment syndrome according to ICD CM9 codes. In contrast to the significant decline over time in the annual incidence of admissions with codes for child maltreatment syndrome in England found in González-Izquierdo et al.'s study (González-Izquierdo, et al., 2010), there is a very different pattern in Hong Kong, with an upsurge in admissions with codes for child maltreatment syndrome. Considering the effect of the changes in the child population during the study period, the annual incidence rates were calculated by dividing the number of admissions coded for child maltreatment syndrome by age-specific population estimates for each calendar year. The annual incidence followed an almost liner curve, increasing from 32.5 per 100,000 in 2001 to 73 per 100,000 in 2008 (R-square = 0.96, $p < 0.0001$). Thus, in spite of the similarity between the hospital admission and child protection systems in Hong Kong and the United Kingdom due to the fact that Hong Kong was once governed by Britain, Ip and his colleagues (Ip, et al., 2010) found a very different pattern in Hong Kong. In addition, preliminary analysis has shown a very peculiar distribution of child abuse cases in different districts of Hong Kong; child abuse cases are clustered in deprived areas with low socioeconomic status and inadequate service provision. This trend of an increasing annual incidence of child maltreatment is also confirmed by another set of official data reported to the CPR of the Hong Kong Government which showed that the annual incidence increased by 65% from 2001 to 2008 (Child Protection Registry, 2009). The alarming rise in child maltreatment and the unequal distribution of cases in our Chinese city demonstrates the need to recognize child abuse as an important social indicator in our community, one which warrants further investigation to delineate its underlying causes and recommend appropriate prevention strategies.

An effective surveillance system also allows professionals to recognize the trends in case notification and the changing patterns in the epidemiology of child abuse. For example, an analysis of hospital admissions of cases of child abuse over an 8-year period from early 2000 showed a distinct seasonal admission pattern, with abuse cases clustering in the months that coincided with the two major examination periods in Hong Kong. This trend was not observable in preschool children and was less obvious in late adolescence, which could be explained by the stress parents experience and the cultural expectations on children related to the demands of school work and examinations. On the other hand, there is a clear sex difference in admissions related to child abuse in different age groups. In young school-aged children, boys are more likely to be admitted because of physical abuse. However, in adolescence, girls are more likely to be abused, even when child sexual abuse is not included in the analysis. These interesting observations may be largely due to the peculiar parenting practices among parents in South China, where corporal punishment is practiced as a common discipline method for young boys and closer supervision and behavior monitoring by parents are more common for adolescent girls as parents seek to protect their daughters from negative peer influences to adopt risk behaviors.

Child Abuse Statistics – An Important Social Indicator in Hong Kong

According to the evidence from the surveillance of child abuse risk factors overseas, the relationships between child maltreatment and socioeconomic and environmental factors show that levels of child maltreatment are sensitive to social, economic, and environmental factors. This calls for an analysis of data by the geographic location where the maltreatment occurs (e.g., by residential locations of the victims or perpetrators). Such data clustered at the geographical level provides the unit of analysis that matches the unit of the size, wealth, and health of the population from the national census or other demographic surveys. The relationship between child maltreatment and the prevailing socioeconomic or structural factors can then be examined and illustrated.

Commissioned by the Central Policy Unit and funded by the SWD of the Hong Kong Government, the authors of this chapter and their colleagues are currently conducting the first research in Hong Kong to study the epidemiology of child abuse and child abuse admissions (trends, risk factors and geographic distribution) by integrating the existing databases from the HA, the SWD, and household surveys. The study started in 2011 and the analysis is expected to finish by 2012. The authors intend to test the hypotheses that the variation and trend in child abuse can be used as important social indicator of different districts in Hong Kong and that the integration of existing child abuse databases would maximize their functions and allow the better identification of child abuse risk factors. The results will allow service providers and professionals to have a more comprehensive picture of child abuse cases in Hong Kong while ensuring that the privacy of personal data is well protected.

The research aims to study (a) the incidence, trends, and risk factors of child abuse hospital admissions in Hong Kong; (b) the correlation and comparison between child abuse cases managed in public hospitals and those reported in the CPR of the SWD; and (c) the epidemiology (including geographic distribution) of child abuse cases integrated from multiple sources (i.e., the HA database, the CPR of the SWD, and Violent Household Surveys (2005 and 2010)) using geo-mapping. The research also intends to identify the variations among different districts in Hong Kong and their correlation with the social indicators obtained from the Census and Statistics Department. The investigators will study and evaluate all hospital records of child (under 19) admissions in the HA database using the computerized CDARS and the AEIS records with diagnostic codes for child abuse and child maltreatment from January 2001 to December 2010. The demographics, socioeconomic status, risk factors, referral patterns, length of hospital stay, geographic distribution (including specific hospital admitted to, 7 HA clusters, 18 administrative districts, and 162 districts of residence), trends and seasonal admission patterns (overall and in each district), mortality figures, and the complications and disabilities of child abuse cases admitted to hospital and/or attended to in accident and emergency departments will be matched and correlated with the database of the SWD's Child Protection Registry. The profiles, family characteristics, service utilization, and medical presentations of unmatched cases will also be investigated in greater detail by delving into the personal and family factors in order to provide insights on the early identification of children and families at risk. In order to provide a clearer picture of the distribution of child abuse cases in Hong Kong and its correlation with community factors, and matching it with services in different districts, the data will be analyzed using Geographic

Information System software which allows the geo-mapping of child abuse data and enhances the quality of analysis and the interpretation of this important issue. The distribution of child abuse cases will be compared with the social and health service provision (e.g., IFSC, other social service center, health center, and medical clinics) available within the same area or in convenient reachable geographical areas in order to determine the potential discrepancy in demand-service provision. The epidemiology of child abuse cases can then be studied and further correlated with the social and economic indicators of each administrative residential district available from the census and other community databases (e.g., population, child population, income and comprehensive social security assistance recipient, education level, single parent, new immigrant, unemployment, crime rate).

From a scientific point of view, the study will explore the epidemiological characteristics, socioeconomic effects, and geospatial determinants of the child maltreatment group. It will also help to bridge the knowledge gap in relation to the local geospatial attributes, characteristics, and risks of the maltreated child population. This knowledge will help us to further explore the characteristics of unique cases in various areas of the community and across the territory.

Health care professionals in Hong Kong work closely with academics in the fields of medicine and social work, and during 2011, they have collected prospective data on child abuse admissions from all public hospitals in Hong Kong. This has involved the commitment and the close collaboration of the MCCA in every major pediatric unit in Hong Kong. This longitudinal project is expected to provide reliable and comprehensive data on child abuse cases admitted to hospital on the individual case management level; it will also provide hard core data on child abuse surveillance and generate a clearer picture to guide policy making and service planning in the region.

Hong Kong's Peculiar Position and Role in Chinese Societies

Hong Kong used to be a British colony; it was under British governance for more than 100 years until 1997 when it became a special administrative region of China and part of China again. It is a city with a blend of cultures that originated in the East and the West; the resonance and disharmony that arises from this makes Hong Kong a rather unique place. In most Hong Kong families, the traditional Chinese way of parenting is practiced; this emphasizes discipline and close supervision of children. In contrast, the medical, education, and legal systems in Hong Kong, in many ways, follow the British system as these models were developed during the period of British governance and are thus rather different from systems in the rest of China.

On the one hand, being influenced by traditional Chinese culture, Hong Kong shares many similarities with other parts of China. On the other hand, its sociopolitical economic structure is quite different: Hong Kong is regarded as a place with a very high Human Development Index (HDI), while China is considered as a country with a medium HDI. Being a major southern city in China heavily influenced by western culture, Hong Kong plays a very strategic role in, and provides a very good platform for, studying the feasibility of new models and piloting a comprehensive surveillance system which may benefit the well-being of children in greater China if an effective data capturing and surveillance system for child protection can be successfully established.

SITUATION IN CHINA

Responsibility for child protection and related services is shared among different departments and divisions in China, where a comprehensive policy on child protection is still lacking. The current laws of China have made provision for prohibiting child abuse; for example, the Primary Law governing Child Protection; the PRC Law on the Protection of Minors; Protection of the Rights of Women and Children within the PRC Law; the Law on the Protection of Children; Article 49 of the Constitutional Law of the PRC; and Article 3 of the Marriage Law. The enforcement of laws and policies at various levels (i.e., national, provincial, local) in greater China is a challenging issue that is beyond the scope of this chapter.

Child protection in China at the national (governmental and departmental) level involves the National Working Committee on Children and Women, the Social Welfare and Affairs Department, and NGOs such as UNICEF-China Combating Violence against Children Project and SOS Children's International Village. However, an effective surveillance system and population-based data for child abuse have yet to be established in greater China. Previous surveillance tactics have mainly involved community-based surveys of children. So far, there has been no comprehensive national survey on this important issue.

A community survey showed that one quarter of young Chinese people have had at least one unwanted experience of some form of sexual harassment or abuse before the age of 16 (Dunne, 2008). In addition, sexual abuse involving physical contact was reported by 8.9% of girls and 5% of boys (Chen, Dunne, and Han, 2006). Although psychological abuse and neglect is a focus of research in many countries, relatively little is known about this problem in China. In a survey of adolescents in six Chinese provinces, around 1 in 10 reported experience of emotional abuse (Chen, Dunne, and Han, 2004).

A school survey conducted in Guangzhou (6,593 students aged 12-16) in China found the following half-year prevalence rates: psychological aggression 78.3%, minor physical maltreatment 23.2%, severe physical maltreatment 15.1%, very severe physical maltreatment 2.8%, and sexual abuse 0.6% (W. C. W. Wong, et al., 2009).

CONCLUSION

Considerable foundation work on child abuse surveillance has been done by health care and social work professionals in Hong Kong. The integration of existing official databases from the social service and health care sectors has proved successful in Hong Kong. Such data has provided a reliable and comprehensive platform enabling a series of epidemiological studies of child abuse. The integration of secondary data from existing official databases and prospective collections of primary data (from sources such as the public hospital system) is a feasible and economic way of building an ongoing surveillance system for child protection. The situation in China is quite different from that in Hong Kong. In China, surveillance for child abuse only involves community-based surveys; representative population-based data are still lacking. There is no comprehensive national survey of child maltreatment in China. Hong Kong's successful experience and the lessons that Hong Kong has learnt will serve as a quite relevant example in the planning and establishment of a child abuse surveillance system in greater China and other Chinese societies. Building upon our knowledge, experience, and resources, we need to work closely together and carry on this challenging yet meaningful mission of safeguarding our beloved children.

REFERENCES

Agency, C. I. (2008). The world factbook. *Potomac Books*.

Al Eissa, M., and Almuneef, M. (2010). Child Abuse and Neglect in Saudi Arabia: Journey of recognition to implementation of national prevention strategies. *Child abuse and neglect, 34*(1), 28-33.

Caspi, A., Sugden, K., Moffitt, T. E., Taylor, A., Craig, I. W., Harrington, H. L., et al. (2003). Influence of life stress on depression: moderation by a polymorphism in the 5-HTT gene. *Science, 301*(5631), 386.

Census and Statistics Department. (2010). Hong Kong Crude Birth Rate. Available at: http://www.censtatd.gov.hk/hong_kong_statistics/statistics_by_subject/index.jsp.

Chan, K. L. (2005). Study on child abuse and spouse battering: report on findings of household survey. Hong Kong: Department of Social Work and Social Administration, the University of Hong Kong.

Chapman, D. A., and Scott, K. G. (2001). The Impact of Maternal Intergenerational Risk Factors on Adverse Developmental Outcomes* 1. *Developmental Review, 21*(3), 305-325.

Chen, J. Q., Dunne, M. P., and Han, P. (2004). Child sexual abuse in China: a study of adolescents in four provinces. *Child abuse and neglect, 28*(11), 1171-1186.

Chen, J. Q., Dunne, M. P., and Han, P. (2006). Child sexual abuse in Henan province, China: associations with sadness, suicidality, and risk behaviors among adolescent girls. *Journal of Adolescent Health, 38*(5), 544-549.

Child Protection Registry. (2003). Social Welfare Department, The Hong Kong Government Special Administrative Region. Available from: http://www.swd.gov.hk/vs/english/stat.html.

Child Protection Registry. (2009). Social Welfare Department, The Hong Kong Government Special Administrative Region. Available from: http://www.swd.gov.hk/vs/english/stat.html.

Danese, A., Moffitt, T. E., Pariante, C. M., Ambler, A., Poulton, R., and Caspi, A. (2008). Elevated inflammation levels in depressed adults with a history of childhood maltreatment. *Archives of general psychiatry, 65*(4), 409.

Dong, M., Giles, W. H., Felitti, V. J., Dube, S. R., Williams, J. E., Chapman, D. P., et al. (2004). Insights into causal pathways for ischemic heart disease: adverse childhood experiences study. *Circulation, 110*(13), 1761.

Dunne, M. P. (2008). The evolving evidence base for child protection in Chinese societies. *Asia-Pacific Journal of Public Health, 20*(4), 267.

German, R. R., Armstrong, G., Birkhead, G. S., Horan, J. M., and Herrera, G. (2001). Updated guidelines for evaluating public health surveillance systems. *MMWR, 50*, 1-35.

Gilbert, R., Widom, C. S., Browne, K., Fergusson, D., Webb, E., and Janson, S. (2009). Burden and consequences of child maltreatment in high-income countries. *The Lancet, 373*(9657), 68-81.

González-Izquierdo, A., Woodman, J., Copley, L., van der Meulen, J., Brandon, M., Hodes, D., et al. (2010). Variation in recording of child maltreatment in administrative records of hospital admissions for injury in England, 1997–2009. *Archives of disease in childhood, 95*(11), 918.

Ip, P., Chan, E., Chow, C., Wong, W., Tsang, A., Lee, S., et al. (2010). Upsurging of child maltreatment admissions in Chinese by using ICD codes for maltreatment syndrome: A different experience in the East (Correspondence Letter). *Archives of Disease in Childhood (E publication 27 July 2010)*.

May-Chahal, C., and Cawson, P. (2005). Measuring child maltreatment in the United Kingdom: a study of the prevalence of child abuse and neglect. *Child abuse and neglect, 29*(9), 969-984.

McGowan, P. O., Sasaki, A., Huang, T. C. T., Unterberger, A., Suderman, M., Ernst, C., et al. (2008). Promoter-wide hypermethylation of the ribosomal RNA gene promoter in the suicide brain. *PLoS One, 3*(5), e2085.

Medical Coordinators of Child Abuse. (2003). Management of child abuse in Hong Kong: results of a territory-wide interhospital prespective surveillance study. *Hong Kong Medical Journal, 9*, 6-9.

Scarborough, A. A., Lloyd, E. C., and Barth, R. P. (2009). Maltreated infants and toddlers: Predictors of developmental delay. *Journal of Developmental and Behavioral Pediatrics, 30*(6), 489.

Sethi, D., Habibula, S., McGee, K., Peden, M., Bennett, S., Hyder, A. A., et al. (2004). *Guidelines for conducting community surveys on injuries and violence*: World Health Organization Geneva.

Shonkoff, J. P., Boyce, W. T., and McEwen, B. S. (2009). Neuroscience, molecular biology, and the childhood roots of health disparities. *JAMA: the journal of the American Medical Association, 301*(21), 2252.

United Nations Children's Fund. (2006). The state of the world's children 2007, UNICEF.

Wong, S. K. (2007). 選定海外地方保護兒童的情況. 立法會秘書處資料研究及圖書館服務部

Wong, W. C. W., Leung, P. W. S., Tang, C. S. K., Chen, W. Q., Lee, A., and Ling, D. C. (2009). To unfold a hidden epidemic: prevalence of child maltreatment and its health implications among high school students in Guangzhou, China. *Child abuse and neglect, 33*(7), 441-450.

INDEX

A

B

C

D

E

F

G

H

I

J

K

L

T

U

V

W

Y